PUBLIC MEN
IN AND OUT OF OFFICE

A Da Capo Press Reprint Series

FRANKLIN D. ROOSEVELT
AND THE ERA OF THE NEW DEAL
GENERAL EDITOR: FRANK FREIDEL
Harvard University

PUBLIC MEN
IN AND OUT OF OFFICE

Edited by
J. T. Salter

DA CAPO PRESS · NEW YORK · 1972

Library of Congress Cataloging in Publication Data

Salter, John Thomas, 1898-   ed.
    Public men in and out of office.

    (Franklin D. Roosevelt and the era of the New Deal)
    1. U.S.—Biography. 2. U.S. Congress—
Biography. 3. Statesmen, American. I. Title.
II. Series.
[E747.S3 1972]   973′.099 [B]   76-39131
    ISBN 0-306-70457-9

This Da Capo Press edition of *Public Men In and Out of Office* is
an unabridged republication of the first edition published in
Chapel Hill, North Carolina, in 1946. It is reprinted by special
arrangement with the University of North Carolina Press.

Published by Da Capo Press, Inc.
A Subsidiary of Plenum Publishing Corporation
227 West 17th Street, New York, New York 10011

Manufactured in the United States of America

PUBLIC MEN

IN AND OUT OF OFFICE

PUBLIC MEN

IN AND OUT OF OFFICE

Edited by

J. T. SALTER

CHAPEL HILL · 1946

THE UNIVERSITY OF NORTH CAROLINA PRESS

For

B. D. Adkins
Elizabeth B. Agard
Duncan Aikman
Charles D. Anderson
Leslie E. Antonius
Harry A. Barth
Harold J. Bingham
Jane Cleveland Bloodgood
Henry J. Bohn
E. E. Cottrell
Wallace Edwin Dancy
Edith Dixon
Maynard Dixon
William T. Evjue
Clarence M. Freedman
Harry Fuiman
Ernestine Robbins Griffith
Victor Griffith
Harold M. Groves
Winston F. C. Guest
Howard L. Hall
Van Campen Heilner
John Hunerjager

Stanley Isaacs
Millie Green Jones
Mary Hadrian Jordan
David H. Kurtzman
Robert M. LaFollette, Jr.
John H. Leek
Mordecai Lipkin
E. B. Logan
M. Lynden Mannen
Patricia Lyon Mannen
George Milburn
E. W. Mill
Abner A. Miller
Frederic A. Ogg
Joe Rothschild
Leah B. Rothschild
Paul Salter
Bror Von Blixen
T. Henry Walnut
Raymond Walters, Jr.
Lucien Hynes Warner
Nayan Warner
E. E. Witte

and

Katharine Shepard Hayden

who concretely illustrate the richness, the beauty, the humor, and the strength of our democracy. Each one here pulls his own weight in our free society, and sheds a lustre for the rest of us. Standing in the presence of this lustre, at one or another time, has made all the difference in the world to this editor.

Lincoln was going to Washington to sit, to speak, and to vote under the big white dome, the only Whig congressman from a state in a rough triangle between Lake Michigan, the Mississippi River, and the Wabash. His letters, appeals, speeches, conversations, and explanations had gone to the eyes and ears of thousands of people; he had poured himself out tirelessly to be a congressman. He had written to Richard Thomas of the town of Virginia, "If you should hear any one say that Lincoln don't want to go to Congress, I wish you, as a personal friend of mine, would tell him that you have reason to believe him mistaken. The truth is, I would like to go very much."

He was now what was called a public man; he was trying to read the mind and the feelings of the public, to look under surface currents and find the deep important drifts, and to connect public opinion and feelings with politics. He was reading faces, voices, and whispers; he listened for insinuations, pretensions, truths, in the little changes to be seen and heard in the faces, voices, whispers, he met. He was trying to learn how to tell what men want to live for and what they are willing to die for, by what was spoken in faces, voices, whispers.—Carl Sandburg, *Abraham Lincoln, The Prairie Years,* (Harcourt, Brace: New York, 1926), I, 344.

"I say this with the greater freedom because, being a politician myself, none can regard it as personal."—*Ibid.,* p. 196.

The name of the man had come to stand for what he was, plus beliefs, conjectures, and guesses. He was spoken of as a "politician" in the sense that politics is a trade of cunning, ambitious, devious men ...

There was a word: democracy. Tongues of politics played with it. Lincoln had his slant at it. "As I would not be a *slave,* so I would not be a *master.* This expresses my idea of democracy. Whatever differs from this, to the extent of the difference, is no democracy."—*Ibid.,* II, 310.

INTRODUCTION

TODAY WE ARE IN THE MIDDLE OF THE FUTURE. YESTER-day we were at war. Today we are living in a post-war world. Great questions challenge the voters' attention. While we were at war, buildings of stone and concrete were destroyed in a flash to be rebuilt in a month, or a year, or in the years unfolding. Political arrangements, institutions, and attitudes are more durable. They change under the hammer of war or depression, but who can know how different they will be when the hammer is gone?

The most interesting thing about this fact of the future is that we and all the people of the world—not only the voters of America but also the people of other lands—are living in this new age whether we know it or not. We may try to confine our thinking to our congressional district, but our daily actions will not be walled in. They touch lands out of sight and out of mind and far away. Our thinking has remained singularly parochial for a people that invented the atomic bomb. Our tools of communication have been improved enormously during the last 2,000 years, but whether or not progress has been made in the social and political ideas communicated is a question still under debate. Our Einsteins have certainly outstripped our Aristotles.

And Einstein himself once told me the reason why. A few months before Germany waged war on Russia, Mr. Einstein casually asked me what I thought Russia was going to do. I replied that I did not know. Immediately I asked him the same question, but he, too, said, "I do not know." I next brought up James Harvey Robinson's query on Aristotle. Aristotle wrote about physics and politics, but what he said about physics has been discarded and forgotten. His statements on politics, however, are still good. Aristotle is studied and quoted by the political scientists of today. I asked the famous physicist to explain this—and he did. "That," Einstein replied, "is because politics is more difficult to understand than physics."

This conclusion is likely to seem amazing to a voter who has put off studying relativity, radar, or the nature of the atomic bomb as subjects too involved to understand, but who will vote for the candidate of his choice without any uneasiness. Actually, however, though man has discovered how to split the atom, he has found no certain way of detecting political truth and error—even though his survival value depends upon his politics. He has a personal responsibility here that transcends all else. Man is a political animal today, an informed and *participating* one, or he may be extinct tomorrow. Recent world history underlines this fact.

On his return from the Potsdam Conference President Truman reported to the people. He spoke of our great material resources, our mechanical and managerial skills, our bravery, but he said there was something else more important than that —something that we have just learned about ourselves.

"The new thing—the thing we had not known—the thing we have learned now and should never forget, is this: That a society of self-governing men is more powerful, more enduring, more creative than any other kind of society, however disciplined, however centralized."

Of course, many people have long known, and said, that a society of self-governing men in a land like ours, or England's, or Norway's, for example, where freedom is the accepted condition of life, is the most satisfactory and excellent government in the world. It is well to remember that self-government means exactly what it says—*self*-government. It means government by the selves concerned. Government for the people, and of the people, must be government *by* the people. This fact cannot be stated too often in a free society. Because here the self, the individual, the each one of us in his eachness, has a personal responsibility to know politics and to do something about it. Self-exppression, articulate and unfailing, is the touchstone of a democratic society.

Paul E. Appleby, while Under Secretary, in the Department of Agriculture, let fall a helpful observation. "Whitehead once commented on the importance of the mental achievement reached when someone first saw the relation of five fish and five apples—the relationship of five to five." We must know the pertinent facts and their relation one to another. We should be able to evaluate, to sense the relationship in apparently unlike things, to see general results. To be concrete, what is the candidate's record? What has this administration accomplished? The voter himself must answer these questions.

A society of self-governing men—a democracy—is not only best and strongest but it is also the form and kind of government that is most difficult to maintain. It requires more of the individual. And it does require an individual. Not a mass-individual, or a *bund*-individual, but an individual-individual. One who can say, "Yes," and who can say, "No," too. The kind of a person who can most likely vote for a public man (a politician) devoted to the common good and capable of serving it. The strength of our democracy depends on the individual's ability to do just that—plus his actually doing it. Here, the big fellow is not the President, or the Senator, or the Governor, but it is the sovereign citizen, His Honor, the Voter. And it is to help the voter know, appreciate, and guide this other indispensable agent—public man or politician—that this book of sketches has been written.

Our government is the government of the Constitution and the laws, but a constitution cannot enforce itself and neither can a law. So our government is also a government of men—public men usually called politicians. And it is these politicians that this book is about. It is a voter's gallery of politicians.

President Truman emphasized the fact, as the Second World War ended, that the great tasks of peace are still to be done. The greatest of these is "the implementation of free government in the world." And we in the United States know that there cannot be a free government without free voters and their indispensable institutions: freedom of speech, press, and assembly. Democracy is like tennis; one learns it by doing it, by participation. He cannot learn it out of a book. Time is involved, too. A people born in a free society usually knows more about democracy than does a newcomer to this way of life. This is the "A" in the ABC's of democratic politics.

The "B" is based on the fact that the valuable voter is articulate. He is willing to stand up and be counted, to speak out in public when he finds a reason for speaking out. Disraeli pointed to something essential here when he said: "A wise man asks, a fool wonders." The voter must be able to ask. For by asking he identifies himself. In addition, the people contribute to the formation of a public opinion by asking questions. And when the voters are articulate, the politicians are inescapably reminded that the people are observing them and interested in what they are doing.

"C." The voter can never rest on his laurels. The price of good government, like the price of world security, is vigilance and endless striving.

In addition to these irreducible qualifications for a free voter there is one more, and one without which the other three are of no avail. We now believe, as we never have believed before, that we are our brother's keeper—whether our brother lives in rural France or in Three Oaks, Michigan. The actuality of being interested in the other fellow is implicit in any permanent condition of world security—the only security in the world.

The most important job that the voter has to do is to pick the right politician. It is urgent for all of us to study this ubiquitous fellow. For he is here, and he is here to stay, whether we like it or not. We cannot get along without him. There is a verse in Hosea: "I ask thee to get knowledge, for without knowledge I will reject thee." Knowledge of the politician is essential in a free society unless we choose to be ignorant of what all voters have an obligation to know. The people need the public man or politician in their business—this business of governing themselves.

Voters and politicians are as the bow and arrow—helpless one without the other. A politician without support and guidance from the people is in a vulnerable position. He is subject to the pressure of any group that looks his way. An articulate voter is a pressure group of one. (A state senator explained that he had no idea how he should or would have voted on a certain measure before the senate. But he received a letter from a constituent asking him to vote "No." "So I did," he told me.) If this had been a controversial issue the same principle would probably have applied. Those who exert the pressure call the turn. Those who bend the bow and aim the arrow direct its course. This analogy is possibly more accurate than is at first apparent; a politician is never alone—he is as the people are. This is the basis of the argument in favor of enlightened public opinion in a free society.

Notwithstanding the fact that the greatest war in history is still vividly in our minds, we live most of our years amid the usages of peace. Our daily life is in a world of politics—talk, not bullets; politicians, not generals; voters, not soldiers. The only way we can lengthen the period between wars is to improve our politics, for wars do not come until our politics runs out.

War, some realist once remarked, is politics carried on by other means. If we want peaceful (comparatively speaking) politics, we want freedom of talk, and we want politicians. It might be smart to keep this fact in mind—not to scorn politics unless we want to scorn ourselves. For although we rightly criticize the individual—whether politician or wife—for any personal shortcomings whatsoever, we do not condemn the institution; we do not condemn all politicians or all wives, or womankind, without cutting the ground out from under the feet of the people in a free society. The individual who criticizes all politicians in this political age is as obsolete as is the ideological forbear who came out against antiseptics or vaccination.

Einstein is right. Politics is most difficult. It is difficult because life is difficult; and politics is life. We live in one world, but our frontier is the ballot box. *The frontier of democracy is the ballot box*. The solutions coming out of the ballot box must equal those coming out of the test tube, or humanity is lost. The atomic bomb is only one of the reasons why mankind's number-one problem is political. Its problem is not science; it is politics.

Modern man is not obsolete. But he will be if he does not think with his head instead of his eyes. Printing is more than the graphic arts, and reading is more than looking at pictures. Man, this paragon of animals, has magnificently mastered his non-human environment. Human nature itself, though, is less simple to cope with. Democratic man as an individual does not believe in murder any more, and that is a long stride forward. Peace is the darling of the democracies. But if the democracy is attacked by an authoritarian state its peace is lost. That brings home the inescapable realization that peace is a world question as well as a national question.

The future of civilization rests on the individual voter. Can he see that personality is the most important thing in the world? Can he forever know that man is an end in himself—never a means? That we, and all people, must live together peacefully if civilized life is to continue? Can the voter implement these ideas and ideals when he marks his ballot? I think that he can.

It is written in the Book of Proverbs:

There be three things which are too wonderful for me, yea, four which I know not:
The way of an eagle in the air; the way of a serpent upon a rock; the way of a ship in the midst of the sea; and the way of a man with a maid.

Now, some three thousand years later, there is a fifth thing for man to ponder: *The way of a politician with a voter.*

This may or may not be wonderful, but it is important. For its secret is the secret of democracy—of the people in a free society. That is what this book is about.

For *Public Men* is a pertinent book of twenty-seven sketches and one essay—a book about politicians and voters in their natural political state. There is something of the form and atmosphere of human nature and the democratic process in this work. Here, for example, is the President, Harry S. Truman, who represents the common American tradition right down to its gizzard. And here is Henry A. Wallace, a liberal leader who is interested in education and who came close to the Great Office. Will he ever be so close again? The late Wendell Willkie, who could dramatize himself but not the issue speaks again in these pages.

The bulk of this volume, however, is devoted to members of the House and the Senate. It is an attempt to describe the national legislature in terms of characteristic and representative members of that body. It is a personal approach to a branch of government in which personality means much—but where experience and brains mean more. The Honorable Sam Rayburn, the Speaker, is a happy blend of all three. He is here, and so are the two oldest members of the House, in terms of tenure, the Honorable Adolph J. Sabath, Chairman of the Rules Committee, and the Honorable Robert L. Doughton, Chairman of Ways and Means. These are the three most important jobs in Congress. How do the men who have them compare with the other members of the House? Are the biggest men in Congress the biggest men? The sketches throw light on this question.

The Honorable Jerry Voorhis, who is sensitive to the needs of people out of sight as well as to the fellow who is pulling his coat tail, is here; and so is the Honorable Sol Bloom, Chairman of the Foreign Affairs Committee. Senator Bilbo, who sometimes sees life as a personal struggle with Walter Winchell, comes to life here in his own words. The author of the sketch wisely followed the injunction of the editor, who said, "I will not say that the candidate is mistaken; I will print his speech." Senator Fulbright, Senator Connally, Chairman of the Foreign Relations Committee, and Senator Barkley, Majority Leader, are among the other legislators present in this volume; and so are Senator Ball, Senator Pepper, and Senator O'Mahoney.

Municipal bosses are not so common as they once were. But here is Hague. He rode the depression and the war. What holds him up? There is an interesting story about a disturbed citizen who asked President Roosevelt why he had never gotten rid of Hague. Our late President who knew politicians and voters so well, inquired: "Suppose that Mr. Hague were removed from office today and then there was an election tomorrow. What do you think would happen?" The disturbed citizen quickly replied, "He would be reelected." "Exactly," the President said. "Therefore don't you think this is a problem for the people of New Jersey?"

The best official springboard for the presidency is the Governor's chair in the state. We are including sketches of Thomas E. Dewey of New York, John Bricker of Ohio, Harold E. Stassen of the wide world and Minnesota, Earl Warren of California, and Robert S. Kerr of Oklahoma.

Each biography is written with an awareness of the national and international attitudes and ideas of the subject. In addition to this emphasis, *Public Men* contains three sketches of Ambassadors—our ambassadors to London, to Mexico City, and a sketch of one who served as ambassador to Tokyo for the ten years preceding Pearl Harbor.

The sketches are written by professors and newspaper men. The biographer's indebtedness is to the methodology of a Boswell or a Freeman rather than a Freud or Sheldon. The authors attempt to describe the subject in the life process—in the political situation that is as much a part of the public man as is his foot or his necktie. The sketches are of varying value and importance. Some are examples of creative art and a few are a more literal statement of facts and events. Each sketch, however, deserves a place in this volume.

To my former students, Marilyn Johnson, George W. John, Anita Alpern, M. L. Mannen, Reuben Sand, Barbara Kemp, and Ursula Felton I can give my thanks only inadequately here. Your helpfulness in a variety of ways I again happily acknowledge. Miss Sina Spiker, my publisher's invaluable assistant, has contributed much to this book. I do not know what I would have done without her. Emily Blenis Williams, my sometime secretary, deserves a big E for her efficiency and industry. To Professor E. E. Witte I am especially indebted.

I never talk to this uncommonly wise man without gaining a clearer understanding of the question discussed.

Finally, I thank the contributors. They have the energy and the vision to produce a human document—a book that smacks more of the human than the documentary, a book for a free society.

J. T. SALTER

Gravelly Point, Virginia
November, 1945

CONTENTS

II

IN CONGRESS

III

IN CITY AND IN STATE

IV

INTERPRETATION

I

IN THE NATION AND IN THE FOREIGN SERVICE

HARRY S. TRUMAN

"I Don't Want to be President"

BY EDWARD A. HARRIS

THE IMPOSING ARRAY OF BOOKS IN THE OFFICE OF HARRY S. Truman of Missouri ranges from "The Rape of Palestine" to "So This is Florida," and he's read them all, including an unexpurgated edition of the Arabian Nights—which give him undisguised delight. He is, to put it mildly, an odd bookworm. For while he takes a reasonable amount of pleasure in the works of Rabelais and de Maupassant, he is likely to remark that the greatest story ever told is in the Bible, which he quotes at will.

Truman's reading tastes in a sense define his character. As an adept student of Scripture he maintains a towering faith in humanity and the essential goodness of all races. Indeed, at times he looks and talks like a cleric. He is a God-fearing Baptist and a connoisseur of good Bourbon (mixed with ginger ale), a reverent family man, and a master at quiet profanity; in short, a curious composite of Sabattical idealism and refreshing everyday practicality. "After thirty years of politics," he has remarked, "a fellow learns to temper his optimism with common sense. The vast majority of human beings want to do the right thing, if they know what it is."

The fact that Harry Truman has remained basically an optimist is all the more remarkable in light of the thorny path he traveled to attain his present eminence. When he held the post of chairman of the powerful special Senate Committee to Investigate the War Program he was in a rare position to observe human frailties, notably incompetence, greed, and waste. The name "Truman" carried almost unparallelled weight with the nation's war leaders. And the saga of his rise from obscurity to that position, and later to his present role [1] as heir-apparent to the presidency of the United States, constitutes a sort of cockeyed Horatio Alger story, belying some of our fundamental American precepts and heavily underscoring others.

It should be pointed out, first of all, that Truman did not want the nomination for Vice-President at the Democratic national convention in Chicago in July, 1944. He was pledged to place in nomination the name of his friend, War Mobilization Director James F. Byrnes, dapper little ex-Supreme Court Justice who unabashedly rushed down to the Windy City and buttonholed delegates for their votes. It looked like a rough-and-tumble scrap between Byrnes and Henry A. Wallace, who as incumbent was armed with the Hydra-headed letter of endorsement from Roosevelt.

But Truman's pledge to nominate Byrnes was only a surface obstacle to the Truman bandwagon pullers. The real stumbling block was Truman himself. He passed the word down to the big Democratic bosses and to his friends that he had thought it all over and he was out of the picture. And he meant it. Hard-boiled politicians and overwise cynics winked and mumbled that they'd never known a politician or "statesman" who hadn't wanted to climb the next rung in the ladder. But Harry Truman was one.

The writer well remembers a memorable visit with Truman in his room at the Stevens Hotel in Chicago Sunday evening preceding the convention. The Senator sat alone near a window overlooking the placid panorama of the Lake Michigan shore-line, and as we talked he made known his resolve to keep his name out of the running. It was pointed out to him that as Vice-President he might succeed to the throne. He shook his head and smiled. "Hell," he said, "I don't want to be President." With the sharp memory of a professional historian he proceeded to recall what had happened to American vice-

---

1. This sketch was written and in the hands of the publisher in April, 1945, before the death of Roosevelt. See the Postscript appended to this chapter.

presidents who had moved up to the nation's helm: failure and frustration, scorn and ridicule.

No, said Truman, he would stay in the Senate, where he enjoyed a modicum of prestige. If he were nominated, the opposition party would "smear him"; they would drag out once again his old ties with the notorious Pendergast machine (of course he did not say "notorious"), and no telling what else they'd hurl at him. He had his family to think of, especially his beloved ninety-two-year-old mother. She had counseled him to remain a senator, and he thought a lot of her advice.

Truman was as plain as that, as homespun as an old linsey quilt. As events occurred, however, he was literally drafted for the race. The avowed candidacy of Byrnes was blackballed two days later by Sidney Hillman of the CIO, who made known his preference for Truman if Wallace couldn't gather enough delegate strength to win the nomination. The pressure on Truman became enormous, but he wouldn't budge until the President personally, in a telephone conversation with Chairman Robert E. Hannegan of the Democratic National Committee, insisted that Truman run. By prearrangement Truman listened in on the conversation, and from that moment on, his hat was in the ring.

That same evening correspondents of the *St. Louis Post-Dispatch,* through its radio station, "broke" the nationwide story of the President's preference for Harry Truman, and by midnight it was all over but the balloting. Courageous Henry Wallace, swinging in two-fisted fashion, didn't stand a chance against the organized power blocs of the Democratic convention bosses, who lined up solidly behind the President's choice. And within a few weeks, Truman was being subjected to the very abuse he had predicted.

Truman took the campaign of vilification calmly. When the Hearst newspapers shrilled the unsubstantiated charge that he had once joined the Ku Klux Klan, Truman, on a campaign swing to the West, quietly pointed out that he had fought the Klan tooth and nail when the Klan was a power in Missouri politics. That onslaught collapsed as suddenly as it had started. When his connection with the old Pendergast machine was revived, he merely remarked wryly that Abe Lincoln also got his start in politics with the aid of a party machine. When newspapers printed the fact that his wife, Bess Wallace Truman, was carried on his Senate office payroll, he said she earned every cent the government paid her. To the writer he added a characteristically frank explanation: "We needed the money." Even anti-New Deal writers came to his defense in this attack, asserting that senators are paid inadequately.

On the campaign train Truman remained unruffled, good-humored, candid with reporters to the point of being impolitic. About one Democratic senator whose anti-New Dealism was giving campaign leaders the palsy and who was on the verge of bolting the party ticket, Truman undiplomatically cracked: "We still have two years [in the Senate] to reform him." Meantime Truman joined newsmen at poker almost nightly, attired in uninspiring pajamas and an old flowered dressing gown. When the waiter carried in a deep-dish apple pie he exclaimed happily: "My, the crust is as good as Mummy used to make." At rallies he stood at attention whenever the band played the "Missouri Waltz," thus requiring the audience to stand with him; and he plugged, as befitted a regular party man, all local Democratic candidates. On November 7 he was swept into office in the electoral college landslide that presented Roosevelt with his fourth term, and one of his first public utterances thereafter, in response to a reporter's query, was his announcement that he would keep his old office in the Senate Office Building.

What manner of man had the people of the United States elected to the nation's second-highest post? By now they knew something about him. They knew of his uncompromising honesty, of his simplicity, his modesty and unpretentiousness. They knew, too, of his intellectual integrity and investigative ability as reflected by his work on the Senate war-program committee, and of his strong stand for international co-operation backed by adequate police force, as detailed in his speeches. But they also knew of his stubborn defense of a discredited and vicious political machine. Here was an apparent paradox in his character. Did it carry dangerous portent? Could it be explained?

Truman wants no apologists. He has never sought to analyze his own character. He adheres to the old Popeye cliche, "I am what I am." But if there is one trait that unlocks the door to this contradiction of deep-seated personal morality and his defense of Pendergastism, it is his loyalty. The ultimate test of his fitness for high office, then, would seem to rest on the question: In a conflict of interests, who gets his foremost loyalty—his political associates or his country? Perhaps, in the following recapitulation of his career, an answer may be found.

Truman had rugged beginnings, in line with good American tradition. Born on a farm near Lamar, Missouri, in 1884, son of John A. and Martha Ellen Young Truman, he attended grade and high schools at Independence. He tried to get into West Point but was rejected because of one weak eye. Abandoning thoughts of a college education, he took a job in a drugstore at three dollars a week. He has, incidentally, always regretted his lack of formal education, feeling that it permanently handicapped him; but he likes to quote his mother when the subject comes up (pretending that it would have been futile to have sent him to college): "When you educate a fool you make a bigger fool; when you educate a good man you make a better man." In the spring of 1944, his aged mother still took Harry sternly to task every time she read that he had missed a roll call in the Senate, and demanded an explanation. Her earthy advice and homely philosophy made an enduring impression on him.

Tiring of drugstore humdrum, young Truman wrapped papers for the *Kansas City Star* for a while, and then clerked in a bank until he was twenty-two years old, when he was drawing down twenty-five dollars a week and getting nowhere. His father easily persuaded him to return to the Jackson County farm as a full-fledged partner, and there he remained until 1916, plowing the fields and milking cows. He has often said that these years on the farm were the happiest of his life.

No one thought the Truman boy would amount to much, except possibly as a classical pianist. He practiced long hours after the farm chores were done and nurtured the hope of becoming a professional musician. This idyllic life, however, was rudely interrupted by the First World War, a turning point in his life. He enlisted as a private and a latent talent for organization and direction came to the surface. At first his associates in arms regarded him as an ugly duckling. He was extremely shy, introverted, wore large shell-rimmed glasses, and looked awkwardly out of place in khaki. But he worked doggedly, helped organize the Second Missouri Field Artillery and later the 129th Field Artillery, 35th Division, and advanced swiftly. He led his men through St. Mihiel and the Argonne as a captain, and nipped a panic when German artillery drew a bead on his battery. Soon he was promoted to major, and served at the front until the armistice was signed, earning the respect and friendship of his men. On the homeward voyage his comrades took a kitty out of their crap games and presented him with a loving cup four feet high. Meantime the experience of battle had seared deeply into his consciousness, and years later as head of the Truman Committee in World War II he sought to put into practice his conviction that wars should be fought on an expeditious basis, without the hindrances of waste and graft, so that victory could be achieved at the earliest possible time.

Returning from France in 1919, Truman married his childhood sweetheart, Bess Wallace, and opened a haberdashery in Kansas City. Selling socks and neckties behind the counter of his store, he renewed acquaintance with many of his war buddies, now business men and politicians. After a year Truman and his ex-serviceman partner went broke. Through the ensuing ten years he and his one-time partner paid off their haberdashery debts bit by bit, refusing to declare bankruptcy.

A "failure" at 37, Truman looked up several of his ex-soldier friends in the Democratic political organization of Thomas J. Pendergast, whose octopus lines gripped all of Jackson County. As a Democrat, war veteran, farmer, and Mason, his background was deemed promising, and Pendergast liked him. He was made road overseer, and in November, 1922, was elected Judge of the Jackson County Court, which is not judicial but administrative, and runs the county's business affairs. He studied law at night, passed the bar examination, but in 1924 was defeated for re-election to the court. In 1926 he was elected presiding judge of the same court by a majority of 16,000, and four years later his majority was 58,000. He has always been proud of his county court record, for there was ample opportunity to play the game with Pendergast and his cement-manufacturing company had he wished. "I had charge of the spending of sixty million dollars for highways and public buildings in Jackson County," he has said. "Nobody ever found anything wrong with that, and it wasn't because they didn't look hard enough."

When it came time to select a candidate for the Senate in 1934, Pendergast called Truman to his office one day and told him he was the man. Truman was astonished but obeyed orders. Pendergast has never explained his reasons for giving the nod to Truman in preference to more "deserving" individuals in the machine, but it was generally believed that the Boss saw in him a modesty and respectability that might help cloak the scarlet hues of the machine. In any event, with the machine's aid the election was easy, and Harry Truman, neat and gray and acutely conscious of his inexperience, went to Washington to start the climactic period of his life.

Here again Truman entered upon a new scene as an ugly duckling. He was still reserved, self-conscious, and inept in the parliamentarian ways, but much worse, he came to the Senate as the hand-picked candidate of a notorious political boss, plucked out of obscurity so abysmal that scarcely any of his colleagues in the august body had heard of him. He sat meekly in freshman row, was dubbed "Pendergast's errand boy," but he took the test with good grace and settled down to work quietly. He was content at first to follow the lead of the senior senator from Missouri, Bennett Champ Clark, whose knowledge of the Senate's procedural rules and of the capital itself was prodigious. Truman studied Clark and his other associates and gradually learned. Assigned to the Interstate Commerce Committee, he got his first taste of the Senate's investigative functions. He took an increasingly active part in the inquiry into railroad finance which the committee was conducting, followed closely the tortuous windings of high finance, and ultimately delivered a stirring speech on the floor castigating Wall Street control over the railroads. Soon he became one of the most hard-working members of the important Military Affairs Committee, traversing thousands of miles to inspect military bases and supply stations. He had always been intensely interested in war, an interest intensified by his own battle experience and brought to practical use in the Congress. He had read extensively about the War Between The States, becoming an authority on it, and now his chief interest began to center on the nation's inner workings in the national defense program. Europe was a cauldron of turmoil, and the freshman senator prepared himself for the inevitable explosion.

Meanwhile Truman had to tend his political fences, with another election coming up in 1940. In his home state trouble was brewing for the Pendergast machine. A young United States district attorney named Maurice M. Milligan began digging into the record of the unholy dynasty. Before long he had uncovered vast vote frauds and began sending Pendergast's henchmen to prison. When Milligan was due for reappointment after this worthy public service, Truman lost his customary calm, making one of the bitterest speeches ever heard on the Senate floor. In the face of mounting public disapproval he went further, demanding that Milligan be fired from the government payroll. Milligan, however, won reappointment and later helped send Boss Pendergast to prison for income tax evasion, breaking the spine of the machine. To reporters who pressed him for comment after this debacle, the usually mild-mannered Senator flared: "It's purely political. I won't desert a sinking ship."

With the Pendergast superstructure toppling, Truman was given little chance of re-election in 1940. Opposing him in the primary were Milligan and Lloyd Crow Stark, then Governor of Missouri, who had taken an important role in overturning the Boss. Truman has never forgiven Stark for seeking and obtaining Pendergast's support for the governorship and then attacking him, and he often says the only man in the world he detests is Stark. With this background the Democratic primary

was a bitter three-cornered slugfest, with Truman subjected
to frothy denunciations as a machine-made man. But Milligan
and Stark split the opposition vote; the remnants of the Pendergast organization rolled up a huge vote for Truman in
Jackson County, and when the votes were counted he had been
re-elected with an 8,000-vote plurality.

With this tempestuous interlude out of the way, Harry
Truman resumed his seat in the Senate and renewed his mounting interest in the war effort. Subsequently the sheer force of
his achievements compelled impartial observers to acknowledge
that a political accident had indeed produced a winner. A
malodorous rat-alley had in truth spawned a rose. The *St.
Louis Post-Dispatch,* which had heaved everything at him but
its linotype machines during his re-election campaign, was
typical of the voluntary flipflops. It described him as "one of
the most useful and at the same time one of the most forthright and fearless of Senators."

Back on the job, Truman began to promote the idea of a
special committee to investigate the defense program. By this
time he had lost a large measure of his shyness. He was on a
first-name basis with most of his colleagues and was well liked.
He was still wondrously modest for a senator, and this trait
stood him in good stead in his unobtrusive quest for support
for such a committee. His associates felt reasonably certain he
would not use an investigating body to smear the administration or to puff up Harry Truman. Early in 1941, Truman introduced Senate Resolution 71, calling for creation of a committee to investigate every phase of the war program. As
custom dictated, Truman, as sponsor of the resolution, was
named chairman. His moderate request for $25,000 was cut
to $15,000. No one took the thing seriously at first except
Truman himself. It was thought that, as a faithful New
Dealer, he should be humored. He had little or nothing to do
with the selection of members, which was handled by Vice-
President Wallace, Majority Leader Barkley, and Minority
Leader McNary. As originally framed, the committee consisted of seven Democrats and three Republicans. On the roster
were only two senior senators, and it was believed that the

appointment of inexperienced members of slight influence reflected the slight esteem in which the committee was held at
the time. The committee's phenomenal change in status was
illustrated some time later when one member failed to be re-
elected to the Senate, and a clamorous behind-the-scenes tussle
followed for his place on the committee.

The appointment of rookie senators to the committee was
advantageous for Truman. He found himself working with
youthful and energetic men who still had their spurs to win
and who had not yet succumbed to inflation of the ego. The
chairman availed himself of the talent at his disposal by appointing subcommittees to delve into phases of the war effort
in which they were most interested. It was the chairmen of the
subcommittees, not Truman, who usually presented the committee's supplementary reports to the Senate. Truman, in fact,
went to great pains to avoid any semblance of a "one-man"
committee, and he succeeded in welding together a group
working in such harmony that the committee never issued a
minority report, an unprecedented achievement among congressional bodies. "Get the facts, and the conclusions will take care
of themselves," became the committee's motto. It enabled a
two-party group to work with little if any political bias, and to
avoid a pitfall all too frequent among congressional committees—that of forming a preconceived conclusion and manipu-
lating evidence to support it.

At hearings Truman invariably called upon other members
to ask the initial questions. The atmosphere was dignified but
informal. Smoking was permitted, and cameramen were allowed to flit about with their flash bulbs, but judicial and senatorial courtesies were strictly observed. One peculiarity was
that non-member senators were free at all times to sit in with
the committee and take part in the proceedings. There was a
studious avoidance of dramatics, no hurling of insults or threats
of personal violence that characterize so many other congressional hearings.

To a large extent the committee's conduct reflected the
demeanor of its chairman. Truman was probably the hardest-
working member of the Senate, and he saw to it that no hearing

HARRY S. TRUMAN

"Humility probably would be the first characterization."

GEORGE S. MESSERSMITH

"Became a redoubtable champion of adequate salaries and allowances for our representatives abroad."

JOHN G. WINANT

"Possibly the greatest interpreter of American l
we have ever had at the Court of St. James'

F. Clyde Wilkinson

JOSEPH C. O'MAHONEY

Only once in Senator O'Mahoney's career has underestimated the people's hunger for facts."

Harris and Ewing

GERALD P. NYE

"He ignored the elementary fact that any government must do something positive in some respect."

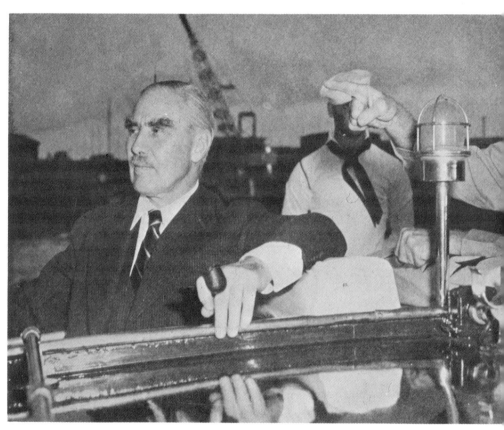

JOSEPH CLARK GREW

"Our sentinal in Japan."

WENDELL WILLKIE

"A keen, unconfused intelligence keeping abreast of the swift march of events."

HENRY AGARD WALLACE

"... hope that somehow the trick of transition from full employment
for war to full employment for peace could be turned. ..."

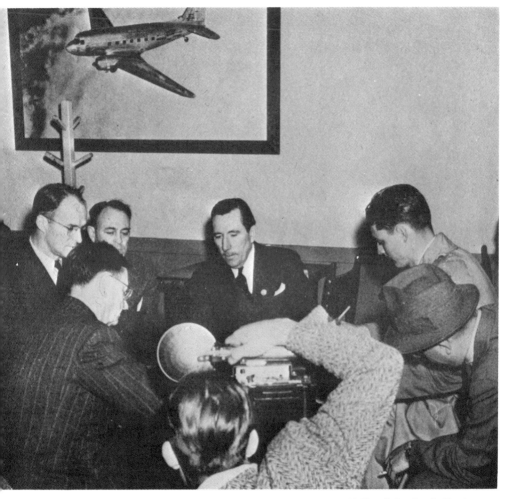

CLAUDE D. PEPPER

"Whatever the verdict of history may be, it will hardly deny him rank as one of the significant men of his day in Washington."

Wide World Photo

JOHN W. FULBRIGHT

"He can be tactful and yielding when it is advisable; he can also be stubborn, exacting, critical, and roughly candid."

Courtesy Mr. Doughton

ROBERT L. DOUGHTON

"Known as the taxpayers' friend, he has taken more money from them than any other chairman of Ways and Means."

ALBEN BARKLEY

"His face is too grim for magnetic smiles, and is features too rugged for glamorous grins— it he can laugh."

SOL BLOOM

"To many, Bloom's failure to speak out is regarded as wisdom; to others it is a sign of mediocre leadership."

Harris and Ewing

ADOLPH J. SABATH

"His place in legislative history must rest on the fact that he was elected more times in a row than anyone else."

Press Ass

HAMILTON FISH

". . . for nearly a quarter of a century had be⟨e⟩ a successful if not a seemly practitioner politics."

THEODORE G. BILBO

To defeat this measure, so help me God, I
ould be willing to speak every day of the
ar!' "

JOSEPH H. BALL

"He feels himself to be representative of a
younger group thinking in terms of the future
rather than of the past."

Harris and Ewing

Press Ass

TOM CONNALLY

ELLISON DURANT SMITH

"After Connally assumed chairmanship of Foreign Relations, he was rated as one of the 'big boys.'"

"A member of the Senate for thirty-six year and last of the 'spittoon Senators.'"

Press Ass'n

Oklahoma City Air Service Command

JOHN BRICKER

ROBERT S. KERR

s record with legislation and the lawmaking
y did not set the Scioto River aflame."

"Even his enemies credited the governor with
doing a good job of selling Oklahoma."

JERRY VOORHIS

"His day of action may come when majority opinion catches up with him."

SAM RAYBURN

" 'The chair is not accustomed to having ruling questioned.' "

THOMAS EDMUND DEWEY

Iore than twenty-one million Americans
roved."

HAROLD EDWARD STASSEN

"Time may very possibly add the rank of
statesman."

FRANK HAGUE

"When he is on his travels he governs by telephone; he never leaves to a subordinate any important degree of discretion."

EARL WARREN

"Careful to emphasize that the desired res could be best achieved by placing Warren the governorship."

was held until all the available facts about a subject had been gathered. The actual hearings could be compared to an iceberg, in that only one-tenth of the mass was visible, while nine-tenths was submerged in the preparatory groundwork of the group. The spark plug of the committee in this groundwork was a youthful, florid-faced former special assistant to the United States Attorney-General named Hugh A. Fulton. It is significant that when Truman was casting about to find a chief counsel for the group, instead of giving the $9,000-a-year post to a political favorite he turned to the Attorney-General for a man and got Fulton.

The committee's work was conducted with scrupulous economy. It was compelled literally to earn its way. After getting its initial appropriation of $15,000, its devastating report on waste in the construction of army camps was rewarded with an additional grant of $25,000. An aluminum investigation brought $60,000 more. As disclosure followed disclosure, all backed up with irrefutable documentation, $100,000 was added on the general record. Three years after its creation, to inquire into a war program rising upwards of 300 billion dollars, the committee had spent little more than $200,000, contrasted with $570,000 lavished on the Dies Committee to investigate un-American activities. Admittedly the Truman group has saved the nation billions of dollars while the attainments of the House Dies Committee have remained somewhat shrouded in mystery.

The committee's technique, as Fulton has pointed out, was that of the rifle rather than the shotgun. It employed precision instead of saturation bombing. "We can stick a pin in here and there," Senator Truman observed once, "but nobody knows where the pin is going to strike next, and that keeps everyone on the alert." But the pinpricks developed the impact of a mule's kick. In its ninety-eight-page report on army camp construction issued in August, 1941, the committee found needless waste of 100 million dollars, attributing the waste to poor planning. The report accused the Army of "fantastically poor judgment" in the choice of camp sites and in its policy of renting trucks, tractors, and other vehicles instead of buying in quantity. General Brehon B. Somervell, chief of the Army Service Forces, commented that this inquiry saved the government 200 million dollars. The unswerving judiciousness of the committee was shown later when, despite Somervell's flattery, it charged the General with "inexcusable" conduct in persisting in the construction of a Canadian oil development known as the Canol project. Somervell had, however, put his finger on the prime usefulness of the Truman Committee. Unlike other committees which often raked up past mistakes, too far gone to rectify, the Truman group moved along with the war effort, turning the spotlight on errors that, in many instances, could still be remedied, or at least could be avoided in the future.

Truman paid the President a visit in January, 1942, to inform him that his committee planned to recommend appointment of one man to run the entire war production program. A day later the appointment of Donald Nelson as head of the Office of Production Management was announced. The Truman Committee then issued its report on war production. Dollar-a-year men in topflight OPM posts were criticized as lobbyists for private business. The report said the task of converting automobile plants into war production had not even started, that defense housing had been bungled, and that shipyards were reaping "unreasonable and unconscionable profits" from Navy contracts. The committee's suggestion for drastic reorganization of the OPM was soon answered by the establishment of the War Production Board.

Truman's action in advising the President in advance of a forthcoming committee report bearing on the executive branch of the government was in keeping with a cardinal principle of the committee. No report was issued until the subject of its criticism had had a chance to read it and point out any inaccuracies it might contain. Truman's committee was the only one on Capitol Hill which indulged in this extraordinary courtesy, but it paid dividends. There was a singular lack of shrieking, of cries of "foul blow" in the wake of committee reports.

By the dawn of 1944, over thirty reports had been made public. It was conceded by this time that the Truman Committee was the nearest thing to a domestic high command. While it had no power to act or order, it got results by focusing public opinion on the men who had the power, and by using Congress' prerogative to look critically and recommend. Cabinet members, generals, admirals, labor leaders, and business tycoons trooped into the committee's hearings with a show of humility accorded few committees. Its outstanding work buttressed Congress' waning prestige. And it catapulted soft-spoken, placid Harry Truman, the freak political accident of Lamar, Missouri, onto a towering pinnacle of prestige and power.

Fame left Truman unimpressed. He was ready to abandon the Senate when the Japs struck at Pearl Harbor, volunteering for service. He was disappointed when Army officials, quite aware that he was a colonel in the National Guard, rejected him for physical reasons. Truman pointed out that he weighed just under 170 pounds, was five feet, ten inches tall, could still wriggle into his World War I uniform, and was well equipped to go into active service; but the argument fell on unsympathetic ears. It was lucky for the war effort.

While Truman's most tangible contribution as a senator was the organization and direction of his investigating committee, he also had a hand in the formulation of many consequential laws. He was, for example, the author of a bill for the federal licensing of operators and motor vehicles used in interstate commerce, and he was chairman of two subcommittees of the Interstate Commerce Committee, one of which dug into the financial status of railroads; the other subcommittee drafted the Civil Aeronautics Act, which brought all civil aviation under the control of the Civil Aeronautics Authority. He helped draft considerable other legislation, but was never known to sponsor bills at the behest of special pressure groups. In placing the public interest before vested interests, he ran into some tough scraps, and at such times showed surprising tenacity and punch. He said repeatedly that he had no criticism of industry or business in general, that the few whom he had to criticize were the exceptions and not the rule. He was still surprised and hurt when the committee was charged with bias or unfairness. When this happened he was likely to dish out, in the committee's behalf, far more than it received.

Most of Truman's targets were impressed with his fairness and moderation. Once he wrote a piece for LaFollette's *Progressive* in Wisconsin tearing into some unsavory practices of the advertising business. Among those who took the article sorely to heart was Frank Braucher, president of the Periodical Publishers Association, who found himself, some time later, listening to the Senator speak at a dinner sponsored by advertising agencies. Braucher was prepared to get pinpricks all over again, but, as he later wrote in a letter to the magazine, *Printer's Ink:*

> It did not turn out that way. I suddenly found myself all attention. . . . I came to some conclusions. Here was a man who appealed to me as not having a demogogic thought in his system. I had to come a long way to arrive at that opinion, but it's mine. The mode and manner so many of us so happily associate with Washington characters we do not like was absent. He did not seem to me to be a salesman of the new order. He appealed to me more as a practical legislator who had faith in the idea that with the application of honesty and common sense, our present system of government furnished ample means for working out our common problems.

Truman's speeches lend support to Braucher's analysis of the man. "My work in Washington," Truman said in 1943,

> has revealed to me in focus the conflicts that exist within the country. Conflict has arisen between management and labor, Congress and labor, race and race, Democrats and Republicans, and even at times between the federal and state governments. These conflicts go back to a basic lack of a uniting, over-arching, positive program, big enough to include all groups, and to require all groups to share and sacrifice alike. True, we have a common war on our hands. Pearl Harbor did much to unify the country. But it would be a bold man who would claim that the war has completed the job of national unity. And remember, the day will come soon when victory for the United Nations will mean that we no longer have a common enemy to hold us together. Our national unity must go deep enough to carry us into the postwar world, trained to think and work together.

And again:

> We know something of what we are fighting against. But too few know what we are fighting for. In our war effort we have been long on

materials, industrial capacity, scientific developments, and all the things that money can buy. But we have been short on the will to pull together, the will to sacrifice—which money cannot buy. Our greatest need, and the basic cure of all our ills, is a faith that unites, a faith that burns—a fighting faith.

William Penn, continued Truman, voiced the classic alternative: Men must be governed by God or they will be ruled by tyrants.

When, in the summer of 1943, Truman toured the nation in company with other progressive congressmen to hammer home to the people the need for post-war collaboration with other powers, he was merely projecting his own personal philosophy to the needs of the world. "To win a military victory alone," he said in state after state, "would be futile unless we lay a foundation in our post-war world that will secure for all men everywhere their basic rights." He once remarked to a friend with genuine regret that he wished he were thirty years younger so that he could see for himself how long-term post-war plans actually worked out. He believes there will be, there must be, a "moral reawakening of the world," and that things will work out all right.

Smooth-shaven, smooth-thinking Harry S. Truman is not dynamic, nor is he a great leader of men. He cannot justly be categorized as a left-winger or rightist. He is incredibly modest; he is simple, honest, straight-forward, and practical. In Congress he was a striking symbol of democracy at its best, for he demonstrated what a plain, level-headed man of quiet integrity could do. He was living proof that the best representatives of the public are not necessarily the most brilliant, the most cultured, or the most gifted oratorically. He showed what could be accomplished by sweat and sincerity and the will to do the right thing. And as a plain man who achieved results far beyond those of his rhetorical, ambitious contemporaries in the halls of Congress, Truman indicated the pressing need for more legislators of his stamp. This would appear to be the lesson of his legislative service, and as such it is more significant than his concrete accomplishments.

But what of Harry Truman as Vice-President, or as succes-

sor to the nation's highest honor in the event of the resignation, incapacity, or death of Franklin Roosevelt? From
Truman's record it is wholly reasonable to surmise that, whatever the future holds for him, he will remain a man of incor-
ruptible honesty and basic integrity. That record bears out
the fact that, with the lone exception of the Pendergast-Milli-
gan affair, he has placed public interest above party interest.
He is proud of being a party man, a "regular," and he points
out that Roosevelt "is the shrewdest politician ever to sit in
the White House." He has often remarked: "A politician is
the ablest man in a government, and when he's dead they call
him a statesman."

When, as frequently happens, the Pendergast blot on his
escutcheon is held up to him, he is ready with an answer: "Tom
Pendergast never asked me to do a dishonest deed. He knew
I wouldn't do it if he asked me. He was always honest with
me, and when he made a promise he kept it." The only time
Pendergast ever asked a favor of him as a Senator, Truman
recounts, was when the Boss telephoned him one day from
Colorado Springs, where he was resting, and asked him to vote
for Pat Harrison for Senate Majority Leader instead of Alben
Barkley. "Pendergast said the White House had just called
him and begged him to get me to vote for Barkley. I told
Pendergast I was sorry but I'd already pledged my support
to Harrison. He just laughed and said: 'I told the White
House you were the contrariest cuss I knew.' And he let it go
at that."

Few will blame Truman for refusing to trample on the Boss
when he was down. As to his efforts to prevent the reappointment of District Attorney Milligan, he charges that Milligan
was over-ambitious, personally-motivated in the prosecution,
and unworthy of reappointment. Milligan, it should be pointed
out, was talented enough to crack one of the most iron-ten-
tacled political monsters ever nurtured on American soil.
Finally, Truman denies that the Pendergast machine lifted him
into politics. In a letter to a Missouri small-town publisher he
once wrote: "I was first elected to office on the strength of the
fact that I had been a battery commander in World War I,

and at the time of the election was running a farm in the southern part of Jackson County."

But Harry Truman does not deny he is a politician. Only a politician, he points out, could have been elected to the Senate in the first place. And, he adds, he would be loyal to the Pendergast organization today if it existed. Truman treasures the Bible, looks upon it as the best guide to practical living. And the Bible, he says, teaches honesty, faithfulness, and—above all—loyalty.

POSTSCRIPT

When Vice-President Truman hurriedly took the oath as President of the United States on that tragic afternoon of April 12, 1945, millions of plain people all over the nation, who had felt secure in the belief that "things could be left to Roosevelt," realized with a shock the enormity of the job facing the new chief executive. Mixed with the stinging grief over Roosevelt's death was world-wide curiosity about the new President; statesmen and writers and speakers hastily looked up his record and studied every line that had been written about him.

In his speeches and his Senate voting record they found that he had been a leader in the fight for a world security organization. He had been a friend of labor but had opposed any break in the inflation-blocking "little steel" formula. He had favored tax simplification and the removal of many governmental controls at the end of the war. He had spoken out against "bureaucracy" and for sane, practical post-war planning that would insure a minimum of administration interference with industry and a maximum of employment. In plain language he had denounced international cartels and the concentration of business in monopolistic hands. He had supported social security legislation and had pleaded for tolerance and an end to racial discrimination.

What did his Senate record show? He had voted for the Social Security Act, for adherence to the World Court (as far back as 1935), for the Wagner Labor Relations Act, for federal loans to tenants to buy farms, for extension of the Reciprocal Trades Act, for the Byrnes amendment to condemn sit-down strikers, the Wage-Hour law, for expansion of low-cost housing programs, for the Lend-Lease Act, for repeal of the Neutrality Act, for price control, for continuance of the Farm Security Administration, for continuance of the National Youth Administration and the National Resources Planning Board, for the St. Lawrence seaway and power project (fought by private power interests), and for the Connally Resolution advocating an international security organization.

He had voted against shelving the President's plan for re-organization of the Supreme Court (in 1937), against the exemption of water carriers from regulation by the Interstate Commerce Commission, against the reduction of non-defense appropriations by half a billion dollars (in 1940), against limiting the use of armed forces to the Western Hemisphere (in 1941), against increasing the corporate income tax rate from 40 to 50 per cent, against tax exemption for state and city bonds, against the blanket draft deferment for farm labor, against the Smith-Connally anti-strike bill, against raising the "little steel" formula, against liquidating of the Fair Employment Practice Committee, and against Congressional control of the Tennessee Valley Authority.

This was an excellent record, but great pressures would be placed upon the new President. Would he measure up to the task? From Missourians like Roy Rogers of the *Kansas City Star* came incisive appraisals: "Humility probably would be the first characterization. Then loyalty, perhaps excessive loyalties that sometimes get high officials into trouble; common sense; deep patriotism; and above all an abiding faith in his country and its democratic system."

Others were pessimistic, especially the great body of honest liberals who had been so disappointed when Truman won the vice-presidential nomination from Henry A. Wallace at the 1944 Chicago convention. But within a few months after the Missourian had moved into the White House most of the same liberals, to their own amazement, were singing Truman's praises.

With a combination of humility and great strength, the new President demonstrated his determination to place public interest above party interest, to carry on the ideals of Franklin Roosevelt. Everyone applauded his Cabinet changes, for the Cabinet under Roosevelt had included some weak sisters. Over the bitter protest of Senator Kenneth McKellar of Tennessee he reappointed David Lilienthal to the TVA. He moved swiftly to cut off overlapping administration agencies and to streamline and reorganize others. He urged the extension of the OPA, chastised a congressional committee for blocking passage of a bill to make the FEPC permanent, slapped the farm bloc by vetoing a bill to exempt farm workers from the draft, ordered an inquiry into the misuse of patents, vigorously supported the Bretton Woods monetary agreement and extension of reciprocal trades pacts, inaugurated weekly conferences with congressional leaders and noticeably strengthened the ties between the executive and legislative branches of the government. Institutional government took the place of personal government. After six months it was still too early to judge Harry Truman as the nation's thirty-second President and its second from west of the Mississippi. But as a Missourian, he was "out to show them," and he had made a good start.

2

GEORGE S. MESSERSMITH

"The Diplomacy of Intelligence"

BY GRAHAM H. STUART

I

THE STORY IS TOLD THAT THE DUKE OF TUSCANY COM-plained that Venice had sent as ambassador a person with neither judgment, knowledge, or personality. When the excuse was offered that there were many fools in Venice the Duke replied that they also had fools in Florence but took care not to export them.

Ever since the peoples of the world have established states the vital problems of peace or war have depended largely upon the character and ability of their diplomats. Diplomacy is not only an art, it is also a profession. The old definition of a diplomat as a privileged spy, or an honest man sent abroad to lie for his country is no longer fitting. The diplomat of today is not a foppish socialite, bedecked in white spats and a cane. He is no longer a lame-duck politician nor a wealthy contributor to the right party's campaign chest.

The successful diplomat of this era is a keen, hard-headed, shrewd business man. This is so because diplomacy is the conduct of a nation's business abroad. A nation's business is a large enterprise. It is not merely an economic or financial transaction. It is also a political undertaking which requires delicate adjustments, intelligent understanding, and far-seeing co-operation. Successful diplomacy must be based upon the fundamentals of justice so administered as to be mutually advantageous.

Although the United States has followed a hit-or-miss policy in the choice of its representatives abroad, on the whole its diplomats have held their own often under very difficult conditions. Benjamin Franklin would have graced the foreign service of any country in the world, and his colleagues John Adams, John Jay, and Thomas Jefferson would be outstanding in any diplomatic corps. The remarkable work of Charles Francis Adams, American Minister to Great Britain, in maintaining peaceful relations during the critical period of the Civil War, was a diplomatic feat of the first water. More recently, Myron T. Herrick in France, Dwight Morrow in Mexico, and Joseph Davies in Russia have improved relations and enhanced their country's position in the eyes of the states where they were stationed.

Of American representatives abroad George S. Messersmith, the Ambassador of the United States to Mexico, may be said to fit the ideal requirements for the modern diplomat. Of primary importance is the fact that he knows his subject both in theory and in practice. His is the thorough knowledge obtained by experience in every phase of diplomatic and consular work in all parts of the world. He is an ambassador who has reached the highest rung of the service from the lowly position of consul, and who in the course of his climb, has served as Assistant Secretary of State. Consul at posts in the West Indies, Europe, and South America, Minister to Austria, Ambassador to Cuba and to Mexico, he has run the gamut of representation abroad.

As a result of his consular experience Ambassador Messersmith is familiar with economic and financial problems which loom so large on the international scene of today. His administrative work as assistant secretary in the Department has given him valuable training to meet the problems of co-ordinating the work of the many agencies of the United States government which are found in all the important capitals of the world. Finally, his philosophy of diplomatic conduct is based upon the promotion of a policy of enlightened self interest. As he himself has phrased it: "Any arrangement between states which carries too overwhelming an advantage for one of them is bound to bear bad fruit." He has been able to stand by his principles because he candidly declares that never has he been asked to make nor has he ever made any arrangement on behalf of our government with another state in either an important or minor matter which was not equitable to both.

Mr. Messersmith did not prepare for the foreign service in college as many do today but entered it after a successful career as a teacher and administrator in the public school system of Delaware. The first post assigned to him on June 25, 1914, was that of vice-consul in Fort Erie where he remained about two years before he was transferred to Curaçao in the Dutch West Indies. It was at this second post that he had to face the serious problem which our foreign service officers so often have had to contend with, namely, to find a suitable place to live upon a wholly inadequate salary. The salary for the lowest rank in the career foreign service was $2,000 without any allowances for housing. Mr. Messersmith found that all of his colleagues representing other governments received higher salaries and that for a married consul to live on $2,000 a year would mean inadequate quarters in an unsuitable part of town. He would not be able to entertain in even the simplest way. In fact he would have to live below the level of the ordinary mechanic in the United States. Considering that the job required at least half a day at the consulate every Sunday in addition to overtime often on week days, such a situation did not seem reasonable.

With George Messersmith, to see an injustice was to try to remedy it. He wrote the Department of State that he had to spend all of his salary and at least $500 a year out of his own funds to maintain his position at the most modest level. Would the Department kindly allow him at least $2,500 a year. Surprised at the temerity of a lowly vice-consul, the Department forthwith raised him to Class VIII and gave him the $2,500 he asked. Furthermore, considering the higher costs due to the war, he was given a temporary post allowance of $500.

From this time on Mr. Messersmith became a redoubtable champion of adequate salaries and allowances for our representatives abroad. But the Congress was slow to act, and it was not until 1924 that a real start was made when the Rogers Bill, the Magna Carta of our present foreign service, raised the general level of salaries, provided for small representation allowances for diplomatic missions, and for the first time granted retirement pay and disability allowances.

But even the Rogers Bill did not help the situation in posts where the cost of living was disproportionately high. When Messersmith was sent to Buenos Aires as consul general in 1928, he had already reached Class II, which meant a salary of $8,000 a year. But Buenos Aires was noted among foreign service officers for the fact that the cost of living was the highest in the world. The new American consul general discovered to his dismay that a modest house without heat or light cost $3,600 a year. He and his wife budgeted their accounts carefully and found that with little entertaining and with no provision for clothing or leave expenses, they were spending $17,000 a year. He thereupon asked for an allowance for his house in addition to his $8,000 salary. He was refused upon the ground that it was not practicable to give allowances to officers whose salaries were over $5,000 a year.

Mr. Messersmith now took up the cudgels in real earnest. He pointed out that consular officers did not enjoy the same privileges as diplomats—consuls paid automobile taxes, club dues, admission fees—yet the diplomat received a post allowance. If a consul failed to keep up his end, it was the government that suffered a loss of prestige. This almost chronic situation crippled very considerably the usefulness of consuls. As a remedy he suggested that the Department collect specific data as to the cost of living of consular officers in all consular posts, then make an allotment based upon the salary plus the cost of living. The Department appreciated the situation and in the appropriation bill for the Department of State for the fiscal year ending June 30, 1930, provision was made in the contingent expenses "to furnish the officers and employees in the foreign service with living quarters, heat, light, and household equipment in Government owned or rented buildings at places where it would be in the public interest to do so." The act of June 26, 1930, put these requirements on the statute books. A first step had been taken to lift the financial burden of those who wished to serve Uncle Sam abroad.

Unfortunately, the economic depression began almost immediately following the good effects of this legislation. Salaries
were reduced 15 per cent, post and representation allowances
were abolished, rental allowances were reduced 65 per cent,
and finally the dollar was depreciated. The results upon the
foreign service were utterly disastrous. Mr. Messersmith was
now consul general in Berlin, where the situation was worse
than in many other countries because the cost of living was high
and the exchange rate was against the dollar. This was equivalent to approximately another 15 per cent reduction in salary.
Mr. Messersmith pointed out to the Department how impossible it was to support a family under these conditions. In his
own case as a Class I foreign service officer at $9,000 with
post and rent allowances amounting to $2,620 the decrease in
income was about 25 per cent, not counting the loss in purchasing power due to devaluation. The effect was far worse upon
the men in the lower grades. In fact in some cases life insurance policies were sacrificed, children taken out of school, and
even necessary food was not always available.

Congress was finally prevailed upon to remedy the situation.
In the appropriation for 1935, rental allowances were increased, post allowances to equalize the cost of living were
authorized, and the so-called Exchange Bill of 1934 provided
for the payment of American officials stationed abroad in dollars equivalent to their approximate conversion before the
United States went off the gold standard. This long fight which
George Messersmith had waged to make it possible for the
man without a private income to serve his country abroad in
either the diplomatic or consular service was won.

II

The French statesman and diplomat Talleyrand is reputed
to have said that it required a great deal more knowledge to
be a good consul than to be a successful diplomat. It was in
the varied activities of the consular service that George Messersmith first made his reputation. After his preliminary work
in Fort Erie and Curaçao, Mr. Messersmith was given the

important post at Antwerp in May, 1919. Here he remained for nine years, first as consul, then as consul general, and finally as dean of the consular corps. One reason for his long sojourn in this post was the remarkable results which he achieved in building up the trade and shipping of the United States. Promotion of trade is just as much a part of a consul's duties as protection of trade. But the means of accomplishing it are left to the initiative and the ability of the consular representative. He must be constantly on the lookout for new outlets for his country's products. Not only does he answer trade inquiries and prepare the periodical and special reports required by the Department, but he may range far afield with voluntary reports on matters which might prove useful and profitable to American business and finance.

Consul Messersmith made himself more than *persona grata* to Antwerp municipal authorities. On one occasion when the Burgomaster was dining with the American consul, the subject of a local strike was raised. Mr. Messersmith suggested a possible plan of settlement. The Burgomaster came to the American consulate the next morning and discussed in detail Mr. Messersmith's ideas regarding the means of reaching an agreement between the disputing parties. The strike was settled the same day. In recognition of his services, Mr. Messersmith was given the signal honor of receiving from the Burgomaster a set of woodcuts which could only be given to honor a citizen or distinguished writer after a vote of the Board of Aldermen. In the history of the city only forty-three sets of this series had ever been made. When Mr. Messersmith left Antwerp to go as consul general to Buenos Aires he was the first consular officer to be given thanks of the city at the Hotel de Ville.

But the Americans also appreciated the work which their consular representative had accomplished. This attitude was expressed by the president of the American Club in Antwerp at the farewell party held for Mr. Messersmith September 4, 1928. After noting the fact that the Club itself had been organized through Mr. Messersmith's initiative, he declared that "the consulate general at Antwerp had become an outpost of the United States where every problem of Americans abroad received prompt, personal, and sympathetic attention."

Mr. Messersmith spent less than two years as consul general in Buenos Aires and during a considerable part of this time he served as inspector. This gave him the opportunity to visit most of the important consular posts in South America, including Rio de Janeiro, São Paulo, Montevideo, Rosario, Santiago, Valparaiso, and Asunción. Wherever he found conditions unsatisfactory he minced no words in his report. For example, he found the consular quarters in Rio de Janeiro very unsuitable; the building itself was small and inadequate, the furniture was worm-eaten. He urged entire new quarters on the ground that the United States government suffered both in its prestige and in its activities. The situation was remedied and today we have in the Brazilian capital not only very adequate consular facilities but a magnificent embassy and a very fine chancellery building.

Americans are often quite careless in the matter of expressing appreciation for favors or assistance rendered to them by public officials. Our foreign service officers never expect to be thanked for doing their job well; yet while he was consul general at Buenos Aires, Messersmith received copies of many commendatory letters which were written by American businessmen in appreciation of the excellent services rendered to them by the consulate. A New York company congratulated the Department on having officials who could and would give all the information desired. A Boston concern wrote that they had often sought information from American consuls regarding the development of their business and usually received satisfactory service, but "we never before experienced receiving such efficient service and such complete information as was furnished by the consul general in Buenos Aires."

Mr. Messersmith's last post as consul general was in Berlin, where he served from 1930 to 1934. His experience as an inspector had shown him the complete lack of co-ordination between capital and provincial posts. The idea occurred to him that it would be a fine thing if in countries where there are a number of important consular posts both the ambassador and the consul general should visit them on a general tour of inspection and mutual acquaintance. He was authorized to try this out in an experimental way in Germany to see whether he could bring about closer co-operation between the consular establishment in the capital with those of the other cities.

Ambassador Sackett was persuaded to visit all the cities of Germany where the United States had consulates. To make the trip the more effective, Mr. Messersmith had it arranged so that the party would pay a special visit to each city at the invitation of the municipal authorities. Both the ambassador and the consul general were accompanied by their wives. The trip to Stuttgart was the first visit by the chief of a foreign mission since 1918. Not only did the visits increase very materially the friendly relations between the American representatives and German authorities but it permitted the consul general to make an inspection of all the consulates. In fact, it was found to be an ideal way of making the supervisory function of the consul general really effective.

It was while he was consul general in Berlin that Mr. Messersmith pressed for a reform that was to increase to a considerable extent the efficiency and the economic operation of the foreign service administration. The economic situation was very serious at the time, and if the chancelleries and the consulates could be combined in the various capitals, it would save considerable building space, reduce the size of the clerical force, simplify the problems of stenographic help and telephone service, and permit the two establishments to be run as an efficient unit. Since both the Rogers Bill and the Moses Linthicum Act provided for dual commissions and interchangeability of diplomatic and consular officers, the authority to combine was already available. Mr. Messersmith urged that the reorganization go further and incorporate the commercial and agricultural attachés into the foreign service under the Department of State. As he pointed out, the expansion of the Department of Commerce Attaché Services had brought about a very considerable duplication of work—a result definitely not in the public interest. There seemed to be no reason why consuls could not perform the functions of the commercial and agricultural attachés. The Department, however, was un-willing to proceed quite so rapidly and contented itself with permitting a gradual amalgamation of diplomatic and consular staffs in capitals where it seemed to be feasible. The consolida-tion of the commercial and attaché services was not made effective until Mr. Messersmith became Assistant Secretary of State and was able to work upon it from the inside.

The most spectacular accomplishments of Consul General Messersmith in Berlin were brought about by the rise of Adolph Hitler and his determined effort to exterminate the Jews. Inasmuch as a German-American consular convention provided that consular officers might address national, state, provincial, or municipal authorities to protect their country-men, the consulate general and consular officers generally took jurisdiction in cases of protecting American citizens in Ger-many.

A case of protection which received wide publicity in the United States was that of Walter Orloff, a Brooklyn medical student at the University of Greifswald, accused of communis-tic activities. The matter was brought to the attention of Con-sul General George Messersmith by two American fellow students. At first the consulate attempted to get Orloff de-ported, but the authorities declared it was too late since the wheels of justice had already started turning. The consulate thereupon emphasized the severity of the accusation, the youth of the prisoner, his long imprisonment before the consulate had learned of his incarceration, his ill treatment, the fact that no counsel had been allowed him, and the effect the case was having on American public opinion. The German authorities finally agreed upon deportation and Orloff was sent back to the United States.

The work of the American consulate general to protect Americans, both Jew and Gentile, was very successful, and numerous letters of heartfelt appreciation were received. The State Department commended Consul General Messersmith highly for his outstanding services in Berlin on behalf of Ameri-cans and elevated him to the post of Minister to Vienna.

III

The appointment of Consul General Messersmith to the rank of minister was an exceptional procedure on the part of the Department of State in that the tendency had always been to appoint foreign service officers with diplomatic rather than consular training. At first it was planned to send Mr. Messersmith as Minister to Uruguay but Under Secretary of State Phillips thought that his intimate knowledge of the Nazis and their psychology should be utilized and that Vienna could serve as an excellent observation post if manned by a keen and well informed diplomat. While consul general in Berlin, Mr. Messersmith, as early as 1933, had noted the military spirit arising in Germany and warned that "this country is headed in directions which can only carry ruin to it and will create a situation here dangerous to world peace. . . ." He showed prophetic insight when he reported from Berlin, November 23, 1933, that "the leaders of Germany today have no desire for peace unless it is a peace which the world makes at the expense of complete compliance with German desires and ambitions."

In Vienna, Minister Messersmith could see the Nazi menace even more clearly and he envisaged their program of domination of Europe with remarkable accuracy. Writing from Vienna on February 8, 1935, he declared: "There is no use in having any illusions as to what Hitler and the Party want. They have their eyes on Memel, Alsace-Lorraine, and the Eastern frontier. They nourish just as strongly the hope to get the Ukraine for the surplus German population and to get the fertile lands which Germany 'must have.' Austria is a definite objective, with absorption or hegemony over the whole of southeastern Europe a definite policy. . . ."

Although Mr. Messersmith and other representatives of the United States in Europe foresaw the danger to the peace of the entire world, it seemed impossible to bring the matter home to the American people. But President Roosevelt and Secretary Hull realized the situation and decided to reorganize the Department of State and the foreign service to meet the critical situation ahead. Inasmuch as Mr. Messersmith had pioneered in the field of administrative reorganization he was recalled to Washington and named Assistant Secretary of State.

In addition to being charged with the administration of the Department and the Foreign Service, Mr. Messersmith was appointed budget and fiscal officer, which meant that he had to prepare estimates of appropriations and present them to the Congress. In presenting his first estimates to the Congress in December, 1937, Assistant Secretary Messersmith showed that the State Department received far less than any of the other departments, in fact scarcely one two-hundredth part of the appropriations for the ten executive departments, yet in importance and position it was the premier department in our government. Mr. Messersmith emphasized the crying need for more personnel in the Department. For example, in 1938 the employees put in over 113,000 hours of overtime for which no payment was allowed. He also urged the need for more prompt promotions for our foreign service officers, better representation allowances, and living wages for the underpaid foreign clerks. The new Assistant Secretary was pleased to find that the Congress was very sympathetic to the needs of the Department when properly presented.

The outstanding development while Mr. Messersmith was serving as Assistant Secretary of State was the Reorganization Act of 1939 which transferred the activities and personnel of the foreign service of the Department of Commerce and the Department of Agriculture to the State Department. This consolidation which Mr. Messersmith had advocated for many years made for unification of effort and reduced to a minimum the duplication of services abroad. It was estimated by Mr. Messersmith that in addition to the far greater efficiency of operation, the net savings effected by the consolidation by the end of 1941 would amount to over $100,000.

In the Department itself Assistant Secretary Messersmith made a complete study of the organization with a view to improving its administration in the entire political and economic field. Although no abrupt changes were made in his two and one-half years incumbency, all but two of the thirty-nine divisions were reorganized to meet the greater responsibilities facing the Department. In addition, two entirely new divisions were established which have since proved their usefulness—the Division of Cultural Relations and the Division of International Communications.

IV

The ultimate goal of every foreign service officer's ambition is to serve as ambassador at a post where there is an opportunity to bring about more cordial relations between the two countries. George Messersmith has had two such posts, and he has used his unique opportunities in both of them to strengthen the bonds of sincere friendship. Undoubtedly his keen appreciation of the sensibilities of weaker countries has been most helpful in his service as ambassador in both Cuba and Mexico. The Platt Amendment is still a vivid and unhappy memory with many proud and patriotic Cubans. Our recognition policy of the past has not been entirely forgotten by our neighbor south of the Rio Grande. Ambassador Messersmith, who was born and reared in a small town and in his early work dealt with community problems, had learned the interdependence of human relationships. This appreciation of the other person's point of view has constantly conditioned his dealings with the representatives of other sovereign states.

Early in 1940, just before Colonel Batista, Cuba's political strong man, was elected president, Mr. Messersmith was sent as ambassador to Cuba. War was already threatening to engulf the Western Hemisphere and the United States desired and needed the support of its Latin-American neighbors. Ambassador Messersmith made it his first duty to settle all outstanding claims between Cuba and the United States upon a mutually equitable basis. He lent his support to obtaining a loan from the Export Import Bank of $25,000,000 to diversify Cuban production and considerable sums under the Lend-Lease Act for the purchase of war materials for the defense of the island. In 1942 he worked out an arrangement for the purchase of Cuba's entire sugar crop at a price mutually satisfactory and advantageous. The arrangement proved so sound and equitable that it has been renewed for the years 1943 and 1944.

When Mr. Hull put through his famous trade-agreement program the first country to sign was Cuba. The result was to increase trade between the two countries more than 200 per cent. The war made certain readjustments necessary, and Mr. Messersmith, just before leaving Cuba, succeeded in negotiating a revised agreement which took care of the changed conditions. Cuba's quick entrance into the war against the Axis powers after Pearl Harbor was followed by an all-embracing agreement between the two countries co-ordinating military and naval measures upon a basis of reciprocity for the duration of the war. The Good Neighbor diplomacy of the United States cultivated with skill and understanding by Ambassador Messersmith in Cuba has borne good fruit in abundance.

Josephus Daniels, United States Ambassador to Mexico, resigned at the age of eighty after nine years of excellent service. It was vital to name in this key post of the Western Hemisphere a diplomat who could be counted upon to cement the already friendly relations between the two countries. George Messersmith was a logical choice, and he has more than proved that the confidence was well placed. The situation in Mexico City was doubly complicated by the fact that numerous autonomous agencies of the United States, such as the Board of Economic Warfare, the Defense Supplies Corporation, and the Coordinator's Office had their own representatives in the Mexican capital. The result was unnecessary duplication and inexcusable waste of effort. Ambassador Messersmith quickly realized the need of centralization in procurement and the advantages which the Embassy possessed in co-ordinating these activities. He sent a strongly worded dispatch to the Department and at the same time put pressure upon the representatives in the field. As a result, a single official was made responsible as the channel for the entire procurement and development program and this official had to clear with the Embassy. Although this policy was criticized by some of the agencies as being high-handed, the consensus of opinion, even among representatives of the procurement agencies, was that the American Ambassador in Mexico City had produced the best co-ordinated program in Latin America.

Other achievements of a noteworthy career have been Ambassador Messersmith's outstanding efforts in furthering Mexico's emergency food program, his work with the Railway Commission to obtain prompt movement of railway cars with through shipments, the setting up and financing of a 100 octane gasoline plant, the construction of the Inter-American Highway, the procurement of vessels for the shipment of bananas, and the successful solution of many other problems which have daily challenged his skill and resourcefulness. But above all he must be given credit for making a valiant effort to obtain a final settlement of the vexatious petroleum question which has been the *bête noir* of the State Department ever since the Mexican Constitution of 1917 declared that ownership of all minerals and petroleum was vested directly in the state. At the Inter-American conference held in Mexico City in the spring of 1945, Ambassador Messersmith was one of the principal architects of the Act of Chapultepec.

The Second World War has proved that the world can no longer afford to settle its disputes by force. The prevention of future wars is the responsibility of the world's diplomats. They must dissipate misunderstandings between nations before they become serious. They must protect their country's interests by equitable adjustments based on immutable justice and human need. Diplomacy will play a more vital role in tomorrow's world than in the past. It must be the diplomacy of intelligence, of character, of justice, and it must be practiced by diplomats who exemplify these qualities. George S. Messersmith has proved his right to a high rank in such a diplomatic corps.

3

JOSEPH CLARK GREW
"Decade of Infamy"

BY CHARLES E. MARTIN

WITH ONE-THIRD OF HIS LIFE FIRMLY ANCHORED IN THE nineteenth century, and with upwards of two-thirds of it spanning the twentieth, Joseph Clark Grew, one of America's great diplomats of this generation was born on May 27, 1880. His father was Edward Sturgis Grew, a Boston businessman, and his mother was Annie Crawford Clark. The best of New England is found in his ancestry, environment, and education. His family had both economic substance and social position. It stems from British and Revolutionary origins and was connected by marriage with the first families of New England.

His education followed a traditional pattern for the young men of his region and station in life. Entering Groton at the age of twelve, he finished in 1898. And as night follows day, he matriculated at Harvard, graduating in 1902. His education, while satisfying and fruitful in every way, does not appear to have been strikingly eventful. It was in preparation for, but not prophetic of the dynamic career, in the midst of power politics, which was to follow.

To "top off" his education, and to broaden his perspective before entering upon the accustomed family business responsibilities, young Grew set out to "see the world," which meant, in the main, hunting in the jungles of Asia. This journey was filled with a variety of experiences, including fortune and adversity. In the Malay peninsula he contracted malaria and had to repair to India to recuperate. There he did some exciting hunting of minor game. It was in China that he bagged his tiger. These hunting experiences inspired his book entitled, "Sport and Travel in the Far East," published in 1910. It illustrates the by-products of the career of diplomacy which are sometimes as interesting as the diplomatic game itself. Finishing his tour in Japan, which did not provide the excitement of his South Asia experiences, he returned to his home in Boston. But it was to be only a sojourn. The ends of the earth had made their call. So had diplomacy. Young Grew answered in the affirmative. There was no turning back.

To prepare himself for the newly chosen career, he secured some business training at home and studied languages in France. Passing examinations did not then, as it does not now (but for different reasons), mean an appointment. Urged by a friend upon President Theodore Roosevelt for a consular appointment, the suggestion bore no fruit until the successful tiger hunt in China was called to the President's attention. At length designation to a clerkship in the consulate general at Cairo was made, and Grew immediately cabled his unconditional acceptance. Great careers and the fate of nations have been known to hang on less worthy causes than hunting prowess.

Grew entered upon his career in 1904. To be sure, it was a modest beginning, low in rank and salary, and with a working assignment of the most routine and uninteresting sort. Yet he was not discouraged. He did secure leave of absence in 1905, and married Miss Alice Perry, whom he had met in Boston prior to his departure for France. As a direct descendant of Benjamin Franklin and of Commodore Oliver Hazard Perry she was well fitted for the diplomatic life, and to this day she has been her husband's constant companion and counselor, sharing obscurity and fame, adversity and fortune alike. To them were born four daughters, in different parts of the world. Edith, the eldest, died in 1924. The others, in turn, made diplomatic marriages. One is the widow of Jay Pierrepont Moffat, former minister to Canada. Another is Mrs. Robert C. English, whose husband has seen service in Siam, Canada, and other places. A third daughter is Mrs. Cecil B. Lyon, whose husband has served both in Washington and in the field.

Leaving Cairo, where he had become deputy consul general, Mr. Grew advanced rapidly through the several grades of secretary of embassy at Mexico City, St. Petersburg, Berlin, and Vienna. He played return engagements at the latter two capitols, but as counselor of embassy. He was also chargé d'affaires at Vienna when the United States severed diplomatic relations with Austria-Hungary in 1917.

Called to Washington under much less dramatic circumstances than in World War II, he acted as chief of the division of Western European Affairs. During the post-war years of 1918-20, he was secretary successively to the American delegations at the pre-armistice conference and the formal peace proceedings at Versailles; and was finally named to the International Secretariat of the Peace Conference. He sat among the mighty while the course of the world was charted anew— and was destined to observe the foundation then laid crumble to earth from as challenging a vantage point as any in the world.

No diplomat is satisfied with service in Washington, no matter how distinguished or rewarding. It is something like an army desk assignment in Washington when war is being waged at the front. Nor is a diplomat satisfied with a consular post abroad. He always looks forward to his first chief-ship of a mission.

This came to Grew in 1920 when he was appointed Minister to Denmark. The next year he was appointed to the legation at Berne. He returned to Washington, serving as Undersecretary of State from 1924 to 1927, giving special attention to the reorganization of the Foreign Service under the Rogers Act. The call of the profession in the field again triumphed, and Grew spent five years (1927-32) as Ambassador to Turkey. Now the rewards of life began to flow in. Everything he did in Turkey seemed a prelude to destiny. He formed a fast friendship with Mustapha Kemal. He found a lasting place in the hearts of the Turks by acts of personal heroism. Representing the United States at the Lausanne Conference in 1922-23, he negotiated and signed the Turkish treaty of 1923. While Ambassador he negotiated and signed two treaties of the highest importance, which became the basis of our relations with the Turkey of today, so significant to world politics.

Diplomatic clouds were gathering in the Far East. President Hoover and Secretary Stimson sought diligently, and even desperately, to hold Japan to her pledged obligations under the Limitation of Arms Treaty, the Four-Power Pact, the Nine-Power Treaty, the Limitation of Naval Bases Treaty, and the Treaty for the Renunciation of War. Mr. Stimson attempted to outlaw war by a new interpretation of the Renunciation of War Treaty; he sought and obtained the collaboration of the League of Nations against Japanese action in China; and made a bold bid for British support in addition to the collective efforts of America and the League. President Hoover proclaimed a new doctrine in international law—the "non-recognition" of regimes coming into power in violation of pacts of peace. To hold Japan at bay, and to uphold the treaty-law of the Pacific, there was need of a man cast in heroic mould, who understood the technique of diplomacy and the wiles of Machiavellian politics; a seasoned veteran who could play the diplomatic game with the best, but for results and not to the galleries; and for legitimate American interests and world peace rather than power politics and imperialism. The choice fell to Mr. Grew, who received his appointment as Ambassador to Japan in February, 1932. Franklin D. Roosevelt and Cordell Hull wrought fundamental changes in America's foreign policy as President and Secretary of State. They also made sweeping changes in government personnel. Among acts of theirs which were highly applauded and which yielded great returns to our country was the retention of Mr. Grew at Tokyo, where he remained from 1932 until war broke out on December 7, 1941, when after six months of internment he returned to the United States.

Mr. Grew's first task in Japan was the assumption of the role, released by former Ambassador Forbes, of protesting against Japan's course in Manchuria, and of protecting American interests there from discriminatory treatment. He reported on June 23, 1932, to Secretary of State Stimson that General Araki had declared Japan's unwillingness to withdraw troops within the railway zone as set forth in the League resolutions, and that Japan did not "recognize the authority of the League of Nations' Inquiry Commission to recommend solutions of the Manchuria problem." In the next month, Mr. Grew, after talking with General McCoy, predicted that the findings of the Lytton Commission would reveal Japan as using false premises in (1) upholding her claim of self-defense in Manchuria; and (2) in asserting that the new regime in Manchuria was based on a legitimate exercise of the principle of self-determination. All evidence to the contrary appeared to be "window dressing." Mr. Grew doubted whether objection to the Japanese recognition of Manchukuo would, at the time, serve any purely practical purpose.

In August, 1932, Mr. Grew reported the hostility in Japan to Mr. Stimson's address before the Council on Foreign Relations on August 8. The Foreign Office used it to fan the flames of public animosity against the United States. Public resentment against foreign nations in general, and the United States in particular, was being built up to strengthen the military in its Manchurian venture against foreign, and especially American opposition. He made a brilliant analogy between Germany in 1914 and Japan now, the victim of a "hot-headed military clique." Continuing the analogy, the Ambassador declared: "The Japanese military machine is not dissimilar. It has been built for war, feels prepared for war and would welcome war. It has never yet been beaten and possesses unlimited self-confidence. I am not an alarmist but I believe we should have our eyes open to all possible future contingencies. The facts of history would render it criminal to close them." And in September, he reported that "the Japanese regarded the United States as their greatest stumbling block" in the realization of their aims.

The reactions of Japan to the report of the League of Nations' Commission were dispatched by Mr. Grew on October 3, 1932. The report was favorable to China and unfair to Japan, said the Foreign Office spokesman, especially on Japanese claims of self-defense and as regards the "puppet state." In February, 1933, the Ambassador summarized, with prophetic vision, the factors which entered into the Japanese "national temper": (1) the independence and prestige of the military; (2) face-saving, with its implications; (3) the concept of Manchuria as Japan's "life-line"; (4) dissatisfaction with China's non-performance of her treaty obligations; (5) the profligacy in military expenditures of the Manchurian campaign; and (6) Japanese inability to understand the sanctity of international engagements.

Throughout these negotiations, Mr. Grew tried to protect American interests in Manchuria against discrimination. These discussions resulted mainly from the creation and operation of a petroleum monopoly in Manchuria, which would endanger, if not exclude, the operations of American interests. The Japanese government uniformly replied that treaties between the United States and China were inapplicable, since Manchukuo had become independent of China; that the matter was one exclusively between the United States and Manchukuo; that Japan could not prescribe the measures of control to be exercised by Manchukuo over its economic activities. Thus the economic and military imperialism of Japan pursued its sordid course.

There were further evidences of Japanese penetration, economic and political, into China during 1934-36. Mr. Grew's share in opposing this course was, in part, his report to the Department of State, on April 20, 1934, of the circumstances under which the celebrated "Amau Statement" had become released to the press. Mr. Amau was chief of the Bureau of Information and Intelligence of the Japanese Foreign Office. He issued on April 17, 1934, an "unofficial statement" regarding Japanese opposition to foreign assistance to China. The statement, said Amau, had been approved by the Minister of Foreign Affairs. The statement set forth Japan's reasons for leaving the League of Nations, and declared that Japan's attitude toward China, considering "Japan's position and mission," could not be evaded. The alleged Chinese practice of playing one power against another was opposed. Joint operations by foreign countries, even as financial or technical assistance, would take on political significance. This would include supplying China with war planes and aerodromes, military advisers and instructors, and loans for political uses. Against this reservation of China to herself, Japan, the outsider, did not cease to protest. How could Japan express her solicitude for China's unity, order, and territorial integrity in one breath; and in the next deny her that measure of co-operation from the friendly nations by which these things alone could be realized?

Mr. Grew conducted many of the negotiations which, through no fault of his, led to Japan's abandonment of joint efforts for the limitation of naval armament. In advance of the 1935 Naval Conference, which was to negotiate a treaty to displace the London Naval Treaty of 1930, the Ambassador discerned the hostile attitude of Japan on this question, and the punishment meted out to those, especially naval leaders, who had supported the London Naval Treaty. The naval building by Japan, plus demand for naval parity, would place Japan on a parity basis because of America's non-building program. Our announcement to build to treaty limits caught the Navy leaders unawares. The Washington Naval Treaty was wholly inadequate, said the Minister of Marine, and a change of ratios would be demanded. In September, 1934, Mr. Grew was told of Japan's intent to denounce the Washington Naval Treaty. In the exploratory conversations, held in 1934, preparatory to the 1935 conference Japan argued for a "common upper limit" as regards any contractual limitation, and insisted that "qualitative" and "quantitative" limitation must go hand in hand. She also urged her usual claims. Mr. Norman H. Davis, head of the American delegation, insisted that the principal question was whether the equilibrium established by the system set up in Washington treaties should be continued or upset. Moreover, Japan should realize that by denouncing the Naval Treaty, she was jeopardizing "the entire collective system which had been set up by the Washington Conference for the promotion of peace and stability in the Far East." Mr. Grew in Tokyo, Mr. Hull in Washington, and Mr. Davis in London struggled valiantly to prevent this course by Japan and to save the system of the Pacific. But it was of no avail. Mr. Grew notified Mr. Hull of the Privy Council's approval of the abrogation on December 19, 1934, and on December 29, Ambassador Saito officially informed Mr. Hull of the action of his government.

Further negotiations over naval limitation were in line with the futility of the foregoing attempts at agreement. In 1935, Japan formally withdrew from the London Naval Conference of that year, called under Article 23 of the London Naval Treaty of 1930. In 1936, Mr. Grew, in view of American permission granted two Japanese government ships to visit harbors in Alaska and the Aleutian Islands not open to foreign commerce, asked permission for the American destroyer *Alden*, on a basis of reciprocity, to visit the Pacific Islands under Japanese mandate. This request was never answered. In 1937 Mr. Grew requested the Japanese government, at Mr. Hull's direction, to agree to the limitation of gun caliber for battleships. Japan denied the request on the ground that "qualitative" limitation could not be adopted short of "quantitative" limitation as well. In 1938, Mr. Grew, together with his British and French colleagues, requested a reciprocal exchange of naval construction information, since it was feared that Japan was building in excess of the limits of the London Naval Treaty of 1936. Japan replied that she contemplated no armament menacing others, and that a failure to reply to a request of no concern to the United States should not be so interpreted.

From mid-year of 1937 until the end of 1938, Mr. Grew, along with other officials, struggled valiantly to bring Japan's undeclared war against China to an end, and also to stay further armed penetration by Japan. This extended from the time of the Marco Polo Bridge incident until the tragic failure of the Brussels Conference. It is impossible to follow in any detail the chain of events in this struggle. It demanded Mr. Grew's daily attention. On July 22, 1937, he sent to Washington the terms of settlement which Japan demanded of China, which had been signed by General Chang, but not recognized by the Nanking government. On August 11, Mr. Grew offered the good offices of his government in the settlement of the difficulty. The Foreign Minister replied that the way toward such negotiations had already been opened. All along, Japan professed peaceful intentions and declared her aims were solely to protect Japanese interests, restore order, and silence boycotts and organized hatred of Japan. Yet step by step, she continued her penetration, until the danger of military operations to neutral interests in the Shanghai area forced positive representations by the neutral governments. Mr. Grew was of effective service to his colleagues at Nanking in urging American interests.

The bombing of civilians and other acts of Japan which endangered American citizens and their rights in China were subjects of extended negotiation by Mr. Grew. During the years 1937-41, these acts were committed with frequency. Typical of Mr. Grew's activities under this heading was his appeal to the Japanese Foreign Minister on September 1, 1937. What the Japanese were wont to call "incidents" or "isolated cases" might easily one day result in an open rupture of relations both countries had worked for years to maintain. The Ambassador had, a few days before, "reserved all rights" in behalf of American nationals affected by Japanese military action. On September 27, 1937, the League of Nations advisory committee declared that "no excuse can be made for such acts which have aroused horror and indignation throughout the world."

While the sinking of the U.S.S. *Panay*, on December 12, 1937, took place in Chinese waters, the major responsibility for the delicate negotiations in the Far East fell on Mr. Grew's shoulders. Everything to bring on a severance of relations, and even war, was present in this situation. Questions of honor and prestige, motive, plain guilt or gross error, misrepresentation or lame apology, made a strange admixture of diplomacy which many expected to ripen into war. The gravity of the sinking of a public ship of war of the United States, on a mission authorized by a treaty within the territorial state was recognized by President Roosevelt, who demanded that the "Emperor be ... advised of his shock and concern." The Japanese Foreign Minister tried to convince Mr. Grew that the whole incident was purely accidental and due to "poor visibility." The Ambassador, buttressed by reliable information from Secretary Hull and from his colleagues in China, refused to accept any explanations as satisfactory and reserved all rights in the matter for his government until the naval authorities could speak, first as to responsibility, and second, as to the extent of damage. The Japanese government was, for once, happy to make full reparation and "close" the incident. On December 23, 1937, the Court of Inquiry rendered its report to Admiral Yarnell, Commander in Chief of our Asiatic Fleet, who in turn approved the report, holding Japan fully accountable, and our own men blameless. In a three-hour conference at the Embassy, the Japanese Naval officials, while seeking to prove that the events complained of were "mistakes and unintentional," nevertheless were unable to convince Mr. Grew that the bombing was innocent. On April 7, 1938, Secretary Hull informed Mr. Grew that the total indemnification which the United States was prepared to accept was $2,214,007.36. On April 22, Mr. Grew cabled Mr. Hull that the full amount had been paid. Thus ended another incident on the road to "infamy," during which negotiations the Ambassador had acquitted himself with dignity, honor, and respect. It had fallen to him to guide us through one of the delicate peace-time problems in our history. Other bombings continued to occur and were protested, practically up to the outbreak of war.

Another diplomatic service attempted by the Ambassador, over the years 1935-41, was to secure respect for American treaty rights in China, and especially to prevent violations of the principle of equality of commercial opportunity. The treaty rights were guaranteed by a number of engagements with China. Equality of economic opportunity was not only incorporated into treaties but was our leading foreign policy in the Far East, to which Japan had agreed. Acts of interference by Japan were legion. Typical of these were the seizure and retention by Japanese military and naval units of the University of Shanghai and the refusal of Japan to allow American businessmen and missionaries to return to their businesses and mission stations in the lower Yangtze Valley. There was widespread interference with American trade in petroleum products.

Infractions of American rights in China, as claimed by Mr. Hull and Mr. Grew, included eleven classes of interferences

of an economic character and seven classes of damage resulting
from military operations and cognate matters. The United
States claimed (1) that our citizens were entitled by treaty to
engage in these economic rights in China, without Japanese
interference; (2) that Japan planned an economic structure
in China, beneficial to her alone, and discriminatory to the
commerce of other powers; and (3) despite assurances to the
contrary, Japan continued to destroy these rights. Foreign
Minister Matsuoka complained to Mr. Grew that (1) a three-
year war had been in progress in China, and it was unrealistic
for American citizens to remain wholly undisturbed in their
economic activities; (2) America, while refusing to supply
Japan with certain objects, complained of Japan's effort to
acquire them within her own sphere; and (3) the United States
totally ignored what the Japanese army and navy had done
to avoid "the recurrence of untoward events." The setting up
of economic monopolies continued, and there was no abatement
of Japan's interferences with our treaty and commercial rights.

From 1939 to 1941, Mr. Grew conducted, from Tokyo,
negotiations which were a part of the increasing tension in
American-Japanese affairs. His efforts were concentrated on
making clear and unmistakeable the American point of view.
The most celebrated attempt to allay these increasing tensions
was his address before the America-Japan Society in Tokyo,
on October 19, 1939. After the usual felicitations, the Ambassador plunged into an exposition of America's view of Japan's
policy, stark in its reality, and marked by its courage and frankness. Arguing against the "fallacy" of a purely "legalistic"
approach to Far Eastern affairs, he declared American principles to be (1) an aspiration for peace with all countries; (2)
respect for the sovereign rights of all countries; (3) belief
that wars cannot be waged without affecting non-combatant
countries; and (4) belief in equality of economic opportunity.
He also rejected the fallacy that America did not understand
"the new order in East Asia." He discussed the "order" in the
light of Japan's practices.

During this period Mr. Grew repeatedly, in oral and written
statements, urged the position of the United States upon

Foreign Minister Arita. The most direct and devastating representation was made on July 11, 1940, when the Ambassador asked of the Foreign Minister: (1) Will Japan exploit neighboring impoverished peoples for her own advantage, or join other countries in lifting their living standards and economies? (2) Will Japan join the countries now acquiring their territory by force? No reply seems to have been given to these questions.

The appointment of Mr. Matsuoka as Foreign Minister was the beginning of even more exasperating experiences for the Ambassador despite the Minister's profession of good will at the outset of his term. On December 19, 1940, in a luncheon address before the America-Japan Society in Tokyo, in which he presented Admiral Nomura as a Japanese Ambassador to the United States, Mr. Matsuoka made a number of intemperate declarations about American policy. Japan, despite contrary American opinion, was waging a moral crusade in China. Japan would, under all conditions, remain loyal to her allies (Germany and Italy), bound together in the Three-Power Pact. American views of its hostile purpose, whether wilful or otherwise, were mistaken. American interest in China's fate was sentimental; that of Japan was realistic and fundamental. So ran Matsuoka's argument.

Mr. Grew had a difficult task, in responding, to follow the Foreign Minister and the new Ambassador. He rose to great heights in a few words. The hope for peace and the desire for calm judgment, he welcomed. But he rejected the statement that America's interest in China was merely sentimental and called for concrete evidence of friendship rather than mere declarations. For with nations as with men, "By their fruits ye shall know them." Before the Budget Committee of the Japanese House of Representatives, Mr. Matsuoka declared on January 26, 1941, that America had no right to object if Japan should dominate the western Pacific, and Japan could not change her goals to accommodate the American viewpoint. The Ambassador had an interview with Mr. Matsuoka on May 14, 1941. The Foreign Minister accused the United States of unmanly, indecent, and unreasonable conduct in its aid to Britain and discrimination against Germany, and said that the "manly, decent, and reasonable thing to do was to declare war openly against Germany." Mr. Grew denied these charges with resentment, reminding him of Japan's atrocities and illegal practices in China, and justifying the American cause under international law. Seldom has so jingoistic a charge been made by one country against another. In a private note, Matsuoka informed the Ambassador that he had meant to say "indiscreet" instead of "indecent." Such was the prelude to "infamy" by the Japanese minister.

The adherence of Japan to the system of Axis Powers, thus disclosing her aims of power politics, conquest, aggression, and war, hitherto denied, was one of the most intriguing events which compelled the attention of Mr. Grew. The first step was the conclusion of a dual anti-Comintern pact by Germany and Japan on November 25, 1936, followed soon thereafter by the adherence of Italy in the form of a tri-partite protocol. The Japanese government, in explanation of both of these protocols, declared that the Comintern had singled out Japan, among other countries, as a field ripe for Communist activities. Japan, as the guardian of peace and order in eastern Asia, was forced to take certain precautions. Since the activities of the Comintern had become international, Japan was forced to attack the menace on an international basis. Mr. Grew, in a letter to Mr. Hull, declared that this "anti-Communist triangle placed Japan in the so-called fascist block of nations and emphasizes Japan's abandonment of her alignment with the democratic powers." The anti-Communist countries, he declared, oppose the policies of the democratic powers, seek to upset the *status quo,* and seek to rally all the so-called "have-nots" under this convenient banner. The threat of this alliance to the life line of the British Empire was pointed out with an accuracy rare in the field of political prediction.

On February 8, 1939, Mr. Grew informed Mr. Hull that Japan was negotiating a military and political alliance with Germany and Italy and expressed the view that Japan should be induced to consider its effect on relations with the United States. Upon Mr. Hull's authorization, Mr. Grew made personal representations to the Foreign Minister. Denying all along that the anti-Comintern pact was an association of totalitarian states directed against the democracies, the Three-Power Pact was concluded by the Axis powers at Berlin on September 27, 1940. Mutually recognizing the leadership of the Asiatic and European members within their own continental areas, Article 3 was directed against the United States, should it become a party to the European or the Sino-Japanese War. Mr. Grew regarded it as a "gamble" by Japan on Germany's victory over Great Britain. He told the Foreign Minister that Japan would become a satellite of Germany, no matter how the European war ended. Mr. Matsuoka repeatedly declared that the article was not directed against any single country. The official position of the United States was stated definitively by President Roosevelt in a radio message on December 29, 1940. The Axis pact, the President said, was a threat of united action against us, should we interfere with their expansionist plans. Our interests were identified by the President with those of the democratic powers, and were lined up against those of the Axis powers. This address, more than any other pronouncement, fixed the future course of the United States.

The visit of Mr. Matsuoka to Moscow resulted in a pact of neutrality between Japan and Russia, signed on April 13, 1941. Mr. Grew communicated to the Department of State Prime Minister Konoye's opinion that it settled the outstanding disputes between the two countries and meant a real contribution to world peace. The Secretary of State regarded it as merely descriptive of a situation existing for some time.

The United States, in the quest for peace, perhaps delayed unduly certain measures which could have impeded Japan's imperialistic course. Some have called this "appeasement." Mr. Grew called it "constructive conciliation." The application of certain economic measures against Japan would have led to war at a time when we were not ready. President Roosevelt, in a remarkable statement on July 25, 1941, declared that the export of oil to Japan was, in part, to prevent a war from breaking out in the South Pacific. Nevertheless, the President, through the exercise of export controls, narrowed down the critical materials exported to Japan until the war effort of Japan was considerably curtailed. These controls, directed from Washington, did not engage Mr. Grew's attention so much as that of the Department of State and the Japanese Ambassador.

Mr. Grew was especially concerned to prevent Japan's realization of her "new order for Greater East Asia" by discouraging her penetration into southern Asia and South Pacific territories. To the assertion of Japan's concern over any change in the *status quo* in the Netherlands Indies, Mr. Hull added the interests of many other countries, and called attention to the extension to the Netherlands Indies of the provisions of the Four-Power Pact, by an exchange of notes. Japan progressively began a series of departures from the commitments of December 13, 1921, culminating in her South Seas aggression. The Japanese government, under its mission to construct a new order in East Asia, brought pressure on the government of Indo-China, under the pretext of bringing the China war to a close. A treaty between Japan and Thailand, signed at Tokyo on June 12, 1940, gave Japan "progressive" aid in its task of establishing the New Order in East Asia. The denial of the rights of third states as well as the political objective of these arrangements with French Indo-China and Thailand were protested by Mr. Grew.

Japan's attempts to penetrate into the Netherlands Indies were checkmated by that government. Mr. Hull and Mr. Grew insisted on the importance of this area to the United States. The real policy of Japan was revealed by Mr. Matsuoka, in a bombastic statement before the Japanese Diet on January 29, 1941. Ascribing difficulties between French Indo-China and Thailand to Anglo-American maneuvering, and attacking the Netherlands Indies government for an uncompromising and unreasonable attitude, he declared it Japan's right to "lead Greater East Asia in accordance with the idea of 'Hakko Ichiu,' which represents our traditional racial aspiration," and is the "mission of the Japanese nation."

Despite rejections by Mr. Grew in Tokyo and Messrs. Hull and Welles in Washington of the Japanese interpretations and pretensions, Japan was headed aggressively toward the South Seas.

The "decade of infamy" in diplomacy was brought to a close by a series of extraordinary conversations carried on at Washington between the Department of State on one hand, and the Japanese ambassador, Admiral Nomura, and Mr. Saburo Kurusu, sent by the Japanese Foreign Office to aid in the conversations, on the other. Simultaneously, the Japanese high command was preparing for its attack on Pearl Harbor. Mr. Grew's part in these matters, while important, was clearly secondary. He secured from Japan a disclaimer of any intent to go to war with the Soviet Union. He pressed the Foreign Minister to encourage the adoption of President Roosevelt's suggestion of regarding French Indo-China as a neutralized country, should Japan withdraw her troops. Mr. Grew, on August 18, 1941, had a two and one-half hour private interview with the Foreign Minister, Admiral Toyoda, who, instead of meeting America's claims, stressed the prospects of war and suggested that Prince Konoye meet President Roosevelt at Honolulu in order to bring about an agreement. On August 27, Prince Konoye made a direct request to President Roosevelt for such a meeting. Mr. Grew suggested that the proposal "not be turned aside without very prayerful consideration." He conveyed to his government Japan's expressed desire for the conference, and conveyed to the Japanese government Mr. Roosevelt's insistence upon Japan's answer to certain basic questions, without which a meeting would be pointless. In a note of September 29, 1941, while admitting his role of "transmitting agent" during the Washington conversations, Mr. Grew fully reviewed the situation as he saw it, concluding that peace would not now result from a demand from Japan of specific commitments in the form of a treaty. Either a military defeat, or a "regeneration of Japanese thought and outlook through constructive conciliation" would bring peace in the end. That the military alternative would be elected by Japan, making "constructive conciliation" impossible, could not then be definitely foreseen.

On December 8, 1941, Mr. Grew was summoned to the

home of the Foreign Minister at an early hour and was told officially that the Japanese government considered it impossible to reach an agreement through further negotiations. The Minister thanked him personally for his efforts to preserve peace. Nothing was said about the outbreak of war. Later that morning the official declaration of war was sent to the American Embassy. The President within a few hours made his memorable address to Congress. The "decade of infamy" in diplomacy gave way to Japan's infamy of war.

Nine months after the termination by war of his eventful ten year's mission, Mr. Grew returned to the United States on the exchange ship *Gripsholm*. He was appointed Special Assistant to the Secretary of State, giving invaluable counsel to our government on all things Japanese—diplomacy, conduct of the war, the peace to come, and the fate of Japan. In addition, through many articles and addresses, he has disseminated information of the highest value to the American people.

4

WENDELL WILLKIE
"The Party's Embarrassing Conscience"

BY WILFRED E. BINKLEY

THE GREATEST JOY IN LIFE IS TO KEEP ONE'S THOUGHTS uncontrolled by formulas. I won't be dropped into a mould. I want to be a free spirit. If I wasn't one, I would still be sitting on a cracker box in Indiana." Strange words were these to fall from the lips of the president of a great holding company, The Commonwealth and Southern, as he sat in his New York office. But then Wendell Willkie was no conventional corporation executive. His whole career was that of a maverick —one that never could be caught and branded. The liberal publicists who, in 1940, showered him with righteous scorn on the assumption that he was only an errand boy of the "interests," had to eat thousands of their rash words before his career had closed.

Given the tribal history of the Willkies and the treasured traditions of the family, Wendell could scarce have been other than a free lance. One by one his four grandparents had reached America as refugees fleeing from German oppression. Such matters might soon be forgotten in some families. Not so with the history-minded Willkies. In this family they constituted persistent dynamic factors of personal motivation. Wendell said that his European ancestors had been in frequent conflict with their governments. "Those who did not observe the restrictions under which they were forced to live got into trouble; one had to flee his native land because he believed in the principles of the French Revolution. Still another was jailed for expressing his opinions."

It was the French Revolution of 1848, spreading into the

German states and finally suppressed by Prussian bayonets, that got his grandfather Joseph W. Willcke, as the name was then spelled, into the difficulties that impelled his migration to America. Wendell knew well the story of his maternal grandmother—how Julia von Hessen-Lois had been aroused from her slumbers by her father one unforgettable night in 1848, how the family had been rushed by coach to the docks, had hidden in a fishing boat and been spirited to England in a lap of the journey to refuge in America. Her rich merchant-father had supported the abortive liberal revolution, and so left Germany only a lap ahead of the secret police. So both the paternal and maternal forebears contributed to the great tide of the "Forty-eighters"—the German refugees who made such a notable contribution to American liberalism in the middle of the nineteenth century. The culminating effect of all these converging lines of ancestral experiences and influences on the present generation was summarized in Wendell's statement that he and his brothers and sister were the first of all the generations of their blood to know from birth the blessings of freedom. Implicit in this fact was a personal conviction of a family tradition amounting to an obligation that must not be betrayed.

Wendell's father, Herman F. Willkie, had arrived in America as a child of four. In this land of opportunity he grew up, managed, while teaching in Indiana schools, to get a college education, cultivated his inherent intellectual interests, became a superintendent of village schools, and married an Indiana schoolmistress, Henrietta Trish, a daughter of the aforementioned Julia von Hessen-Lois. Schoolmaster Willkie is still remembered as a strict disciplinarian—"Hell Fire Willkie," the Elwood school boys called him, because of his insistence upon attention to studies.

Busy as he was, Superintendent Willkie somehow found time to read law, was admitted to the bar, and developed a lucrative practice in the boom town of Elwood where the discovery of what seemed to be an inexhaustible supply of natural gas doubled the population again and again. On the side, lawyer Willkie invested heavily in real estate and accumulated a modest competence. Presently the enterprising mother too took up the reading of law, and she is believed to have been the first woman to be admitted to the Indiana bar. It is said that she once won a case in court against her husband as an attorney. Ordinarily, however, they worked together in the practice of law. Into such a setting Wendell Willkie was born in 1892.

Teacher-lawyer parents then were fundamental factors in the development of Wendell's personality. Here was an atmosphere that stimulated the growth of enduring intellectual interests. At times the family came near impoverishing itself buying books. Five or six thousand well-selected volumes were accumulated in the family library, and they became well worn. No regimented home life frustrated the unfolding personalities of the Willkie children. Good-natured, lively argument was a never-ending family diversion, and discussion came to be the very breath of life to Wendell. Among his schoolmates the bull session came to be an element as natural to him as water to a fish.

When Wendell was but a child the failure of the natural gas pressure cut short the Elwood boom, hitting hard the growing lawyer family with its real-estate investments. So his wits were to be sharpened by the experiences of a boy in a family that sometimes struggled to make ends meet. A man will not soon forget his childhood experience managing to earn ten cents a day, using a large horseshoe magnet to recover nails from the trash on a factory floor. So he sold newspapers, drove a bakery wagon, became, as a young man, a barker for a South Dakota tent hotel, worked with migratory threshing crews from Oklahoma northward, moved houses out from declining Elwood, and worked in a steel mill. In 1940 he fairly took the breath of a campaign audience by remarking that the last time he had come to that place he had arrived on a freight train. One summer between high-school terms he worked in the searing heat and deafening clatter of the big tin-plate plant in Elwood where the arrogant attitude of the management fixed permanently in him the point of view of the worker.

The elder Willkie's gratitude for his escape from Prussian regimentation to the freedom of America found unique forms of expression here. He must have been occasionally pointed out to strangers on the streets of Elwood as the incomprehensible lawyer who would never ride on a railroad pass. At a time when the typical lawyer lived for the day when a corporation would mortgage his talents with a retainer's fee, Herman Willkie could not be induced to accept one, no matter how pressed for money the big family might be. On the contrary, he became a conspicuous defender of the underdog, and local labor knew the lawyer on whom they could always depend to plead their cases.

While still a high-school boy, Wendell returned home at the close of a summer's work of all sorts in the West to find Elwood in the midst of a prolonged strike of the Amalgamated Association of Iron, Steel, and Tin Workers. As strike breakers poured into Elwood, the tension grew and the laborers' attorney, Herman Willkie, was finding his time and talents severely taxed to prevent a court injunction from paralyzing the strikers' efforts. Wendell knew first-hand the workers' grievances and offered to help. So the father engaged him as office assistant and, what seemed to the boy unnecessary, as a bodyguard. However, one dark night two notorious local bullies employed as strike breakers made a violent physical attack on the father and son, and the Willkies, aged fifty-one and seventeen, were acquitting themselves well when the police arrived.

Presently Wendell accompanied his father and local labor leaders to Chicago to seek the aid of Clarence Darrow in fighting the injunction. He saw his father interview the great lawyer, get his promise to assist, and was then staggered at the impossible fee asked—twenty thousand dollars plus one thousand dollars for each day spent in court. Wendell proudly cherished the memory of how his father carried on the injunction fight alone to a successful conclusion at twenty-five dollars a day.

Out of this family background went Wendell with two brothers and a sister to the University of Indiana. Here the monopoly of campus control by the fraternities so irked Wendell that he set out to organize the Barbarians, as the non-fraternity students were called. If, after some signal success, he did in the end pledge with a fraternity, it was not without some harrowing searching of the soul. "Why don't you go ahead and join?" asked his roommate, who found him one night pacing the floor as he wrestled with the dilemma. "If I don't join Beta," came the answer, "I'll lose my girl, and if I do I'll lose my soul." The girl believed he needed the subduing influence of the fraternity. The token pledge ultimately given was a compromise executed just before graduation in deference to the girl but late enough not to harm the Barbarians.

It is puzzling how anyone so extraordinarily active on the campus had time for anything else. Yet the Willkie intellectual interests were as evident as ever. He haunted the stacks of the library nights and week ends pulling out and browsing in whatever volume caught the fancy of such an omnivorous reader. Dr. W. A. Jenkins, the librarian, said, "I don't see how Wendell does it. He leads his classes, is in the midst of every campus activity, and causes the faculty endless trouble; yet he has read more widely than any other boy I have ever known."

Whether or not he merited it, Willkie came to be regarded as a "red-sweatered, campus radical spreading socialistic ideas, including abolition of all inheritances as unfair to those who inherited nothing." In explanation of this reputation, he said later, "I had read everything I could get my hands on, including *Das Kapital* by Karl Marx, and I was enormously impressed by it. I wondered why we did not have a course in socialism. A faculty member told me he would conduct such a course if I could drum up ten students in it. I had to buttonhole almost every one in the university before I could get ten. No wonder they thought of me as a socialist." Willkie always insisted that he was a disciple of the elder La Follette in his social philosophy.

It was no doubt fitting that the campus career of this maverick should culminate in a crisis on the day he was graduated from the Law School. For three years he had been at the head of his classes in law, and he was consequently elected class orator for the commencement. Present were the law faculty and the Supreme Court of Indiana as he rose to speak. His subject, "The New Freedom," was alone sufficient to cause the lifting of eyebrows, for by 1916 this Wilsonian slogan had about as completely run its course as had the New Deal by 1944. Some opening remarks, doubtless intended to be facetious, were interpreted as caustically critical of the law faculty. Then the inspired orator plunged into a glowing tribute to his hero, President Wilson, who had broken the power of the great economic interests. Not yet satisfied, he took up the then red-hot issue of the revision of the constitution of Indiana, and to the consternation of the conservatives demanded the calling of a constitutional convention. It was all thoroughly Willkie-esque, but he did not at once receive his diploma.

Admitted to the bar, Willkie had not much more than got settled down to the practice of law with his father at Elwood when war was declared. Enlisting as a private, he received officer's training and as a captain arrived in France only a month before the armistice.

Many a story came out of the army revealing the peculiar Willkie personality. For example, his colonel was overheard reprimanding the young captain for his familiarity with men in the ranks, which had to stop. "Nothing doing," was the prompt reply. "I am associating every day with men I'd be proud to look up in private life." His contempt for distinctions became conspicuous as enlisted men in trouble turned to him confidently for advice. "It is true," wrote Willkie in 1944, "that after the Armistice I voluntarily defended before courts martial, in France, boys, mostly from my own regiment, who, the fighting being over, relaxed their respect for some of the military regulations and saw no reason why they should not slip off now and then for a night in Paris. But this activity won for me no recommendation of promotion from my superior officer. ... On the contrary, my immediate superior suggested that on account of it I was a nuisance and should be demoted."

Out of the army, Willkie resumed the practice of law, this time locating in Akron, Ohio. "I represented all sorts and conditions of people," he wrote, "individuals, corporations, and partnerships involving every kind of problem—all those types of business that a lawyer in general practice in a city of two hundred thousand normally handles." But the son of Herman F. Willkie is said sometimes to have fairly taken the breath of the officials of a corporation he was representing in an important case by appearing against them as counsel in a personal damage suit brought by a working man. At the moment when the Ku Klux Klan had reached the peak of its power and public men were cowering before it, Willkie led successfully the fight to prevent it from dominating Akron school policies. Moreover one of his two main purposes in becoming a delegate to the Democratic national convention in 1924, he said, was "to put the Democratic Party on record against the Ku Klux Klan."

Was this grandson of German refugees from tyranny, this son of the persistent Elwood champion of the underdog, cast out of character in the role of president of the Commonwealth and Southern? There are those who think so. George Soule suspected "he would probably give a good deal to have that part of his career forgotten." As he mingled with utility men his ideology began to respond to the climate of opinion of the Pullman car and the business club. In the consequent confusion of thought we find him, in October, 1937, attacking the Post Office Department as inefficient because it did not make a profit and later contending that if a corporation were to take over the Post Office "this service would be as efficient as it is now and there would be no deficit." In May, 1940, he was comparing the New Deal with the French Popular Front which he was blaming for the weakness of France with all the engaging naïveté of an ultraconservative. Yet here was an upstart who only a little earlier had left a group of utility men fairly gasping by challenging to his very face an opinion just uttered by the then fabulous Samuel Insull. The mighty holding-company magnate wanted the "radicals" who were criticizing his system hushed up. Willkie quite characteristically expressed the opinion that criticism is a good thing. Insull closed the colloquy with the game observation: "Mr. Willkie, when you are older you will know more."

Certainly it was no self-centered organizer of an inner ring ready to exploit the main chance that had become president of the Commonwealth and Southern. Even a proposal to increase his salary was repulsed with the remark that he was already receiving as much as the President of the United States and under depression conditions the corporation could scarcely afford to pay more. Instead of milking subsidiaries as holding companies were wont to do, he even had turned over to the Central Illinois Light Company $700,000 gain from the sale of that company's bonds which the Commonwealth and Southern had a perfect right to retain as its own profits. With a keen sense of the trusteeship of his position he sought to create earnings with which to declare dividends for the hitherto neglected common stockholders. Five hundred new salesmen were sent forth to sell electrical equipment with which to create increased demand for current. He believed it was absurd for the utilities always to be fighting their customers. "When I became president of the Commonwealth and Southern, the domestic rates of the system were far from the lowest among the major systems, and the use was far from the highest," he declared in 1944. "When I retired, after seven years with the company, the rates were the lowest and the use was the highest of any major private system in the country." This is fortified by the testimony of TVA director David Lilienthal that Willkie "has done a real job of selling electricity at low rates."

The crowning personal achievement of Wendell Willkie was his getting himself nominated by the Republican national convention in 1940. The pre-convention build-up was, of course, great, but it was not constructed by magicians out of a personal cipher. Even Fred Rodell, in his frigid analysis of Willkie published in *Harpers,* admitted that "it was not—as often claimed—the wildly cheering well-to-do packed in the galleries, but Willkie in person, talking to delegates, and talking to pests, radiating charm and confidence and sincerity, who clinched his own nomination." Nor did the wily ones at Philadelphia catch him off guard. The party boss who sent an emissary with a proposal for a deal in delegates got the prompt reply, "Tell him no. As we say in Indiana, I didn't drop off the berry bushes yesterday."

What was there about the ways of Wendell Willkie that

accounted for such a phenomenon as the miracle at the Philadelphia convention? Keen observers were wont to report that the first impression Willkie gave was that of a big touslyheaded, excited and spontaneous Indiana boy. A habit of running his hand through his thick, brown, unruly hair contributed to an air of dishevelment. Sincerity fairly oozed out of him, and John Chamberlain observed that people "prepared to dislike him often come away from a first meeting with Willkie with a feeling of positive shame for their suspicions." Unconsciously he suggested Will Rogers, who never met a man he did not like. Stanley Walker was convinced he "would be as much at ease, maybe more so, in the company of a derelict bum, who came to his back door—and many do so—as with his college mate, Paul McNutt, and—which is far more important—so would the bum." To another newspaper man he was "as approachable as a Pullman porter, as democratic as a candidate for sheriff." So when he sat still and chatted all day at a picnic and was chided for getting no exercise, he explained, "But I'm having fun."

Through years of studying, meeting people, arguing, listening, and conciliating, Willkie developed his talents to a high degree of proficiency. He was blessed with an intuitive love of crowds which stimulated him. Heckling seemed to help him think on his feet. Moreover, he was blind to fear. It never once occurred to him as a campaigner to avoid an egg-throwing district, and no rancor lingered after the lively episode.

In conversation Willkie did not develop an argument systematically with a first-, second-, third-point logic but sniped at the matter from all sides and, as someone put it, "finally grabbing hold he rolls it up in a ball, and throws it at you." Meanwhile he "telescopes words together, dropping syllables like freight cars piling up on an engine." Surplus internal energy apparently induced the fussing and fidgeting as he talked. Thoroughly aroused, the slight stoop came out of his shoulders as he rose up to his full six feet, one inch, the blue eyes lit up, the facial lines became expressive, both arms began swinging in emphatic gestures, and one beheld something of an exhorter in action. Yet no matter how violently he may have disagreed, the argument over, no spite or rancor remained. "I've found you can convert anybody," he said, "if you're right, so long as you don't make him mad."

Even if Willkie did call his seven-room New York apartment "just a clutter of books," they constituted a well-chosen library of novels, histories, essays, biographies, etc., selected for use and whatever he read was stored in his tenacious memory. Facts positively fascinated him, and he employed dates and data with an exactness disconcerting to whoever chose to take issue with him. Apt at illustration, he found the Bible and Shakespeare familiar resources, while long passages of Bryce's *American Commonwealth* were at his tongue's tip. "I think I could pass a test in English Constitutional history with a mark of at least 95," declared this omnivorous reader. For historical insight, balanced judgment, and sheer felicity of expression, how many amateur historians, or even professionals for that matter, can match this paragraph from Willkie's review of *The Young Melbourne* in the New York *Herald Tribune Book Review* in the summer of 1939: "It is refreshing to read a book like this whose author poses no world problems, debunks no great reputations, and attempts to prove no social theory—but is content to make the final years of the Whig regime vivid and alive in a style lucid and engaging, with a scholarship exact but unobtrusive."

After his debate with Robert H. Jackson in the Town Meeting of the Air in January, 1938, no national leader cared to accept a challenge from Willkie for another such contest. Jackson was being groomed as the Democratic candidate for governor of New York. His speech, according to Raymond Moley, went off well enough, but Willkie so utterly outclassed him that "the Jackson build-up dissolved into the elements from which it came." The usually temperate Moley concluded: "Willkie is as literate as Winston Churchill, as redolent of the American scene as William Jennings Bryan, and as full of driving energy as Theodore Roosevelt. It is hard to find his parallel as a debater." Willkie's proposal in 1940 that he and President Roosevelt revive the tradition of the Lincoln-Douglas debates was doubtless made in good faith. Drew Pearson's proposal of debates between the Republican candidates in the spring of 1944 brought an acceptance only from Willkie, and it was a prompt one.

One searches Willkie's speeches and writings in vain for the clichés that constitute almost the stock in trade of many a campaigner. He packed into a sentence more substantial content than many a publicist put into a paragraph. While an excited orator was shouting the shibboleth "bureaucracy" and making nothing clear except that he hated Franklin Roosevelt, Willkie got to the heart of the real issue with the remark, "There are many competent men in our government. But they are frustrated by bad management. They are not given clear-cut, outright authority which permits them to be as good as they are capable of being." Another paid lip service to "liberty" while Willkie minced no words in blistering the poll taxes that disfranchise poor whites as well as blacks. He let others shed their crocodile tears over outraged "free enterprise." On the contrary, handling the subject without gloves, he declared, "The trouble with the free enterprise system has never been the enterprisers but the men who talked about 'free enterprise' and then went ahead and violated all the rules of enterprise.... A free enterprise system does not belong to a few at the top— that is a vested enterprise system. A free enterprise system belongs to everybody in it." Nor was this at all an attack on the capitalistic system but the view of one whose pattern of social integration was the idea of the essential harmony between the interests of business and those of the community as a whole.

"Men and women all over the world are on the march physically, intellectually, spiritually," said Willkie in the spring of 1944. On foreign no less than on domestic issues he revealed an acute awareness of latent social forces being released by the impact of World War II—forces that have shattered the status quo beyond any hope of restoration and rendered fantastic the dream of a return to international "normalcy." His success in collecting the material that went into *One World* was due, as Lindsay Rogers perceived, to the fact that he knew what questions to ask. The phenomenal sale of this book seemed to mark him as the evangel of a dawning sense of inter-national responsibility among our people.

Why did so notable a national figure, endowed with such superb personal talents achieve so little as a party leader? Evidently that kind of leadership requires a rare skill to be acquired, even by gifted persons, only through long and per-sistent practice—practice that Willkie never even sought to develop. Moreover he began his first campaign with a handicap the nature and magnitude of which he did not quite apprehend. Only four months before the convention Gordon Hamilton's article in *Current History* had reported Al Smith as following a suggestion of Willkie as possible presidential timber with the remark, "I understand he's a Democrat, but I don't know." The new edition of *Who's Who* had not yet, at the time of his nomination, completely displaced the issue, still reporting him as a Democrat. The candidate even had difficulty saying "We Republicans." When he addressed the convention that a few hours earlier had nominated him, was it a Freudian slip that betrayed him in the closing sentences into saying, "So *you* Re-publicans, I call upon you to join me," etc? Here was a con-vert not yet sure enough of his conversion to boom out the hearty greeting, "Fellow Republicans."

For two long generations Republican presidential candidates had been men saturated from childhood with the grand tradi-tion of the party. When the candidate was not himself a Civil War veteran he was usually the son or grandson of one. How-ever hazy as to details or even at variance with the facts of history his political ideology may have been, it was none-the-less a complex of convictions constituting a driving faith. Under God the Republican party had saved the nation in its direst crisis against the enemies of the Republic all of whom, whether Southerners or Northerners, he believed were drawn from the Democratic party. In any case the nation could never be quite safe in the hands of the Democrats. Such ideas get into the very bone and marrow of Republicans.

Whoever assumes that such matters can be lightly dismissed by a candidate must have skipped a good many pages of human psychology. Willkie not only lacked all this but, what is worse, had from childhood been indoctrinated around the parental Willkie dinner table in the Democratic faith. Episodes such as when the elder Willkie had sat half the night discussing the campaign with his guest, the presidential candidate William Jennings Bryan, had made their permanent impressions upon the memory of eight-year old Wendell. Nor can one casually knock off some Saturday afternoon and become a Republican of the kind demanded in a national leader. Now and then, as Willkie campaigned, he had the words—but he never quite got the Republican tune and at any rate he sounded off key to Republicans saturated with their party mythology.

Say what you please, the genius of the Republican party is strikingly different from that of the Democratic party. Its group-composition, if not its ideologies, would insure that. In its very inception in the 1850's the emerging Republican party had swallowed up the vast hordes of the fiercely anti-alien American or Know Nothing party. Ever since that decade, immigrants have tended to shun the Republican party. The great-grandchildren of the Know Nothings to this very day betray their lineage, for they are still "Americans." Something besides geography contributes to the Republican tendency toward "isolationism"—an inherent distrust of Europeans whether on this or that side of the Atlantic. The center of gravity of the Republican group aggregation is in the older native stocks, largely Protestant. Outside the South the Democratic party is heavily weighted with the Celtic and more recent immigrant stock, largely Catholic. When a man whose entire practical party experience has been with one of these ethnic combinations moves suddenly into the other he has something to learn. Nor is he likely to get it in a day.

So, whether he knew it or not, candidate Willkie in June, 1940, was an alien among a strange people many of whom were wondering whether he would ever get his naturalization papers. In his wide reading he may never have run across the extraordinarily shrewd observation of Shailer Mathews in his *French Revolution:* "The very 'ward healer' with his 'gang,' is today, by some strange paradox of American politics, a guarantee that government by the people shall not perish from the earth" Party organizations perform an estimable public service in maintaining their parties as going concerns. Such Republican leaders as Lincoln, McKinley, and Theodore Roosevelt worked with politicians unashamed. In 1940 this element in the Republican party required Willkie's special cultivation—not his neglect. After all, was this late Democrat merely utilizing the Republican party to gratify a personal ambition to get into the White House?

The very nomination of Willkie had shattered the rule that preferment ought to be the reward of long party service, normally starting in the precinct. Had Willkie ever heard of the Republican maxim, "The party is greater than any man"? There was something portentous in the candidate's brusque declaration that no ghost writer would prepare any of his speeches. This implied that they would express the personal convictions of a free lance instead of party opinion arrived at through conference and mutual concession. Joe Martin's early appeal to him for harmony's sake, to co-operate with the Republican congressmen whose constituents were not yet ready for a peace-time draft measure was cavalierly ignored and the acceptance speech advocated that very policy. The difficulty of getting the candidate on the stump to use the public address system until his voice was worn out augured ill. His decision to continue the Willkie Clubs provided a gratuitous and continuous affront to the regular party organizations. The struggle of the local committees to get the candidate to play ball with them went on until, as Max Lerner put it, "between the party boys and his own entourage there was a war of annihilation." Consequently when Willkie set out three years later to seek a second nomination, he felt impelled to confess his shortcomings and promise local party leaders to work with them. By this time, however, the Republican politicians had pretty completely given him up.

Willkie's drive for a second nomination in the spring of 1944 took the form of a vigorous speaking campaign that ended in the debacle of the Wisconsin primaries and his prompt withdrawal. Why did he fail to capture a single Wisconsin delegate in this contest against three candidates who did not even appear in the state? Newspapermen who accompanied him were prompt to note his failure there to capture the confidence of the local party leaders. It was an open secret that he was appealing to the party rank and file over their heads. Thus he would show the professional Republican politicians they did not know their own business. While he certainly had no idea of undertaking such a hare-brained venture, he nevertheless permitted to circulate, without denial, the rumor that he might, as a last resort, start a third-party movement. This looked like the threat of a club to be wielded by a man who had not yet even securely established his Republicanism. There were even strange slips of the tongue that seemed to betray a subconscious uncertainty as to his own Republicanism as, for instance, in his Green Bay speech when he is alleged to have declared, "Unless you Republicans uphold my hands your party will be on the way to certain defeat and possible dissolution." The tell-tale pronouns were fraught with significance. While organization men wanted to sit tight and let the voters punish the Democrats for their sins, Willkie kept insisting that the Republicans not only ought not but also could not win without a program. Meanwhile the persistent drift of the congressional by-elections convinced the party politicians that the Republicans could win without a program.

Blaming the Republican organization does not begin to explain Willkie's failure in 1944. The regular Republicans did not want Herbert Hoover in 1928. "He's a Democrat" they kept insisting and even George W. Norris, of all Republicans, protested Hoover's nomination on the ground that he had no right to seek the presidency on the Republican ticket. But Herbert Hoover then stood out in clearcut relief before the common man as the "Great Humanitarian." He came in "packageable form." His advent heralded the "New Era" with two cars in every garage and a chicken in the pot on Sunday. The masses could understand things as concrete as those.

No such luck as Hoover's came to the intellectually agile Willkie. He deluged the public with a flood of stimulating and wholesome ideas that fascinated the intelligentsia but left the man in the street bewildered and asking "Just what does he stand for?" This leader who in 1940 had vied with President Roosevelt in assuring the electorate that he would keep the boys out of Europe had turned into a super-lend-leaser even before Pearl Harbor. The candidate who had swept the isolationist counties in 1940, and not much more, was presently preaching the "elimination of narrow nationalism" and proclaiming the vision of *One World*. He criticized British imperialism, promoted Zionism, urged co-operation with Russia, condemned Darlan, and befriended China. On domestic matters he blistered the reactionaries in both parties, championed civil rights of minorities—laborers, Negroes, Jews—and even won before the Supreme Court of the United States a case that kept the federal government from deporting a Communist. He demanded "real enterprise," not just "free enterprise," insisted upon good administration and demanded taxation twice as heavy as the Roosevelt administration asked for and eight times as much as Congress was willing to vote. Thus can a keen, unconfused intelligence, keeping abreast of the swift march of events, produce a fine running commentary that leaves the man in the street puzzled and confused by the barrage of ideas.

Every successful American political leader on a nation-wide scale has managed sooner or later to master his art, integrate his ideas, and bring them to a sharp focus. Thus Jefferson made himself the symbol of agrarian justice, Jackson the champion of the common man against a ruling class, and Lincoln first the exponent of "Free Soil" and then of the "Union." Ignoring the history of American party symbolism Willkie devised no slogan with which to captivate the feelings, such as the "Square Deal" of Theodore Roosevelt, the "New Freedom" of Woodrow Wilson, the "New Era" of Herbert Hoover, or even the "New Deal" with which Franklin Roosevelt won smashing victories again and again.

Ideologically Willkie's difficulty in 1944 was the fact that both on domestic and foreign policy he was still the Wilsonian Democrat. His plea for real economic enterprise and the freeing of individual opportunity from the menace of monopolistic and governmental restraints was but the "New Freedom" of

Woodrow Wilson whose disciple he never ceased to be. This pattern and tradition had to be suppressed as he faced Republicans to whom the name of Wilson was poison.

Willkie's vision of a well-ordered post-war world was again that of a Wilsonian Democrat. Even during the Wisconsin primary, in replying to Fred Rodell's article, he published in *Harpers* the fact that he had gone as a delegate to the 1924 Democratic convention in order "to secure a straight-out plank in the platform indorsing the League of Nations."

Could Willkie have utilized Republican traditions in urging his program? John Chamberlain thought so and cogently expressed it when he wrote that "the tragedy of it is that he has an idea to sell that could have been put forward in the garments of ancient Republican respectability. The relation of tradition to party is important, and if a man establishes his 'regularity' he cannot be opposed on purely whimsical ground. If Willkie had got the idea across that he was the heir to something vital in Republicanism, there would have been no clack about him being a 'me too' adjunct of the party of Roosevelt. He might have been the Republican Moses, the man to lead his party out of the Egypt in which it dwelt throughout the 1920's."

William McKinley within the shadow of the assassin, proclaiming the end of an era of exclusiveness and the hoped-for relaxation of prohibitive tariffs was no isolationist. Neither was John Hay as he sought through a bold diplomatic stroke to save the integrity of China and American trade through the "Open Door" policy. Theodore Roosevelt and William Howard Taft were anything but isolationists as they promoted participation in Hague conferences and the making of arbitration treaties. Neither were Elihu Root and Charles Evans Hughes isolationists as they promoted and participated in the Court of International Justice. Here were names with which to conjure before Republican audiences and that is precisely what candidate Thomas Dewey did in the campaign of 1944. Missing no historic party precedent he utilized the prestige of every notable Republican who had ever played an important part in world co-operation. Thus he endeavored to convince doubting fellow-partisans that a post-war international organization was in keeping with sound Republican tradition. This could be done with ease by the grandson of a founder of the Republican party, but the same words would have sounded hollow if uttered by an unconverted disciple of Woodrow Wilson.

Willkie was a political evangelist rather than a politician-statesman of the type required for national party leadership. Given the maverick, the politician-statesman or group co-ordinator is almost out of the question. Lincoln's keen, cool, calculation as to the issues that would integrate a heterogeneous party combination was not to be cultivated by such a restless spirit as Wendell Willkie. Nor was Lincoln's infinite patience in private conference—reasoning, conciliating, winning over doubting fellow partisans—possible for one who was happiest on the platform haranguing the multitude and calling them to repentance.

Utterly freed from the fetters of a candidacy by the Wisconsin primary, Willkie could resume without restraint his predestined role of a free lance. In this he grew in stature month by month. On the eve of the Republican convention he published the series of articles that represent a high-water mark in the discussion of political issues. So he became to the Republicans what Dorothy Thompson pronounced "the party's embarrassing conscience." Not all the ostentatious show of indifference on the part of the delegates to the Republican convention could quite conceal the ever-haunting question, "What will Willkie and his following do?" Let those who assume that he achieved nothing turn again to the articles he published in June, compare them with Dewey's campaign speeches, and note how week by week the candidate drew closer and closer to the program promulgated by the departed leader.

5

JOHN G. WINANT

"Interpreter of American Life"

BY MONTELL OGDON

I

L ET US WORK TOGETHER AS FRIENDS," GOVERNOR WINANT
said to the legislature of New Hampshire in his first inaugural address on January 8, 1925, "co-operating one with another for the common good of all and so keep faith with those
who with high hope elected us to office." This theory, embodying the idea that public officials derive their authority from the
people, leads to the conclusion that persons in local, state,
national, or international positions of public trust have a basis
for finding a common purpose in their policies if they are
sincerely anxious to serve the public interest. Perhaps no man's
career in public life in America today throws more light on
the possibilities of progress on this basis, in local, national,
and international affairs, than does the career of Ambassador
Winant.

John G. Winant was born in New York City on February
23, 1889, graduated from St. Paul's School, Concord, New
Hampshire, 1908, and was a member of the class of 1913 at
Princeton. After teaching history for two years at St. Paul's
School he began his political career with election to the 1917
session of the New Hampshire House of Representatives, receiving the support of both organized labor and business in his
campaign. As soon as he had completed his first session in the
legislature in the spring of 1917, he went to Paris, France,
where he enlisted in the A.E.F. as a private. He flew with the
First Aero Squadron, became commander of the Eighth Ob-

servation Squadron, and was honorably discharged with the
rank of captain in April, 1919. While he was still with the
Army in France he heard that Mr. Samuel Gompers was in
Paris working on a plan for an international labor organization. He was able to obtain leave to go to Paris where he conferred with Mr. Gompers and participated in the preliminary
conferences concerning the plans for the proposed I.L.O.

During the years immediately following the war Winant
engaged in private business to some extent, but divided the
greater part of his time between the New Hampshire legislature and graduate study in economics and public administration. In 1920 he was elected to the state senate for the session
of 1921; in 1923 he went back to the House of Representatives;
in 1925 he received the M. A. degree from both Dartmouth
College and Princeton University, and began the first of his
three terms as governor of New Hampshire.

While serving in the legislature Winant worked closely with
Governor Bass in support of progressive legislation. His
achievements in the fields of labor and social security have
brought him much well-earned praise. As governor and as
president of the Council of State Governments Winant worked
successfully for measures that would raise standards of living.
He looked at a single legislative problem in its interrela-
tion to other sectors of the economy and wherever possible
sought to work out a solution on a co-operative basis. The milk
problem was one which affected more than a single state since
more than 90 per cent of the milk consumed in the Boston
area of Massachusetts came from Vermont, New Hampshire,
and Maine. Winant therefore advocated an interstate co-
operative approach to the problem. "If we are to stabilize the
milk market in those States," Winant said, "it is necessary to
work out an interstate arrangement which may possibly be incorporated in a formal interstate compact."

One of Governor Winant's first acts as president of the
Council of State Governments was to sign a joint proclamation
convening the Second Interstate Assembly to consider means
for harmonizing federal and state tax systems, and "to develop
more effective co-operation between the States in their dealings

with each other and with the Federal Government." He worked steadily as a member of the legislature and as governor to maintain and improve services of the railroads and utilities to the public, and to keep rates down to reasonable levels.

Governor Winant must be given much of the credit for enactment of minimum wage and maximum hour legislation in the state of New Hampshire and for the work done in this field by the Interstate Compact Commission composed of Eastern states. In 1917, at the age of twenty-eight, while a member of the legislature, he introduced the first forty-eight-hour bill in New Hampshire.

While governor, Mr. Winant obtained the passage of both a minimum wage act and a forty-eight-hour-week act. In connection with the minimum wage legislation he instituted cost-of-living studies for the state, which were carried out in conjunction with the Bureau of Labor Statistics of the U. S. Department of Labor. To date these studies stand as among the most comprehensive ever carried out in any state on living costs.

In preparing a legislative program and plans for the necessary state administrative organization to carry out labor legislation, Winant consulted with the most outstanding people in the field, in both state and national affairs, including such persons as Professors Frankfurter and Landis of Harvard Law School, Justice Brandeis, and Secretary of Labor Perkins.

On the suggestion of Governor Winant, the subject of an interstate compact for the purpose of harmonizing state labor laws was discussed at an interstate conference on labor legislation held in Boston in January, 1933. A committee to consider the form for a labor compact was created and Governor Winant was appointed as chairman. Governor Winant and State Senator Henry Parkman, Jr., of Massachusetts, worked together in the matter of planning succeeding conferences and in getting agreement upon an interstate minimum wage compact. "In recognition of the service of Governor Winant in furthering the compact plan, the Minimum-Wage Compact was signed in Concord, New Hampshire, on May 29, 1934, by the representatives of the Governors of seven States." [1] The compact was subsequently ratified by several states and approved by the Congress, and is still in operation.

II

Governor Winant's role in helping to bring about a settlement of the nation-wide textile strike called by the United Textile Workers in September, 1934, is an exemplary lesson in the handling of employer-employee relationships. The strike, which was the most destructive in the annals of American textile employer-employee relationships began on the Tuesday following Labor Day in certain Southern mills and soon spread through other important textile-producing states. It resulted in serious rioting in several states, with at least fourteen persons killed and a large number injured, the calling out of the National Guard in seven states and a loss of some $15,000,000 in wages alone. After the strike had placed more than half of all the textile workers in the country out of work, the National Labor Relations Board reported to the President that it had been unable to effect a settlement and recommended that the President create a special board with full authority to investigate the causes of the strike and to propose a just basis of settlement.

The President by Executive Order on September 5 created the Textile Board of Inquiry and appointed Governor Winant chairman with Marion Smith of Atlanta and Raymond V. Ingersoll of New York as the other members. The Board was requested to inquire into the general character and extent of the complaints of the workers and the problems confronting employers, and to consider ways and means of meeting those problems and complaints. The President gave the Board until not later than the following October first to report its findings and recommendations.

Governor Winant communicated with the other two members of the Board and arrived in Washington by air on September 6. Labor leaders, textile industrialists, and the press

1. Ethel M. Johnson, "Interstate Compacts on Labour Legislation in the United States," *International Labour Review*, XXXIII (June, 1936), 795, 800.

were either apathetic toward the Board or skeptical concerning its ability to effect a settlement. But the Board went into its task with vigor and, beginning on September 7, successively called in the principal representatives of labor and employers for conferences.

On September 20, two weeks after Winant arrived in Washington, the report of the Board was in the hands of the President and the Secretary of Labor. The report was as brief and concise as it could be made. It contained a recognition of the problems of both labor and industry in four specific recommendations. (1) For the more adequate protection of labor's rights under the collective bargaining and other labor provisions of the textile code there should be created an impartial board of three members to be known as the Textile Labor Relations Board. (2) In order to obtain necessary data upon the ability of the cotton, silk, and wool industries to support an equal or greater number of employees at higher wages, it was recommended that the President direct the Department of Labor and the Federal Trade Commission to investigate and report on the situation at the earliest possible time. (3) For the purpose of regulating the use of the stretch-out system it was recommended that a special committee be created under the Textile Labor Relations Board to supervise the use of the system and that until February 1, 1935, no employer should extend the work load of employees except in special circumstances with the approval of the stretch-out committee. (4) To aid in the enforcement of code provisions relating to wages above the minimum and to serve as an aid and a guide in the making of collective agreements it recommended the gathering of further information which would be made available to labor and management.

President Roosevelt and Secretary Perkins on September 20 were reported as feeling that the report furnished the basis for the peaceful settlement of the textile strike. The President commended the report as excellent—a good example of the practical way in which industrial problems could be calmly discussed and solved under a republican form of government.

On September 21 and 22 most of the mills reopened, and on

the latter date the Executive Council of the United Textile Workers and local leaders declared the strike at an end and asked textile employees to return to work. Thus, two weeks after the Winant Board attacked the problem of the textile strike, management and employees had by their action accepted the report and the mills were again operating.

III

Mr. Winant's work in the field of health and social security developed from certain primary social and economic principles which sprang from his sympathy for his fellow man during suffering or distress and his will to take constructive steps that would be effective in relieving individuals from want and insecurity.

A long-time and broad economic security program he considered as being essential. By tending to maintain a steady level of economic activity and purchasing power, social security measures would mean increased production and consumption. He has repeatedly declared that the prosperity and living standards of one state depended upon the standards of other states, and the standards in one country depended upon the standards and conditions in other countries.

Of the many achievements of his administration as governor of New Hampshire Mr. Winant ranked those which relieved human suffering as the most important. Children and dependent mothers deserve first consideration, he told the state legislature. Consequently, he felt justifiable pride in the legislative record during his governorship, which included the adoption of an enlightened and humane policy of protecting dependent children through increased mothers' aid, a vocational rehabilitation act, old age pensions, schooling and aid for the blind, and hospitalization for tubercular and cancer patients.

Governor Winant co-operated closely with the national government during 1933 to 1935, though much of the type of legislation labelled as "New Deal" had already been a part of his state legislative program before 1933. The New Hampshire plan which he developed followed principles for relieving unemployment that were later among those used in the National Recovery Act. As a Republican governor he was criticized for co-operating with the Democratic administration in Washington. His principles of economics and humanity were too deeply engrained, however, to be shed for partisan reasons. Where he considered the "New Deal" program beneficial to the state, he co-operated promptly. He lost no time in keying the state's institutional building program into the Federal Works Program. This he deemed to be good business, because the buildings were needed; the projects meant employment to people who preferred jobs to doles; the state would share financially from the national funds which it helped to supply, and the projects indirectly would stimulate business activity in the state.

The trend toward centralization in the United States, Governor Winant felt, was due to the fact that people turn to the federal government for action when and because they fail to get satisfactory action by the states. The only way to stop such centralization he alleged, was to provide in some way for the efficient handling of such matters by the states. He did not, however, look with fear upon so-called encroachment of the federal government upon the state governments, or of the state governments upon local affairs as long as the problems were handled efficiently and in accord with the will of the people. Each of us individually, he declared, "is a citizen of the federal government, the state government, and the local government, and there can be no intelligent quarrel within ourselves as to whether we are representing at any given moment the federal government or the state government or the local government. If our form of government fails," he declared, "it will be because that government failed to react efficiently to the wants of the people."

Mr. Winant felt that we as a nation had not in the past developed enough co-operation between the federal, state, and local governments. In an address delivered before the Second Interstate Assembly in the spring of 1935, he said:

Our mistake has been in failing to put sufficient thought on the problem of an intelligent adjustment of the functions of these various levels of government—and "intelligent," in this case especially, connotes an adaptation to the needs of modern times. We are too prone to imagine that a form of government set up more than a century ago will, without effort on our part, automatically meet all the changes that have taken place in social and economic conditions. We must have some imagination and some initiative ourselves if we are to implement those governments which were established to protect individuals and communities and national life.

The achievement of the purposes of the Social Security Act of 1935 was dependent upon effective co-operation between the Social Security Board and the states. States not having satisfactory social security programs had to set up such programs and to appropriate funds therefor before they could receive the federal aid provided for in the Social Security Act. Winant, who had achieved eminence in interstate co-operation and had been in charge of social security as assistant director of the International Labor Office, was appointed by the President as the first chairman of the three-man Social Security Board.

He previously had been appointed by the President to the Advisory Council which assisted the Committee on Economic Security in weighing the proposals developed by the committee's staff and the Technical Board, and in arriving at a judgment as to the practicability of proposals to be incorporated into a social-security bill.

The record of the Social Security Board under Mr. Winant's chairmanship is a remarkable one. During the first six months of its existence the Board was not able to organize its own staff or to make the grants-in-aid provided by law, because of Congress' failure to appropriate funds. However, through co-operation between the Board and various other agencies, particularly the Department of Labor, the Board was housed and granted a loan of personnel numbering approximately 160 persons. It set up a functional organization with three operating bureaus and the necessary service bureaus and offices.

The Board and members of its staff held numerous conferences with state governors, members of state legislatures, and officials of the states which had not yet enacted the necessary legislation. Draft bills of different types were prepared for the consideration of the officials of those states. Each type provided a variety of alternatives that made it possible to meet the needs and major differences of opinion in the respective states.

During the year 1936, as a result of the hard work and whole-hearted co-operation of the Board members and staff as well as state officials, the state legislatures perhaps achieved an all-time record in the enactment of social legislation.

On December 15, 1936, 40 States and Hawaii and the District of Columbia were co-operating in the provision of public assistance for needy aged persons. Twenty-six States and the District of Columbia had approved plans for aid to dependent children, and 27 States and the District of Columbia were co-operating in the provision of public assistance for needy blind persons.[2]

On December 31, 1936, a total of thirty-five states and the District of Columbia had unemployment compensation laws with an estimated coverage of 18,000,000 gainfully employed workers.

Chairman Winant resigned from the Board in September, 1936, when it was under fire during the Presidential campaign, in order that he could be free to reply to the political criticism without hindering the work of the Board or embarrassing the Board in any way. The speeches which he made effectively answered the campaign charges that the Act was a fraud on the workers and should be abandoned. After the campaign he resumed his post as chairman of the Board at the request of President Roosevelt and served in that capacity until February 19, 1937, when he resigned in order to return to the International Labor Organization as the Assistant Director.

IV

In his work with the International Labor Organization, as a delegate to the twentieth conference held in 1936, as assistant director in 1935, and 1937-39, and as director in 1939-41, Mr. Winant followed many of the same principles that he had adhered to as a supporter of improved labor standards in the state of New Hampshire and among the several states of the

2. *First Annual Report of Social Security Board,* fiscal year ending June 30, 1936.

United States. He conceived of the I.L.O. as a democratic association of nations, the objectives of which included "the advancement of labor standards on an international scale," and "the promotion of world peace." Long before becoming associated with the organization he had accepted the tenets of its sponsors that the standards of working and living conditions enjoyed by the workers in any one country depend upon the labor standards of the other nations.

Mr. Winant was appointed by the President to head the United States delegation at the twentieth International Labor Conference, of which he was elected Vice-President. He and Miss Frieda Miller, the second United States delegate, were able to show the Conference that their government, though a federal system, could do much in international co-operation. They jointly submitted three significant draft resolutions to the Conference. The first was concerned with measures to combat diseases due to dust, the second with freedom of association, and the third with unemployment.

Mr. Winant strongly supported a draft convention on reduction of hours of labor in the textile industry, and urged that a fact-finding meeting be held that would go into the merits of the forty-hour week in textiles. He held that the forty-hour week was justified on economic and humanitarian grounds. It was one means of attacking unemployment and was also imperative as a humanitarian measure against the increased tension resulting from the speed and specialization of modern production techniques. He felt that the forty-hour week in the United States had tended to maintain employment and maintain purchasing power.

The I.L.O. was a working international institution when Mr. Winant became its director. He is noted, however, for having strengthened its foundations, extended its effective work, and for having transferred the office against great odds to Montreal, Canada, where it could be of use during and following the war. Neither the employers' or workers' groups knew quite what to expect from an American director. But Mr. Winant was able to dispel any uncertainty they may have had with respect to his steadfastness of purpose and his ability to obtain co-operation in carrying out the role of the organization.

Winant deserves much of the credit for the development of social security as one of the important functions of the I.L.O., and for the establishment of a permanent social security organization for the western hemisphere. On the occasion of the inauguration of the Workers' Hospital at Lima in December, 1940, Mr. Winant participated in a series of meetings that laid the plans for establishment of a permanent international social security organization for the western hemisphere, which was behind the industrial countries of Europe in the enactment of social legislation. Following his endorsement as director of the International Labor Office, an Inter-American Committee to Forward Social Security was established at the Lima meetings. It was designed to work closely with the International Labor Office in making possible a systematic and continuous exchange of information among the social security institutions of the American countries, and to prepare the ground for the institution of a permanent social security organization among the American countries.

The First Inter-American Conference on Social Security, an outgrowth of the plans laid at Lima, was held in Santiago de Chile, in September, 1942. The I.L.O. performed the important task of preparing certain of the draft reports and draft agreements for the consideration of the Conference. The purpose of the Conference as stated in Article I of the statute is to "facilitate and develop the co-operation of the social security administrations and institutions." The procedure provided for is definitely democratic in nature. There are no compulsive features in the organization—but procedures are outlined and facilities rendered conveniently available that make it possible for countries to work together and to help each other in the improvement of living standards of their people.

The most dramatic and most important act of Director Winant in relation to the I.L.O. was his removal of the Office from Geneva to Montreal. As the blitzkrieg swept across Holland, Belgium and France in the Spring of 1940, the decision had to be made quickly. There was danger that much of what had been accomplished in the way of higher labor standards and co-operation between workers, employers and governments might be lost. The I.L.O. would render a signal service to humanity if during the war it could preserve its achievements in social progress, further promote co-operation between workers and employers in the free countries, and help to win the fight against fascism.

Sometime prior to the move, reductions in the budget had already made necessary a reduction of more than two hundred in the Office staff. The selection of those who had to be dropped and their notification were difficult and unpleasant tasks which Mr. Winant could have delegated to others in the organization. This, however, was not his way. He personally made the decisions as to who should be released and he broke the bad news to each of them personally. How Mr. Winant took time to see that these persons who were left behind were taken care of, and how he helped those to get away who were trying to get across France before the Nazi Army had blocked the only exit, provide a clue to his most outstanding characteristic, namely that of taking time to help people, oftentimes without their ever knowing it. Many of the most vivid incidents connected with the evacuation from Geneva cannot be told as yet —but members of the I.L.O. staff have likened Director Winant's action in looking after people before he left to that of the skipper who is the last person to leave a ship.

Through the good offices of Prime Minister Mackenzie King, the International Labor Organization was able to establish its seat in Montreal. Emergency headquarters were set up in a Montreal church. The Canadian government gave the Office diplomatic status, which entitled the officials and staff to the privileges and immunities necessary for the performance of the Office's functions. McGill University in Montreal gave quarters and other facilities. By November, 1940, the Office was established in its new location.

It was Director Winant's desire that the Office, operating from Montreal, should carry on as many of its varied functions as possible. This it has done, particularly with respect to rendering assistance to governments, maintenance of research, and preparations for post-war reconstruction. During the very year in which the transfer was made from Europe, the Office issued a number of special reports and has since continued to issue its principal periodicals. Since 1941, it has also been able to produce some important economic reports, which were begun while Mr. Winant was still the director. These include *Wartime Developments in Government-Employer-Worker Collaboration* (1941), which describes the institutions and procedures set up or developed during the war, *Food Control in Great Britain* (1942), *Intergovernmental Commodity Control Agreements* (1943), and *Man-Power Mobilization for Peace* (1943), which considers the problem of demobilization after the war of persons serving in the armed forces and in war industries and their re-employment in peace work.

It was Director Winant's view that the Organization should use its machinery to help lay the basis for a democratic post-war international organization. The Labor Organization could help to plan toward an orderly and socially desirable demobilization of war and defense industries. It could furnish a forum in which workers would have a chance to discuss their plans for the post-war period with the workers of other countries and to test their ideas of the social objectives of peace and for meeting post-war problems against representative and alert international opinion. Finally, Mr. Winant felt that the International Labor Organization provided the means, through the use of scientific knowledge and democratic processes, by which social justice might be achieved. Hence he considered it to be "the duty of the I.L.O. to help formulate a practical social program that will assure to the people recognition of their needs and to each member country sound social and economic institutions." [3]

As soon as the Office had been established at Montreal it set about, under Mr. Winant's direction, to assemble data and to plan the work for succeeding labor conferences that would help to pave the way for post-war reconstruction of the social order. The Conference of the International Labor Organization which met in New York City from October 27 to Novem-

3. *International Labour Review*, XLII (Oct.-Nov., 1940), 173-74.

ber 5 and in Washington on November 6, 1941, was in large part the result of plans which Mr. Winant helped to lay before he resigned as director on February 15, 1941, to accept the American ambassadorship to Great Britain.

The 1941 conference adopted a number of resolutions dealing with various phases of post-war reconstruction. Resolution C, which epitomized the opinion of the conference, was proposed by the government's, employers' and workers' delegates of the United States, and adopted in an amended form. It provided in effect that the I.L.O. should participate in the task of implementing the social and economic principles of the Atlantic Charter, but there was no exact definition as to what form this participation should take or how far it should go. The twenty-sixth session of the International Labor Conference which convened in Philadelphia on April 20, 1944, to consider the program, status, and policy of the I.L.O. in the post-war world, was visualized by Mr. Winant as a new constitutional convention. Writing in *The Saturday Evening Post* for April 15, 1944, Ambassador Winant expressed the opinion that "the history, the record and the organizational structure of the I.L.O. give solid ground for hope that its advice and its help will be of service to the governments of the United Nations."

The work that the International Labor Organization has done in the war of the United Nations against fascism, the contribution which it is making to the establishment of a sound post-war social structure, and the service to mankind which it may render as a functional United Nations organization are due in no small part to the efforts of Mr. Winant. The second resolution of the 1941 conference was adopted as a tribute by the International Labor Organization to the Honorable John G. Winant, former Director, for being successful in having preserved "the life, spirit and freedom of the organization."

V

The matters with which a wartime and post-war ambassador must deal in the post at London cover a wide range of subjects, and many of them involve problems of state of great import to the United Nations in the war effort and in building the post-war international organization. The various problems with which the embassy is concerned, besides such routine matters as standing reports and arrangements for the coming and going of a constant stream of American officials, include public morale, military and naval matters, lend-lease, maintenance of health and social welfare, most efficient use of manpower and resources, and such post-war problems as relief and the relaxation of trade barriers. Ambassador Winant was particularly well qualified for dealing with the public problems that were basic to the success of our joint military undertaking against fascism.

The Ambassador had known and worked with Anthony Eden, Ernest Bevin, and many other people in English public life on the laborer's welfare, health, and nutrition. Mr. Eden pointed out that service to humanity had been Winant's life work, that he had in all his varied activities devoted himself to providing greater freedom and a fuller life for mankind, and added that never in the history of the Anglo-American relations had the English people been so fortunate in the representatives sent to them from overseas. The hope which was felt among Englishmen of all classes upon the appointment of Ambassador Winant was expressed by the poet laureate, John Masefield, when he welcomed Mr. Winant as follows:

Two with like laws and language should be friends.
Whatever enmities have marred a past,
A future with goodwill may make amends
And build a new world happier than the last.
Your coming and your friendship are a cheer.
If yours and ours will but understand,
Earth's future children will not live in fear,
Nor deed of spirit die by deed of hand.

Prior to the war the organization of the embassy staff was comparatively simple. Besides the ambassador it consisted of a counselor of embassy, the career secretaries of embassy, the attachés, a number of officers concerned with administrative and other matters, and the necessary clerks and messengers. The total personnel normally numbered about 250. By the time D-day came, there were some 1,500-odd officers and employees of the embassy, representing more than twenty departments and agencies of this government. Some of the special missions employ more personnel than did the embassy prior to the war, and they are housed not only in the handsome six-floor embassy building but in numerous buildings around Grosvenor Square and in adjoining blocks. There has at no time been a conflict between the policies being pursued by our embassy at London and the representatives who head the special missions. Ambassador Winant himself has worked closely with the heads of the special missions and with the career men, as well, such as Dr. H. Freeman Mathews, senior career member of the embassy, and counselor of the embassy from 1940 to 1943. He immediately put across the idea that everybody, career diplomat, special representative, or clerk, was a member of one team which had an all-important task to perform.

Instead of occupying the magnificent embassy residence and entertaining in the diplomatic style, Ambassador and Mrs. Winant, together with the children when they were still at home, have modestly lived in a five-room flat on an upper floor of the embassy. Mrs. Winant shares the Ambassador's simplicity, kindness, and intense desire to help people and in her own right has contributed much to the same cause.

Among Mr. Winant's greatest achievements as ambassador is the job of morale building which he performed within the first few months after his arrival in England. The battle of Dunkirk had taken place; the blitz was in full swing; London had been largely evacuated of children and also of many other persons; English soldiers and civilians were manning the beaches, and the danger of invasion had by no means passed. Englishmen realized that ours was a friendly neutrality, but their peril was great and they found it hard to understand why America did not consider herself in danger.

When Mr. Winant spoke to them his words were appropriately those of the ambassador of a neutral nation, but they came from the heart of a man who would never cease fighting for freedom; their courage revived in the knowledge that

American ideals were the same as those for which Britain was fighting. Here was a man who spent his nights during the air raids out in the streets of London going about lending a hand to anyone who needed it. He revived their faith in America and in mankind. They knew that they would not long have to fight alone. Prime Minister Churchill, whom many considered to be one of the great fountains of courage, declared that Winant gave him strength.

Ambassador Winant is possibly the greatest interpreter of American life we have ever had at the Court of Saint James's. He believes in the people he represents, and he understands and appreciates the people among whom he resides. In a very brief period he had gained the confidence, the respect, and the affection of the English people. He is, of course, called upon to make many public addresses. These he limits to a few minutes in length, but he has something specific to say to each of the many different types of groups with which he comes in contact.

There are many ways in which the Ambassador assisted in the solution of military problems. For example, in the exchange of American destroyers for bases in British possessions, one of Winant's tasks, in co-operation with the Army and the Navy, was to secure the rights, powers, and authority necessary for the construction and operation of those bases by our armed forces, with adequate safeguards to protect the communities in which they were located. After Pearl Harbor this task was expanded to cover arrangements for use by American military and naval forces of bases of operations and lines of communication in British territory all over the world.

Ambassador Winant has been helpful in promoting good relations between our armed forces in the British Isles and the British forces and populace. He pays tribute to General "Ike" Eisenhower, as being "a supreme master of teamwork." The Ambassador himself also deserves credit for smoothing the way for welding the forces of the several allied countries into a single force. He recognized the inevitable problems in the presence of hundreds of thousands of foreign soldiers in a country no larger than the United Kingdom. He has co-operated with the American commanding officers in suggesting ways to help the American boy adjust himself to English ways, and with the English in suggesting ways of making our boys feel at home and avoiding friction. It is believed that Englishmen now have the highest regard for Americans that they have ever had, many reports of differences notwithstanding. Each day the American visitor hears from the lips of some Englishman or woman the following words: "We did not understand Americans before, but that is changed now." Our troops, Ambassador Winant declares, are the finest ambassadors there are. Large numbers of them have come into contact with the English people and each have found that they could get along together.

When Lord Beaverbrook heard Winant express his views on an important subject for the first time he stated his immediate reaction in the following words: "I know that man means everything he says." Ambassador Winant has proved the truth of Beaverbrook's remark. Some of the cases which have brought out Winant's forcefulness and effectiveness are still of a confidential character, but certain instances are well known in London and increase the respect which official Britain has for this "Yankee Ambassador."

Ambassador Winant's background and forcefulness of character have been of great value in making effective the policy of his government to obtain the most efficient use of United Nations resources in the war effort and the application of the principles laid down in the Atlantic Charter in vital decisions concerning the post-war structure. Mr. Winant had a carefully selected group of experts of the embassy staff devote themselves to the task of gathering information on the wartime problems faced in Great Britain, such as rationing, prices, and manpower, and of the methods employed by the British government in solution of these problems. The embassy has consequently furnished valuable information for the guidance of our own government, enabling it to profit from British experience and to avoid many mistakes which they had made and corrected. This work, Ambassador Winant believes, has borne fruit by increasing our own industrial contribution to the total war effort while at the same time we retained our democratic processes.

By keeping himself personally well informed concerning production and manpower in Britain Mr. Winant has also been able to render valuable aid to the British government in the joint effort to make most effective use of available resources. During a coal strike in England in June, 1942, Mr. Winant was asked by Mr. Bevin to talk to the men on strike with view to persuading them to return to work. Winant was qualified to make such an appeal. He had not only brought about the settlement of a more difficult strike in 1934 in the United States, but he had been through the hardship and tragedy of the last war; he had seen the cruelties of depression and unemployment, and he had experienced the Nazi blitzes on London.

Ambassador Winant went to Durham and talked to the miners in their association hall, after which they went back to their jobs. In a brief speech of fifteen minutes, simple and sincere, he talked of the critical stage of the war, the necessity of enduring courage, and the objectives of the living democracy which we are fighting to preserve. He associated all democratic peoples together in the war effort and the social reconstruction effort that must follow the war. The fight for post-war social objectives, he said, was not something we shelve for the duration; "it is a part of the war."

Ambassador Winant closed his speech to the miners by urging the faith and philosophy which guide his own public action.

Just as the peoples of democracy are united in a common objective today, so we are committed to a common objective tomorrow. We are committed to the establishment of service democracy. This is the democracy that brought Britain through the blitzes. This is the democracy that is manning our forces. This is the democracy that is bringing ships, planes, tanks and guns in growing volume from your factories and from ours. This is the peoples' democracy. We must keep it wide and vigorous, alive to need of whatever kind and ready to meet it whether it be danger from without or well being from within, always remembering that it is the things of the spirit that in the end prevail, that caring counts; that where there is no vision people perish; that hope and faith count and that without charity there can be nothing good.

Ambassador Winant has not only staunchly defended the principles of the Atlantic Charter but has worked for the establishment of the necessary international machinery to assure their fulfillment. He has been conscious of the need and the difficulties involved in the social, economic, and political reconstruction. The people of this country and of Europe have been fortunate to have a man of Ambassador Winant's capacity and integrity to deal with these problems. It is such men as Ambassador Winant, who have the love for their fellow man, the faith in democracy, and the courage to act on that faith that enable us to enjoy the full fruits of a democratic life. His achievements are proof that problems in the international sphere as well as in local affairs can be solved through friendly co-operation on the basis of social justice.

6

HENRY AGARD WALLACE
"People Are More Important than Pigs"

BY PAUL SIFTON

I

THE MORNING OF THURSDAY, JANUARY 25, 1945, WAS clear and cold. In Washington, D. C., thousands of homes were chill because of a shortage of oil and coal. The nation's transportation system was slowed down by the worst winter in twenty years. War production in Pittsburgh and other industrial centers was slowed down by lack of coal and raw material deliveries. In Europe, American armies fought yard by yard toward the heart of industrial Germany. On the Eastern front, Russia had resumed the drive toward Berlin. In the Pacific, MacArthur was on Luzon, only a few miles from Manila, and B-29's were pounding Japan itself. The U.S.A., the arsenal of democracy, was producing for war at the rate of seven billion dollars a month—ten million an hour, around the clock. Twelve million young Americans were in the Army, Navy, and Merchant Marine; fifty-two million more were employed, twenty million of them in direct war production; and jobs, essential and non-essential, were going begging. President Roosevelt and high officials of his staff were "out of town," although the press was not allowed to say so, *en route* to Yalta where the terms of European peace were to be drafted with Churchill, Stalin, and their staffs. The nation slogged through the snow and icy mud, thinking of the sons, brothers, husbands, sweethearts fighting far away. People had in their hearts hope of early victory and peace in Europe, hope of a speed-up in the long march up the Pacific islands to Tokyo. There was elation in the air in Washington and wherever else it was known that the Big Three were meeting and "something was cooking." But there was fear, too, and a wild fierce hope, fear of peace itself and the unemployment that it would bring; hope that somehow the trick of transition from full employment for war to full employment for peace could be turned, that "freedom from want" would not become as sour on the tongue as "safe for democracy" had become twenty-five years before.

The previous day, Monday, January 24, an aged, bad-tempered banker named Jesse Jones had advised the Senate Commerce Committee to split off the fourteen-billion Reconstruction Finance Corporation from the Department of Commerce before confirming the nomination of his successor, who had loaned more money, in smaller sums, to more borrowers and collected a higher percentage of it than had Mr. Jones. Jones had come into the Senate Caucus Room through the Committee door, thereby avoiding contact with the Common People crowded into the great chamber. He had advised the Committee that "the Government's investment in plants and facilities, and in raw materials, represented by billions of dollars of the taxpayers' money, should not be made the subject of careless experimentation."

Jones did not state, and no senator was rude enough to remark, that, to get him to finance and buy much of the plant and materials, it had been necessary to apply the blowtorch of public opinion to the seat of his ample pants.

Boiling with outraged pride because he had been fired in favor of the man who had applied the torch eighteen months earlier and who had been fired for doing so, Jones threw this Sunday punch: "Certainly the RFC should not be placed under the supervision of a man willing to jeopardize the country's future with untried ideas and idealist schemes.

"The lending agencies of the Government can be administered, as they have been, on a purely non-partisan basis for the benefit of all the people [31 per cent of the RFC-financed manufacturing, military and housing facilities went to Texas] or they can be used to destroy what we have built up in this nation in our 170 years of independence. That, to my mind, is the issue which this committee and the Congress must decide."

And then the corny disclaimer of intent to hit low: "It must decide all of this without any regard whatever to any individual, including myself."

The gentlemen of the press called it a wonderful build-up to a big let-down.

The next day a crowd began to assemble in the marble corridor outside the Caucus Room at 9:00 o'clock. When the big doors opened at 10:15 men and women and a few children were lined around the rotunda and down another corridor. In contrast to the crowd of the preceding day, which had been heavily salted with RFC employees, these people were excited, elated, laughing, eager in their anticipation. They filed in and filled the room. As on the preceding day, the press tables were crowded with working reporters and white-haired Washington "observers" seldom seen outside their offices and clubs.

Shortly before 10:30, the hour set for the hearing to resume, the Committee filed in through the Committee entrance. The crowd waited. The clock hands above the chairman's head stood at 10:30.

A tall, gangling man, hatless, wearing a topcoat and carrying a briefcase, appeared in the big side doorway through which the Common People had come into the room. He was alone. He came in fast, at an easy walk.

Handclaps, cheers, whistles, cowboy and rebel yells started at the instant he came through the door and grew in volume as he passed through the crowd, down between the press tables to the witness chair and table.

Senator Bailey was pounding with his gavel. The ovation rolled over the committee, up against the wall, back and forth. The hearing record reads—and this will be news to those who could not hear the nearly always inaudible Senator Bailey:

"THE CHAIRMAN [after the arrival of Mr. Wallace]. There will be no further demonstration. The demonstration you gave is entirely satisfactory; there is no complaint, but the committee is now in session. It is very important that we should proceed in the most orderly way possible."

With the bases loaded, a smart pitcher doesn't wind up. And Henry A. Wallace is a smart pitcher. He was a smart pitcher in the Iowa bush league, in the national league, in the international league. And now he was pitching for the right to play in the post-war world series. He always had a deceptive awkwardness, particularly when he bent over toward his shoe laces in starting a real wind-up. But the body, shoulder, and arm action, and the final wrist twist were easy. Now, facing a committee determined to cut him down and bury him as so many had tried to do for twelve years, he grinned—that damned boyish apologetic grin of a friendly farmer in town for the day, prices up, and the missus getting a new dress at the dry goods store.

Straightening in his chair, you could see a man setting his spikes in the dirt, getting the sight on the plate. He pulled back and let go. It was an Iowa fire ball, high and inside, right across the letters on Jesse Jones' shirt:

"There are some who have suggested—perhaps in an effort to save my feelings or face—that this separation of the lending functions from the Commerce Department is desirable because of my alleged 'lack of experience' in such field. Let me say that this talk does not fool either me or the American public. You know and I know that it is not a question of my 'lack of experience.' Rather, it is a case of not liking the experience I have."

The next ball was waist-high, with a fast in-break: "Let me be specific: For eight years I was Secretary of Agriculture. During that period the Commodity Credit Corporation, the Farm Security Administration, the Farm Credit Administration, and the Rural Electrification Administration were under my supervision. During that period these agencies loaned over six billion dollars. We made 11,500,000 separate commodity credit loans and 1,208,000 rural rehabilitation loans. We arranged the financing to permit 20,814 tenant farmers to buy their farms. . . ."

The third pitch was the fireball again, this time with all the force Wallace could crowd on, smoking straight across the center of the plate. It was thrown less than two minutes after he began. Here it is: "The real issue is whether or not the powers of the Reconstruction Finance Corporation and its giant subsidiaries are to be used only to help big business or whether these powers are also to be used to help little business and to help carry out the President's commitment of 60,000,-000 jobs. In other words, the question is really one of whether this committee, the Congress, and the American public want these enormous financial powers utilized and invested in a free America—in a prosperous America.

"This is not any petty question of personalities. This is a question of fundamental policy. It is the question of the path which America will follow in the future. So that there can be ho doubt in anyone's mind where I stand on these fundamental issues, I would like to take this opportunity to discuss with you the future which I feel is in store for America."

Then for five solid hours Wallace spread out before the committee a war and post-war program for the nation that, in sweep and specific detail, exceeded the capacity of most of them. Conditioned by their training and environment to distrust government responsibility for full employment, some members were so blocked by their prejudices that they became bored and impatient. Strangely enough, the Common People in the back seats and most of the Press seemed to understand what Wallace was saying and to eat it up. As he spelled out the application of Roosevelt's economic bill of rights, they followed point by point, as intently as a crowd at an Iowa-Nebraska football game, breaking in with applause again and again. When he finished his prepared statement, the ovation was so explosive and prolonged that Chairman Bailey, pounding for quiet, said rather plaintively, "I am glad you gave expression to your feelings. I hope you won't repeat it."

All that Bailey could get out of the cross-examination that followed was a feeling that Wallace proposed to get full employment by government lending and spending of more and more millions, *ad infinitum*. In this, Bailey was not wholly to blame. Wallace was walking wide of the subject of taxation. At one point, he said that such a program as he had outlined "can provide America with a national income of such size that it will be possible to reduce the tax rates still further on personal incomes, on business profits and on consumption, and still collect enough tax revenue to meet the needs of the government, including orderly retirement of the public debt."

At Seattle, February 9, 1944, he had been more precise: "There is just one basis for judgment of our taxation in the post-war period and that is, 'Will this system of taxation over a period of years give us the full employment of people producing the kinds of things which the people of the United States need and want?'

"Undoubtedly we shall have to continue with heavy, steeply graduated taxes on personal incomes after the war. But in the case of corporations it would seem to be wise policy to tax in such a way as to force corporation reserves either into the building of plant and equipment or into distribution as dividends. Huge corporate reserves, beyond legitimate business needs, which are held out of use are subtracted from the purchasing power of the nation. *In time of unemployment each billion dollars stored up as savings means at least half a million men unemployed for a year."*

Unwilling to attack his goal of full employment, his enemies on the committee had to work around the edges, questioning his method.

When Senator W. Lee (Pappy-Pass-the-Biscuits) O'Daniel asked for a statement of his business experience, Wallace cheerfully filed a statement that filled nine pages of small type.

When Bailey cited the growth of debt under the wartime British Prime Minister William Pitt, Wallace took from his brief case a quotation from Lord Macaulay describing eloquently the simultaneous growth of debt and prosperity, and concluded with a quotation from a Connecticut Yankee, Senator Danaher: "If you are satisfied that you get your money's worth, the Federal budget can be said to be balanced."

When Bailey pressed him on regulation of farm production, Wallace remarked, "I remember how eager the Senator was to have restrictions put on potato crops some years ago." Bailey said that he then thought the legislation was bad but he acted to protect potato growers against invasion by farmers driven out of corn and cotton.

When pressed to state his views on the balance of foreign trade, Wallace joyfully whaled away at the high tariff of the 'twenties.

"After World War I when we emerged as a creditor nation, and a very great foreign trade drive was put on through the Department of Commerce, I felt very critical because simultaneously with that very powerful foreign trade—and I think it was very skillfully done—we raised our tariff, and I used to go around the country saying to the farm folks, 'There is going to be a great deal of trouble coming to the farmer, because here is the United States, a creditor nation, saying to the outside world with regard to the debt the outside world owes to the United States, "Come here and pay up," and saying it in a very mean and very dirty tone of voice through all the newspapers, and congressional speeches.'

"*Then we put a pitchfork against the bellies of these foreign nations, saying, 'No, you don't, you so-and-so, stay away from here, we won't let you pay up.'* I said that kind of thing was bound to produce irritation, bound to create the most serious kind of trouble in those foreign nations.

"I really think it was the fundamental cause of the rise of Hitler, the fundamental cause for a great deal of disturbances we have had all over the world. I have felt that most deeply."

Twitted by Senator Brewster with FDR's bald letter to Jesse Jones saying that Wallace had to be rewarded for his tireless 1944 campaigning, Wallace brought down the house by saying, "I am glad to be recognized as having some competence in the political field, which hasn't always been recognized hitherto." A moment later, he spoke approvingly of former Democratic National Committee Chairman Jim Farley's methods in recommending men for jobs but never forcing them on administrators.

"Jim thought that if there were a Democrat with equally high qualifications he should be given a break. . . . 'If 53.6 per cent of the people of the United States are Democrats, it seems to me that they have the right to 53.6 per cent of jobs'—meaning government jobs."

Four days later Wallace spoke at a testimonial dinner in

New York. Before he went on the air, Mrs. Eleanor Roosevelt, who might qualify as an expert witness, wished him luck as *"the* leader of the courageous American people," in meeting the problems and opportunities of peace as FDR had been the leader in dispelling fear in 1933. In this famous "lost speech," Mrs. Roosevelt warned that "the people will get the leader they deserve."

Wallace's speech, the last before he became Secretary of Commerce, showed a new aggressiveness, an awareness that dark forces in the political and economic deeps of the nation were coming to the surface in the convulsive struggle to shape a new nation of fully employed and happy people and a world peace that, based on political and economic justice, could endure.

"There are two issues in this fight. The first is jobs for all after the post-war boom is over. And the second is like unto it. *The common man of America can and therefore must be better off in time of peace than he was in time of war....*

"The Nation must not be subjected to an economic Munich or Dunkirk.

"Men represent issues. And the issues are so important that all of us sooner or later will have to stand up and be counted....

"The time has come to fight back."

II

Henry Agard Wallace was, as of spring, 1945, the undisputed progressive leader in the U.S.A. That is what Mrs. Roosevelt meant when she called him *"the* leader of the courageous American people." Remember that it was Mrs. Roosevelt who, flying to Chicago in 1940, met Jim Farley at the airport, went into the riotous Democratic convention and, by sheer force of character, impressed upon the delegates the fact that Franklin D. Roosevelt insisted on Wallace. He wanted Wallace as life insurance for the New Deal, already being "put on the shelf while we took down the atlas of war." In FDR's view, Wallace alone had the mental breadth and moral stamina to keep the organization and administration of a people's peace on a level that would hold the imagination and hot loyalty of many peoples around the world.

In 1940, it had to be Wallace because in a very deep and subtle sense he was Roosevelt's pledge to his own conscience. Already, in the five-year amortization agreement on new war plans, FDR was preparing to bribe and buy industry's co-operation in equipping the nation for another war. When it was over, "all the shanties were going to come down"; the march of progressivism would be resumed; Wallace was the best man in sight to lead that march.

In 1944, deprived of Wallace by the advice of politicians afraid of the New Deal and of Wallace's grasp of economic fundamentals, a conscience-stricken Roosevelt watched the political corpse rise from the scene of the assassination stronger than ever before, transformed into a political power in his own right, carrying with him the charm of a superman, whom no political bullet or poison could harm. FDR saw this walking miracle go up and down the country, like a Johnny Appleseed in seven-league boots, campaigning months on end for the man who had abandoned him, winning back the support of millions of progressives who had been outraged by the job done at Chicago. The cold anger of FDR's dismissal of Jesse Jones is a gauge of his remorse over the "sacrifice" of Wallace. That "sacrifice" made Wallace a free man in his own mind and in the sight of progressives. The son-father relationship with FDR had been broken.

As this is written, Wallace is in eclipse. If Truman goes to the right or fails to master the awful task of changing over from full production for war to full production for peace, progressives in both parties may turn to Wallace in 1946 and 1948. If Truman stays progressive, Wallace will stay on his team and pitch, whether or not he is his 1948 running mate, as he did for FDR in 1944. His present job as Secretary of Commerce is a thankless but vital task; he is trying, quite simply, to save free enterprise by making it really free, free of monopoly, free to obtain the latest patents, free to get a fair share of a bigger and bigger full-employment bill. Whether the Pooh-Bahs of business will ever really trust and co-operate with him is doubtful; too many of them speak of liberty when they mean license, of freedom when they mean monopoly. As long as they are fat and sassy, they won't co-operate; if they become lean and fearful, they may. Whatever Wallace's fate in his present job, Truman isn't writing him off as a political force and asset in years to come.

III

The surest formula for a successful American play or novel is the success story itself. In Broadwayese, "the sap makes good" plot is always good box office. It is the twist that American democracy gives to the Cinderella theme. Instead of the Prince as destiny, in a just society a man can rise to security and honor by virtue and/or luck.

Henry Agard Wallace is no sap and never has been. But the caricature drawn by his enemies in both political parties and in the caves of Wall and LaSalle streets has portrayed him as a super-sap, a moon calf, a buck-toothed goof dangerous to leave in the vicinity of the great switchboards of modern industry where his idly poking fingers might short-circuit the whole complicated power grid.

This label of sap may turn out to have been his greatest political asset. Remembering the label and feeling a helplessness in the maze of modern life, listening to his words of hope and cheer mixed with hard facts and Old Testament anger against the exploiters, millions of Americans have felt kinship, sympathy, new hope, and a fierce partisanship crossing party and sectional lines.

As the eternal sap who makes good, the hick who tells off the city slickers, the political corpse who won't stay buried, the shy, smiling man with the hair that won't stay combed, the one politician who talks jobs, food, land, airplanes, patents, monopolies, freight rate discriminations, decent housing, and the world-wide brotherhood of man, Wallace adds up for millions in this and other nations to the average man's dream of what he himself might be and say and do. Wallace's very awkwardness, his breaking of the rules of the political game, his ability to do things the hard way and the wrong way and get away with it, are assets in that they seem to many to make him, but for the grace of God, themselves.

Actually, Wallace comes pretty close to being an intellectual aristocrat. He is an expert in the fields of pure and applied statistics and in plant genetics. His record as a successful business man and administrator of the Department of Agriculture and of the Board of Economic Warfare is incontrovertible. In 1943 an applauding Congress increased the BEW appropriation thirty days before he and Milo Perkins were fired. As Senator Lister Hill said in the debate on his appointment to be Secretary of Commerce: "It is evident that the question is not whether Mr. Wallace is incompetent. The proposition is that he is too competent; he is too able and effective for the views which he holds." Throughout Latin America, he is admired and trusted, partly because he went to the pains of learning Spanish well enough to speak directly to the people there. His reading public is world-wide, probably as great as that of any man now using the English tongue.

Wallace wears his learning as carelessly as Roosevelt, an economic aristocrat, wore his campaign hats. He is truly educated in that he has learned the long words and then learned how to express their meaning in short words. His mind has gone through the fiery furnace of science. Early worship of facts and the scientific method has been tempered; economics in itself is "mere machinery"; the important job is synthesis of facts and a moral sense of direction in their use. Science must be the tool, not the master, of man; man can assert this mastery by bringing to bear the logic of philosophy and the intensity of religion. Wallace is among the most genuinely learned men in American public life since Benjamin Franklin and Thomas Jefferson. His field of knowledge is broader than Wilson's, who thought of economics and the natural sciences in terms of history and political science.

He has a fierce love for *people,* but until very recently has seemed shy and luke-warm with *persons* beyond an intimate circle. This is changing. As he senses the warmth of feeling that others have for him, he is beginning to respond with a disarming open-faced frankness and a detached humorous attitude toward himself, his Scotch-Irish background of thrift and reserve. At times he makes embarrassing mistakes in judging other people, as when he said in his New York speech that he was sure every member of the Senate liked and respected him as a man.

When Wallace first went to the Senate as its presiding officer, he tried to be one of the boys. Instead of using a refrigerator where blows for liberty could be struck with bended elbows, H.A. tried to "unlax" with the senators by playing handball and tennis. Since he is good at both, far too good for most senators, and would consider it morally dishonest to slow down to let a senator win oftener than he deserved, his athletic overtures came to naught. He seems never to have developed facility in the handling of conversational small change. It is now probably too late for him to learn. At the rate his career is developing, it doesn't seem to matter very much.

In his tireless campaigning up and down the back roads of the nation in two presidential campaigns, he has developed an easy naturalness that mows them down in Wisconsin, Iowa, or New York City. In October, 1944, for example, while being driven from one speaking date to another near Eau Claire, he got out to talk with two Wisconsin farmers husking corn. He shucked back the husk from an ear, guessed "about 46 per cent moisture." They agreed. He asked how they would vote. One said, for Dewey; the other wouldn't say. Wallace took the dried silk from the ear of corn, held it under his nose and asked, "Now do I look like Dewey?"

A few weeks later, speaking in a small Iowa town, he found the auditorium packed, an overflow meeting downstairs and a loudspeaker in the street for more. "You can't fool me," he began. "This isn't a meeting of Democrats. I know the figures for this county and there aren't this many Democrats. You're Republicans and I'm not going to make a Democratic speech. Suppose you just ask me questions and see how many I can answer. First question?"

It worked. H.A. made it work. When a shrewd question was put, instead of trying to answer it, he said:

"That's a good question. You've got me beat. Next?"

"What about the little pigs?" he was asked.

"Now that's a fine question," he replied. "That's the best question you've got. If I were a Republican I'd concentrate on that question and nothing else."

Then, turning serious, he lit into his passionate denunciation of the economics of scarcity under which restriction of pig iron production in the late 'twenties and early 'thirties made inevitable the butchering, but not the total waste, of little pigs.[1]

What people outside of Iowa don't understand is that Wallace is no political accident, no biological sport. He is in the tradition of agricultural America and of his family. He is a veteran of the farm wars of the 'twenties. His ability to go from the particular to the general and back to the particular, to relate corn to weather to hogs to market to employment to finance to tariffs to government policy to the making of war and peace and all of this to his *summum bonum,* the "dignity of the individual human soul" is the result of his family and school environment.

For many generations back in this country, in North Ireland, and in Scotland, the Wallace family has been of the land. They were farmers in Scotland, in Ireland, in western Pennsylvania, and in Iowa. They were pietistic Psalm-singing Presbyterians. They related religion to their daily lives, to their farming, to schools, to the evils of railroad monopoly and freight discrimination. Their creed was boiled down to the motto of *Wallace's Farmer:* "Good Farming—Clear Thinking—Right Living."

His grandfather, Henry Wallace, was a great man in American agriculture. He can be said to have made three Secretaries of Agriculture: "Tama Jim" Wilson, whom he recommended to McKinley and who served for sixteen years; his own farmer-teacher-editor son, Henry Cantwell Wallace, who fought Secretary of Commerce Hoover's foreign trade policies in the Harding and Coolidge cabinets, thereby hastening his own death in 1924, and his grandson, Henry Agard Wallace, who,

1. The full factual story is given in his book "Democracy Reborn" (pp. 104-6), and is worth reading as political polemics, economics, or literature. It makes even the souls of the little pigs rise to fight for an economy of abundance in the years to come.

on January 25, 1944, was to avenge his father by telling a Senate committee that the Hoover-Harding-Coolidge foreign trade policies had "put a pitchfork against the bellies" of the debtor nations and brought on Hitler and World War II.

As the twig was bent, so the tree inclined. Henry Agard began his corn breeding experiments and his writing for the family paper while still a student at Ames, becoming an associate editor upon graduation in 1910.

The line of descent is plain in the three Henrys, similarly, the genetic quirk of "grandfatherism," strengthened by the association of the very old and the very young Henrys. Plain, too, is the part played by the Iowa State Agricultural College, an intellectual center of the state. (This was long before the butter-oleomargarine fight.)

Wallace is the first great man of the coming American Renaissance. His interests are broader than Da Vinci's, as the horizons of today's world are broader than Da Vinci's. His patron is the People, as Da Vinci's was the Duke of Milan. Even to sample fairly his various interests in farming, genetics, statistics, economics, engineering, fiscal policy, taxation, foreign trade, and the structure of a People's peace would require more space than the present essay allows.

Because he has been called impractical, it is good to note that while a hard-headed banker was dozing in the Department of Commerce, Secretary of Agriculture Wallace on April 13, 1939, arranged to trade 600,000 bales of surplus cotton for 90,500 long tons of rubber—enough to make 18,000,000 tires; and that on October 27, 1939, he said, "In case of a world war our lack of this product [rubber] is likely to be our Achilles' heel."

Because he has been accused of wanting to regiment the nation, note also that, speaking of eugenics, he has said, "our need is for diversity rather than uniformity," and has suggested improvement of environment so that "normal people will have the greatest opportunity for developing and leading happy and useful lives."

Because he has been accused of fuzzy generalities in proposing post-war full employment, note the preciseness of this 1938 statement and compare it with Sir William Beveridge's "Full

Employment in a Free Society," published in February, 1945:
"For my own part, I do not think that civilizations when they
mature have to commit suicide. I believe they can, by taking
thought, maintain their full vigor for many hundreds of years.
The United States has an enormous vitality, but is subject to
violent alternations of fever and chills.

"To end these fevers and chills, some clearing agency should
be devised to proportion the housing activities, the buying of
railroad equipment, the building of factories and the buying of
public-utility equipment more uniformly over the years. In the
late twenties this nation produced an average of more than
thirty billion dollars of durable goods annually. This was too
much and was certain to lead to a depression later on. In the
early thirties this nation produced less than twenty billion dollars' worth of durable goods annually. This was too little and
resulted in stagnation which produced the utmost misery. In
1937 we produced five million automobiles, or many more than
were needed for replacement purposes. Therefore in 1938 we
shall not produce nearly as many. *The jerkiness in our heavy-
goods industries is responsible for much of the recurring unemployment which leads to recessions in farm prices.*

"This is a problem which must be solved if capitalism is to
survive.

"The chief way of modifying the capitalism of the future
will be through constructively changing the relationship of the
corporation to the government and to labor. Also there is the
possibility of substituting the co-operative for the corporate
form of organization in those lines of activity where the co-
operative form of endeavor can eventually prove to be more
efficient.

"In all efforts of this sort the goal should be not merely to
get greater efficiency in the long run but also to bring a larger
number of human beings into a feeling of intimate joyous
responsibility in their work. In many cases the corporate form
of organization will serve this double purpose better than the
co-operative. In some cases government ownership will serve
the purpose best. In other cases the purpose may be best served
by breaking up overhead financial controls which stifle local
initiative."

Because Walt Whitman, Lord Dunsany, John Donne, or Wallace's own grandfather would have liked it very much, note this poetic excerpt from his last radio piece as Secretary of Agriculture, entitled "The Strength and Quietness of Grass":

"I have always had a great affection for grass. It seems to stand for quietness and strength. I believe that the quietness and strength of grass should be, must be, permanently a part of our agriculture if this nation is to have the strength it will need in the future. A countryside shorn and stripped of thick, green grass, it seems to me, is weakened just as Sampson was. An agriculture without grass loses a primary source of strength.

"It is only recognizing the truth to say that in the past we have been lured by the Delilah of profits to destroy grass covering recklessly. . . . Now we are beginning to see the weaknesses of an agriculture stripped of grass. More and more we are turning in thought and practice toward an agriculture in which grass will act as the great balance wheel and stabilizer to prevent gluts of other crops—to save soil from destruction —to build up a reserve of nutrients and moisture in the soil, ready for any future emergency to create a more prosperous livestock industry, and finally to contribute to the health of our people through better nutrition."

And because it tells the nature, range, and height of the future he sees, note this excerpt from his frankest recorded public statement, a rambling talk at his own school, Iowa State College at Ames, one night in October, 1936:

"I think we are coming—by fits and starts of course—to a time when there is to be infinitely more co-operation than we had in the past, when the law of the jungle does not prevail to the same extent as it did in 1929. I think the New Deal faintly foreshadows certain ultimates in that direction."

Finally, because it would fit under his bust wherever placed, note the homeliest, simplest statement of his creed that he has ever achieved, taken from his white-hot "Pigs and Pig Iron" speech of 1935:

"People are more important than pigs."

II

IN CONGRESS

7

JOSEPH C. O'MAHONEY:
"His Answer to the Enigma"

BY JULIAN SNOW

O NE EVENING LATE IN THE SUMMER OF 1934 I WAS DINING in the Occidental Restaurant in Washington with Joseph C. O'Mahoney, lawyer, ex-newspaperman, Massachusetts-born United States Senator from Wyoming. The conversation turned that night to the reasons for the industrial collapse of 1929 and the tremendous recovery program then under way. The Seventy-third Congress had been appropriating deficit dollars at the rate of a billion a month in an unprecedented effort to speed recovery. General Hugh Johnson and his NRA were endeavoring to regulate the shaken economy of 130,000,000 citizens. In Europe a ranting, political agitator, financed to power by the Fritz Thyssens of Germany, had made totalitarian government the answer to security for other millions of human beings.

"Is America preparing to fly the swastika?" I asked the Senator that night. "Government exists only for the purpose of making it possible for people to serve themselves," he replied. "When America's economy stalled the government had to act. But all we are doing now is only a palliative. It does not reach the cause of the sickness. It offers no permanent solution." He paused, and then remarked, as though to himself, "But there *is* an answer."

"The answer" O'Mahoney had in mind has developed into the theme of his career in the United States Senate. We find it boiled down to this ten-word concept of democracy which he has written in his own distinctive, rapid script across thousands of leaflets, visiting cards, and photographs for which autograph seekers besiege their congressmen: *There can be no permanent political liberty without economic freedom.*

This concept is the yardstick he seeks to apply to legislation on the floor of the United States Senate and behind closed doors in Senate committee rooms; to addresses before national conventions of farmers, working men, economists, small businessmen, or top-flight industrialists. It is reflected in the reforms he proposed to his Temporary National Economic Committee. We find it as the theme of his recommendations as chairman of special Senate sub-committees on war contracts and on industrial reorganization after the war and in the plan he announced in February of 1945 for co-ordinating the work of the various standing special committees of the United States Senate studying national policies and programs for the disposal of more than nineteen billion dollars in government-owned plants and facilities.

Joseph Christopher O'Mahoney, whose father, Dennis, came to America from county Cork, is slight of build, blue eyed, bushy browed, dynamic, eloquent, persuasive, with the Irish love to do battle for great causes. "Joe is at his best fighting for minorities," Agnes O'Leary O'Mahoney, his wife, remarked one day after watching her husband battle vainly for hours to win Senate approval of his amendment giving Congress a voice in our trade agreements with foreign countries.

The political armistice between the New Deal and Wall Street in the first year of the Roosevelt administration had ended in the summer of 1934 when the Securities Exchange Bill was enacted. The *Wall Street Journal* and similar publications characterized the bill as a menace "to the foundations of representative government" and "handcuffs for industry." In later years O'Mahoney was to hear the same sort of criticism directed from the same source at his National Charters for National Commerce Bill.

O'Mahoney, who had taken his seat in the Senate by appointment January 3, 1934, was facing a campaign that fall. He had supported the administration throughout those early months, even voting to sustain the President's veto of the current Soldiers' Bonus Bill. Returning home that summer he found

himself dubbed a "rubber stamp," and "yes man." Although
the opposition candidate was a Republican congressman known
as the "best vote getter in the state," O'Mahoney was elected
by a majority of 11,800. In 1940, running against another
Republican opponent with "vote appeal," he received the largest vote ever given a Wyoming candidate for United States
Senate and headed his ticket even though 1940 was a presidential year. His majority that time was 20,000.

Whatever justification his political opponents in Wyoming
may have had for branding O'Mahoney an administration "yes
man" in the early days of his career, his disagreements with
the President on fundamental issues since then have relegated
to the ridiculous any such claim today.

His leadership in the historic battle in 1937 which ended in
the defeat of the President's plan to increase the membership
of the United States Supreme Court with judges more to his
liking; the position he has taken on the reciprocal trade agreements question; his unceasing opposition to law by executive
order and bureaucratic mandate; the heights he achieved as
sponsor and chairman of the Temporary National Economic
Committee throughout the three years of its existence; and his
record on legislation affecting the West have made of him what
radio commentator Fulton Lewis, Jr., described in March of
1944 as "something of an institution in Wyoming, a distinct
personality who has a heavy following among Republicans and
Democrats alike."

O'Mahoney's activities in the national field used to be of
concern to close friends in Wyoming who had not yet sensed
the pride of their fellow citizens in the national prestige of
"Senator Joe." Some of these friends argued that when a man
becomes a national figure, he has no time to attend to small
chores at home. Directly or indirectly they sought to remind
their senator that many prominent legislators have been known
to fail of re-election because they had overlooked the hard,
prosaic fact that what one does for the folks at home is vital
to what "Cactus Jack" Garner once termed "continuity in
office." Practical politician that he is, O'Mahoney has always
kept in mind the ABC's of continuity in office, although he has

reasons to doubt it as a hard and fast rule for political success.

In 1938, for example, he had campaigned vigorously throughout Wyoming in behalf of a Democratic governor and a Democratic congressman, both close personal friends of the Senator. The governor had established a splendid record for his businesslike administration and the Congressman could and did point to many public works projects which he had helped to secure for his state. With "the record" of achievement weighing heavily in their favor, wagers posted by Democrats went uncovered. Confidence oozed from Democratic headquarters and defeatism, real and feigned, cast a heavy pall on the Republicans.

Early on the morning of November 8, O'Mahoney cast his vote in Cheyenne and left immediately by plane for New York City to address the National Academy of Political Science. By midnight it was apparent that the Democrats with "records of achievement" had been ousted by Republicans with records yet unknown. While Democratic leaders, dazed as though shell shocked by the political bomb, stood benumbed in the lobby of Cheyenne's principal hotel, O'Mahoney's secretary intercepted him en route with a telegram advising him of the upset. On the evening of November 9 he appeared before the Academy and delivered extemporaneously a brilliant address on "Industrial Organization and the American Ideal of Living." Not even the major political upheaval in his own state twenty-four hours earlier could throw him off beam.

But O'Mahoney does not rest upon the laurels he has won on the national stage. Instead he is recognized as a spokesman for the livestock industry, for Western agriculture in general and sugar beet growers in particular, as well as for Western oil operators from whose leases on the public lands flow millions of dollars of royalties into the Reclamation Fund and to Western roads and schools. "He not only does what you ask but he does more than you expect of him," is the way one Republican constituent, a stockman, expresses it.

Early in 1942, when the Japs were reported to be following their armies into the Dutch East Indies with oil equipment and drilling crews to tap new oil pools and replace the wells destroyed by the retreating Allies, O'Mahoney acted. He introduced a bill reducing public domain royalties on production from newly discovered oil deposits to a flat 12½ per cent. The legislation was signed December 24 of that year, and by the end of 1943 drillers had tapped new oil-bearing sands in Wyoming with such success the *Oil and Gas Journal* estimated that of 800,000,000 barrels of newly discovered oil reserves throughout the nation, Wyoming had a total of 312,000,000 barrels, or about 40 per cent.

In addition to the problems of the Western oilmen, the demands upon the Senator's time from the stockmen and the sugar beet growers are never ending. When, for instance, the woolgrowers complained that the army and navy were using too much foreign wool, O'Mahoney called a meeting of his special Senate committee on wool production and marketing to meet with officers from the Army and Navy and heads of the OPA, UNRRA, Commodity Credit, the Department of Agriculture, and the Reconstruction Finance Corporation to remedy the situation. And, when the OPA despite protests of the cattlemen, proposed price ceilings on live animals, he not only pleaded their case with the officials in charge, but he delivered a national radio broadcast to support the stockman's contention that the ceilings edict would mean less meat, not more.

Wyoming is the state from which head the tributaries of the Missouri, the Colorado, and the Columbia rivers, so he joined with other Western senators and after lengthy studies, was successful in obtaining enactment of the so-called O'Mahoney-Milligan amendment to the Missouri River and Flood Control Acts of the Seventy-eighth Congress by which priority water rights for domestic, agricultural, and industrial uses were secured for Wyoming and other Upper Basin states.

Again, acting in behalf of the citizens of his own state, he joined with Congressman Frank Barrett of Wyoming in securing enactment of a bill to abolish the Jackson Hole National Monument which had been created by executive order of the President. The President, however, vetoed the bill.

Senator O'Mahoney was born in Chelsea, Massachusetts, in 1884, one of eleven children, and when he left Columbia

University in 1908 to make his home in the West he carried his Boston accent with him. Although thirty-seven years as a Westerner have erased much of it, his Eastern pronunciation of such words as "calf" might prove political dynamite in the ranch country were it not that he pleads the stockman's case so effectively in Washington.

When, in 1917, he left a newspaper desk in Cheyenne to return East as secretary to the stockman-senator John B. Kendrick of Wyoming, he made good use of his opportunity to become acquainted with the problems of his adopted state, assisted Kendrick in work on the Packers-Stockyards legislation and absorbed much of the old Senator's homespun political philosophy.

In 1920 he was graduated from Georgetown University Law School where he was president of his class, and returned to Cheyenne to hang out his shingle and to dip into Democratic state politics. He was an early pre-convention supporter of Roosevelt for President, and as Democratic National Committeeman from Wyoming, attracted the attention of party leaders in the Chicago national convention of 1932, where he had a hand in the drafting of the party platform of that year.

After Roosevelt was nominated O'Mahoney worked with National Chairman Jim Farley at party headquarters. Upon Roosevelt's election O'Mahoney came to Washington as First Assistant Postmaster General. Nine months later, in November, 1933, Senator Kendrick died and Governor Leslie A. Miller appointed O'Mahoney to succeed his old boss. He now occupies the same offices in which he had served his apprenticeship under Kendrick.

Upon taking office he inherited all five of the Kendrick committees—Appropriations, Public Lands and Surveys, Irrigation and Reclamation, Indian Affairs, and Post Offices and Post Roads. Since then, he has relinquished the Post Offices and Post Roads assignment and has added Judiciary, Military Affairs, and Patents. He is chairman of the Indian Affairs Committee and of four special senate committees—the special committee to investigate the domestic and foreign oil policies of the United States, the Military Affairs sub-committee on war contracts, the sub-committee on industrial reorganization of the Senate post-war planning committee, and the sub-committee on appropriations for the District of Columbia. He was also chairman, throughout its existence, of the joint Legislative-Executive National Economic Committee to study the concentration of wealth.

In 1935 O'Mahoney introduced the first of what have since become known as the National Charters for National Commerce Bills. O'Mahoney and Borah had similar proposals in Congress. Later they combined their bills to become co-sponsors. Borah has since died, but O'Mahoney is continuing to urge upon Congress and the country the national charters solution to the enigma of how to preserve the economic freedom of the individual in an economy of huge interstate enterprises.

The idea was not original with either of its sponsors. The suggestion had been made over and over again by statesmen of the last fifty years and had been rejected because of the fear that it would lead to political domination of the states by federal government, and because many businessmen feared it would mean another bureau in Washington. O'Mahoney continually seeks to allay these fears and says that in the absence of legislation of this kind it will be impossible to escape the continued multiplication of government boards and commissions. His theory is that we should establish standards of management and responsibility to which corporations should adhere.

He believes that a National Charters Law such as he proposes could effectively prohibit interlocking directorships and thereby eliminate one of the principal causes of concentration and save both business and small corporations without injuring the big ones. Such a bill could make corporation directors trustees in fact as well as in law, thus protecting investors, big and little.

The measure could also raise a barrier to business dealings by corporation officers and directors for their own personal profit with the corporation they manage and would protect investors and "all honest enterprise." And it could make corporation officers and directors civilly liable personally for anti-trust law violations which they themselves conceived and directed.

In the National Association of Manufacturers and in the United States Chamber of Commerce where, in 1935, big business had looked down its nose when the first of the National Charters for National Commerce Bills was introduced, there is now a noteworthy change of attitude, brought on in part by the discovery that the author of the bill is not such a wild-eyed radical after all, and also because, as one N. A. M. employee expressed it, "Compared with the present methods of federal regulation, O'Mahoney's National Charters Bill has changed in the eyes of many business executives from a tiger to a house cat."

In support of his philosophy of government O'Mahoney often cites not only the Constitution of the United States, but also the Constitution of his own state. One provision of the Constitution of the state of Wyoming reads: "Arbitrary power exists nowhere in a republic, not even in the largest majority." O'Mahoney made such effective use of this statement of moral principle during his fight on the administration's court packing proposal of 1937 that Mark Sullivan remarked: "When we founded our government we were so familiar with this principle we took it for granted. Here is the foundation stone of the American conception of government—yet it was not written explicitly in the federal Constitution nor in any of the state ones except that of a sparsely settled mountain commonwealth." And he might have added that here was an example of the second least populated state in the Union successfully asserting, through her chosen representative in Congress, that arbitrary power exists nowhere in a republic, not even in the White House.

Although subsequent events born of the war have relegated to comparative unimportance the drama-packed battle in 1937 over the administration's Supreme Court Reorganization Bill, it provides us with a vivid picture of the subject of this sketch in a moment of high resolve and unshaken faith in his concept of a fundamental principle of American democracy.

Despite Senator O'Mahoney's close questioning of Attorney

General Homer Cummings and other key administration spokesmen who appeared before the Senate Judiciary Committee, many veteran Washington observers could not believe that the one time aide and personal friend of Big Jim Farley would break with the President on so important an issue. For example, Harold Brayman, seasoned Washington correspondent for the *Philadelphia Ledger,* flatly predicted, a day before O'Mahoney announced the course he would pursue, "He will desert the President about the time Jimmy Roosevelt does. Those who have jumped to the conclusion he will oppose the President fail to appreciate his background and inclinations. They forget that for the first year of the Administration he served as a first assistant to Jim Farley. He and Farley became great friends and he would no more think of turning against the Administration . . . than he would of jumping off a cliff."

But the prediction was wrong. To Farley, who warned him not to "get behind the eight ball," O'Mahoney smilingly replied, "I must vote my convictions, Jim."

O'Mahoney found himself allied with nine other members of the Judiciary Committee—Borah, King, Van Nuys, McCarran, Hatch, Burke, Steiwar, Austin and Connally. When the final vote was taken, the committee voted ten to eight to prepare an adverse report. O'Mahoney wrote much of the document, which was jubilantly heralded by the partisan *Chicago Tribune* as "the second Declaration of Independence." The communistic *Daily Worker,* however, characterized Senator O'Mahoney as one of the decoy liberals who are leading the forces of reaction in the crusade against Supreme Court reform.

The Wyoming senator believes that men in public life should stand on their own feet and not be mouthpieces of behind-the-scene operators. When the American Bar Association invited him to participate in a radio round table opposing the bill and offered to write his script, he replied, "I appreciate your offer to co-operate, but not even the American Bar Association is going to ghost write for me."

In the adverse report of the committee and in all his speeches, O'Mahoney meticulously avoided personalities, calmly disposing of the disputed bill, section by section, with the dispassionate logic of a jurist.

"It matters not what the inscrutable future may hold for Senator O'Mahoney, good or ill, it will never dim July 12, 1937," wrote Charles Brooks Smith of the Wheeling (W. Va.) *Intelligencer* from the Senate Press Gallery on that day. "By a great speech on the Court issue, in which he opposed the proposed change, he vaulted to the forefront of Senate statesmanship, as it rates today. He lifted debate ... from mediocrity to a high plane. You could see in the faces of his colleagues, whether with him or opposed to him on the issue, admiration mounting. ... Occasionally he neatly dropped a questioning heckler back to his seat, with a reply which at no time dropped below the par of his argument in the main. It was apparent that the dapper youngish looking (53 years) Massachusetts-born Senator from Wyoming had all the answers. The questioners started early, beat a retreat, surprised and crimson with embarrassment."

With the Court Bill doomed to defeat by the rising tide of opposition from throughout the nation, Democratic leaders were faced with the necessity of healing the party breach with a compromise substitute acceptable to both the administration and the senators who had rebelled. A historic session of the Senate Judiciary Committee called by Chairman Ashurst met behind closed doors. Those present suggested many alternatives for a substitute. There was no stenographer present, so O'Mahoney, armed with a pencil and a Senate memorandum pad, jotted down the points as they were agreed upon. Newspapers the next day characterized his memorandum as "reminiscent of the James Madison notes of the Constitutional Convention."

Although O'Mahoney frequently extols fundamental theories in government, he is one of the most practical men in the United States Senate. His clarity of thought and his newspaperman's ability to boil down a story to its essentials are his outstanding characteristics. Throughout his public career his untiring search for facts and his skill in presenting them so the people can understand is why, for instance, he can hold the attention of his audience, whether he is addressing a gathering of farmers and small merchants in Wheatland, Wyoming, a national convention of manufacturers in New York City, or listeners on a coast-to-coast radio network.

His debate with the then Senator Worth Clark of Idaho on a Town Meeting of the Air program in New York, in October, 1943, is an example of the last. The subject of debate that night was "Does the Two-thirds Rule of the Senate Impede United States Foreign Policy?" with O'Mahoney maintaining it did and Clark holding fast to the Constitutional "safeguard." The debate, with the audience joining in at the close, was in effect a preview of the national picture tomorrow. O'Mahoney's argument followed the same pattern of presentation as he had used in the "Court Fight" debate on the floor of the United States Senate six years before—dispassionate, factual, succinct, devastating.

Only once in his career has O'Mahoney underestimated the people's hunger for facts. When, as chairman of the Temporary National Economic Committee, he predicted at the outset of the inquiry that the study would be "dull but important," not even he foresaw that public interest in the millions of words of dry economics would rocket the eighty-four volumes of hearings and monographs to a Government Printing Office best seller. Nor did he foresee its full import as an authoritative source of research not only for congressional committees, government departments, universities, and economic foundations, but also for the United States Supreme Court and lesser tribunals. The fact that the TNEC monographs have been trickling through to the courts is particularly obnoxious to the National Association of Manufacturers which did some "monographing" of its own in "Fact and Fancy in the TNEC Monographs".

The Temporary National Economic Committee, commonly called the Monopoly Committee, is important today not only because of the voluminous data compiled during its two years and nine months (1938-41) of searching inquiry into the nation's economy, but also because of the part many of its recommendations will play in the America of tomorrow. The

Resolution creating the inquiry stems from President Roosevelt's message to Congress April 29, 1938, recommending an investigation of concentration of economic power. The economy-minded Wyoming Senator, with the background of the extensive hearings he and Senator Borah had conducted on their National Charters Bill, had a rough draft of the resolution completed before the Senate reading clerk intoned the President's final words: "Idle factories and idle workers profit no man." What was intended to be solely an executive investigation O'Mahoney turned into a joint enterprise with the legislative power in the driver's seat. He saved the power of Congress before most observers realized that any clash was impending.

The immediate problem was to apportion the committee membership so that both the legislative and executive branches would be represented to the satisfaction of Congress and the departments downtown. The answer was a twelve-man joint committee, with the Senate and the House each having a representation of three, and the executive branch a membership of six. The twelve met and named O'Mahoney, the sponsor of the resolution, as their chairman.

But organization of the committee was trivial compared to the problem of keeping the unwieldy boat on an even keel. Jittery businessmen, egged on by a cynical press, thought at first they saw a witch hunting expedition in the making. Predictions that the six department members of the group would vote together while the congressmen members would not, vied with rumors that this or that long range planner with communistic leanings or fascist concepts, was brewing plots to wreck the American capitalistic system.

The Temporary National Economic Committee was deliberately designed by O'Mahoney as "temporary" to distinguish it from self-perpetuating agencies so common in Washington. On the original committee were Hatton Sumners of Texas (vice-chairman), Eicher of Iowa, and Reece of Tennessee from the House; and Borah of Idaho, King of Utah, and Chairman O'Mahoney of Wyoming from the Senate; for the executive branch of the government were trust-buster Thurman Arnold of Justice (now Associate Justice of the Court of Appeals, District of Columbia), William O. Douglas, Chairman of the SEC (later a Justice of the United States Supreme Court), Garland S. Ferguson, Chairman of the Federal Trade Commission, Isadore Lubin of the Labor Department, Richard Patterson, Assistant Secretary of Commerce, and Herman Oliphant, General Counsel of the Treasury Department. Leon Henderson, executive secretary and later a member of the committee, was, with Arnold, one of the departmental mainsprings of the group.

The inquiry examined patents, life insurance, petroleum, iron and steel, prices, investment banking, profits, investments, technology and concentration of economic power, cartels—everything under the economic sun. Raymond Moley, writing critically of the first two years of the studies, predicted ominously in the *Saturday Evening Post* that the TNEC, far from being no more than a damp firecracker, would prove to be a time bomb which would explode with devastating effect in the months to come.

"Witnesses emerge from the hearings convinced O'Mahoney has the inquiry well in hand," wrote Moley. "The picture of O'Mahoney, so palpably earnest, so obviously sincere, blacks out the picture of Henderson, Arnold and others toiling upward in the night." And then, apprehensive lest he be accused of tarring O'Mahoney with the same brush he had been using on some of the other members of the committee, Moley adds: "Like Sir Henry Ellis, once chief librarian of the British Museum, O'Mahoney is a fair and honest man. And no one holds Sir Henry responsible because either Thomas Carlyle, Thomas Macaulay, George Grote, Karl Marx or John Stuart Mill worked in his Reading Room."

Today the skeptics who once saw the work of the TNEC as a meandering hodgepodge of theory and fact, now have a clearer focus on the over-all picture and they have reason to wonder whether the leavening process started by that committee will end in their lifetime.

For example, in the first year of its existence, the committee had recommended certain material modifications in the patent laws, and some of these recommendations have since been placed upon the statute books. The O'Mahoney National Charters for National Commerce Bill is back in the Senate Judiciary Committee supported by a resolution of the TNEC approving it in principle. It has been made part of O'Mahoney's recommendations to the special Senate Committee on Post-War Economic Policy and Planning.

The TNEC studies of cartel agreements between such huge American and European corporations as Standard Oil of New Jersey and I. G. Farben industries of Germany were personally planned by O'Mahoney and are the basis for his subsequent bill requiring all cartel agreements to be registered with the attorney-general of the United States. The committee also approved the principle of incentive taxation as a means of stimulating the investment of private capital in new, independent business. It was also recommended by O'Mahoney in his report to the Post-War Policy group.

In a Jackson Day address in Baltimore in 1945, Senator O'Mahoney gave what many regarded at the time, as the answer to a question asked by millions of Americans: "Why are we fighting this war?" O'Mahoney had just referred to a letter he had received from his nephew, a captain in the United States Army then in Germany, who wrote of visiting a Nazi torture chamber—evidence of how Nazis treat men who dissent from Nazi views.

"By what fortunate circumstance," cried out the Senator, "by what divine providence does it happen it was some defenseless European, some poor Ethiopian, some trembling Asiatic who endured the torture instead of me? If we tolerate arbitrary power anywhere on earth, we invite it here! That is why we fight this war! that is why we labor to shape a new world in which there shall be no thralldom for the human spirit."

Typical of O'Mahoney was his reaction to the trend of debate on post-war reconversion bills in the Senate in August of 1944. "We are concentrating our thoughts, not upon creating new jobs, but upon providing doles for the unemployed," he told his colleagues. "The only question apparently is the size of the doles.... I do not like to talk in terms of 10,000,000 unemployed or 18,000,000 unemployed in times which are to follow cessation of hostilities because I do not believe it necessary to talk in those terms. It is a defeatist attitude." The only solution, he said, was to provide the opportunity to work, and as a step in that direction he introduced an amendment, later accepted by the Senate, designed to more freely release materials for small business. In still another bill, relating to the disposition of surplus properties after they were no longer needed for war purposes, he wrote the provision, since enacted into law, by which millions of acres of government-owned real estate, now tax free, may be returned to private ownership, with veterans given high priority.

In the O'Mahoney offices in Washington, where the staff had become weary of the three years of hearings which their boss had conducted in the TNEC inquiry into the economic structure of the nation, the announcement that their senator, as chairman of Senate committees on industrial reorganization and on war contracts, was preparing to launch another gigantic economic committee study, called the new enterprise "a super duper TNEC." Richard L. Strout, veteran Washington correspondent of the *Christian Science Monitor*, in an article explaining the new O'Mahoney program for joint studies, characterizes him as "one of the most powerful figures in Congress and the key man in one of the post-war problems."

"Conservatives charge the possibility of a collectivized state in the present Government ownership of plants, factories, and giant industries running all over the United States," said Strout. "Left-Wing groups, on the other hand, assert that an effort is already under way to turn these mighty instruments of production over to existing monopolies."

After conferences with the chairmen of other Senate committees engaged in a study of the stupendous economic problems expected to confront the nation after the war, Senator O'Mahoney announced on February 22, 1945, plans to coordinate the work of the various Senate groups to formulate national policies and practices for the disposal and utilization of more than $19,000,000,000 worth of government-owned plants and facilities.

Reminiscent of the joint legislative-executive pattern of the old TNEC days was the program of past-war planning which he initiated in 1945 as chairman of the Senate subcommittees on Industrial Reorganization and Surplus Property. Round-table discussions by business leaders and representatives of executive agencies of the government were mapped by O'Mahoney to secure co-operation instead of conflict.

The program presented by O'Mahoney had the approval of Senator George, Chairman of the Senate Post-War Economic Policy and Planning Committee, and Senator Murray, Chairman of the Senate Small Business Committee, Senator Thomas, Chairman of the Senate Military Affairs Committee, Senator Mead, Chairman of the Senate National Defense Program Committee, Senator Pepper, Chairman of the Senate Committee on Patents, Senator Kilgore, Chairman of the Senate Military Affairs Special`Committee on Technological Mobilization, Chairman Gillette of the Surplus Property Board, Attorney General Biddle, and officials of the defense plants corporation, were also consulted. Various industry groups and organizations which have been giving attention to the problem are included in the O'Mahoney program.

Equally characteristic of the Wyoming Senator is the battle he began in 1943 against a lobby-inspired proposal to exempt the insurance business from the provisions of the Sherman Anti-Trust Act. Said the *New Republic* in May of 1944, "Senator O'Mahoney deserves a Congressional Medal of Honor for statesmanship. Few men have ever worked more effectively on a matter of high public interest, in which the public has shown little or no interest, than the Senator from Wyoming." A month later following the decisions of the United States Supreme Court holding that insurance when conducted across state lines is commerce in the meaning of the Constitution, an official of a National Association of Insurance Agents warned the members of the industry that "any attempts to override the stand taken by Senator O'Mahoney, would embarrass the entire insurance industry in the eyes of the public because on its face it appears now that the insurance business in asking to be exempted from the Sherman and Clayton Anti-Trust Laws wishes to be free to indulge in monopolistic and trade restraining practices."

In the past decade O'Mahoney himself has probably used the phrase "free private enterprise" more frequently than any other member of Congress. But to the novice who would follow the O'Mahoney lamp, pitfalls, and blind alleys are many. "Now, just what do you mean by 'free private enterprise'?" the Senator asked a naïve enthusiast one day. "It is a phrase everybody is using now. It means all things to all people. General Electric is for free private enterprise and so are huge monopolies like the Aluminum Company of America. It has become a shibboleth—'Quote the Bible and serve the Devil.'"

What, then, does this man variously termed radical, liberal, and sagebrush senator have in mind?

He believes, first, that the great evil of our time is the centralization of economic power which, in turn, has produced centralization of government. He now sees government falling of its own weight.

Second, he believes that the salvation of the people does not lie in building up government to regulate them, but in preserving opportunity for work to all groups and individuals.

Third, he believes that economic independence must be re-established or, without it, people's government will perish.

"What I am trying to do," he once explained, "is to find a rule whereby regimentation in both government and business will end, and the individual will be saved from being throttled."

How? Read his National Charters Bill. Read the TNEC recommendations. Read his report to the Senate Post-War Economic Policy and Planning Committee. Read his addresses before the annual meeting of the National Academy of Political Science in New York City, November 9, 1938, and before the American Marketing Association, November 23, 1943. Boil them all down and you will have the O'Mahoney program to retain political liberty and economic freedom:

1. Incentive taxation to promote investment of private capital in new, independent enterprise.

2. Laws to protect private enterprise thus established from arbitrary control by monopoly.

3. An administrative law to prevent government bureaus from regimenting business.

4. Enactment of a National Charters for National Commerce Law.

5. Encourage the people through their state and county governments to exercise local power to foster full utilization of local resources.

These are the salient points of his answer to the enigma of how to adapt industrial organization to the American ideal of living.

8

GERALD P. NYE
"Essentially Negative"

BY J. L. SAYRE

I N THE FALL OF 1936 SENATOR NYE SEEMED TO HAVE attained the rank of one of the great men of the times. He had completed the munitions investigation which aroused not only American public opinion, but also world-wide attention. Similar investigations were demanded in Great Britain, Canada, Argentina, France, and Sweden.[1] He had forced admissions from J. P. Morgan, from Du Pont officials, and from a host of other important industrial leaders that led people to the conclusion that the traffic in arms was a dirty business which must be strictly controlled in order to lessen the likelihood of future wars. His name was intimately associated with the passage of the first Neutrality Act. In recognition of this work he received the Cardinal Newman award for distinguished contributions to international peace.

Three years later, in July of 1939, he was one of the senators most instrumental in defeating the request of President Roosevelt for revision of the second Neutrality Act. From then until Pearl Harbor he was a vigorous champion of American isolation. Today he is probably as thoroughly discredited as any man in the country, and he was defeated in the general election of 1944 in the state that was once proud of him.

Nye's career has been much like that of a rocket—a rapid rise accompanied by some bursts of light that give promise of what is to come, then a brilliant display followed by a burning descent. He was born December 19, 1892, in Hortonville, Wisconsin, the son of a small-town editor and the nephew of the

1. A. Nevins: "British Munitions Inquiry," *Current History*, Mar., 1936, p. 619.

once famous humorist, "Bill" Nye. His boyhood was spent in another Wisconsin town, Wittenberg. These years saw the growth and development of the "Wisconsin Idea" under the leadership of the elder Robert M. LaFollette. Many Wisconsin people were at that time sympathetic to reforms of an economic, social, and political character. LaFollette provided the political acumen and perseverance necessary to translate the progressive sentiment into law. Largely because of his influence, income and inheritance taxes were adopted, labor was helped by workmen's compensation legislation, railroad rates were regulated, the conservation of natural resources was begun, and the direct primary was established. Naturally these changes were vigorously debated throughout the state, and Nye's interest in public affairs was intensely aroused. It is easy to understand that Nye acquired an outlook from these lively years that colored his later life in politics.

When he was less than twenty, he went back to Hortonville to run the newspaper there. For the next twelve years he was engaged in journalism of one kind or another. For a few months he worked for the *Des Moines Register,* but he preferred a small town and a less conservative climate than that of the Iowa capital. In 1919 he became editor and publisher of the *Sentinel-Courier* at Cooperstown, North Dakota.[2] There he remained until he went to the United States Senate in 1925.

Shortly before he came to North Dakota, a wave of agrarian discontent swept over this state. The farmers felt they were being exploited by the bankers, the railroads, the large elevators, and milling concerns. The legislature alternately ignored and thwarted their demands. In 1915 Arthur C. Townley, together with a few close advisers, formulated the idea of the Nonpartisan League to give effect to the farmers' aims. It had a five-point program: (1) a grain grading law, (2) state hail insurance, (3) a state bank, (4) a state mill and elevator, and (5) exemption of farm improvements from taxation. The movement was rapidly and overwhelmingly successful except in the eastern counties and a few of the cities. When Nye came

2. E. F. Brown, "Crusading Mr. Nye," *Current History,* Feb., 1935, p. 521.

to Cooperstown, the League was at its zenith. Nye joined the League and gave it vigorous support in his paper. Since the Nonpartisans had little support from the press at first, his advocacy of their cause gave him considerable prestige among them.

The Nonpartisan League suffered a decline in the early twenties, but Nye remained loyal to the organization. His loyalty was rewarded by a nomination for Congress in 1924. He was defeated, but his very failure on this occasion was a principal factor in winning for him his big opportunity the following year when Senator Ladd died. The incumbent governor, A. G. Sorlie, wanted to be a United States Senator himself but had laid his plans for the election year, 1926. He could not appoint himself to the office, and it seemed unwise to call a special election since to do so would result in eliminating what he regarded as his own best chance for the following year when regular nominations would be held. After some delay, Sorlie appointed Nye for the unexpired term. Governor Sorlie felt that Nye would be grateful for a reward far beyond his reasonable expectations, and that the Cooperstown editor would gracefully step aside in Sorlie's favor a year later.

When the young appointee arrived in Washington and presented his credentials, he met a sharp rebuff from the Senate. The conservative Republicans were by no means anxious to have another radical agrarian in their midst. They therefore proceeded to question the authority of Governor Sorlie to make the appointment under the laws of North Dakota.[3] Nye had supported LaFollette in the 1924 election and consequently his Republicanism was in some doubt. Finally he was seated in January, 1926, by the close vote of 41 to 39. From then until 1938 Senator Nye's political career was marked by an increasingly important series of successes and good fortune.

Governor Sorlie had died in 1926, and Nye found it comparatively easy to win election to the Senate in his own right. President Coolidge attempted to deny the North Dakotan his share of patronage, but Nye fought back and won. Coolidge never fully forgave Nye for the heresy of having supported

3. *New York Times,* Jan. 3, 1926, p. 6.

LaFollette, and Nye once said that the password to the Coolidge cabinet meetings was "knub" which meant bunk, spelled backward. Nye's anti-administration bias resulted in his being given comparatively poor committee assignments—among them the Committee on Public Lands. Nye struck out for himself by joining the farm bloc and working for the McNary-Haugen Bill which was cordially disliked by the President. Then from the Public Lands Committee he found his role in national affairs. He did a first class bit of inquiry into the operations of the Continental Trading Company, a concern set up to bilk the stockholders of Standard Oil of Indiana and the Sinclair Oil Company for the benefit of a few of the high officials.[4] Furthermore, the Continental Trading Company was unpleasantly connected with the Teapot Dome oil scandals. The latter had been exposed by the late Senator Walsh of Montana and his counsel, Owen J. Roberts and Atlee Pomerene. The public's faith in the integrity of high government officials and leading businessmen had certainly declined when one sickening revelation after another was published: Secretary of Interior Fall guilty of taking a bribe, Secretary of the Navy Denby guilty of gross stupidity if nothing worse; Doheny, Sinclair, and Stewart, all big businessmen in oil enterprises, were regarded as dishonorable. Ugly rumors about former President Harding continued and spread. Then by refreshing contrast stood Walsh and Nye as honest and capable defenders of the national interest. The two senators gained widespread esteem.

Senator Nye, in common with the late Senator Borah, has done most of his fighting against the ultra-conservative element in the Republican party in the non-presidential years. In 1928 he was opposed to Hoover before the convention, but after Hoover was nominated, Nye supported him in the campaign. During the first few months of the new administration, the North Dakota senator was a strong friend of the President. Nye felt that the Federal Farm Board might be a large part of the answer to the problems of agriculture, and that Hoover was sincere in wanting to improve the economic position of the farmer. As the depression deepened it became increasingly

4. *Cong. Record*, 70th Cong., 1st Sess., Vol. 69, Pt. 10, p. 10530.

clear that neither the President nor the conservative Republicans in Congress intended to undertake a vigorous program of relief and recovery. Nye broke with Hoover and became a hostile critic as conditions went from bad to worse. When the President succeeded in obtaining congressional consent to the moratorium on reparations and the war debts, Nye was one of the farm bloc group who demanded that the farmers' debts be scaled down. Although he was unable to accomplish much for farm relief, the elections of 1930 provided him another opportunity to gain prestige in his forte—investigations.

Senator Norris induced the Senate to establish a select committee to investigate campaign expenditures in the senatorial races (both for the nominations and for the elections) of 1930.[5] Nye was made chairman, with Dale of Vermont, Patterson of Missouri, Wagner of New York, and Dill of Washington as the other members. The committee was bipartisan in character—the first three members were Republicans and the last two were Democrats. The committee was given sufficient authority and funds so that an adequate investigation could be made. It is fair to anticipate the account of the work of this committee at this point to say that Nye did most of the work. He did get some real help from Senator Dale, but the others did very little. Charges of fraud and corruption were so common that year, Nye soon found it would be impossible to give proper attention to every case. The principal hearings concerned nominations and elections in ten states: Colorado, Delaware, Illinois, Kentucky, Nebraska, New Jersey, North Carolina, Pennsylvania, Tennessee, and Virginia. The evidence showed political skullduggery of a minor character in six states. For example, the Crump machine in Memphis had given large numbers of Negroes poll tax receipts so that they could go to the polls and vote "right" in the primary. In the other states the hearings read like a series of detective stories with Nye playing the part of Sherlock Holmes.

The Delaware case must give pause to those who would abandon the direct primary and return to the convention system. Josiah Marvel was a greatly respected leader of the bar

5. *Ibid.*, Senate Resolution 215, 71st Cong., 2nd Sess., Vol. 72, Pt. 7, p. 6841.

who had apparently a majority of the delegates to the Democratic convention pledged to him. The night before the convention met, a dinner was given to the delegates by some of
Marvel's opponents. The next day the convention nominated
Thomas Bayard by a fairly close vote.[6] Nye did not pursue his
investigation in Delaware as thoroughly as might be wished.
He did, however, find several trails that led to the influence
of the Du Pont family. He did not trace these effectively, and
he was frustrated in obtaining the real explanation of the
Bayard nomination. Quite possibly the stalemate experienced
on this occasion lingered in his mind until the munitions investigation a few years later. Then the Du Pont interests developed
more respect for Nye's inquisitorial skill.

If the Delaware inquiry had shown politics to be mean and
petty, the events in Illinois furnished a very dramatic comic-
opera relief. Nye had been investigating the campaign expenditures made by and for Ruth Hanna McCormick, then candidate for the U. S. Senate. While the agents for the committee
were trying to uncover evidence about Mrs. McCormick's expenses, they found they were being shadowed. The news reached
Nye that his past career in North Dakota was receiving the
careful attention of strangers. Nye himself was followed when
he took a brief vacation in Glacier National Park. When the
North Dakota senator taxed Mrs. McCormick with responsibility for this counter espionage, she admitted it without reserve. She declared she did not enjoy having her private affairs
pried into in what she thought was a highhanded manner, and
that if Nye was going to pillory her before the public, she
would give him a taste of his own medicine. After the first
furor had died down somewhat, it seemed to be a rather graus-
tarkian episode. Mrs. McCormick's investigation of Nye had
revealed nothing to his discredit, and consequently this acted
as a boomerang against her. On the other hand many people
did not fully endorse the ethics of hiring government agents
to spy on a woman's personal affairs. It appeared that some
$319,000 had been spent in her behalf [7] and the news of this

6. Senate Report Pursuant to Sen. Res. 215. Delaware.
7. *Ibid.* Illinois.

large sum probably did not help her cause with the Illinois voters. In any event she was defeated in the fall election by James H. Lewis, the Democratic nominee. A careful analysis of the reasons for her loss indicates that the Nye hearings had little to do with it. She took an equivocal stand on the questions of prohibition and the World Court. She lost some votes because of her sex. The political pendulum was swinging away from the Republicans at that time anyway. Finally she was closely associated with the *Chicago Tribune*—a newspaper that is not as influential with the voters as it pretends to be.

The Nebraska primary was the occasion of a peculiarly contemptible bit of chicanery. Senator George W. Norris was seeking the Republican nomination, and it seemed highly probably that he would get it. His public career had been marked by a very independent and progressive attitude that did not endear him to the conservative Republicans in his state or elsewhere. He had also been a severe critic of the privately owned public utilities. The latter combined with certain Republican leaders (most particularly Victor Seymour and W. M. Stebbins) to encompass the defeat of Norris. A grocery clerk of Broken Bow, Nebraska, was persuaded to lend his name to the enterprise. The grocer was named George W. Norris. The plan was to have the grocer file for the nomination at the last minute. Then there would be two persons named George W. Norris on the primary ballot at the same time. It was expected that this device would force the election officials to divide the vote equally between the two men, and that such division would result in the nomination of the third candidate, Stebbins. The scheme failed because of a technicality as to the exact time for filing nominating petitions.[8] The Chief Justice of the Nebraska Supreme Court rendered a decision that eliminated the grocer Norris. The Nebraska investigation was the most effectively handled of all those that Nye undertook at this time. Undoubtedly his heart was in this inquiry. He was helping his friend, Senator Norris, and at the same time he was making the ultra-conservatives and the "interests" squirm by his revelations. It was work well done.

8. *Ibid.* Nebraska.

The work of the Nye investigation in Virginia was of a different character from the others in that the political activities of Bishop Cannon in the 1928 campaign were being examined rather than matters connected with the then current contests. It was found that Bishop Cannon of the Methodist church had felt very little enthusiasm for the candidacy of Governor Alfred Smith for the presidency in 1928. The Bishop took an active part in trying to defeat Smith in Virginia. The plan was to have an anti-Smith Democratic ticket so that good Virginia Democrats could (1) refrain from voting for a Catholic, (2) refrain from polluting themselves by voting for a Republican, and (3) still vote as Democrats. Bishop Cannon was not only engaged in devious politics but also in devious finance since he maintained seven bank accounts during the critical period and shifted funds from one to another in a bewildering manner.[9] Although most of the account from Virginia was by then an old story, still it is fair to say that Nye helped to write finis to a page of our political history of which we cannot be proud.

The select committee had done well on the whole. The public was interested in the results and anxious to have at least the worst abuses made illegal for the future. Nye did introduce a Corrupt Practices Bill that would have improved the quality of our elections if it had been passed and honestly enforced. Unfortunately, it soon became plain that Nye was a good investigator, but a poor legislator. He gave little vigorous effort to obtain remedial legislation. For this failure there are three explanations: first, that he had obtained excellent publicity for himself and that that was sufficient; second, that he sounded out other members of Congress and found there was no hope of getting a Corrupt Practices Act passed that had real teeth in it; third, that other more pressing matters quickly claimed his attention. These reasons are not mutually exclusive, and it is probable that the truth consists of a mixture of all three.

In 1932 both Roosevelt and Nye carried North Dakota by handsome majorities, and the Senator returned to Washington with high hopes that the New Deal would be to his liking.

9. *Ibid.* Virginia.

With a few notable exceptions, it was not to his liking at all. He was against the NRA chiefly because it would help large business as against small business, indeed he feared it would foster monopoly. He was against the AAA. This is not as remarkable as it might seem. The AAA more largely reflected the aims of the American Farm Bureau than of any other farm group. The Bureau was the largest farm organization in the country but was not important in North Dakota where the Farmers' Union was dominant in the agricultural field. This latter body was not pleased with the Triple A provisions. Despite Nye's disappointment over the measures for industrial and agricultural recovery, he and Roosevelt reached agreement on a new undertaking. The munitions makers must be investigated.[10] America was disgruntled over the international developments that followed the First World War. In 1917 we were "The gallant starry Republic," "generous Uncle Sam," and the "idealistic Americans." By the middle 'twenties we were "Uncle Shylock." That hurt. We had fought to make the world safe for democracy, and Europe had raised a crop of dictatorships. The poppies sold yearly by the American Legion served as a bitter reminder that American boys had died for ends we failed to achieve. A large number of publications such as the book by Walter Millis, *The Road to War*, seemed to show that since certain persons made money out of war, it would be to their interest to foment and prolong wars. As a result of this attitude, the munitions investigation was authorized by the Senate.

The story of the Nye inquiry into the many and far-reaching ramifications of the traffic in arms is sufficiently fresh in the minds of most people to make a long account inappropriate here. Nye was at his best in this work. He extracted from unwilling witnesses admissions of the gravest import. Du Pont of America, Vickers-Armstrong of England, Schneider-Creusot of France, Krupp of Germany, Skoda of Czechoslovakia had enough sins to account for, as the public soon discovered. The truth was damning enough, but Nye fostered the view that these firms were linked in a gigantic conspiracy to promote

10. *News Week*, Apr. 21, 1934, p. 3.

wars and international hatred all over the world, and to make a long period of peace impossible.

The hearings produced a series of sensations on the public opinion not only of America but of foreign nations as well. The impression was created that countries and their rulers were mere puppets in the hands of the "merchants of death." It was brought out that in the First World War factories and vital properties of the munitions makers in Germany and France miraculously escaped being hit by air or artillery bombardments although near-by cities and military installations were shelled and bombed with great accuracy. Trading with the enemy even in contraband material went on during hostilities with the consent of the British, French, and German governments. At the same time that enormous profits were being made by the manufacturers of ships, steel, and explosives, large territories were laid waste, women and children were left poverty stricken and hungry, and millions of the best young men in the world died on the battlefields of Europe.[11] Even a personal villian was found in Sir Basil Zaharoff, salesman extraordinary of munitions, who crawled like a loathsome spider in the dark on the web of international fear, hatred, and intrigue. If one country bought two submarines, then Sir Basil was soon whispering to the war and finance ministers of a neighboring state with the result that the latter bought four destroyers. It was even hinted at one point that King George V of Great Britain had used his influence in behalf of the arms makers. American admiration for the integrity of European diplomacy did not rise perceptibly during this investigation.

In August of 1914 President Wilson had opposed loans to any belligerent nations on the grounds that loans were essentially an unneutral act. He soon weakened his stand on this matter, however, and agreed that the American Government would not object to credits being extended to the warring nations. Nye called J. P. Morgan to the hearing to testify in regard to certain financial aspects of the war. The New York banker was asked what difference there was between loans and

11. Senate Report No. 944. Special Committee on Investigation of the Munitions Industry, U. S. Senate, *passim*.

credits. When Morgan replied that they were substantially the same in effect and purpose, the natural conclusion was that President Wilson had been either gullible or something less than honest in making so early a reversal of American policy. The successive steps by which America's economic interest became more and more closely bound up with victory for the Entente were made clear. The Allies bought large quantities of munitions and other goods in the United States, and paid for them at first. This stimulated American business and employment. Then the Entente pleaded they had no more money to spare, and unless they got generous credits, they would have to cease their purchases. They obtained the credits. This resulted in more prosperity for America. A reluctance to lend more money was met with the statement that cessation of war purchases would bring an economic depression here. Thus foreign nations had maneuvered American business into a position where our own commercial welfare seemed to require American financial sources to lend the foreigners more and more. Then came the inevitable plea that if we did not enter the war on the side of the Allies, they would never be able to pay us at all. We entered the war. When it was over and peace had been made, we soon heard the now familiar charges that we "had made money out of their misfortune," and that "anyway the money had been spent in the United States for war goods at high prices, so that really we had only loaned the money to ourselves to stave off a depression"! There was a considerable element of truth in this, though it is plainly less than the whole truth of the problem. It was easy to show that the makers of war goods had made huge profits—far above what they normally made in times of peace. If the "merchants of death" made great sums of money because of a war, it seemed to follow that war was a good thing for them financially. If war benefited armament manufacturers, then perhaps they had had much to do with starting and prolonging the war. Perhaps they were opposed to any long period of peace. Perhaps they would endeavor to sabotage international attempts at disarmament for the sake of their own greed.

Evidence was placed in the records that tended to substantiate these suspicions. One William B. Shearer, representing certain American manufacturers, attended the Naval Disarmament Conference of 1927 at Geneva. The conference failed. It failed completely. Shearer was there as an "observer" or perhaps as a lobbyist. So far there is no doubt as to the facts. It was made to appear that Shearer had so worked upon the fears, jealousies, and suspicions of the conferees that he had caused the failure of the meeting. This last point was not satisfactorily established—the worst that can fairly be said is the Scotch verdict, "Not proven." Nevertheless the impression remained with the public, or large segments of it, that the munitions makers had wrecked the Geneva Conference.

Hitler had just risen to the status of dictator of Germany. His promise to rearm the Reich was well known in this country. It was found that French bankers had contributed to the Nazi campaign funds which made the rise of Hitler possible. Their reasoning in justification of such donations was that if Germany rearmed, then France would have to arm further. French military preparation meant that Schneider-Creusot would get big orders and gain large profits. This would help the bankers who were financially interested in the French munitions concern. Enough evidence was in the record to insure a verdict of guilty against the munitions makers charged with having tricked America in World War I, wrecked the Geneva Conference, and financed the rise of Hitler.

Nye had won his case before the bar of public opinion. Agreement was general that new legislation was needed to control the activities of private manufacturers of arms and munitions of all types. The American Legion was only the most prominent of hundreds of groups that endorsed the plan to take the profits out of war. America must not again be led step by tricky step to take part in any war that did not directly concern her. Europe and Asia could stew in their own juice; we would mind our own business unless actually attacked.

The Neutrality Acts of 1936 and 1937 were the natural and logical outcome of the public demand for an isolationist policy which Nye had done so much to arouse. Now he was famous. Speaking invitations poured in upon him. He received the

Cardinal Newman award for distinguished contribution to peace.[12] The people of foreign nations demanded that their own governments investigate munitions makers as Nye had done. It was something for a radical agrarian from a small state to conduct three important Senate investigations in the face of considerable hostility. It was even more that he had apparently taken the control of American foreign policy out of the hands of an able and popular President. Republican leaders seriously discussed the possibility of nominating him for President in 1940. He had made a brilliant record before he was forty-five, and still greater opportunities seemed to lie waiting for him in the future. He looked forward confidently to continued success.

When he returned to North Dakota to campaign for re-nomination and re-election in 1938, he found a hard fight awaiting him. Governor Langer decided to contest the Republican primary against Senator Nye. Langer was a powerful figure in the Nonpartisan League, and appealed especially to the less wealthy farmers in the state. In fact, Langer was much stronger with the League than was Nye. The Senator was able to put together a coalition of political forces that won for him both in the primary and in the general election which followed. The conservatives preferred Nye to Langer and supported the former strongly. Most of the independents, some Nonpartisans, and a few Democrats joined with the conservatives in this contest with the result that Nye won by rather narrow margins in the June primary and again in the November election. The loss of farm votes in this election was due chiefly to the belief that although their senator had made a name for himself, he had done little to help agriculture in North Dakota. The great majority of farmers who voted against him in 1938, agreed with him on isolation and neutrality but felt that he had become a publicity seeker who neglected the interests of his constituents in order to further his own career.

In the summer of 1939 President Roosevelt asked Congress to revise the Neutrality Act, and based his request on the grounds that an outbreak of war in Europe seemed imminent.

12. *New York Times,* Jan. 15, 1936, p. 8.

The Senate Committee on Foreign Relations refused to report out the bill which contained the substance of the President's request. In September the Second World War began, and Congress was called into special session to consider again neutrality revision. From then until Pearl Harbor the isolationist-interventionist controversy was the outstanding political question for the United States. The fight became increasingly bitter between the two groups as the war spread in Europe and Africa. The dispute cut sharply across party lines. President Roosevelt, Secretary of State Hull, Senator Pepper found vigorous allies in Wendell Willkie, Governor Stassen, and Frank Knox. On the other hand the Republican isolationist leaders, Nye, Johnson, and Borah were quickly comrades-in-arms with Senators Wheeler, Clark of Idaho, and Clark of Missouri. The colleges were divided—President Butler of Columbia was outspoken for the interventionists and Hutchins of the University of Chicago for the isolationists. The press reflected the prevailing doubts when the *Saturday Evening Post* changed sides in a sudden reversal and the late William Allen White did likewise.

The two years of discussion produced great bitterness on both sides. The isolationists were accused of being pro-Hitler, pro-fascist and cowardly. The interventionists were charged with an eagerness to sacrifice the lives of America's young men in an imperialist war that continued only because the British Empire was unwilling to make peace with moderate concessions. One party urged that we sell war goods to the anti-Axis nations and help them to preserve their way of life as democratic countries, but the other party declared that China and particularly Russia were as thoroughly totalitarian states as were Italy and Germany. The economic motive was twisted to fit the arguments of both disputants. The Roosevelt group made the point that the sale of war material to Great Britain and her allies would stimulate American industry and provide jobs for American workers. The Nye answer was that Britain was our chief rival for international trade and had always been unscrupulous in trying to get the best of us financially. The isolationists emphasized that if we went to war, we would become for all practical purposes a dictatorship ourselves, certainly for the period of actual conflict and perhaps permanently. We should therefore stay out of war and keep our democracy while we still could do so. How could we preserve our cherished institutions by giving them up? The reply was that if we refused to help our friends when they needed help badly, we would be hated by both sides when the war was over and the Axis had won. Furthermore, in order to protect America and the western hemisphere, we should have to become a permanently armed camp to resist probable aggression by Germany and Japan who had frankly embarked on a course of world conquest. There is no need to analyze the controversy further in this essay. Nye, and the people who followed him, were clearly wrong, as we now see.

Step by step America moved toward preparedness and toward participation in the war, and step by step Senator Nye fought the administration's foreign policy. He opposed the fortification of Guam, he opposed the exchange of the American destroyers in return for naval bases in the Atlantic and Caribbean, he opposed lend-lease, he opposed the extension of the drafted Army's term of service, and he opposed convoys for supplies to Britain. He was wrong, and the course he wanted the United States to pursue was neither wise nor statesmanlike. Still, like the Confederate leaders in the Civil War, he fought hard for his cause. By the late fall of 1941, it was obvious that the isolationist strength was slipping, and that only an unexpected peace in the very near future could prevent America's entry into the world conflict. Nye was becoming exceedingly unpopular, but he stuck to his guns to the last. On the very day of the Japanese attack on Hawaii, he was speaking against intervention in Pittsburgh. We must concede that he was not lacking in courage in standing up for his convictions.

When we declared war on Japan, Nye voted for war. No patriotic American could have done otherwise, but in a very real sense, he missed his great opportunity at this time. If he had declared that isolationism was finished, that he would support necessary legislation for the successful prosecution of the war, and that when it was won he would work to have America take a leading part in the framing of a just and durable peace, he would stand much higher today in public esteem. Unfortunately, he pursued a course that is hard to admire. It was very largely carping criticism rather than the advócacy of constructive measures. His comments on Great Britain and Russia have done little to improve harmonious understanding among the United Nations. He voted against price control, he opposed the Farm Security Administration, he became so warped in his bitter attacks on Roosevelt, Churchill, and Stalin, that his speeches were discounted in advance. Worst of all, in the opinion of the author, is his opposition to any really effective collaboration by the United States with other nations now that the war is won. Nye has become so thoroughly opposed to all major policies that prevail today that he has lost his perspective. He ignored the elementary fact that any government must do something positive in some respect, and so today he is not associated with a single positive plan of any kind.

Senator Nye sought renomination in the Republican primary in North Dakota in June of 1944. Congressman Usher L. Burdick was running for the nomination with the endorsement of the Nonpartisan League. A faction of the conservatives and independents had induced Lynn U. Stambaugh, former national commander of the American Legion to seek the senatorial nomination of the Republicans in the same primary. The three way split made it possible for Nye to get the prize by the narrow margin of 952 votes. The League vote and the labor vote went chiefly to Burdick; the conservative and independent vote was split between Stambaugh and Nye, with the former receiving the larger share. Nye did obtain some League votes especially in the German-Russian section of the state. This racial group was the most strongly isolationist element in North Dakota before Pearl Harbor. He got some conservative votes —principally because of his anti-administration attacks. He also received some sympathy votes from independents who felt he was being made a martyr unjustly because of his pre-war isolationism. Still his prestige declined enormously as compared with what it had been in 1932 and 1938.

After a bitter campaign in the summer and fall between Nye
and Stambaugh (who had entered the race this time as an independent), the voters chose the Democratic governor of the
state, John Moses, to replace Nye as United States Senator.
The reasons are not hard to find. First in the public mind was
his extreme isolationist stand. Soldiers who returned from
Guadalcanal and told their families and friends about the hardships they encountered at the outset there did not help the
political cause of the man who opposed preparedness in the
Pacific. Then his record in the Senate seemed to many to have
been entirely too much concerned with getting favorable publicity for Gerald Nye, and too little devoted to furthering the
legitimate aims of agriculture and of North Dakota. Finally
his unwillingness to take a strong stand for some form of
world organization endowed with really effective powers to
maintain peace in the future was almost incredible on the part
of a man who had spent years denouncing war.

Besides the foregoing reasons directly related to public policy that affect Nye's position with the voters, there are a number of personal considerations which must be examined since
they throw light on his character and capacity. In his favor it
must be said that he is honest in the financial sense—it does
not appear that he has ever been accused of graft or of taking
money for improper services. He is sincere within limits. He
really is against monopolies and trusts: his vote against NRA
was based on a real fear that little business would suffer
thereby. There is reason to believe that his attack on the munitions makers and on the interventionists did come from the
heart. He thoroughly disliked President Roosevelt and his administration. Nevertheless, when it is recalled that he went to
Washington as a progressive agrarian anxious to do something
for the underprivileged, his record is less admirable. He has
been against the policies of Coolidge, Hoover, and Roosevelt,
and he has not been actively for any alternative plans. The
feeling has grown that his success went to his head and he
felt safe in ignoring the interests of his former friends.
Certainly it is true that few people regard him as a real progressive now—the progressives in his home state do not follow

him, and the conservatives accepted him with some misgivings about his past, but accepted him temporarily because of his anti-New Dealism.

It is generally conceded that he can be a very effective speaker. He is nearly always well, but not too well, dressed. His voice is by no means unpleasant, and he has it under excellent control during an entire address. He usually begins in the modest, disarming manner of a small town business man who has been pushed forward by friends to present a few facts on some problem of local importance. He is not pompous nor overbearing in his manner. An opening statement of his topic is usually followed by a humorous story to put the audience at ease. Then little by little, and fact by fact, he marshalls his case. He has learned, as Demosthenes did, to put the weak part of his case in the middle of the speech. He usually states the position taken by the other side with superficial fairness— just fair enough so that at the moment the average listener will think he is being very decent about it, but not fair enough to stand careful analysis. Then the main thread of the argument is caught up again as he nears his climax. The former senator is a master of the effective pause, and he uses it just before two or three high points in his addresses. After the climax, he speaks faster and with frequent use of emotionally charged symbols as he continues to an apparently inevitable conclusion. Perhaps it is in the public speeches of Mr. Nye that his real character is most manifest. Emotionally they are well done, sometimes superbly well done, but the reasoning is strained and incomplete. When it comes to attacking some abuse, only a handful of public men today can do it as well as Nye. When, however, it is a matter of making a constructive proposal, of analyzing fairly the alternatives, of convincing his hearers he is advocating a sound plan for positive action, he does badly.

It is upon his fame as an investigator that his reputation was made and chiefly rests. Up to a certain point he handled his most important hearings with great skill. He assuredly understands publicity values. He selected skilled agents to do the preliminary work so that he would not get off on the wrong track. He was above the average in adroitness in questioning witnesses, and was excellent in eliciting pertinent facts that dramatized an abuse. He is well aware that the public likes to think in terms of persons rather than things or systems—perhaps he feels this way himself. In any event, once an investigation was well under way, some villain was quickly found who could be publicized as a modern Nero or a real Iago. Within reasonable limits, the more villains the better for the success of the inquiry. We must be fair to Senator Nye—this much of his technique was a necessary part of attracting attention to some current evil so that sufficient interest would be aroused to make correction possible. It was after the seriousness of some wrongdoing had been exposed, and many of the culprits had been found, that Nye weakened. He has not been interested in sending malefactors to prison, nor—with the exception of the Neutrality Acts—has he seemed either willing or able to press for remedial legislation. In short, he has not followed through to a real conclusion. It is only natural that the paucity of results should lead people to believe that Nye was principally anxious to obtain favorable publicity for himself.

The North Dakota senator's weaknesses have already been indicated, but it will be appropriate to summarize them here. In many ways he seems petty. His opposition to Roosevelt's policies made him so bitter that he permitted himself to tell stories of doubtful accuracy at the expense of the late President. He frequently did not answer letters from his own political followers in North Dakota. This cheap discourtesy was most unwise since his friends, whose help he needed for electioneering, resented this neglect. He did not do his fair share of committee work in Congress and consequently his effectiveness as a legislator was lessened there. At social affairs he has been known to snub newspaper publishers who had opposed his stand on public policies.

Fundamentally he is emotional rather than thoughtful, and this has been, as much as any factor, the explanation for his rise and decline in public esteem. He did not like the agricultural programs of any administration during the last nineteen years. They were all bad in his view. Very well, he would expose the evil forces menacing the farmer. He did so and then relaxed, content apparently to believe that to denounce someone was to solve a problem. He found political abuses in senatorial campaigns. Good. He publicized, he questioned, he denounced, he introduced a bill, and he quit. Strangest of all was his refusal to be realistic about the coming peace that will follow this war. Twice in a generation America has taken part in world wars. The nations are becoming more and more intimately and vitally concerned about what happens to their neighbors, and the international anarchy that has characterized relations among "sovereign" nations must give way to a high degree of co-operation. Sovereign countries were free to do as they pleased, and this included the right to go to war with one another. The history of several thousand years has shown beyond cavil that nations did go to war with each other frequently. If there are not to be more wars in the future, then plainly the various independent states of the earth will have to limit this right to go to war whenever they please. Nye favors peace against war of course, but refuses to agree to the essential restriction of sovereignty that must be made if wars are to cease. This was not good sense on his part.

He has lacked perspective and has been content with shallow or superficial solutions to complicated and far reaching problems. The answers to questions of war or peace require much more than a knowledge of the Neutrality Act. Agricultural difficulties are too deep seated and involved to be dismissed with any one simple plan like the McNary-Haugen Bill, or the benefit checks of the AAA. In the last analysis, Nye is essentially negative in his approach to national affairs. His lack of a positive program is his real tragedy. If he had devoted himself to a cause that meant definite accomplishment, in short if he had been a creator as well as a critic, his fame would have been secure. In several ways Nye resembles John Randolph of Roanoke who was at the height of his fame more than a century ago as a sharp critic and brilliant speaker. He was not a constructive leader in Congress and so his real usefulness was soon over. The same can be said for Nye.

9

SAM RAYBURN
"He First Tries Persuasion"

BY FLOYD M. RIDDICK

SAM RAYBURN AS SPEAKER OF THE HOUSE OF REPRESENTA-
tives is a powerful figure in shaping the destiny of our
federal government. The renowned Thomas B. Reed, three
times Speaker of the House, stated that the office "had but one
superior and no peer." The power that the office commands,
however, depends upon the personality of the incumbent as
well as upon the prerogatives of the office. In Rayburn's case,
a strong and unwavering personality has contributed to the
making of an outstanding Speaker. As a self-made man, he
has exercised that determined will to obtain his life's objective
—the speakership. He always knows where he is headed and
concentrates his energies to that end. As Speaker, he uses every
prerogative at his command to carry out the scheduled legislative program. Speaker Rayburn does not hesitate to refuse
recognition to a colleague if that refusal becomes necessary to
enact the legislation prescribed by the Democratic leadership,
nor does he question calling a representative to order if the
decorum of the House is at stake. Sam Rayburn seldom indulges in debate and he hates oratory, but if his party's victory
is at stake, he goes down into the well of the House and de-
claims to the majority membership. He tells it what to expect
and what is expected of it.

Mr. Rayburn rose to power in the House in accordance with
the seniority rule of that body, having served as a representative for twenty-seven years before becoming Speaker. However, he is the first chairman of the House Committee on Interstate and Foreign Commerce to become Speaker. From the

Cannon regime to the election of Mr. Rayburn, the chairman-ships of the committees on Ways and Means, Appropriations, and Rules had served as the stepping stone to the floor leadership and then to the speakership.

Speaker Rayburn, a career legislator, was born in Roane County (Clinch Creek), Tennessee, January 6, 1882, the eighth of eleven children of William Marion and Martha Waller Rayburn. The Rayburn family moved to Fannin County, Texas, when Sam was five; there Sam was reared on a farm producing cotton primarily for a livelihood. In Tennessee, his father had been a corn farmer. The first year of farm life in Texas was almost disastrous for the Rayburn family; everyone worked, but the amount of cotton produced was only sufficient to give the family a meager existence. Thus Sam's early life was filled with labor, deprivation, and poverty. He told the House membership one day: "I was reared on a farm where I have picked cotton, gathered all kinds of crops, and ploughed and hoed from sun to sun." [1]

He grew up in an atmosphere known only to those who toil so long for so little a financial return. He acquired a love for the land but a dissatisfaction with farming for a livelihood. Seeking a way to realize his childhood dreams and to unfold his innate powers, he announced to his father at the age of seventeen that he wanted more from life than just to stay on the farm. With his father's consent and financial support to the extent of $25, Sam Rayburn entered East Texas Normal College from which he emerged two years later with a teacher's certificate. He then taught in public schools for two years and at the age of twenty-four was elected to the Texas state legislature. After four years there (at the age of twenty-nine) he became Speaker of its house of representatives. Two years later he was elected to the United States Congress, already a long way down the road to his childhood ambition—he had announced to his high-school classmates that he expected to serve in the state legislature of Texas and later go to the House of Representatives of the United States and become Speaker of that body.

1. *Congressional Record,* Sixty-fourth Congress, First Session, p. 1043A.

While Mr. Rayburn seldom has anything to say about his youth, he told the House during his first term in Congress:

It has always been my ambition since childhood to live such a life that one day my fellow citizens would call me to membership in this popular branch of the greatest lawmaking body in the world. Out of their confidence and partiality they have done this. It is now my sole purpose here to help enact such wise and just laws that our common country will by virtue of these laws be a happier and a more prosperous country. I have always dreamed of a country which I believe this should be and will be, and that is one in which the citizenship is an educated and patriotic people, not swayed by passion and prejudice, and a country that shall know no East, no West, no North, no South, but inhabited by a people liberty loving, patriotic, happy, and prosperous, with its lawmakers having no other purpose than to write such just laws as shall in the years to come be of service to human kind yet unborn.[2]

In matters of interstate commerce, Mr. Rayburn grew to towering stature. While he denies any claim to brilliance, he is intelligent, has an excellent memory, and has enjoyed twenty-four years of experience on the Committee on Interstate and Foreign Commerce. He was a member of that committee from 1913 to January, 1937, and its chairman from 1931 to 1937. During those years the committee not only reviewed all of the federal laws on interstate commerce, but witnesses testifying before it discussed nearly all aspects of the subject in general, acquainting the committee membership with all details of interstate commerce. Most of the existing government agencies set up to supervise and regulate interstate commerce were created during the period from 1913 to 1937. Mr. Rayburn took advantage of this experience. Out of this opportunity, he accumulated a knowledge of commerce and of business intricacies which surprised even the brain trusters, in their dealings with him in connection with the enactment of the New Deal interstate commerce regulatory laws.

As chairman of the committee, Mr. Rayburn was the author of many bills on transportation. He fathered the Securities and Exchange Commission Act; and he managed through the House the bills to liquidate holding companies and to create the Rural Electrification Administration.

2. *Ibid.*, Sixty-third Congress, First Session, p. 1249.

As a legislator, Mr. Rayburn has made a definite contribution, primarily in the field of interstate commerce. With a rich background on which to build, he has molded a governmental philosophy that is neither conservative nor liberal. In fact, Mr. Rayburn cannot be associated with any of the popular labels used to mark the social philosophies of public men and writers. On the other hand the speeches he has made in Congress since 1913 reveal that he has been amazingly consistent in his conception of the duties, powers, and prerogatives of the government. But he must find himself in a difficult position in defining the line of demarcation between the jurisdictions and powers of the state and federal governments since he has been forced to make decisions in an era during which there has been an unprecedented shift to a centralized government. As chairman of the Committee on Interstate and Foreign Commerce, floor leader, and then Speaker, he has supervised or engineered through the House more legislation centralizing power in the federal government than has anyone else in American history. At the same time he has insisted on various occasions for the rights and powers of state governments. In 1921 for example, he made the following statement:

I am getting sick and tired of the Federal Government everlastingly sticking its hands into the affairs of my State and I am against any more building up of bureaus and of bureaucracy in Washington to reach out into the different States and tell the people of those States what they shall and what they shall not do. . . . One of the greatest issues in this country is coming within the next few years, and it is going to be as to whether or not the individual citizens of the several States of this land are capable in some way of managing at least a small portion of their own business . . . instead of having to run to Washington every time they want to know whether we can or whether we cannot do a thing.[3]

His conception of a strong federal government, however, dates back to his entrance in Congress. In 1914 he declared to the House that Congress not only had the power under the Constitution to regulate interstate commerce but when "brought to the necessity" Congress has the power "over all matters that affect the carrier in trying to carry out its con-

3. *Ibid.*, Sixty-seventh Congress, First Session, p. 3089.

tracts with the public to do an interstate business. There is no proposition better settled in law," he said, "than that when the Federal Government has the right to enter a field of legislation, and does enter that field, it then occupies it exclusively." [4] During World War I he sponsored legislation to make a strong executive and a highly centralized federal government including the bill by which the federal government took over the railroads. Immediately after the war he opposed both government ownership of the railroads and an indefinite tenure by the government, and favored a repeal of all of the war-power measures. In 1920 while discussing the bill to return railroads to private industry, he said:

> Mr. Chairman, this is only one of the many measures that I want to see passed in this and the succeeding Congress. I want to see all of these war powers repealed and the Government get out of these expensive and socialistic businesses. I want to get back to normal. When these matters are attended to then I want to see our Americanization law strengthened. I believe in an America for Americans. This country is too small for any man or set of men who pay allegiance to any other Government or any other flag. This is no place for the man who violates our law—be he high or low, rich or poor. The anarchist and the Bolshevist shall go. This is a mighty good country because 99 per cent of the people, regardless of section or party, are good citizens and loyal. And when a crisis comes, they will stand together. When the red hand of anarchy and lawlessness is thrust toward the throat of liberty, patriots will forget their differences.[5]

Consequently, it seems that Mr. Rayburn's decisions concerning the line of demarcation between the federal and state governments and the jurisdictions and powers to be exercised by the government are influenced and basically determined by the facts of the case.

Mr. Rayburn favors a controlled capitalistic social order; he is an opponent of state socialism. He distrusts the domination of big business or of big government, and does not think that the law should be used as an instrument of revenge. He believes there is room in this country for free men and free

4. *Ibid.,* Sixty-third Congress, Second Session, p. 9687.
5. *Ibid.,* Sixty-sixth Congress, Second Session, p. 3209.

enterprise. He told the House on one occasion when his party was in power:

The Democratic Party is not the enemy of capital or of big business. We know that there must be large aggregations of capital to carry on the great and growing business of the country; hence we would be more than foolish to do anything that would hinder or retard the growth of the country.... We intend to do simple justice to business, and, on the other hand, we are determined that business shall deal justly with the people. No honest man will ask more, and no man, be he honest or otherwise, may expect less.[6]

Soon after becoming a representative, Sam Rayburn disclosed an insight into government control in the future over business. In his first term, he proposed that the Interstate Commerce Commission not only regulate freight rates but that the Commission should likewise supervise the issuance of all stocks and securities of the railroads. In proposing his stock and bond bill in 1914, he said:

Hereafter before any railroad of this land shall issue any new securities, put them on the market, it shall come before the Interstate Commerce Commission and under oath set forth the reason why it desires this issue, and before it can issue and put on the market these securities the Interstate Commerce Commission, a capable governing body, must itself pass upon the question.

He further stated:

I believe that the interlocking of directorates of great corporations of this country has been one of the greatest of the evil tendencies of the times.... We have instances on record where one man will be the president of many corporations. In some of them he will have a small amount of stock; others in which he will have, in many instances, a controlling interest in the corporation. These corporations buy from and sell to each other. It is as natural for a man who controls these corporations to work for the interest of the one in which he has the greatest pecuniary interest as it is for water to flow downhill.[7]

He proposed as the true doctrine advocated and adhered to by the Democratic party since its coming into existence "to levy taxes so that they will bear equally and equitably on all prop-

6. *Ibid.*, Sixty-third Congress, Second Session, p. 9689.
7. *Ibid.*, p. 9688.

erty in all sections, and so that the greatest burden will fall on those most able to pay." [8]

He believes firmly in the Reciprocal Trade Agreements program of the administration, so much so that on May 12, 1943, when the Trade Agreements Act was up for a three-year extension,[9] he used all of his influence as the Speaker of the House to get the Act extended without modification in the existing law. He took part in the debate in an effort to block dissension within his own party ranks.

Mr. Rayburn is an advocate of an intelligent long-range flood control, power, and water conservation program. Long ago he saw that the waters of our great rivers were blessings if they could be harnessed to serve instead of to destroy. Early in his legislative career he pointed out the importance of building dams and reservoirs. On March 30, 1944, in a speech in San Francisco, he declared that "low-cost power will put industry that is now used for war into the new uses of peace. You will be able to find a workable balance between farm and factory." [10]

As to congressional procedure, Speaker Rayburn is a stern believer in the seniority rule; that, by and large, it is the best system for making promotions in Congress. Otherwise, he says, there would be endless fights which would be hurtful to the political parties as well as to the enactment of the legislative program. He believes in the standing-committee system and feels that good legislation cannot be written in the House Chamber; the groundwork, he thinks, must be performed by the respective standing committees; the committees were designed for that purpose, he declares. The standing committees should be left to function on their best judgment; he is an opponent of the famous Discharge Rule requiring committees to report bills.

He is not opposed to investigating committees; on one occasion he stated: "I do believe that when the white light of pub-

---

8. *Ibid.*, First Session, p. 1247.

9. See procedure on H.J.Res. 111 of the Seventy-eighth Congress, First Session. The bill was amended to extend the Act for two years instead of three.

10. *Congressional Record,* Seventy-eighth Congress, Second Session, p. A-1908 (daily issues of *Record*).

licity is thrown upon the business transactions and associations of men it will be one of the greatest factors in causing men to cease doing many of the reprehensible and unwise things that they are now doing." He feels the need of special investigating committees so much that he took the initiative in 1944 in getting the House to adopt two resolutions [11] authorizing the Speaker to appoint two committees to study post-war problems, with the objective in mind that they would recommend to Congress the enactment of legislation to prohibit a post-war debacle in our domestic economy as well as in the family of nations. He stated on one occasion:

Only recently I appointed a committee of 18 men to study post-war planning. We must get ready to do the great job of peace as our soldiers are doing the terrible work of war. I asked the members of this committee to consult with those in Government, in industry, in labor, and in agriculture in order that the best and soundest ideas may be put into our recommendations to the Congress. . . .

We must have a military policy in the United States after this emergency is over. On Tuesday of this week I appointed a committee of 23 members to study post-war military policy. . . . I do not know what all of our post-war military policy will be, but some of it I do know, and may I repeat that we are not going to destroy all of our munitions factories, we are not going to tear down our airplane plants, we are not going to sink our Navy.[12]

That does not mean, however, according to Speaker Rayburn, that investigating committees should be used to embarrass unduly the administration or business.

Sam Rayburn, after a bitter contest, was promoted to the floor leadership on January 3, 1937, from the chairmanship of the House Interstate and Foreign Commerce Committee. Four representatives announced their candidacy but the only real opposition was found in John J. O'Connor, at that time Chairman of the Rules Committee. Mr. Rayburn was at a disadvantage in the fight since in the first place it was unprecedented during recent years for the chairman of the Committee

11. H.Res. 408 of the Seventh-eighth Congress authorized the creation of the Committee on Post-War Economic Policy and Planning; H.Res. 465 of the same Congress authorized the creation of the Committee on Post-War Military Policy.
12. *Congressional Record*, Seventy-eighth Congress, Second Session, p. A-1908.

on Interstate and Foreign Commerce to be promoted to the floor leadership; the previous floor leader had been chairman of the Rules Committee. Secondly, Mr. Bankhead of Alabama was uncontestedly being made Speaker, a condition which invoked the argument that all of the top political posts should not be given to Southern Democrats. To Mr. Rayburn's advantage, however, was the fact that John J. O'Connor was not favored by the administration since as chairman of the Rules Committee he had blocked the consideration of legislative proposals sponsored by the administration.[18] Moreover, according to the general opinion of the House membership, Mr. Rayburn, a Southern Democrat, was progressive while Mr. O'Connor, a Northern Democrat, was conservative—these attributes are usually reversed. Finally, Mr. Rayburn secured his promotion when Vice-President Garner (it is believed at the request of President Roosevelt) threw all of his strength and support behind Mr. Rayburn. At that time Mr. Garner was very popular and influential among the House membership.

From the very beginning as floor leader, Mr. Rayburn conducted himself as a true party leader. He had stated upon accepting the new assignment that he expected to "make it his business to try to put through the program in connection with the Speaker" and other responsible leaders of the House, and he worked closely with the President to see that the administration's legislative program was enacted.

Representative Rayburn as a leader of the House was not very loquacious. He was regularly in attendance when the House was in session, directing the program and overseeing the membership of his party just as a coach does for the membership of his team in a contest. With a determined attitude and a firm conviction of the importance of his task, he always directed the House membership so as to expedite the legislative program. He never spoke unless he saw that his party was faced with a close or losing fight. If the outcome on a piece of legislation was questioned, he did not hesitate to participate

13. By way of explanation, it should be noted that it is impossible to consider in the House controversial non-privileged bills unless the Rules Committee sees fit to grant a special rule to that effect.

156 PUBLIC MEN IN AND OUT OF OFFICE

in the debate. But when he spoke he did not mince words; he did not assume that it was his job to discuss the merits of the legislation. He did remind the members of his party of their responsibility, of which the following excerpt taken from his speech on May 27, 1937, in discussing the 1938 Work Relief Bill, is a good illustration:

I take the floor at this time to appeal to the reason of my colleagues on this side of the aisle; not to their patriotism, because they are always full of patriotism; but we have reached a point in the consideration of this bill where I believe that the temper of this House is not such that we are likely to have reasoned legislation. Our friends over on the other side of the aisle, under patriotic and able leadership, are in a state of absolute glee this afternoon because they think that somebody will say that with their help committees and leaderships have been overthrown. We are badly split up, many amendments have been adopted in heat. . . .
I never quote the President of the United States, but within the hour I have been in conversation with him. I believe that on these three major amendments that have been adopted—frankly, I am opposed to each and every one of them in their present form, and the form of each of them is unfortunate—I believe that within a few hours we can get together with the man who must administer this law and with the members of his own party in the Congress of the United States and adjust this whole thing so that we can all win a victory and not be defeated.[14]

As floor leader, he was successful in expediting the legislative program. He accomplished this by objecting to extraneous discussions which were irrelevant to the bill under consideration. He commented to the House one day that "I can remember, the Speaker can remember, when I came here and the other members of long service, that it took from 3 to 5 days for us to pass a major appropriation bill. We have not spent upon one of these major appropriation bills, according to my recollection, more than two days during this session of Congress."[15]

He had not been floor leader long before he introduced the practice of prohibiting endless brief speeches at the beginning of each session before the House proceeded to the day's legislative program. Early in 1937 he served notice on the House

14. *Congressional Record,* Seventy-fifth Congress, First Session, p. 5082.
15. *Ibid.,* p. 4552.

membership that he would object to speeches of more than
a minute's duration until each day's legislative business had
been disposed of. He stated:

Mr. Speaker, reserving the right to object, and I am not going to
object this time, but a few days ago Members got in the habit of asking
unanimous consent to proceed for 1 minute; then it was 2, then 3, then 4,
and now it is 5. There is not a great deal of difference between 5, 6, 7,
or 10. I may say that hereafter to requests to address the House for more
than 1 minute before the legislative business of the day has been concluded
I shall object.[16]

Mr. Rayburn worked rather closely with the minority floor
leader, getting his co-operation in putting through a legislative
program. Experiences in Congress had taught him the wisdom
of this decision; he had learned that the majority could always
win in a final showdown, but an obstinate minority could certainly delay to no end the enactment of legislation.

Mr. Rayburn definitely merits a place in history as a strong
Speaker and a loyal supporter of his political party. In these
qualities no one has excelled him since the Cannon regime. In
fact, it is easy to believe that Mr. Rayburn models his Speakership after those of Thomas B. Reed and "Uncle Joe" Cannon.
On October 18, 1939, he told the House that he had always
admired Mr. Reed and Mr. Cannon for one thing especially,
"that is, they had the ability, they had the confidence in themselves to believe that they could exercise well all the power
that went with the great office of the Speaker under the rules
of the 'House of Representatives," and that he had always
looked up to "a man with iron in his backbone and brains in
his head." [17]

During his long tenure of office before becoming Speaker,
he learned "party ways," and blended his unique personality
with party loyalty. As Speaker, he has used the office to the
advantage of his party when that could be done in accordance
with the rules and precedents of the House.

16. *Ibid.*, p. 8004; see also *ibid.*, Third Session, p. 517.
17. *Ibid.*, Seventy-sixth Congress, First Session, p. 570.

His efforts have likewise been directed to enhance the position of Congress in the federal government. The Speaker admits that "we must have team work between the executive departments and the legislative branch of the Government; this co-operation must be mutual and understood by all of us." On the other hand, Mr. Rayburn is very jealous of the powers and prestige of Congress. He has charged in the House and to the press on various occasions that the attacks on Congress in recent years have been a studied effort to destroy the faith and confidence of the American people in their representatives. But, he assuringly added, there has never been a dictatorship built up in any land until the faith and confidence of the people had been destroyed in the legislative branch and the legislative branch itself had been destroyed.

In his defense of Congress, he served notice on the administrative agencies in his address upon re-election to the speakership in 1943 that "before determinations are reached or proposals are announced, those in positions of responsibility up on the Hill must be consulted." Personally, he has resented administrative agencies sending up to Congress involved and detailed legislative programs even before consulting with the chairmen of the committees concerned.

Mr. Rayburn has done little to change the rules and parliamentary procedure of the House. In fact, he has viewed the rules and precedents of the House as "pretty nearly perfect." It has been his endeavor as Speaker to see that the membership lived by the intent of the House rules. When questions have arisen as to the proper procedure under the defined rules of the House, he has endeavored to render decisions from the chair in strict accordance with what have been the practices of the House. He will tell you that he has not endeavored to read into the rules any new parliamentary procedure. With the use of the up-to-date volumes of Hinds and Cannon's *Precedents,* making the practices of the House since 1789 on all procedural matters available within a moment's notice, it has not been so difficult for recent Speakers, with the assistance of the Parliamentarian, to apply the practices of the House to all procedural issues as they have been raised.

In the chair, Mr. Rayburn has made no pretense at being overly diplomatic. He has always stated his case as he saw it. Sometimes his manner has seemed unnecessarily irritable when he has cut off some obstreperous member with a hefty rap of the gavel and a firm "The Chair is not accustomed to having its ruling questioned." But that does not mean that Mr. Rayburn goes out of his way to antagonize the House membership; specifically he is not an irritable man. If he were, he would not be Speaker. Sam Rayburn is very popular among his colleagues. His performances as Speaker have merely been Sam Rayburn presiding over the world's greatest legislative body in the manner he thinks the job should be done.

The House membership has learned his firmness and trustworthiness; it has been aware of the fact that he knows how to be hard boiled; and from all appearances, the representatives have feared to abuse their rights and privileges under the rules because of the possible outcome with the Speaker. Of course the Speaker is a reasonable man; he first tries to use persuasion with the membership and particularly with his party; if that does not get results he knows how to get tough quickly. Mr. Rayburn is the administration's chief spokesman and leader in the House, but he knows how to talk with the administrative officials if their dealings with Congress are not in accordance with what he thinks they should be.

Sam Rayburn has gained the confidence of the House membership and there can be no question but that his presence has a considerable influence on the House procedure. President Roosevelt has recognized this power of the Speaker so much that in a personal letter to him on February 19, 1942 (shortly after the United States declared war and Congress was faced with much emergency legislation), he wrote the Speaker requesting that he cancel an appointment at Fort Worth, Texas, to speak the following Monday night at the George Washington dinner. In the letter, the President stated: "I feel it is my duty to ask you to stay here with me until the House has disposed of the much needed legislation. In other words, the nation needs you a lot more than Texas does right now."

On different occasions, he has displayed a distinct and determined leadership. On August 12, 1941, his performances were such as to secure for himself the credit for having made possible the enactment of the bill [18] for the extension of the Draft Act, and had this bill been killed, the whole defense program of preparedness for World War II would have been disrupted. The Speaker knew, with the aid of his party assistants, that it was doubtful if a majority of the representatives would vote for House passage of the bill; and he knew that it was his responsibility to do something to assure a continuation of the defense program. Thus he called upon Secretary of State Cordell Hull and the top officials of the armed forces for letters to read to the House in order to impress its membership with the seriousness of the situation; and during the closing minutes of the debate before the roll-call vote was taken, he exerted all of his influence as Speaker by taking the floor and appealing to his party membership for support. Beyond that, he utilized his knowledge of parliamentary procedure during the few moments of confusion as to what had happened to freeze once and for all time the announced bare majority vote of 203 yeas to 202 nays, by which the bill passed.[19] This vote was determined by making last minute pleas to doubtful colleagues.

Late in 1943, disunity over the war effort was spreading throughout the country. The incident of General Patton slapping a soldier in the Italian campaign was being rehearsed in newspapers, over the radio, and even in Congress, at the expense of the war program. The men responsible for the conduct of the war were much concerned and feared what might be the outcome of disunity among the civilian population. Again, Speaker Rayburn took the floor in the House on December 9, 1943, to halt or to eliminate, particularly in the House, hurtful criticism, which was only breeding disunity among the people. He warned the representatives and the country that "we are getting in a dangerous situation." [20] The Speaker spoke so firmly and with such assurance that the members of the

18. See procedure on H.J.Res. 222 and S.J.Res. 95 of the Seventy-seventh Congress.
19. See *House Journal*, Seventy-seventh Congress, First Session, p. 599.
20. See Senate Document 142 of the Seventy-eighth Congress.

House took the warning; they were impressed. The abrupt change in the nature of speeches made in the House of Representatives subsequently revealed the influences of what the Speaker had said so authoritatively.

In brief, it must be said that Rayburn has done an impressive job for his party as Speaker of the House. While he has presided impartially over the House membership, he has led members of his own party to support legislation desired by the Roosevelt administration in the face of almost insurmountable opposition. On many occasions from 1941 through 1944, he accomplished unbelievable legislative feats in the House with the Democratic majority, which was permeated with dissension and disunity. Toward the close of 1944, he could claim only a bare majority of the total House membership, and they were united in support of only a very few issues.

The innovation of the important weekly conference at the White House between the President and the Vice-President, the Speaker, and the floor leaders of the House and Senate was made soon after Mr. Rayburn became floor leader. These meetings between the President and the congressional leaders have become an important instrument in the relationships between the President and Congress, and bridge a gap of long standing under our governmental system of independent arms. Sam Rayburn has played no small part in the development and success of these conferences.

This practice of weekly meetings between the President and the congressional leaders became necessary because of the strained relationships between these two arms of the government. It had been common during the early part of the speakership of Mr. Bankhead for the Speaker to announce to reporters at his morning press conference that he did not expect any message from the White House during the day. Then after the lapse of an hour a message from the White House to Congress would arrive, an embarrassing predicament for the Speaker. Further, the President was regularly making legislative proposals to Congress which were so far-reaching and unprecedented without first consulting the leaders that they were unable to sell such bills of fare to the membership; in fact, it was embarrassing to present them. The "packing of the Supreme Court" recommendation illustrates the case.

At these weekly meetings the congressional leaders always advise the President of the legislative schedule for the week ahead; and the first subject of discussion, unless some emergency prevails, is the pending programs of the two houses. Subsequently, the discussion moves to matters of long-time planning, international and national problems, particular bills pending in Congress, and the like. The conversation in each instance is dependent upon the time and the character of the week's program. Major bills frequently provoke long discussions as to content and strategy of enactment. The system actually serves as a clearing house for legislative-administrative problems. The practice without question improves the relationship between Congress and the President, not only because it forces compromises and better understandings between the two arms of the government, but the members of the House and Senate feel that they have been consulted through their respective leaders.

No records are available as to the origin of these conferences, but since they were started with the rise of Sam Rayburn to the floor leadership, it is only natural to believe that Mr. Rayburn's contribution to their conception and development is not secondary.

The Speaker further advocates close co-operation between the various divisions of the administration and Congress. To illustrate: On October 14, 1943, he appointed representatives from four House standing committees to confer with Secretary Morgenthau on post-war stabilization of international currency, and members of the House Committees on Interstate Commerce and on Merchant Marine and Fisheries to confer with the State Department officials concerning communications and shipping problems, respectively.

Sam Rayburn is a dynamic individual, trained primarily in the school of experience. He had to fight his own battle for recognition in public life.

Outside of law-making he has shared two passions—the production of white faced Hereford cattle and the study of the lives of Robert E. Lee and Thomas Jefferson; from these, he has acquired the true prospective of a Jeffersonian Democrat and believes that the soil is one of the greatest sources of security for a healthy nation. Throughout his career as a legislator he has advocated that "any legislation that will cause more citizens of this country to become home owners will be legislating to help the Government. Nothing could go further to make this the ideal country in which to live than for some action to be taken that would cause the men who till the soil to own the soil that they till." [21] He feels that nothing helps so much in the making of good citizenship as for the people who make up the government to think that they are a part and parcel of that government, and that the government is instituted rather to help than to hinder the citizenry from enjoying the fullest liberties and fullest freedom. His creed:

One of the strongest motives in human endeavor is the hope of acquiring title to a house and to certain aids in making a livelihood. Small and privately owned farms, gardens, shops and stores have existed through the ages, and will continue to exist. The people who own them and operate them are the bulwark of civilization.

Mr. Rayburn has greatly influenced the legislative program in the House particularly following his rise to the position of chairman of the Committee on Interstate and Foreign Commerce; at all times, he has placed personal enhancement secondary to the prestige of his party; he is truly a party man, ever fighting to carry out the program of the Democratic party. That does not mean that Mr. Rayburn is a yes man, yielding to every desire the Democratic administration has expressed; it means Mr. Rayburn believes in party government. Specifically, he has been known to differ on various occasions with members of his party and even with the late President in whom he had much faith and for whom he fought unceasingly. But he believes that his fights should be kept within the "family." He does not feel obliged to think on all public issues as do all the members of his party; but in determining government policy he proposes that the responsible party officials talk the matter

21. *Congressional Record*, Sixty-fourth Congress, First Session, p. 1043A.

over "within the family" and reach an agreement so that the party can present its position to the public in unison.

The courage of Speaker Rayburn to announce and to defend his views and opinions within the party, regardless of the desires and wishes of his superiors, was evidenced in 1940 when he, with an unblemished record in behalf of the New Deal, announced his support for the nomination of Garner as Democratic candidate for President as opposed to a third term for Roosevelt. Some people were a little surprised at Mr. Rayburn's stand in supporting Mr. Garner, a man whom the President is known to have opposed personally.

The coming of World War II has presented Sam Rayburn in a new capacity; i.e., a high governmental official having to participate in international affairs. To equip himself for such an undertaking he has for the last several years developed a close association and friendship with former Secretary of State Cordell Hull; he frequently dined and consulted with America's number one man in foreign affairs. In fact, he is an admirer and student of the life of Cordell Hull. He demonstrated his regard for the man on January 22, 1944, at the Jackson Day dinner. Mr. Rayburn, in reflecting on President Andrew Jackson, said that if Jackson should walk "among us today [his] eye would be drawn to two great figures. . . . I have not come here just to call names, . . . I would rather deal in issues than in personalities. But some names, through greatness of spirit, outgrow these limits and become a force in the world. And so it is with these two—these two heroic figures who would bring the light of satisfaction into the eyes of our forefathers. One of these Americans is Franklin D. Roosevelt." And then after a prolonged silence before his audience of over 2,000 top government officials, and after a long look at the Secretary of State, he added: "The other is Cordell Hull."

Mr. Rayburn is disappointed in the aftermath of the last war, but he still wants a peace organization based on the structure of the League of Nations. Just as important, he is concerned with conditions at home after the war. Out of this interest, he is solely responsible for the creation of the House Special Committee on Economic Policy and Planning, headed by Representative Colmer, and the Special Committee on Post-War Military Policy, headed by Representative Woodrum. He wanted these House select committees, equipped with staffs of experts, to study and to draft plans and recommendations to aid Congress with its task of determining legislative policy after the war. His concern in post-war problems is expressed in the following excerpts from his Jackson Day dinner address, referred to above:

First, we are not going to meet our debt to the boys who have gone abroad and fought our battles for us by hoping that when those boys get back jobs for them will just happen. We are not going to forget those men and their families when the parades have passed and the bonfires of victory are cold. It is not enough to shower them with torn telephone books. There are no calories in confetti.

Second, we are not going to deprive our people of the right to work. We are not going to leave that right in the lap of chance or tie it to the chartline of a boom-and-slump economy.

We are pledged to preserve for our country its system of free enterprise. We can save that system by making it work; and by that I mean making it work for the well-being of all our people....

We are not going to hold out to our people the sorry mirage of isolationism....

In referring to the closing of war plants after the war, he said: "We also have different ideas about the closing of those war plants. We have the idea of converting them to the production of peacetime needs of our people—of more production, not less—and of keeping our workers in jobs."

Speaking on March 30, 1944, of our policy in the Pacific, he said: "In the world of tomorrow, with its new tools of war as well as of peace, many [of the Islands of the Pacific] will take on new strategic importance.... The day will come when it will be up to us, not the Japs, to decide what shall be done with them...." He continued:

It must be our intention to safeguard our national security in the Pacific Ocean after this war in any manner and by any means that may be necessary. We know now that treaties and agreements, presuming a sense of honor in both parties, do not accomplish this in the case of the Japanese because the Japanese are not an honorable people....

But there is one language that they can understand. Our battleships, our planes of war, our tanks, our fighting men, speak that language. Our 16-inch naval guns speak it fluently. So do our block busters and our torpedoes. And with this kind of language, we want to be ready at any time, now and forever, to talk to the Japanese in case they don't get what we mean.[22]

Thus, according to the standards of the average American, Mr. Rayburn has been exceedingly successful. He is indeed an important but unassuming man of simple faith and impeccable integrity. He is impatient but kind, and he understands the men around about him. His integrity, dependability, and loyalty are beyond reproach. He has not excelled in learning nor has he attempted to direct the political thinking of America, but he has contributed greatly in the taking of ideas and has molded them into a mode of life by which we may live. He is an excellent example of the frontier spirit, self equipped and daring to obtain an objective in life at any cost.

22. *Ibid.,* Seventy-eighth Congress, Second Session, p. A-1907.

IO

ROBERT LEE DOUGHTON
"Hard Work with No Vacations"

BY ROBERT S. RANKIN

THE CHAIRMAN OF THE COMMITTEE ON WAYS AND MEANS in the House of Representatives is a powerful figure, not only in Congress, but in American political life. The usual descriptive term that is applied to the Committee on Ways and Means is that of "all powerful." If this appellation has been deserved in the past, the importance of the committee and its chairman, Robert Lee Doughton, in this day of huge budgets and higher taxes is indeed hard to measure. The size of the United States budget today makes the job of determining the nature and the extent of taxation one of the most important in Washington. Claude Kitchen and Joseph Fordney, past chairmen of this committee, thought they had done good jobs when they raised a billion dollars. Today Congress approves revenue bills that raise nearly fifty billion dollars in taxes. The job of determining the nature and extent of taxation is shared by many, but it falls particularly upon the broad shoulders of Robert Lee Doughton, the Chairman of the Committee on Ways and Means.

Each year as the budget grows in size, new and heavier taxes are made necessary. The need for additional revenue today is always present. No matter how much money is raised, the government invariably demands more. Each year the taxpayer, as he scans the mounting spiral of expenditures, realizes that his tax bill in the year to come will be much greater.[1] Is there a limit to the amount that the government should collect be-

---

1. Ninety-six per cent of present taxes are used for war expenditures and the peacetime budget is only 4 per cent of the present revenue.

yond which the source of income might be destroyed? To Bob Doughton, more than to any other man, is given the duty of saying just how much can be raised by taxes and the best way of securing this amount.

The individual who determines the rates and the type of taxes is torn between two fires; he must have the confidence of the taxpayers and be thought of as the taxpayers' friend, and at the same time he must get as much money from them as he possibly can. His success is measured largely by how painlessly he extracts the money. Bob Doughton has performed this difficult task in a manner satisfactory not only to his party but to most Americans. Known as the taxpayers' friend, he has taken more money from them than any other chairman of Ways and Means. His position in the political world merits close scrutiny, particularly so at a time when the war emergency has placed extra burdens upon him.

To the Committee on Ways and Means are referred all revenue measures. It has jurisdiction over "subjects relating to the revenue and measures purporting to raise revenue and the bonded debt of the United States." [2] It is admittedly the most important committee in the House, although in size its membership of twenty-five is today eighteen less than that of the Committee on Appropriations. Democrats, particularly, are desirous of places on this committee, for its democratic members constitute the Committee on Committees for the party and make all Democratic committee assignments. Their membership on the Committee on Ways and Means is determined by action of the party caucus, usually after very spirited contests. It is no wonder, then, that the chairman of this committee occupies a place of vital importance in the organization of the House and in the strategy of his party.

It is an interesting commentary on American government that Bob Doughton, never having planned a political career, has been a member of Congress since 1911, and, never having gone to college or having been trained in finance or taxation,

2. Clarence Cannon, *Precedents of the House of Representatives,* VII (1935), 1723. For a brief description of the Committee on Ways and Means, see Floyd Riddick, *Congressional Procedure* (1941), p. 125.

has been chairman of the Committee on Ways and Means for a longer period of time than any other person. In spite of these records for longevity, Mr. Doughton did not enter political life until he was forty-five. His home is in the Blue Ridge Mountains of North Carolina. His father died when young Bob was approaching manhood and he was, therefore, placed on his own. He continued to live in his own section of the state and did very well as a farmer, stock raiser, horse trader, and storekeeper. About the time he became interested in politics he was made president of a small country bank. His entry into the political world was as a member of the North Carolina Senate. Serving one term, from 1908 to 1910, during which he was a member of the Finance Committee, he next ran for a seat in the House of Representatives. Winning this election in 1910, he has served continuously in the House since that date.

When Bob Doughton took his seat in the House, he preferred membership upon the Agriculture Committee. He was, however, because of his banking experience, placed on the Banking and Currency Committee. Later he served as chairman of the Committee on Expenditures in the Department of Agriculture.[3] In the Sixty-ninth Congress a vacancy developed on the Committee on Ways and Means because of the death of Claude Kitchen, a member from North Carolina, and he secured this appointment. He was aided in securing this position because geography still plays an important part in the selection of the Democratic members of the Committee on Ways and Means. In 1933, seven years after his appointment to the committee, he was chairman—an interesting example of the way of seniority rule. Doughton was way down the list with little chance of becoming chairman. However, Garner, who was the ranking member during Republican control, was elected speaker. Collier, the next in line, who served as chairman during the Seventy-second Congress, became disabled, which caused Crisp of Georgia to serve as acting chairman for the remainder of that Congress. Crisp, however, left the

3. He has also had long service on the Committee on Roads and the Committee on Education.

House to run against Dick Russell for the Senate. Rainey, the next-ranking member was elected Floor Leader; Cordell Hull of Tennessee, who had outranked Doughton in the Seventy-first Congress, was elected to the United States Senate; and thereupon Doughton became the chairman of the committee at the same time that the Democratic party had control of the House, the Senate, and the executive branch of government.

His elevation to this high position has not been without criticism. E. Pendleton Herring, in commenting upon this point said: "Chairman Doughton . . . a man of sincerity, public spirit, and fidelity, was expected to direct his committee in their consideration of measures far outside his background, experience, and philosophy as a country banker and North Carolina farmer."[4] Bob Doughton has lived and learned, until today it is difficult to find criticism of his work except that which is political in nature. Undoubtedly he has the respect and admiration of both the Democratic and Republican members of the House. This does not mean that he refrains from poking fun at or criticizing the Republicans. On the contrary, he rather enjoys it. One of his closest friends is Mr. Treadway of Massachusetts, formerly the ranking Republican member of the committee. Yet his description of a speech by Mr. Treadway was that it consisted of "gesticulations, gyrations, fulminations, and hallucinations."[5] Again, after listening to speeches upon the tariff by Republican members, his description of their position was "the most extreme on the tariff I ever heard expressed. They out-Fordneyed Fordney, out-Cumbered McCumber, out-Smooted Smoot, and out-Hawleyed Hawley, and, if possible to do so, out-Treaded Treadway."[6] Nevertheless, his following is so strong in the House that, according to one commentator, this tax-scarred veteran has only to growl and the representatives blink and growl too. Tributes to Bob Doughton appear frequently upon the pages of the *Congressional Record*, and, while some are several columns in length, a recent statement by the same Mr. Treadway reflects the opinion of his

4. E. Pendleton Herring, *Presidential Leadership* (1940), p. 31.
5. *Congressional Record*, LXXX, Pt. I, 948.
6. *Ibid.*

committee. "No committee," he said, "ever had a more able, more fair, or more conscientious chairman." [7] Certain individuals think the respect of the House membership is due to some extent to his age, others to his rough-hewn and simple virtues, and still others because of his success as chairman of this important committee.[8] Whatever its basis may be, certainly no member within recent times has received in the *Congressional Record* more letters and statements of respect than has Bob Doughton.

Possibly one of Mr. Doughton's greatest political assets is that he has many of the characteristics dearly loved by Americans. Some are the basis for nicknames—many in number—but all showing affection and esteem, not derision. To North Carolinians he is known as "Farmer Bob." He has received this name not because he farms for pastime but because he is a genuine dirt farmer. This name makes him a brother to his constituents, for his district is largely rural. The terms "Muley" and "The Great Stern Face" are based primarily upon his stubborn character and on the fact that once he thinks he is right he stands by his convictions. Snell once said, "If the gentleman says he is sure about it, I know he thinks that way, for he says what he thinks." [9] His word is law to both friend and foe. Yet, in spite of this stubbornness, Knutson of Minnesota, who, if the Republicans obtain control of the House of Representatives, will probably be the next chairman of the Committee on Ways and Means, recently stated, "In all the time I have known him, I have never seen him do an ungenerous act." [10] Farmer Bob would probably add a few words to the motto of Davie Crockett, so it would read: "Be sure you are right, and then go ahead in spite of any influences that might be brought against you."

Many friends of Mr. Doughton think that he does not know how to take advantage of opportunities for publicity. In fact,

7. *Ibid.*, LXXXVIII, Pt. V, 6265.
8. See the following sketches of R. L. Doughton: Max Stern, "Farmer Bob," *Today*, June 25, 1935; George Creel, "Man of Iron," *Colliers*, July 13, 1935; Gerald Movius, "He'll Take a Bite Out of You," *Saturday Evening Post*, Jan. 17, 1942.
9. *Congressional Record*, LXXX, Pt. X, 10584.
10. *Ibid.*, LXXXIX, 9375.

it is not ineptitude, but a genuine lack of interest in publicity. He never seeks the limelight; while dislike of publicity is a pose assumed by many politicians, this is not true of Mr. Doughton. In the controversy over the President's veto of the 1944 tax bill, Senator Barkley received nationwide attention for his words condemning the veto message, while the remarks of Mr. Doughton, no less caustic, passed with a bare notice and little fanfare.[11]

His independence approaches stubbornness. At a time when President Roosevelt and Mr. Doughton were in close harmony with respect to their financial views, Drew Pearson, the columnist, made the statement that his tax vote had been influenced by Johnnie Hanes. This observation incensed Mr. Doughton no end. He called Mr. Pearson to his office and in very forceful language stated his independent position and his opinion of columnists who are careless in their accusations. After the interview, Mr. Pearson made the statement that "Mr. Doughton thoroughly convinced me that Mr. Hanes had not influenced his vote, and, furthermore, that not even the President of the United States could influence his vote unless 'Muley Bob' found that the President's views coincided with his own carefully considered conviction." [12]

Mr. Doughton's physical vitality is remarkable. Despite his eighty-one years, he is vigorous and active. While he is a little hard of hearing, he frequently hears things that he is not expected to hear. The tremendous vitality of this eighty-one-year-old statesman has been the subject of much comment. It has been attributed to the fact that he neither smokes nor drinks and is regular in his habits, going to bed at nine o'clock and rising at daybreak. He himself bases it upon the goodness of Providence, heredity, and hard work with no vacations.

David Harum and Farmer Bob Doughton have much in common. Both were horse traders *par excellence*. The favorite story about Farmer Bob is that once a stranger bought a team by mail from Farmer Bob for four hundred dollars. Later he

11. It is true, however, that it is more unusual for a floor leader to differ with the President than for a committee chairman to do so, particularly where Barkley and Doughton are involved.

12. Drew Pearson, "Washington Merry-Go-Round," Dec. 12, 1942.

wrote that the team was not satisfactory, and he would not pay the price agreed upon. Mr. Doughton stopped at the man's place of business one day and said he was in the market for a good team of horses. "I'll show you the best pair in the state," said the dealer, leading out the team in question. He then quoted a price considerably higher than four hundred dollars. Whereupon Mr. Doughton introduced himself and had little difficulty in collecting his four hundred dollars.[13] With respect to one deal he made while on a visit to the Philippine Islands, he is not sure which party came out ahead. He was attracted by a large set of caribou horns, beautifully finished and hand carved, and asked the price. "The best I can do is $12.00," said the native. "I will give you $4.00," bargained Mr. Doughton. "Sold," was the immediate reply of the native.[14]

One last characteristic is his ability to express fundamental truths in simple language—another trait well liked by Americans. When he thought taxes were getting so high as to approach confiscation, his statement was, "You can shear a sheep many times but you can skin him only once." Taxes, he said, would be levied "to get the most feathers with the fewest squawks from the goose." [15] Once, in commenting upon the fact that men of privilege make biting remarks on public affairs, he wrote: "The importance of a man's opinion on national affairs is not necessarily determined half so much by the chair in which he sits as by the manner in which he got to that chair." [16]

As Chairman of the Committee on Ways and Means, Mr. Doughton is largely responsible for the present tax policy of the United States. Holding this office since 1933, a period longer than that held by any other chairman, he has reported more tax bills than any chairman in the history of the country. This record is particularly impressive when we consider the critical period in which these tax measures were introduced. It is well to review Mr. Doughton's views on taxation, for

13. See *United States News*, June 21, 1937, for one version of this story.
14. *Allegheny* (North Carolina) *Times*, Dec. 12, 1935.
15. See syndicated article by George Peck, "Awfully Close to the Skin," Thursday, Nov. 25, 1943.
16. Robert L. Doughton, "The Relations of a Business Man with his Congressman," *Dun's Review*, May, 1937, p. 7.

they have affected profoundly the tax policy of the nation. In the first place, taxation for Bob Doughton has only one purpose—revenue. He has informed his committee that "we have no constitutional right to levy taxes for any other purpose than to raise revenue." [17] If social reform can go along with the raising of revenue, that is all right, but the controlling purpose of all taxation is to secure revenue. In the second place, he prefers a middle-of-the-road position with respect to taxation. He has his suspicion of tax reformists who hope to solve tax problems by sweeping reforms and changes. He considered the Townsend Plan a racket, and he listens with a really deaf ear to the attempts of one group to soak another. In brief, this is his own description of his position: "I've got no sympathy with the idea of soaking the rich. Neither have I any sympathy with the policy of burdening the poor. There is a middle ground where revenue can be obtained from sources that can most easily supply it." [18] As one member of the committee puts it, "with Bob Doughton as chairman, we will never substitute the wringer for the eagle on our coat of arms." [19] Throughout his chairmanship, Mr. Doughton has objected to a national sales tax, which he thinks sins against every sacred principle of taxation, and to a higher excise tax on tobacco. In his position with respect to both taxes, Farmer Bob has the full support of his North Carolina constituency. Today he opposes the abolition of renegotiation, and is urging localities to reduce their tax burdens as much as possible to help the taxpayer to meet his heavy federal taxes.

Mr. Doughton has accepted the pay-as-you-go plan of payment of income taxes,[20] but he recognizes the great cost of collection and the difficulty of making many taxpayers, such as farmers and small businessmen, pay income taxes that cannot be determined to any degree of accuracy at the time the tax payment is demanded. He is largely responsible for the simplification of income tax reports for 1945, admitting that he secured help in preparing his tax report for 1944. The tax simplification bill became law without hearings, a procedure that is unusual in the preparation of a tax measure. This was done because everyone both within and without the committee desired tax simplification and the task was a mechanical one necessitating no change in tax policy. The chief criticism of the Republican party to the work of Bob Doughton is really not a criticism of Bob so much as it is an attempt to indict the entire Democratic party. According to Joseph W. Martin, the need today is for a well-balanced, integrated tax system.[21] Undoubtedly Mr. Doughton would support all moves to secure this end, but it is indeed difficult to adjust a well-balanced tax program when an imperative need for additional revenue is always present.

While the war continued, the planning for post-war taxation, though intriguing, seemed hardly practical to this tax veteran. Nobody knows what amount of money will be needed, he states, and nobody can anticipate what will be the attitude of a new Congress to any proposed tax program.[22] Mr. Doughton has recently been made chairman of the Joint Committee on Internal Revenue Taxation which is busily engaged in making a study of this post-war problem. In anticipation of recommendations that were to come from the committee. Mr. Doughton in a speech prepared for the National Tax Association outlined his position with respect to post-war taxes. Admitting the serious situation that now exists, he said, "I am of the opinion that we have reached or are approaching the point where further tax increases may result in diminishing returns rather than increases in revenue." [23] He then stated that any post-war tax program must be very elastic and subject to change as new conditions arise; that while taxes should be reduced, he sees little hope, in view of the size of the national debt, to reduce taxes to the degree proposed by some; that governmental expenditures must be examined and those not absolutely essential

21. For an overall indictment of the Democratic administration by Mr. Martin, see *Ibid.*, LXXXIX, A4034-37.
22. For a brief summary of Doughton's tax views, see "C.N.C. Profile," *Washington Close-Up*, Sept., 1943.
23. *Congressional Record*, XC, A4303.

be eliminated; that the new tax plan must remain unchanged for a sufficient length of time to permit business to plan intelligently, and, lastly, that the government must be run on a sound financial basis and its credit maintained first in all the world. Once Bob Doughton takes his stand on a tax question, he remains adamant. His objection to altering the 1944 tax bill as suggested in the President's veto message is not due to the fact that the additional money could not be raised by taxes, but that such a raise in rates would be unfortunate from both an economic and a political viewpoint. Such an increase would make necessary raising the income tax payments of persons in the lower brackets and, from the economic standpoint, he hesitates to increase further taxes that have, in some cases, already been raised in the last few years as much as 5,000 per cent. Once a tax program is approved, however, he believes in collecting the tax without any cut-rate incentive. From the time the Ruml plan was first suggested, Bob Doughton was opposed to it.[24] For this position he was roundly criticised, for it was contrary to the desires of many taxpayers. The *Philadelphia Inquirer* maintained, "It's Doughton against 40,000,000." [25] He never gave in, for he thought the support of the forgiveness of taxes feature was based on the hope of not having to pay taxes that were honestly due the United States government and which were sorely needed.

In the preparation of a tax bill, Mr. Doughton, as chairman of the Committee on Ways and Means, is constantly between two fires. If swift action is taken on a revenue measure, he and his committee are criticized for not giving this important legislation proper consideration. On the other hand, if the bill remains in committee for a lengthy period of time, the committee is accused of delay and dilatory tactics. The Revenue Bill of 1942 was debated by the committee for over four months, and revenue bills since then have received practically the same amount of attention.[26] It is possible for the committee to be guilty of either of these two charges, but obviously, with

24. *Ibid.*, Mar. 31, 1943.
25. *Philadelphia Inquirer*, Apr. 7, 1943.
26. *Congressional Record*, LXXXVIII, Pt. V, 6262.

respect to a tax measure, it is impossible to satisfy everybody. Notwithstanding the fact that a tax bill is approved by the whole committee, Mr. Doughton has been accused by the Republicans of railroading a tax measure through the committee and through Congress, while President Roosevelt criticized the committee for delay in bringing in the tax bill of 1944.

Looking back over his years in the House, Bob Doughton takes pride in the part that he has played in formulating the tax program of the nation. He also derives satisfaction from his part in making the dream of a Blue Ridge Parkway a reality, his championship of the reciprocal trade agreement policy of Cordell Hull,[27] and his part in securing the passage of the Social Security Act.[28] His interest in social security has never diminished, and to his committee has been recently assigned the duty of preparing the Reconversion and Demobilization Bill. This measure is a little outside the usual routine work of the committee but was referred to the committee because it provides for amending the Social Security Act. Looking toward the future, Farmer Bob is concerned with the growing national debt and the establishment of a bureaucracy. Notwithstanding the fact that the winning of the war came first, it was not with satisfaction that he introduced measures raising the national debt limit. In 1940 he went on record, while recognizing that increased borrowing would be necessary, as favoring a pay-as-you-go system to as great an extent as possible. He has not changed his position radically since then.[29] His dislike of bureaucracy is a natural outgrowth of his great pride in the work of his committee. He thinks the control of the purse strings should be in the hands of the people's representatives and not bargained away into the hands of the bureaucracy. Once, when asked how long it would take to prepare a new tax

27. He considers that reciprocal trade agreements "constitute a definite stride back to world sanity."—*Ibid.*, LXXX, Pt. I, 950.
28. With respect to the Social Security Act, one writer states that it is a "good example of careful administrative preparation followed by minute congressional scrutiny."—Roland Young, *This Is Congress* (1943), p. 57. Doughton himself says, "It is a measure of the practical good sense and skill with which Congress and its advisers translated that vision into the workable, and working, terms of the present law."—*Congressional Record*, LXXXIII, Pt. V, 5645.
29. *Congressional Record*, LXXXVI, Pt. XVII, 4958.

bill, he is reported to have replied that he could not tell for "we aren't a group of bureaucrats who can just put a tax bill together and dish it out to the country." [30]

Like all good representatives, Mr. Doughton never neglects his own district. He was originally elected from the old eighth district of North Carolina. In this district the Democrats and Republicans were fairly evenly divided and alternated in sending men to Congress. Farmer Bob changed this. He was elected first in 1910 by "talking to little groups, talking to individuals, talking everywhere," [31] while his opponent made addresses. He has won all succeeding elections, some after stiff battles. The state of North Carolina has been redistricted since 1933, and he now represents the ninth district. He is just as popular here. His district does not have an overwhelming Democratic vote; it is in the shape of an inverted question mark and stretches from the mountains in the west to the middle of the Piedmont section. This peculiar-shaped district was drawn to include the Piedmont counties where the Democratic party is stronger in order to absorb a sizable Republican vote from the mountain counties. In 1940 he won the election by the greatest majority in history, and in 1942 he was unopposed, his opponent withdrawing because he thought it "the patriotic thing to do in view of Doughton's service to his district and the country as a whole." [32] In the last analysis, Farmer Bob's success in his own district is due to the following factors: He never neglects his district; he remains a farmer and takes real pride in his profession; and he runs on his record, knowing that it is a good one.

Farmer Bob is therefore a tough man to beat. This, coupled with the prospect of his possible retirement by next election time, has been responsible for the lack in recent years of high-class opposition. Democrats would rather not run against Farmer Bob in the primary, and Republicans hesitate to oppose him at election time. In each instance political suicide might result. Good political strategy makes these men put off running until the next election, when Mr. Doughton will retire. Ordi-

30. See statement of Mr. Treadway, *Ibid.*, LXXXVIII, Pt. VI, 7872.
31. See statement of Cameron Morrison, *Ibid.*, LXXXIX, 9374.
32. *Statesville* (North Carolina) *Daily Record*, Aug. 10, 1942.

narily this would work, but Farmer Bob seems to gain in vitality as the years pass. Much to the chagrin of these office-seekers, but to the delight of his supporters, he won his last political campaign for re-election and it will take a Republican landslide to uproot him.

During his long period of service in the House of Representatives, Bob Doughton has always been a strict party man. Accepting the benefits of party allegiance, he in return has given loyal support to party measures. President Roosevelt, as the leader of the Democratic party, commanded his respect and his loyalty.[33] From 1933 until 1945 very close and very friendly relations existed between the President and the Chairman of the Committee on Ways and Means. The first real difference between these two men developed over the veto of the tax bill of 1944.[34] To Mr. Doughton, his position was in harmony with the desires of his committee, the House, and the Senate, and could not be classified as disloyalty to the party although he refused to vote to sustain the President's veto. He stated his position in the following words: "I have endeavored at all times, so far as I consistently could, to be helpful to the party with which I am affiliated, and where there has been doubt in my mind about the position of the Executive or my own party, I have always resolved that doubt in favor of going along and supporting the policies of the administration. ... I accord the President the right to veto any tax bill and to assign his reasons therefor, but, Mr. Speaker, I do not feel that he should attempt to dictate what should go into a tax bill. I must part company with the President of the United States when he

33. Farmer Bob had been asked to run for the office of Governor of North Carolina in the election of 1936. He did not do so because President Roosevelt wanted him to keep his seat in the House. Although many accounts of what actually took place between Doughton and the President have been given, the following probably comes close to the truth of the matter. Hearing of the contemplated retirement from the House in order to run for governor, President Roosevelt sent for Doughton and "after a fifteen minutes chat in the White House, he [Doughton] emerged announcing he had changed his mind. 'I got the idea,' he drawled after the conference, 'that I would be more useful in my present position, so I decided to stay on.'"—*Winston-Salem* (North Carolina) *Journal and Sentinel,* June 6, 1935.

34. Previously, it is true, Bob Doughton had disagreed with President Roosevelt over the filing of joint income tax returns.

dictates what we shall do." [35] This is no new position for Mr. Doughton, for all along he has been jealous of the powers of his committee. In July, 1941, he had sounded a warning of his position when President Roosevelt, in a letter addressed to "My dear Bob," outlined the criticism of the Treasury Department to the work of the committee. In reply, Farmer Bob expressed surprise at the President's position, and, instead of agreeing with the President and the Treasury Department, he reaffirmed the previous position of his committee.[36] Again, he has reiterated the independence of the Committee on Ways and Means by saying that "it should be clearly understood that the Committee on Ways and Means is not going to delegate to any department, agency, person, or persons its duties and its responsibilities." [37] Although denied by the President, the chairman thought that the veto message reflected upon his integrity and that of his committee, and he resented deeply "the circumstances, the methods, the reasons, and the language of this veto message." [38] In spite of this difference, Mr. Doughton will continue a strict party man and, except when a fundamental principle is at stake, will hesitate to take any overt action that might intensify a break between the party's chief and the congressional leaders.

For the Democratic party Bob Doughton sees a bright future if it maintains the road of reform and change, tempered by wisdom. Probably his best utterance on party policies was made in a speech delivered in his home state and in his own district. He said: "There is but one way to keep our party useful, and that is to keep it strong and in power. There is but one way to keep it strong, and that is to keep it united and clean. There is but one way to keep it clean, and that is to be ever vigilant in a scrutiny of its standard bearers and its aim and purposes." [39] In this statement he shows both the love of a practical politician for unity and power and the desire of a statesman for a clean, vigorous, and progressive political party.

35. *Congressional Record*, XC, 2013.
36. *Ibid.*, LXXXVII, Pt. XIII, A3764.
37. See *Washington Close-Up*, Sept., 1943, p. 3.
38. *Congressional Record*, XC, 2013.
39. *Ibid.*, LXXXIII, Pt. X, 1418.

11

J. WILLIAM FULBRIGHT

"Hell-bent on His Objective"

BY MAX HALL

U NOBTRUSIVELY INTO CONGRESS IN JANUARY, 1943, stepped a highly educated and self-possessed young Arkansan, Bill Fulbright.

New members are supposed to be seen and not heard. They should be attentive, run errands for constituents, keep out of trouble, respect tradition, trust their elders, watch, wait, and pray. If re-elected enough times they may be in a position to influence important legislation.

Fulbright was soon sharply conscious of the limitations which the seniority system imposes upon a new man; yet he somehow was able to take the lead in an important undertaking, that of putting the House of Representatives on record for post-war collective security. Before he had been a congressman nine months, the House by a vote of 360 to 29 approved the one-sentence Fulbright Resolution, calling for United States participation in international machinery having "power adequate to establish and to maintain a just and lasting peace."

This was the first declaration by either branch of Congress that America stood ready to co-operate in preventing future wars, and though cynics noted that it omitted the details of how wars were to be prevented, commentators generally viewed it as an historic event, a first step in reversing the nation's traditional policy of isolation.

Congress had found its voice on world organization, and America had found a new and different-looking star in its political skies. Fulbright of Arkansas became better known to the country at large than the great majority of his elders in the

House. In the spring of 1944 he was sent to London by Secretary of State Hull to serve as chairman of a United States delegation to an international conference on education. That summer he went to Arkansas and campaigned for the United States Senate against three determined opponents—the incumbent senator, the governor, and the state's leading industrialist. Fulbright was elected.

In the fall of 1944, the senator-to-be was again in the headlines with another one-sentence resolution, the first to be offered in favor of world freedom of the press. When he took the oath as senator at the beginning of 1945, he was not quite forty years old. A few newspapers in the South had already begun suggesting him as Democratic candidate for President in 1948.

Some in Congress, constantly impressed by the remarkable system of legislative bottlenecks by which the elders protect the republic against the presumptuousness of youth, were still wondering about the Fulbright Resolution of 1943. How could a mere first-termer maneuver such a potent measure through the committee-dominated House? Why was his name permitted to remain on the document even after the Committee on Foreign Affairs had focused its collective intellect upon it for revision?

It is a story not only of determined convictions, but also of practical politics. The fact is, a prize scholar, a "professor," turned out to be a shrewd tactician, hell-bent on his objective but methodically taking it a step at a time, careful not to antagonize persons with power for obstruction, and accepting frankly the dictum that in politics it is necessary to compromise.

James William Fulbright entered Congress from an Ozark Mountain district. It was his first adventure in politics. Yet he was hardly inexperienced in worldly affairs. He had studied abroad, lived six years in Washington, been a college president, and to counteract the politically-damaging "professor" label could justifiably call himself a lawyer, businessman, and farmer.

Spanning his career was his progress from president of the

University of Arkansas student body in 1925 to president of the University of Arkansas in 1939. In the interim he studied political science at Oxford as a Rhodes scholar, traveled for a year on the continent of Europe, studied and then taught at the law school of the George Washington University, composed briefs in the anti-trust division of the Department of Justice, and returned with his Philadelphia-born wife to Fayetteville, Arkansas, where he not only joined the law faculty of the university but settled on a 115-acre farm and took active direction of a lumber company and other business interests which he and his five brothers and sisters had inherited from their father. Mrs. Fulbright, product of a well-to-do Republican family, turned out to be amazingly adaptable, and her ability to make friends was helpful in his two political campaigns.

Fulbright is a strong-looking man with blue eyes, dark hair, and a slow, deep voice. Despite a casual, friendly manner, he is far from "soft," either physically or intellectually. His views are well defined and he is at his best in a discussion or argument. He has little patience with what he regards as ignorance or stupidity; he hates appeals to emotion and in his speeches usually asks the audience to take the attitude of cold self-interest. He can be tactful and yielding when it is advisable; he can also be stubborn, exacting, critical, and roughly candid. In monetary affairs he is capable of "driving a hard bargain." In college athletics he was a star halfback. Publicity pleases him, but the charge that the Fulbright Resolution was "highly press-agented" was untrue. He is a moderate liberal who showed signs of growing more conservative during his second year in Congress, a trend possibly related to his increasing concern over the views of his constituents.

"There are two ways to be a successful politician," Fulbright said to a friend after his first election in 1942. "One is to keep quiet on major issues and pay careful attention to the wishes of every constituent. The other is to do something big enough so that the people will be proud of you and willing to overlook the lack of personal attentions. I am determined to try the second way."

That is, he would try to be a national congressman. And he did not have to search for a national issue. In his mind the war and the peace overshadowed all other subjects. The Representative-elect told the Arkansas Democratic Convention that the war was being handled well but if the party expected to retain the direction of the nation's destiny it must not only win the war but "evolve some program for the government of the world that will prevent these recurring wars." He was fond of saying that isolationism was not dead and would try to rise again.

His impatience with isolationists was nothing of recent origin. In the black summer of 1940, when France had fallen, Fulbright asserted in a speech at the University of Oklahoma that the "weasling, timid, and fearful policy of our isolationist Senators," whom he listed by name, "was one of the greatest dangers to our true interests."

"The hope of the world for centuries to come rests upon our decision in the present crisis," said Fulbright, who was then thirty-five years old. He said that without our help it was doubtful that Britain could survive. "If individual liberty of the human personality is worth fighting for, I do not know why we are waiting, except that some of our leaders are blind and ignorant."

Though the senators he assailed were no doubt unaware of his existence at the time, it is interesting to note that three years later the Fulbright Resolution, after passing the House on September 21, 1943, was sent to the Senate and promptly tossed in a pigeonhole where it is still collecting dust. The Senate followed the lead of the House and passed a similar resolution later in the fall, but preferred to write it with a senatorial pen.

Fulbright's congressional journey toward recognition began with his appointment to the Foreign Affairs Committee. If he had not been a member and thus in a position to work within the committee, there is little chance that the Fulbright Resolution would have received serious consideration. After the committee, Democrats and Republicans, approved it unanimously on June 15, 1943, there was never any doubt of House approval. True, action was postponed until after the summer recess at the request of leading Republicans, and this depressed Fulbright, who believed the world was watching for a sign from America; but the delay was designed not to muster opposition but to solidify Republican support. Republican leaders viewed the resolution, simple and free from controversial details, as a fine opportunity to demonstrate the unworthiness of attempts to identify the party with isolationism. Even Hamilton Fish made a speech for the resolution.

Fulbright probably would not have been assigned to such an important committee at the outset had not another young Arkansan, Wilbur Mills, just been named to the Ways and Means Committee. The Democrat members of that powerful group determine who shall fill Democrat vacancies on all the other committees. The Arkansas delegation unanimously recommended Fulbright for Foreign Affairs, and Mills sponsored his name.

Those first few weeks in the House, Fulbright recorded his observations in letters back home. He said it appeared that twenty or thirty "crackpots" monopolized most of the sessions and the worthwhile members spoke only when they had something to say. He said the internal organization of Congress is "antiquated and inefficient" but reforms are difficult because of "the vested interests of the senior members in their positions of power and prestige."

"After four weeks of getting acquainted, you begin to wonder when the House is going to do something," he told a friend. So he did something himself. Fulbright has always put much stock in the value of discussions. Early in February he invited to his office fifteen vigorous-minded new congressmen of both parties, sharing for the most part a sense of world community. Among the Democrats were Will Rogers, Jr., of California, Howard McMurray of Wisconsin, and Mike Mansfield of Montana, all of whom were new members of the Foreign Affairs Committee. The Republicans, perhaps even more international-minded than the Democrats, included Walter Judd of Minnesota, Christian Herter of Boston, Bob Hale of Maine (like Fulbright, a Rhodes scholar), and Charles

LaFollette of Indiana. They met weekly in Fulbright's office and discussed the leading proposals for world organization.

The only veteran congressman in the group was John Vorys, Ohio Republican, another member of the Foreign Affairs Committee. Fulbright had become friendly with him playing paddleball in the House gymnasium. Vorys had never been considered an internationalist, but he joined in willingly, enjoyed the sessions, and months later made a speech for the Fulbright Resolution.

The Arkansan was well received by his new acquaintances, but Fulbright's reputation as spokesman for a body of opinion dated from his first House speech, which produced his baptismal shower of national publicity. The new Republican congresswoman, Clare Boothe Luce, in her own first speech in the House, had called for a strong national policy in post-war aviation and had ridiculed the administration, particularly Vice-President Wallace, whose ideas she termed "globaloney." Fulbright, annoyed, was energetically criticizing Mrs. Luce in the presence of Luther Johnson of Texas, second-ranking Democrat on the Foreign Affairs Committee, when Johnson retorted, "Why don't you reply in a speech?" Johnson had been interested in Fulbright ever since receiving from Chester Davis a letter (written at Fulbright's request) recommending the Arkansan as promising material for the committee. Johnson talked with Majority Leader McCormack and other Democrats and it struck them as appropriate that a new member reply to a new member. So a time was reserved for Fulbright on February 16, 1943.

He is not a colorful orator; he reads his speeches earnestly, never dramatically. He was speaking sooner than he intended, he said, because although he was not unconscious of the "sparkling beauty and suavity" of the "honorable lady," he was not as susceptible to her logic as some other members had been. "Globaloney," he said, "was a wonderful word which convulsed the gallery and will certainly live for many seasons in the folklore of Broadway." He told the House that she advocated expanding our air routes over the world, at the same time excluding everyone else from our skies, and he called this a "narrow, imperialistic policy of grab." He turned his speech into a profession of faith that a workable system of collective security is possible provided the American people are willing to discard their traditional isolationism, "now often disguised under the name of Americanism."

The time was getting short for developing a program for peace, he declared. "It must be done now, while the minds and hearts of the peoples of this world are concerned with universal and fundamental issues—while dangers and sacrifice give us humility and understanding." He asked the House to authorize the Foreign Affairs Committee to make a thorough study of all proposals for international organization (nothing ever came of this suggestion, which he embodied in the first bill he ever introduced). Insisting he proposed no "sentimental and idealistic enterprise," he said our selfish interests, indeed our survival as a great nation, depend on collective security. Accusing Mrs. Luce of wishing to base our aviation policy on the assumption that a third world war is just around the corner, he declared that he for one believed we could "turn this ghastly, barren tragedy into a tremendous opportunity which, with imagination, intelligence, and determination, will enable us, together with our allies, to create the world of the future."

Mrs. Luce rose icily to defend herself. Standing at twin microphones the two newcomers clashed in a sharp debate. She asked whether he intended that this country relinquish control of its own skies and airports, and he replied, no more than we have relinquished control of our seaports under the policy of freedom of the seas. She scornfully pointed out that in his speech he had said "inferred" when he meant "implied." She demanded that he give precise passages from her text containing the implications of which he had accused her, and he drawled, "Would you like me to read your speech again to this audience?" The Democrats howled.

Incidentally Mrs. Luce was destined to be another of the Republicans who supported the Fulbright Resolution in a floor speech.

The Foreign Affairs Committee in those days of 1943 was

conducting hearings on the Lend-Lease Act, which was up for renewal. The record shows that Fulbright asked each witness substantially this question: "Don't you think lend-lease could be used to promote a political organization of nations after the war?" He had in mind an amendment to the act, paving the way for such an organization, and went to see Secretary of State Hull, Under Secretary Sumner Welles, and numerous friendly congressmen such as Charles Eaton of New Jersey, top Republican member of the committee. Fulbright was told that such an amendment would be unwise lest it endanger the lend-lease program.

But he was more restless than ever. He did not see how the United Nations could lay plans for an orderly world without finding out what Congress thought. Was Congress still isolationist? It had never declared otherwise. Several resolutions had been introduced, but the Foreign Relations Committee headed by Senator Tom Connally and the Foreign Affairs Committee headed by Representative Sol Bloom showed no disposition to consider them, and they could get nowhere without committee approval. Nor had President Roosevelt or the State Department asked Congress for a declaration on peace machinery. Fulbright wrote a short memorandum, thinking he might take it individually to members and get them to sign it. After showing it to Eaton, Johnson, and others, he dropped the idea as impractical. But little Luther Johnson, twenty years a congressman, again gave the young man a push in the right direction. He suggested that the memorandum be made into a resolution. This from such a stalwart of the Foreign Affairs Committee was practically a godsend.

How would Fulbright's measure differ from other post-war resolutions, which eventually numbered above thirty in the House and Senate? Most of them were long and sprinkled with *whereases*. Many contained details liable to set off dogfights diverting from the main issue. Fulbright's would be simple and general; its first requisite would be that it must be capable of being passed—and by a heavy majority. He admired the Ball-Burton-Hill-Hatch peace resolution in the Senate, and indeed when Judd, Herter, and other first-term Republicans of the

House published an indorsement of the B_2H_2 proposal, Fulbright quickly issued a statement on behalf of the freshman Democrats, supporting the B_2H_2 proposal and expressing gratification that the Republican brethren had broken from the "traditional stand" of their party. But he did not believe the B_2H_2 resolution could be maneuvered through the Senate, and certainly not by a convincing two-thirds majority. Before an audience at Constitution Hall he debated this point with Senators Ball and Burton; he said his own resolution had been called "innocent," but "in view of the historic caution and timidity of our illustrious Senate, it is important that it be not frightened by an esoteric or complicated proposal." In fact, said the practical-minded Arkansan, "with so many diverse interests and characters represented in the Congress, anything short of the Lord's Prayer will arouse some opposition."

The original version of the Fulbright Resolution as submitted on April 5, 1943, was:

"Resolved, That the House of Representatives hereby expresses itself as favoring the creation of appropriate international machinery with power adequate to prevent future aggression and to maintain lasting peace, and as favoring participation by the United States therein."

Everything now depended on the committee, which at that time was holding no meetings. Since Fulbright believed that an expression on peace machinery by the representatives of the people would actually help win the war by setting up a positive war aim and further unifying the Allies, he was exasperated with each day's delay.

To be demanding would be out of the question, but he did what he could. This consisted mainly of talking. He made dozens of speeches, not on the House floor, but by invitation over the radio and at meetings in Washington, New York, Boston, Philadelphia, and elsewhere. In these addresses, which he composed alone and with a pencil, he argued persuasively for a "creative war." Deploring that we fought merely to *defend* our way of life, he urged that we "rid ourselves of the hangovers of our appeasement idiocy and our isolationist dream," stop regretting that all this happened to us, and turn the war into a "rare opportunity in the history of the world." We must make up our minds that the goal of the war was not merely to crush our attackers but to achieve a world organization, in which the nations must give up a part of their sovereignty for the common good. The details of the plan, he said, were not as important as the determination of the people to accept the principle. To visualize such an organization and believe it possible would have "an electrifying effect on our national spirit," bring about the "spiritual awakening" of America, and enable us at last to "make our contribution to civilization."

Even more important for the future of the Fulbright Resolution, he talked with individuals. They included Speaker Rayburn, Supreme Court Justice Roberts, and the chief brains of the State Department. The official silence of the latter institution was a factor in the hesitancy of some congressional leaders to rush out with any resolution that might be "embarrassing" to our diplomats. Under Secretary Sumner Welles, however, wrote Fulbright a warm letter, and he promptly passed it among the committee members, who were impressed. Welles wrote that he had talked with Secretary Hull, and that both Hull and the President agreed that the resolution or one like it would be most helpful, though they did not want to indorse any specific measure because that was a matter for Congress to work out. Fulbright's proposal was at first only a House resolution, and when he sought advice on whether it should take another form, Welles was one of several who believed it ought to be a concurrent resolution, which could go to both House and Senate though it would not require the President's signature. Fulbright resubmitted the measure on that basis. Welles also conferred with Sol Bloom, who alone could summon the committee into session, and personally recommended the principle of a post-war peace resolution.

Another who listened sympathetically to Fulbright and took a personal interest in encouraging the committee to consider the various post-war resolutions was Speaker Sam Rayburn, a tower of influence on other members of the House. But the Fulbright Resolution was never stamped as an "administration measure." Had the President originated or urged it, there would hardly have been so huge a bi-partisan vote in its favor. Had Chairman Bloom been one of its early protagonists, the Republicans on the committee were unlikely to have found it so suitable for their purposes. To the House as a whole, Democrats and Republicans, the simple declaration taken from the soil of the Ozarks and forged by the representatives of both parties around a conference table seemed an easy and politically sound solution of an issue that many had feared to raise in Congress because it might stir up bitter controversies in a time of war.

Bloom assembled the committee on June 8. After the several proposals were read and discussed, the Republican James Wadsworth, whom Fulbright once privately described as "probably the wisest member of either House," declared for the Fulbright Resolution. Before the meeting was over, they had thrown the other resolutions in the waste basket and had begun arguing over Fulbright's choice of words. Throughout two more meetings, the members for hours tore the solitary sentence to pieces and put it back together. The net result was that the words "to prevent future aggression and to maintain lasting peace" became: "to establish and to maintain a just and lasting peace among the nations of the world." When on June 15 everyone was satisfied, Wadsworth is reported to have remarked that he assumed Mr. Fulbright's name would remain on the resolution when it went to the House. No one dissented. Chairman Bloom then made public the committee's action and strongly praised the resolution.

One more change was made in the wording. When the summer recess was over and the resolution came up for House action, the committee decided to add four words specifying that participation of the United States should be "through its constitutional processes," an amendment which Fulbright thought was unnecessary. Thus the final form of the declaration as it passed the House was:

"Resolved by the House of Representatives (the Senate concurring), That the Congress hereby expresses itself as favoring the creation of appropriate international machinery with power adequate to establish and to maintain a just and lasting peace among the nations of the world, and as favoring participation of the United States therein through its constitutional processes."

In the two-day debate the opponents were vehement but they could collect only twenty-nine votes. Center of the opposition in the nation was the *Chicago Tribune,* which deplored the House action and charged that Fulbright had been sent to Oxford on a Rhodes scholarship "to learn to betray his country and deprive it of its independence." The newspaper also asserted that "in this instance, as no doubt in many others, Mr. Rhodes appears to have got his money's worth." Fulbright and other Rhodes scholars considered legal action. When asked to comment on the charges, the Arkansan said they were "representative of the fascist, anti-democratic, anti-American element that would like to control this country." He described the *Tribune* as "bigoted and stupid, intolerant, narrow-minded and ignorant."

At the request of the committee, the Library of Congress prepared a report on editorial comment regarding the Fulbright Resolution. Examined were 142 newspapers in 45 states; 204 pertinent editorials were found, of which 150 were favorable, ten unfavorable, and 44 not clear.

Fulbright never intimated that his resolution would assure "lasting peace." During the debate he termed it "just the beginning of the process of building a foreign policy for the nation in this modern world." On January 21, 1944, in a House speech supporting the United Nations Relief and Rehabilitation Administration, he gave his sober view on the possibilities. Pointing to the Moscow, Cairo, and Teheran conferences, which had all taken place since passage of his resolution, Fulbright told the House "a start has been made," and then declared:

"I recognize, of course, that these are only the first gropings of a tortured and suspicious world, and that the road to peace is going to be much longer and, in an entirely different sense, even more difficult of attainment than is a military victory in this war. It will be a long, evolutionary process, made up of many mistakes and constant differences of opinions, yet I still think that the urge to peace is so strong and the alternative so disastrous that eventually our reason will triumph over our prejudices and emotions."

Near the end of 1944, in a speech before the New York State Chamber of Commerce shortly before taking his seat in the Senate, Fulbright appraised the Dumbarton Oaks report as "an excellent beginning."

He said, however, we should recognize at the outset "that the making of peace does not consist merely of a treaty, a conference report, or a magic formula. The making of peace... is a process, continuing from day to day and from year to year so long as civilization lasts. While it is essential to have the machinery, as a vehicle for continuous consultations and cooperative action,... yet the supremely important element is the character and ability of the men who operate the machinery."

He asserted: "We must take great care and pains to supply, as our representatives, men of broad vision and profound wisdom. The scarcity of such men in public office is unfortunately the greatest weakness of our nation."

This has been a favorite theme of Fulbright's for many years. As a teacher of law he constantly urged his best students to enter politics. He made his own decision to run for Congress after a former pupil confronted him squarely one day with his own philosophy.

Fulbright said in the New York speech that aside from the major difficulty of the scarcity of able leaders, he believed present circumstances were more favorable than ever before for creating an effective organization for peace. The horror and destruction of this war, he said, have "finally induced a genuine and sincere desire for peace among the vast majority of the peoples of the world." There is nothing inherently insuperable about the problem of collective security; the element heretofore missing has been the will, the positive determination by a strong enough combination, to suppress aggression. He said the people who cite past failures to make peace as evidence that it can't be done "are no different from those who throughout the ages have questioned and opposed every progressive step taken by man."

As a member of the House, Fulbright found it easier to

apply pure reason to foreign policy than to some of the domestic matters with which he had to contend. While devoting most of his time to the problem of "these recurring wars," he could not ignore the political aspects of his other duties. Bills came up to be voted upon; he discovered that swapping favors with other members—the "human relationships of politics"—was "part of the game"; even personal errands for constituents took up more and more of his time. A congressman, he concluded, is always faced with this: "You've got to compromise, not only to please your constituents but to get along with your fellow-congressmen. I don't believe it's possible to stay in public life with only your conscience as a guide—free to do entirely as you please."

The idea, Fulbright observed, is never to compromise on important things, but to give way on insignificant things or issues on which you have no strong conviction. If you don't, he said, you are "stymied" in your own important endeavors. Said he, "If a majority of my constituents thought isolationism was right, I would still work against it and they could defeat me if they wanted." On the other hand, though he felt that farm subsidies are probably necessary in wartime, he had no powerful conviction either way; and since he believed that most farmers in his district were against subsidies because they thought the payments would hold down their prices, he voted against subsidies.

Fulbright was one of the few Southerners who voted against continuing the Dies committee in 1943 and against a bill which removed from the federal payroll three men accused of radical affiliations. He said the Dies committee had performed its usefulness and that the other measure was unconstitutional. He joined fellow Southerners, however, in voting against measures to abolish the poll tax, an issue about which he appeared to be unexcited either way.

In the 1944 senatorial campaign, Fulbright weathered bitter personal attacks and potshots at his voting record by playing up the large issue of statesmanship. He argued that no progress worth while could be made toward solving internal problems of Arkansas and the nation unless the United States could look

forward confidently to an era of peace. "If our economy must
be geared indefinitely to the prosecution of war or to the preparation for war," he said, "then regimentation and eventually
totalitarianism must be our lot." He said all the candidates
professed to be for peace and other desirable objectives; therefore the only important issue was their character and ability to
influence events and get things done.

It happened that in the presidential campaign, Democrat
strategists likewise were preparing to emphasize world affairs
and personal qualities of leadership. Therefore Fulbright's
victory in the August primary, equivalent to election in one-
party Arkansas, struck a national keynote. Though weary, he
went out and made speeches for President Roosevelt. He told
Eastern and Midwestern audiences: "The real issue in this
campaign is which candidate is the most likely to be able to do
something positive and constructive toward making a sure and
lasting peace."

This was substantially the same argument he had made in
his own behalf. Apparently Senator Fulbright is planning further contributions of his own to the "lasting peace" of the
Fulbright Resolution.

12

ADOLPH J. SABATH
"Dean of the House"

BY JOHN R. BEAL

SINCE THE FIRST CONGRESS MET IN NEW YORK, ABOUT 9,000 persons have served as members of the House of Representatives. Of this number only one can boast of having been elected twenty times consecutively—Adolph J. Sabath of Illinois.

There are others who have served in Congress longer. Justin S. Morrill of Vermont served continuously for forty-three years and ten months, first in the House and then in the Senate, from 1855 to 1898. George W. Norris of Nebraska spanned nearly forty consecutive years in the two houses. Joseph Gurney (Uncle Joe) Cannon was in the House a total of forty-six years, although two defeats during his career broke the continuity. Cannon holds the all-time all-Congress record, and there is nothing in the actuarial prospects of the senior members of the Seventy-ninth Congress to indicate that his record will be surpassed within the near future.

Nevertheless, thirty-nine years of unbroken service is long enough to stretch back to Theodore Roosevelt's administration and by itself earns Sabath a niche, however small, in American legislative history. It has importance beyond its interest to amateurs of statistics because of the extent to which the seniority system is imbedded in the U.S. Congress. No member can serve that long without becoming chairman of an important committee, assuming his party controls the House. For Sabath it has meant chairmanship of what the newspapers frequently describe as "the powerful" House Rules Committee.

Sabath at seventy-nine is white-haired, short, stocky, and

has a slightly pompous air. He smokes cigars, and off the floor he generally has a short, half-smoked stub of one in his mouth, extending barely beyond the short cropped hair of his moustache. His pompousness is not offensive and comes from the fact that he holds his five foot, six inch frame erect, shoulders back, and since he weighs 180 pounds, this throws quite a bit of chest out in front.

On the House floor, where his position requires that he take frequent part in debate, he is a poor speaker. Sixty-three years in this country have not cured him of using the *v* sound for *w*, and vice versa. Since he has to make frequent references to an impending "wote" this calls attention to his accent. Once he telephoned President Roosevelt to inform him that if he vetoed a certain bill the House would "upstain the weto." His grammar requires considerable editing by the unsung heroes who proofread the *Congressional Record*.

Sabath is no master of the witty retort, the sharp give-and-take of parliamentary battle. He is easily needled and finds it hard to think of appropriate comebacks when goaded. At such times his face purples, he pulls his shoulders back a little farther in defiance, and he talks a little louder. Clare Hoffman of Michigan is one of the gadflies who find it easy to arouse the old man. John E. Rankin of Mississippi is another.

Sabath is the complete New Dealer. Not only is his voting record 100 per cent, but he was in the forefront of those urging Franklin D. Roosevelt to run for a third and a fourth term. His support of the New Deal, while undiscriminating, was genuine and sincere; his whole record reflects a sympathy for the underprivileged although he personally is well-to-do.

Of the 531 members of House and Senate, what peculiar qualifications have made Sabath dean of them all? What secret of politics does he possess that makes him four years the senior, in point of service, of leathery old Robert L. (Muley) Doughton of North Carolina, chairman of Ways and Means, six years the senior of Speaker Sam Rayburn of Texas? Each of these men wields more influence in Congress than Sabath.

Much of it can be explained by examination of Sabath's personal background.

Adolph was born April 4, 1866, the second of twelve children in the family of Joachim and Babette Sabath, in Zabori, population about 400, in what was then Bohemia, later Czechoslovakia, still later a part of Adolf Hitler's Greater Reich. Joachim was a butcher, and the Sabaths the only Jewish family in a town which was the seat of a Catholic diocese. Since doctrines of racial superiority were not as prevalent in that unenlightened age, and since the Sabaths attended the Catholic church and school, there was nothing to set them apart from other citizens of Zabori.

At thirteen, Adolph was ready to leave the family hearth in search of fortune. He went to a nearby town, Horazdovic, and became apprentice in a dry goods store. His duties included clerking from 7 A.M. to 9 P.M., and after hours he helped care for the proprietor's blind brother-in-law, one Wigl. It chanced that Wigl had lately returned from the United States, from which it follows that Adolph was inspired to save his money for a journey to the New World. He shipped by steerage from Bremen to Baltimore, and chose Chicago as his final destination because a cousin was there. It cost him, as he recalls, a total of $40. His arrival, at fifteen, was in keeping with the immigrant tradition. He had $2.15 left.

For six weeks young Sabath worked for $3.00 a week in a planing mill, but was discharged as too small to handle the work. He got another job, at $4.00 a week, clerking in a Halsted Street store which sold shoes and house furnishings. This proved a better thing financially, since it cost him $3.50 to live. In five years he worked up through the jobs of bookkeeper and cashier to become manager of the store, and at twenty-one he became a citizen of the United States.

By that time Sabath was ready to go into business for himself, choosing real estate with a partner two years older than himself. By degrees he began sending for other members of his family. Migration of Bohemians to Chicago, however, was not limited to the Sabaths. They came over in numbers and gravitated to the southwest side of Chicago, just being developed, so that it became known as the Pilsen section.

Sabath sold them lots. He bought tracts from insurance companies and subdivided. It was prosperous business, for at the age of twenty-six he handled one deal involving $140,000. The depression of 1893 nearly wiped him out, but with the aid of the companies with which he dealt he managed to see it through, and he boasts that he never foreclosed on any of his purchasers.

Meanwhile he attended Bryant and Stratton Business School and took up law to save lawyers' abstract fees. In 1891 he was admitted to the bar, and in 1893 he started to practice. He was a prominent figure in Bohemian-American circles, a fact which led into politics. He borrowed a middle initial from his father's name to distinguish himself from a cousin Adolph. As a representative of his racial group he was appointed justice of the peace, and after two years he was named a police magistrate. This post he held until elected to Congress in 1906, and is the substance for his title, "Judge." He began his service in the House on March 4, 1907.

Sabath today remains a leader in the Czechoslovakian community of Chicago, where reside about one third of the first and second generation Czech population in this country. Seventeen nationalities of immigrants and their descendants are represented in his district. Poles predominate, then Czechs, Lithuanians, Yugoslavs, and others. Illinois has had no congressional redistricting since 1901, so that the district has undergone a minimum of political disturbance, although its population stood at only 112,116 in the 1940 census against a national average of about 304,000 per congressional district. Because of this the Chicago *Tribune,* long his critic, has referred to him as "Half a Congressman" Sabath.

Sabath no longer actually lives in the district, but attempts to defeat him on this score have been uniformly unsuccessful. In 1938 he beat his Republican opponent by 32,104 to 10,842; in 1940 by 35,637 to 14,540; in 1942 by 29,167 to 11,255; in 1944 by 38,370 to 11,929.

It is necessary to add, however, that Sabath's unvarying success at the polls has not been hindered by the fact that he is *persona grata* with the Kelly-Nash political machine. He was satisfactory to Mayor Edward J. Kelly and the late Patrick

Nash not only because he attracted Bohemian-American votes by his presence on the ticket, but also because he proved willing to do what he was told. That he has been able to be a 100 per cent New Dealer and vote thè Kelly-Nash party line is due to the fact that the interests of the Roosevelt administration and the Chicago machine have coincided on most issues, or at least did not clash.

Thus Sabath was able to vote for early New Deal reform, labor, and farm legislation, to stick to Franklin Delano Roosevelt after he had alienated the farm bloc, and to support his foreign policy.

As a congressional freshman, Sabath got off to a good start. He entered in the days when House members had individual desks in the chamber for which they drew by lot. He drew a choice aisle seat near the front, but insisted on yielding it to a man he recognized as a prominent Democrat, who drew one inside. His neighbor happened to be Champ Clark, to whom it was more convenient to operate from the aisle. It was a generous gesture that led to friendship between the two.

With the aid of William Jennings Bryan, whose presidential candidacy Sabath had backed as a convention delegate from Chicago, Sabath got assigned to the Committee on Immigration and that on the Alcoholic Liquor Traffic. It happened that Congress, with little on its immediate schedule when it met in December, 1907, took up a bill to enlarge the immigration station at Philadelphia. James R. Mann of Illinois, then Republican floor leader, suggested to Sabath that since he was familiar with immigration, here was a chance to make a speech.

Sabath demurred: "I'm here only a few days; I'd better wait until I'm here awhile." But after two oratorical fire-eaters attacked the bill, one of them suggesting that it would be more appropriate to burn down the immigration station than enlarge it, Sabath was moved to speak.

"Between you and me, I never in a Turkish bath perspired more," he recalls now. "I dragged myself to the well. I seen before me thousands of great giants, members of Congress." But with Mann and other champions of the bill egging him on, he gradually got started. "I made a pretty fair speech, showing what immigrants had done for this country. The bill was passed and I was a big guy."

He got further attention when he introduced railroad workmen's compensation legislation. Sabath first familiarized himself with systems being used by Germany, England, and New Zealand, and then sent his proposed bill to the Interstate Commerce Commission for suggestions. From a friend in the ICC he was tipped that Theodore Roosevelt had been told about it and wanted some Republican to sponsor an administration version.

Sabath promptly introduced his own bill, with a statement of explanation in which he "gave Teddy a little boost," expressing assurance that T.R. would favor such progressive legislation. A few days later he got a letter inviting him to call on the President. Sabath, while flattered, was too embarrassed to respond. However, it was the practice in 1908 for members of Congress to take business constituents to the White House to shake the President's hand. At one of these receptions Sabath turned up with some men in his district. T.R.'s secretary noted his presence, and whispered to the President. When Sabath reached the head of the line, Teddy bellowed: "Don't go away. I want to see you afterward. Didn't you get my letter?"

"After that they knew who Sabath was," he recalls. "I became known."

The Sabath bill was pigeonholed, but it led to creation of a commission which proposed legislation that eventually was passed. Sabath opposed it on the ground that its rates were too low and it was a railroad relief bill rather than a measure designed for railroad workers.

In 1910 Sabath became an unwitting instrument in the fight led by George W. Norris of Nebraska which unseated Uncle Joe Cannon as czar of the House and resulted in creation of the Rules Committee which he was to head later. Cannon was a complete despot in that he made all committee appointments and exercised exclusive control over the recognition of members, thereby controlling the progress of legislation to the floor.

Sabath had introduced a bill to amend the census act so as

to permit questions in the thirteenth decennial census classifying persons born abroad by their mother tongues. "Lots of people were classed as citizens of Austria Hungary when they were really Bohemians and Poles," he explains.

The only exception to Cannon's control of House procedure was Calendar Wednesday, when committees, in alphabetical order, had the privilege of calling up bills. Cannon was interested not so much in Sabath's bill as he was in breaking down the tradition of Calendar Wednesday. He informed Edgar Crumpacker of Indiana, chairman of the census committee, that he would recognize him on a certain Wednesday to take up the Sabath bill.

Crumpacker, in seeking to interrupt the normal procedure with the census act amendment, claimed that Sabath's bill was privileged under the Constitution, since that document provided for the taking of the census. Norris and the insurgents seeking to unhorse Cannon made a fight on the proposition. They lost their appeal from Cannon's decision in favor of Crumpacker.

Then Norris, using this precedent, introduced a resolution setting up a geographically distributed, bi-partisan Committee on Rules to replace the hand-picked group of five controlled by the Speaker. He likewise contended that his resolution was privileged under the Constitution, since Article 1, Section 5, Paragraph 2 provided that "each House may determine the rules of its proceedings." An historic fight ensued that kept the House in continuous session for twenty-six hours and finally resulted in victory for the insurgents, 182 to 160. Sabath voted with the majority. Since then the Rules Committee, selected in the same manner as other House committees, has governed the flow of legislation from committees to the floor.

During this period Sabath was active in home-town politics. He had been attending Democratic conventions since Bryan made his "Cross of Gold" speech. That Sabath played a minor part in the lusty partisan fights of Chicago is a fair inference from the fact that many a political history of the period omits any reference to him. Yet he carried on a vendetta of sorts with Roger Sullivan, leader of one of the Democratic factions, and for ten years, while Carter H. Harrison served five terms as Mayor of Chicago, Sabath was chairman of the Cook County Democratic Central committee.

In 1912 Sabath went to the Baltimore Democratic National Convention with a Champ-Clark-for-President delegation. Clark had carried Illinois three to one against Woodrow Wilson in the presidential preferential primary, and the delegation was instructed for Clark at the state convention. Sullivan, however, held a rump meeting which named a Wilson delegation, and at Baltimore the credentials committee seated Sullivan and his cohorts.

After Wilson's nomination, the chairman of Cook County Democrats was a conspicuous sorehead. He refused to go to Sea Girt, N. J., with other Illinois Democrats to visit the nominee. "I was sore, piqued, dissatisfied, and disgruntled," Sabath recalls. But under the pleadings of party leaders, Sabath finally agreed to go by himself to meet Wilson.

"I was well received," Sabath says. "The first I knew I was invited to go with him to have a drink in a little pavilion." Wilson asked Sabath what reasons he had for opposition. Sabath replied that he considered Clark more liberal on immigration, labor, and prohibition issues. Wilson asked him to make it specific.

"You have written a book which has done injustice to immigrants," said Sabath. "You referred to 'hordes of undesirable immigrants.' "

"My dear Judge," Sabath quotes Wilson as replying, "I wrote that book not as a candidate but as a historian. By itself that phrase may look bad, but read the context. Read the entire book. Here, I'll read it."

Sabath says that as Wilson read from his "History of the American People" he thought to himself: "Damn you! I was misled on that point because that was what Hearst was hammering on."

Wilson also satisfied Sabath that he was friendly to labor and no bluenose on prohibition—"See, I take a little drink with you." The Chicago county chairman was converted "after spending with him two hours walking here and walking there."

"I was then a well publicized and well advertised man and chairman of the Cook County Central Committee," Sabath reminisces. "The following morning the *New York Times:* 'Sabath goes to Sea Girt to inform Wilson he couldn't support him, but after—' Oh, the papers were full. I'll say this—every promise he made me he carried out."

The promises involved diplomatic appointments after Wilson took office. During the campaign Sabath persuaded Wilson to repudiate Sullivan as a candidate for senator, thus killing the latter's chances and opening the way for election of the pink-whiskered dandy, James Hamilton Lewis.

"Truth of the matter was," says Sabath, "I myself thought I'd run for the Senate, but I thought to myself, 'You'd make a stronger man.' "

In 1917 Sabath voted for war, and the same year he married Mae Ruth Fuerst of Chicago. They had no children.

During 1918 it was reported in Congress that Wilson was considering negotiation of a separate peace with Austria Hungary. This worried Sabath, who favored independence for the racial groups under its rule and who feared that such a course would tend to keep them a part of the Hapsburg Empire. Twice he visited Wilson to urge against it, but felt he had made no progress. Finally, when he took a constituent to the White House on business, Wilson's secretary, Joseph Tumulty, urged him to try again. Sabath did, that afternoon. Whatever may have been in Wilson's mind as to a separate peace, he reaffirmed his policy of self-determination for small nations in a message to Congress two days later. It was not long afterward that revolutions broke out in Czechoslovakia and Poland that led to their later independence.

Sabath also was instrumental in getting Wilson to see Thomas Masaryk. Charles R. Crane, Chicago plumbing magnate, was urging the President to talk to the Czechoslovak leader, but the State Department objected that he could not receive an alien enemy. Sabath, with the help of Tumulty, persuaded Wilson to ignore this technicality. The result of the meeting was Wilson's acceptance of his cause and Masaryk's declaration of independence for Czechoslovakia. It gave considerable satisfaction to the son of the butcher of Zabori to have had a small part in it.

This experience, and his contact with First World War problems as a legislator, made Sabath a confirmed internationalist in outlook. He was a staunch advocate of Woodrow Wilson's League of Nations. An early supporter of recognition for Russia, he introduced a resolution urging this course during the 1920-21 session, and during Hoover's term he sought to promote commercial relations between the two countries.

He was one of the first to take alarm at the rise of Hitler and to see peril for the United States in the formation of the Berlin-Rome-Tokio axis. He supported Franklin Delano Roosevelt's foreign-policy moves of the 1930's and abandoned a former anti-militaristic stand to help enlarge the Navy. Where once he had ridiculed Hobson of Alabama when as a member of the House the former admiral had urged more battleships for defense against Japan, Sabath in 1938 was aiding the fight for the first of the modern naval expansion bills. His was a vote on which the administration could always count in its bitter pre-war battles with the isolationists.

In September, 1943, before the war had progressed to the point where there was much reason for talk about what to do with Germany, Sabath made a speech in the House advocating that the Reich and Japan never be permitted to rearm. He took his cue on economic foreign policy from the administration.

Sabath's greatest legislative opportunity came during the depression when he persuaded the House to set up a special committee, which he headed, to investigate an alleged racket that had grown up in the organization of so-called "protective committees" in connection with defaults on an estimated $8,000,000,000 total in real estate bonds throughout the country.

The impression given in the creation of the committee was that something could be done about recovering funds for those who had invested in the defaulted bonds, preventing the "protective committees" from dissipating such assets as there were, and recommending any reform legislation that seemed appropriate.

The opportunity was flopped completely. The entire investigation was enveloped in confusion and futility. No legislation was recommended. There were even ugly rumors—voiced publicly in the House by Representative Ralph E. Church of Illinois—that the law firm of Sabath, Perlman, Goodman, & Rein was profiting from fees obtained from companies under investigation. Sabath denied the charges in a House speech during which he wept and at the end of which he collapsed. His fellow committee members, including Everett M. Dirksen, Church's fellow Republican from Illinois, joined in defending him. The charges were never proved. While the implications of venality would have a bearing in gauging the worth of Sabath as a statesman if they were proved, the fact that he flubbed the investigation is a bad mark by itself. Sabath lacked the incisiveness to know what he wanted, and allowed a curious assortment of attorneys to work for the committee for nothing.

Sabath became dean of the House on the death of a fellow Illinois Democrat, Speaker Henry T. Rainey, in 1934. He became dean of Congress on the retirement of Senator George W. Norris. He was elevated to the chairmanship of Rules in 1939 after John J. O'Connor of New York was defeated in Franklin D. Roosevelt's attempted 1938 purge of the Democratic party, which was unsuccessful everywhere else.

His election as chairman was not without grumbling on the part of the members. There was some talk of passing him over, but it was put down by Speaker Sam Rayburn, then majority leader, who knew that strict adherence to the seniority rule would avoid opening up a Pandora's box of intra-party trouble in committee selections.

But by that time the day was past when a New Deal chairman of Rules could actually run the committee which controls legislative procedure in the House. Working against Sabath in the last committee was the solid bloc of Republicans: Hamilton Fish of New York, Leo E. Allen of Illinois, Earl C. Michener of Michigan, Charles A. Halleck of Indiana, and Clarence J. Brown, of Ohio. Working with this bloc against all domestic New Deal issues were the intransigeant Southern Democrats: Eugene Cox of Georgia, Howard W. Smith of

Virginia, J. Bayard Clark of North Carolina, Martin Dies of Texas, and William M. Colmer of Mississippi. Against this combination of ten votes Sabath could hope at best for three in addition to his own: John J. Delaney of New York, Joe B. Bates of Kentucky, and Roger C. Slaughter of Missouri, new and relatively untried.

There was little left for Sabath to do but preside. What management, what whipping-into-line of the titular majority was accomplished, was done by Sam Rayburn's strong personality.

The Rules committee-room in the United States Capitol is a dingy chamber in the southeast corner of the House wing, just across the hall from the members' family gallery on the third floor. It is lighted by a large crystal chandelier and the windows to the east look out on the Library of Congress across the plaza. Clerks' desks line the east side of the room, bookcases filled with *Congressional Records* bound it to north and south. Under the chandelier is a long table, about three by fifteen feet, covered with royal blue felt and punctured at regular intervals by ash trays.

Sabath, sitting at the north end of the table, has a chaste bronze desk lamp, a blotter, a wooden block and a gavel as symbol of his authority. Members loll in swivel chairs along the table's length, the Democrats on the chairman's right, the Republicans on his left. Witnesses are members of Congress— committee chairmen and others—seeking permission to take bills to the floor. They testify from the far end of the table.

The witnesses indicate how much debating time they think should be allowed for consideration of their bills on the House floor, and opposition witnesses may appear to urge against bringing them up at all. After the public hearing the committee goes into executive session for its decision. If the bill is approved, the decision takes the form of a resolution making it in order to take up the measure for consideration by the Committee of the Whole House on the State of the Union, with general debate limited to a specified number of hours or days. Debating time is split equally between the majority and minor-

ity. The resolution usually provides that the bill shall be open
to amendments. Sometimes—and it is on such occasions that
the committee uses its power—amendments are prohibited
under a "gag" rule, when the House is forced to vote the
measure up or down as it is submitted.

Such a resolution is then taken to the floor, called up by
Sabath, and after an hour's debate, or less, adopted. Then the
House goes to work on the bill itself. This formal procedure
is required because with the membership grown to 435, the
House is too unwieldy to consider bills under the general rules,
which permit each member to be recognized for one hour.

Without Rules Committee approval it is difficult, but not
impossible, to get any major legislation to the floor.

Public hearings of the Rules Committee can be, and have
been, the most hilarious shows in Washington. To a large extent the committee's job is a routine one, since members recognize that public opinion has attained a force which requires
Congress to come to a showdown on major issues under majority rule.

Consequently many of the hearings merely amount to a letting off of steam. Witnesses express opinions, the volatile Cox
of Georgia works up an emotional fervor of opposition to the
New Deal, the rail-thin Smith of Virginia, with his inevitable
gates-ajar collar, interpolates caustic comments. Amid the confusion Sabath gently taps his block with the handle of his gavel,
murmuring: "Gentlemen, gentlemen!" in mild reproof, and
gives the impression of a man trying to hold back a steam
roller.

The picture is significant. Sabath's personal inclination is to
be kind, polite, gentlemanly, while the post calls for qualities
of toughness and stubbornness. The cruder qualities have
raised many mediocre politicians, through long service, to
positions of power.

Long in politics, Sabath has been pushed around continuously
by those more natively inclined to the rough pastime. He has
skirted around the edges of big events in the nation's history
without exerting much influence on them. Despite his sympathy
for the little fellow, which is genuine, he never has learned the

trick of using the perquisites of long service to do anything very effective to implement it.

The seniority system has elevated others without regard to merit, and developed many of them in the process. It has taught many of those so elevated to wield their power whenever legislation or appropriations came under their jurisdiction, whether their aim was to further the New Deal, checkmate it, or merely get pork and patronage. It has taught them secrets of committee control, by fair means or foul: respect of the members for the chairman's ability, or fear of his arrant demagoguery.

Sabath failed to learn these lessons. For him the seniority system meant a chairmanship for which he was not fitted. His place in legislative history must rest on the fact that he was elected more times in a row than anyone else.

13

HAMILTON FISH

"Crusading Isolationist"

BY RICHARD NELSON CURRENT

"I SUPPOSE," REMARKED HAM FISH, AS HE WAS BEGINNING the last of his twenty-four consecutive years in the House, "my name is as well known as anyone's in Congress." [1] And he was no doubt right. Many of the millions who knew him or knew of him, however, were conscious more of notoriety than of fame. Some, calling themselves liberals, seemed to regard his very presence on Capitol Hill as a standing threat to the future of popular government. But the Gentleman from New York himself viewed Hamilton Fish in a quite different light. He thought of him as a liberal of the first water, and a high-minded patriot to boot. "I've never been a reactionary in my life," he would insist. "I'm a progressive. I'm with Thomas Jefferson."

The record of his congressional career fails to reveal any sign of creative, Jeffersonian statesmanship. The record, as appraised from 1920 to 1941, does give ample evidence of liberalism and patriotism, provided the appraiser is willing to accept the Fish definitions of those terms together with their Fish corollaries, anti-communism and isolationism.

Liberalism of the ichthyic sort was revealed in the congressman's occasional lapses into "progressive" irregularity, as when in the nineteen-thirties he repeatedly threatened a revolt in the House unless his Republican party, abandoning its "reactionary" leadership and ways, should support legislation for

1. This quotation of Fish and all the quotations to follow, except those for which another source is indicated, reproduce his remarks as made in conversation with the author in New York on Jan. 4, 1944.

social security and minimum wages and maximum hours. Again, his liberal proclivities were shown in the many kind words he uttered on behalf of such minorities as the Negroes and the Jews. Two examples must suffice. In 1922 (he was in those days a favorite of the American Zionists) he sponsored the House resolution in favor of creating a Jewish national homeland. In 1937, for the Negroes, he proposed an anti-lynching law, a forerunner of the more widely known Gavagan bill. Perhaps the depth of his liberal feeling was best indicated, however, by the strictures which along with the American Liberty League he laid upon President Roosevelt and the New Deal for their infringements on the old-fashioned individual freedoms. If this be liberalism, Fish made the most of it.

If patriotism consist in monuments for the dead and preferential treatment for the living who have worn the country's uniform, Representative Fish indubitably deserved to rank among the foremost expounders of it, too. After the First World War he appointed himself the special pleader for soldiers recently returned and the chief commemorator of those who were not to come back. In sum, he brought in the bill for honoring the Unknown Soldier, helped lead the fight first for bonus legislation and later for cash payment of bonus certificates, and strove long and successfully to have civil service rules relaxed in favor of war veterans.

Out of his patriotic interests sprang naturally if not inevitably his opposition to the alien philosophy of bolshevism. Not until 1930, however, did he get around to making himself conspicuous as the scourge of the Communist party in the United States. Conscious of his liberalism, he made it clear he did not blame foreign influences or foreign-born agitators for quite all the contemporary ills of the land. "I believe in capitalism as opposed to communism," he averred, "but capitalism shorn of its abuses and ugly greed to exploit labor and mankind for the almighty dollar." [2] Skeptics doubted whether he really meant to shear off the wrongs of capitalistic society.

As Fish put it, he was an "isolationist" only "as regards war" and not at all "as regards peace." He opposed American

2. *New York Times*, Jan. 18, 1931, Sec. 9, p. 2, col. 2.

membership in the League of Nations because he thought it might entail an obligation to fight, but he readily embraced the idea of international action to "outlaw" war and, indeed, became the House champion of the pretentious Kellogg-Briand pact. On missions of world co-operation for peaceful purposes he visited Europe in 1923 and again in 1939. After the outbreak of the European conflict he resisted most of the steps which the Roosevelt administration took to give aid and comfort to the enemies of Nazi Germany, but usually his resistance was equivocal or qualified. He moved to postpone rather than to prevent a peacetime draft. He attacked the lend-lease bill but defended the plan to help England, "short of war," by selling goods for cash. Sometimes he looked like an apologist for the Japanese; at other times he assailed administration leaders for their persistent refusal to prohibit the sale of oil and scrap iron to Japan. In all this he perhaps reflected the confusion of the American people, but he certainly did little or nothing to clarify the issues.

When the Japanese assault finally came (to mar his fifty-third birthday) he announced: "From now on politics is out, and only unity of action to achieve victory is vital to America." [3] This might be taken as a confession that, so far as he was concerned, "politics" had by no means been "out" during the preceding years but had been at least as important as his personal convictions in determining his legislative stands.

Ham Fish was a big man—physically. His height of six feet four, his weight of more than two hundred pounds, fairly well distributed even when he was past fifty, and his broad and massive shoulders made him conspicuous in a crowd. In conversation his nasal, almost whining voice, his fidgety mannerisms, and his perpetually furrowed, frowning, worried look, all belied the prepossessing effect of his towering figure. Apparently he lacked a real sense of humor—that is, a capacity for laughing at himself—and yet in his abstracted way he was jocular and "folksy" enough. Coming into his office from the slushy sidewalks of a January afternoon, he could take off his shoes

3. *Ibid.*, Dec. 12, 1941, p. 5, col. 2.

and socks, replace the latter with a new pair from his pocket, put the shoes on a radiator to dry, and then in stocking feet continue to converse with a total stranger while he banteringly chided his secretary for suggesting it would have been more dignified to make the change in another room. He was no stickler for the proprieties, no snob.

He might well have been one, considering his family background. His grandfather, the Hamilton Fish of the history books, achieved fame as Secretary of State in Grant's cabinet. His aunt, Mrs. Stuyvesant Fish, ruled for years as queen of the socially elect in New York and Newport. Born on the ancestral estate along the Hudson in Garrison, Putnam County, Ham himself was brought up in a style befitting a scion of the Fish clan. In a spirit of *noblesse oblige* he carried on the family tradition of public service, a tradition he used to compare in its advantage with that of another distinguished line of politicians, the Roosevelts.

Although at Harvard he gained distinction not only as Walter Camp's choice for "All American" tackle but also as a graduate in three years *cum laude,* nobody considered Congressman Fish to be one of the profounder or more erudite members of the House. It was characteristic that he could not discuss understandingly the writings of Charles A. Beard, famous advocate of an intelligent form of the very isolationism he himself was proud to espouse. Still, though he once turned down an offer to teach political science at his alma mater and later accepted an invitation to coach football at Poughkeepsie High School, he retained something of a scholar's interest in government as well as a sportsman's enthusiasm for the great American game. On one occasion he even addressed the learned men of the American Academy of Political and Social Science on his specialty, the meaning and menace of communism.

An admirer of Theodore Roosevelt, he served in the New York Assembly from 1914 to 1916 as a "progressive," advocating among other things the introduction of direct presidential primaries in his state. No isolationist in those days, he echoed the "preparedness" demands of Colonel Roosevelt, promptly enrolled at Plattsburg, and later helped to organize a National Guard regiment of Negroes. When war was declared he went overseas as captain of this colored regiment. From France he sent back letters revealing something of the warrior-politician's role which in emulation of T. R. he had conceived for himself. "I believe," he wrote to his father, "if the censorship regulations were abolished, the 15th New York (now the 369th U. S. Infantry) would be as well known as the Rough Riders were in the Spanish-American war, before peace is declared." [4] He emerged from the war with at least a Croix de Guerre and a promotion to the rank of major, if without a swashbuckler's fame comparable to that of the hero of San Juan Hill.

This military experience left a deep and lasting impression upon the personality of Hamilton Fish, as indeed similar experiences did upon the personalities of thousands of his comrades in arms. The veteran who has faced fire may sense, quite understandably, a subtle transformation that sets him apart from stay-at-homes and equips him with a certain type of wisdom they can never share. Only, with Fish, this natural tendency went to unnatural extremes. He came to consider his record for personal bravery (which itself was not contested) as the final retort, the unanswerable refutation, to all aspersions upon his character, his conduct, or his political views. He would reason in much this fashion: Franklin D. Roosevelt did not serve in the front lines; Hamilton Fish did. Therefore, no matter what the issue, Roosevelt must be wrong; Fish is right.

As a self-conscious patriot, Fish was one of the organizers of the American Legion, more particularly, chairman of the subcommittee that wrote the preamble to its constitution. Time and again he acted as a House spokesman for the lobbies of the Legion and other veterans' groups. Not only to conventions of Legionnaires but also to unnumbered school assemblies, church gatherings, racial conclaves, and meetings of nativist societies, businessmen's service clubs, and organized hereditary patriots he carried the various versions of his star-spangled message. In the light of his own conscience he was not going far afield when he spoke to cheering crowds at rallies of the

4. Letter published in the *New York Times*, May 5, 1918, Sec. 5, p. 2, col. 1.

German-American Bund, an organization avowing its devotion
to the highest type of patriotism.

The company Fish kept, and by which presumably he could
be known, included a number of like-minded persons in and out
of Congress. In the House he counted among his intimate
friends most of the Republican oldtimers, like Harold Knutson, who once trumpeted him as a presidential prospect.
Among both senators and congressmen he maintained warm
personal relations with the leading spokesmen for America
First, notably Dewey Short, Burton K. Wheeler, and Gerald P.
Nye. At one time he was as welcome at the presidential mansion as any other guest from the opposite end of the Avenue,
but for several years he saw nothing at all, personally or
socially, of President Roosevelt. Yet he claimed to be on good
terms with many of the underlings and even some of the key
men of the Roosevelt administration, among whom he would
mention Secretaries Jesse Jones and Cordell Hull and, for
good measure, Chief Justice Harlan F. Stone. Outside the government his most conspicuous acquaintanceships were with
Fulgencio Batista, Cuban dictator; with Lawrence Dennis,
foremost "intellectual fascist" in the United States; and with
George Sylvester Viereck, German-born journalist, literateur,
and convicted Nazi propagandist. Of the groups who with
Viereck and Dennis were indicted in 1943 and 1944 for sedi-
tion or conspiracy, Fish said at the time that some were perhaps really "fascists," others probably "crackpots," and the
rest good Americans who happened to be "anti-British, anti-
Russian, anti-Roosevelt, or anti-Jew." But a number of his
nearest associates were Jewish, a fact which he would adduce
as disproof of any anti-Semitism on his own part.

In the role of legislator Fish was active and even influential
—in a negative way. As head of the famous Fish committee
investigating Communist activities (in 1930) he distinguished
himself by his elaborate politeness to the witnesses he called,
his obstinate inability to understand their point of view, and his
utter failure to get the legislation he demanded for eradicating
communism from American soil. As ranking minority member
of the Committee on Foreign Affairs, for several years until

his resignation late in 1942, he took his task to be largely one of obstructing the Democratic majority and antagonizing the chairman, Sol Bloom. He asserted his independence at every opportunity, as when he refused even to attend hearings at which the secretaries of State and War were to give confidential information, his object being to protest the secrecy by his absence and also to remain free to attack the majority's proposals on the floor of the House. As the senior Republican on the Rules Committee he continued in a position highly adaptable to tactics of criticism and delay, for he had the right to use, himself, or to parcel out among his fellow partisans the limited time allowed the minority for discussing each measure in House debate.

On the floor of the House Fish might have been more effective if his oratory, replete with flamboyant irrelevancy and fervid *non sequitur,* had not been so hard for his colleagues to follow. In the fall of 1941, when congressmen were debating an amendment to the Neutrality Act which would permit the arming of merchant ships, a perplexed listener stopped Fish in the midst of a speech to ask: "Would the gentleman be willing to inform the House at this stage in his remarks whether he is going to vote for this legislation or not?" "Certainly," Fish replied, "I propose to vote for it." He went on to explain that he was talking not, as might have been supposed, against the bill before the House but against quite another legislative possibility, the repeal of the whole Neutrality Act! Finally he did indeed vote for the bill—but only after first voting to kill the measure by recommitting it.[5]

On several occasions the question of congressional ethics arose in regard to the activities of Fish. When, during the neutrality debate of 1939, he headed the National Committee to Keep America out of Foreign Wars (on the executive board of which were thirty-six other House Republicans), a Democratic representative accused him of impropriety in creating his own pressure group to influence the deliberations of his peers. Later, when he was called to testify at the Viereck trial in

5. *Congressional Record,* Seventy-seventh Congress, first session (1941-42), pp. 8166, 8249-50.

1942, the federal prosecuting attorney charged him with misusing his rooms in the House Office Building as a kind of mailing center for the Nazi-inspired speeches of isolationist congressmen. This he denied, and he disclaimed responsibility for the actions of a clerk in his employ, George Hill, who went to jail for perjury though not for alleged propagandist enterprises. Again, when materials bearing the Fish frank were distributed by notoriously anti-Semitic individuals and organizations, Fish was said to be abusing his franking privilege, and the national convention of the American Legion in 1943 passed a resolution (later rescinded) censuring him for it. His defense was, in sum, that members of Congress legally may and customarily do send any applicant, without inquiring into his character, batches of their printed speeches for separate remailing. The evidence indicated that Fish at all times had remained within the letter if not the spirit of the law.

As acutely aware as any congressman of the uses of publicity, Fish enjoyed an advantage over most of his colleagues in possessing a short, four-lettered name that was both handy for headline writers and easily remembered by newspaper readers. Yet his dealings with the fourth estate were more haphazard than happy. Ruefully he would remark: "People often ask me why I don't hire a public relations man. I don't need any publicity—sometimes I get too much!" He did hand out an ample supply of neatly prepared press releases; some of the recipients gave him "good breaks," he said, and others did not.[6] Frequently he exploited the radio to reach the public ear; for example, he took the people into his confidence, over the air, to expose the mischief that he thought the Foreign Affairs Committee was about to do (in 1941) in the matter of lend-lease. If, however, Fish had had to depend for support upon

6. Some "crusading" newsmen have weakened their own case by their over-eagerness to malign Fish. This has been true of Drew Pearson, Walter Winchell, Kenneth Crawford, and the protean author of the sensationally advertised *Under Cover*. Crawford, as Washington reporter for the New York tabloid *PM*, once made hasty charges which he soon afterward saw fit to retract. See *PM*, Sept. 26, 1941, p. 9, and Sept. 28, 1941, p. 7. The author of *Under Cover* (pp. 414-16), following reports in the *Washington Post*, gives an account of Fish's conduct at the Viereck trial which is refuted not only by the congressman's own recollection of the events but also by the contemporary report of the correspondent of the *New York Times*. See the *Times*, Feb. 21, 1942. p. 7, col. 1.

his nation-wide reputation, as press and radio fashioned it, doubtless he would not have remained so long the representative of the twenty-sixth congressional district of New York, which was after all the ultimate source of his political strength.

Fish's long hold upon his constituency may best be understood in the light of his campaign for renomination and re-election in 1942, which attracted more national attention than any other congressional canvass in that year. The President of the United States, whose own home lay within the district and who in a campaign speech of 1940 had publicized if not immortalized the Congressman by his reference to the mythical firm of "Martin, Barton, and Fish," again deigned to make known his wish that Ham would be soundly beaten. The titular head of the Republican party, Wendell Willkie, and the prospective leader of the state ticket, Thomas E. Dewey, both declared themselves against their fellow Republican. When nevertheless Fish duly won his twelfth consecutive victory at the polls, the question arose: Why did voters backing the war effort return to office the most conspicuous of the erstwhile non-interventionists?

The answer was, for one thing, that Fish had a large personal following among the Republicans in his district. Their devotion was in part a measure of their gratitude for the many generous legislative services he had performed and the still more numerous and more openhanded gestures he had offered on behalf of the farmers especially, but also the wage earners, the businessmen, the Negroes, the various towns, and other politically conscious groups. These winsome favors largely made up for a lack of the usual congressional patronage, of which Fish enjoyed practically none after the advent of President Roosevelt. Once his party should return to power, he frankly expected to get "plenty of it," in the state of New York as well as in his own locality. How wisely he would use it he had suggested by his record of the nineteen-twenties, when the National Civil Service League accused him of excessive regard for "politics" in his recommendations for postal appointments, and he confounded the reformers with his reply that each and all his candidates were "Republican workers recommended by the entire local Republican organization"! [7]

In addition to the personal following thus gained and held, Fish was able to rely upon the backing of the party organizations of Putnam, Orange, and Dutchess counties (which his district then comprised). In 1942 the Republican committee of Orange County, much the largest of the three, endorsed him with 190 votes to 26 for his outstanding competitor, Augustus W. Bennet, a prominent attorney of Newburgh and a leader of the local Willkie forces in the previous presidential campaign. Thereupon Bennet confessed he could not claim even a "moral victory" over "the powerful Fish machine."

Against Fish, his Republican opponents hoped to make telling use of his legislative and personal record, above all his stand on international questions and his well-known association with such persons as George Sylvester Viereck. But a majority of the constituents, if they seemed to disagree with their congressman in his stand on particular measures such as lend-lease, nevertheless approved his general attitude toward foreign affairs. In the summer of 1941 he had spent $1,800 on a "postcard poll"; he asked his constituents whether the United States should stay out of the war or get into it, and over four-fifths of those replying were convinced the country should stay out. This was the only instance of his sampling public opinion in this way—"too expensive to do it very often"—but he did gather information regularly from his Republican committeemen, from local newspapers, and from letters which the people at home did not hesitate to send him. He in turn kept the people informed by distributing reprints from the *Congressional Record* with what was said to be the most complete mailing list any congressman possessed. He also maintained offices in Newburgh and New York as well as Washington, and in all three places visitors were so welcome that one wonders how he had any time for legislative work in the capital, to say nothing of insurance selling in New York. These many contacts were not fruitless. In the summer of 1942 a study by the American

7. Statement by the head of the National Civil Service League in the *New York Times*, Dec. 4, 1924, p. 3, col. 3.

Institute of Public Opinion indicated that well over half the Republicans in the twenty-sixth district were supporting Fish, despite their familiarity with his isolationist and seemingly pro-German and pro-Japanese attitudes before the event at Pearl Harbor. "Ham guessed wrong," his followers were saying, "but so did a lot of us."[8]

The congressman had another advantage over his Republican adversaries, namely, that as an experienced rough-and-tumble campaigner he was inhibited much less than they were by any thought about the niceties of politics. For example, his readiness to plead in the House for deferment of fathers did not prevent his berating one of Bennet's supporters, aged about thirty-seven and father of three children, because the man was not in uniform. In one of his radio performances he went so far as to sing the old song, "Johnny Get Your Gun," and request his listeners to send white feathers to this man, in an effort to discredit him.[9] Another sample of the *ad hominem* nature of his harangues upon the hustings was the following: "The smear artists, the Communists, radicals, and a few fanatical interventionists who hate my outspoken condemnation of Communists, the left-wing New Dealers, and even some reactionaries in my own party who cannot control me are out to defeat and purge me."[10] Dismissing all references to his legislative past as mere efforts to "play pre-Pearl Harbor politics," he posed as a man of the common people against the "millionaire class," a thing not hard for him to do, considering the fact that the list of local Republicans opposing him included several such names as E. Roland Harriman and Harry Harkness Flagler. He argued, moreover, that if he was defeated the district would lose the advantages of his seniority and his prospective chairmanship of the House Rules Committee. And,

8. Dr. George Gallup, in the *New York Times,* July 26, 1942, p. 32, col. 1. Dr. Gallup's summary and analysis of the Institute's findings has been very useful at several points in this discussion of the relations between Fish and his constituents.

9. Augustus W. Bennet to the author, Dec. 27, 1943, and Jan. 14, 1944. The author is greatly indebted to Mr. Bennet for these letters embodying full, frank, and fair-minded accounts of local politics, even though he does not share Mr. Bennet's point of view in all respects.

10. Report of a radio speech from station WGNY, Newburgh, in the *New York Times,* May 2, 1942, p. 14, col. 2.

finally, he was able to turn to his own account the very attempt of Dewey, Willkie, and Roosevelt to down him. Throughout the district most of the Republican rank and file resented the presumption of outsiders "butting in."

In short, Fish won the Republican nomination in August, 1942, and he won it decisively, by virtue of his large personal following, his "machine" backing, his understanding of popular moods, and his unrestrained and highly effective campaign methods. Having done so, he could look forward to almost certain victory in the November election, for the party rolls in the district listed more than twice as many Republicans as Democrats. The failure of the Democratic leaders and the disaffected Republicans to unite behind a strong coalition nominee virtually brought an end to all hope of stopping Fish. Even so, although 1942 was a "Republican year" and Dewey carried the twenty-sixth district with 30,000 votes to spare in the gubernatorial campaign, Fish won in November by a margin of only 4,000 votes, less than half as many as in the previous election and the fewest in his whole campaigning experience.

In the minds of anti-Fish Republicans the fact of these statistics, together with the assumption of considerable voting out of party loyalty and sheer habit, raised a doubt whether the Congressman really represented the dominant wishes of his constituency. But Fish himself looked upon the returns as a vindication of popular rule. Selfish groups, he said afterward, had spent hundreds of thousands of dollars in a vain attempt to thwart the people's will. "That was a real example of democracy in action—the way my workers worked for me in '42. They can't be bought!"

After the widespread Republican reaction at the 1942 polls, Fish predicted a "snowstorm" of ballots at the next national election which, as in 1920, would smother the wartime administration and obliterate most of its works. Then the New York congressman would come into his own. His personal prejudices would become governmental principles—his family pride, his patriotic self-consciousness, his vaguely "progressive" outlook, his hatred of F. D. R. and all that Roosevelt stood for, and his great fear of bolshevism, which in the beginning may or may not have been a pose but which if only through autosuggestion had formed an integrant of his mentality. And his private ambitions would be either realized or well on the road toward realization.

Probably his ultimate aspirations reached above Congress to the highest office in the land. He had allowed a "Fish boom" to get under way in 1936 and had threatened, momentarily, to run on a peace platform in 1940. To his critics he seemed a man consumed by a ridiculous lusting after the presidency. For years he dreamed of building a new political organization in the South—"let's call it a Constitutional Democratic or a Jeffersonian Democratic or simply an American party"—which would support Democrats in state and local elections and a Republican, presumably one with the initials H. F., in the national campaign.

When asked point blank early in 1944 what his greatest ambition was, he modestly and patriotically replied: "To have a Republican president and Congress and be chairman of the Rules Committee, because in that position I can do best service to my country." He would rather be head of the Rules Committee, he averred, than be a senator or a member of the Cabinet. As chairman he would be one of the high tacticians behind the lawmaking process, for every proposal would require a special "rule" from his committee before it could even be considered in debate. Further, his long-established friendship with the prospective heads of other little congresses within the Congress, notably Ways and Means, would make him an influential member of the whole clique of House leaders. These men could not, by themselves, run the cumbrous contrivance that turns out the laws, but they could cause it to stall if a Democratic president or an uncongenial Republican were attempting to pilot it.

How Fish as chairman would deal with an unsympathetic administration he indicated at the time he left the Committee on Foreign Affairs to confine himself to that on Rules, when he asserted that the latter "should devote its energies and time to checking on the governmental agencies and requiring the bureaucrats to show by what authority of law they are taking over with their own hands the legislative functions of Congress." [11] Between these lines one can read the mingled envy and frustration any ambitious congressman must feel who contrasts the plodding slowness and final limits of his own advancement with the quick and dazzling preferment of many a "bureaucrat." In this same spirit Fish also gave utterance to the fateful thought of impeachment. He foresaw, in the good time coming, not only vindication for those in Congress accused of having Nazi connections in the pre-war period but also obloquy for those in high places who in time of supposed neutrality had conspired with the British at the jeopardy of peace.

As for the Fish treatment of international problems, he along with the rest of the Republicans voted dutifully, after the American declaration of hostilities, for measures essential to the prosecution of the war itself. This did not mean that he had abandoned the basic attitudes that underlay his previous career. Still a Russophobe, he warned against early "commitments" on the part of the United States; they might turn out to be obligations for this country to help "make the world safe for Communism." Apparently he found the Fulbright Resolution toothless enough that he could approve it without a qualm, though he afterward referred to his affirmative vote as evidence that despite his detractors he was no "isolationist" in a bad sense. When in 1944 the first concrete test of sentiment on post-war collaboration came before the House, namely, the bill for an American contribution to the UNRRA, Fish refrained from making an all-out attack, but he did join with those skirmishers who tried, unsuccessfully, to halve the appropriation and, successfully, to make part of it available for the relief of suffering within the British Empire. As if to clinch the argument that he was no incorrigible isolationist, he later spoke approvingly of the work of the "world security" conference at Dumbarton Oaks.

Meanwhile, in the immemorial way of congressional politicians of the party of the outs, he fulminated now and then against presidential tyranny and the destruction of states' rights. But he had nothing intelligible to say about the concrete and urgent problems of demobilization and the main-

11. *New York Times,* Dec. 15, 1942, p. 30, col. 5.

tenance of full employment. He was content merely to side with his fellow Republicans and, except for occasional remarks on Negro rights, with the conservative Democrats. Insofar as he possessed a definite economic and social point of view, he did not differ fundamentally from those in his own party who criticized hím for his notions about foreign affairs.

It was not, then, an upsurge of the crusading spirit of the early New Deal which turned Fish out in the election of 1944 and took from his reach the things he had set his heart upon. His opponents in the twenty-ninth district (formed in the New York redistricting by separating Orange County from the old twenty-sixth and combining with it Rockland, Sullivan, and Delaware counties) succeeded now where they had failed two years before. They united behind a single strong candidate, Augustus W. Bennet, whom Fish had again defeated in the Republican primary. Bennet ran on the Good Government, Democratic, American Labor, and Liberal party tickets. To offset Bennet's appeal to independent Republicans through the Good Government party, Fish organized a Jeffersonian party to catch the votes of disaffected Democrats, but these and the votes of Republican regulars were not enough. He lost.

Good Government won, but did good government win? Those who raised the hue and cry after the incumbent seemed to proceed upon the major premise that wicked men were to blame for bad government and the minor premise that Ham Fish was a wicked man. It would appear, however, that most of the faults they found in Fish were, in actual fact, as much institutional as personal. They accused him of putting "politics" before statecraft, but they forgot to mention that the whole existing system of congressional tenure, representation, and advancement made it urgently essential for an ambitious member of Congress to make "politics" his foremost concern. The friends of Good Government were no doubt politer, more decorous politicians than Fish and his followers could claim to be. But Ham Fish for nearly a quarter of a century had been a successful if not a seemly practitioner of politics. His strenuous efforts made him look like the very caricature of a congressman.

14

SOL BLOOM
"Supersalesman of Patriotism"

BY HUGH A. BONE

THE SCENE WAS THE FLOOR OF THE HOUSE OF REPRE-
sentatives, February 4, 1941; the occasion was a debate
on the lend-lease bill; the speaker was Sol Bloom, chairman of
the Foreign Affairs Committee.

The bill is short, direct and to the point. The people of the United
States with their fundamental horse sense know that. In light of our
clear cut national policy to aid Britain, the bill is the most efficient and
forthright way to execute our policy in a manner consistent with our
long history of the democratic way of doing things.

Three days later near the close of the day, a deadlock developed over the question of placing limitations on the lend-lease
bill, a deadlock which seriously threatened passage. At the
eleventh hour Bloom stepped in to offer an amendment to limit
lend lease to one-tenth of the total appropriations for defense
in the fiscal year of 1941. This compromise "clicked" and the
day was saved when both Republicans and Democrats passed it
with a big vote.

Following through, Bloom went over to the other side of
the Capitol as a daily visitor to observe the progress of debate
on the measure in the Senate. With his gift for colorful expression and flair for quoting statistics, he said: "The Senate
has used in [this] debate three times the words employed in
all of the inaugural addresses and those great addresses of
Washington and Lincoln, plus the famous liberty documents
of all time." He can tell you the number of words in these
addresses as well as those in the Magna Carta and the English
Bill of Rights.

The life of Sol Bloom is a Horatio Alger story. He is a success in business and a success in politics. Putting the two together he is one of those rare souls, a repeatedly re-elected New Deal millionaire. He is now in his seventy-fifth year. One newspaper describes him as "somewhat less than average height, with a lively, mobile face. He looks something like George Arliss. He is a natty dresser, features white vest edgings, complete color ensembles, and a pince-nez with a broad black ribbon." [1]

Sol's busy life has not kept him from being a "joiner." Besides being a leader in several Jewish organizations he holds membership in the Masonic lodge, the Elks, the Loyal Order of Moose, the Red Men, and I.O.B.B., and he occupies several honorary positions.

He married Evelyn Hechheimer in 1897. Mrs. Bloom did much for her husband and assisted him in his work. Since her death in 1940, he has continued to live in northwest Washington with his only child, Vera, who conducted what was, until after Pearl Harbor, his busy social life.

Sol's parents were extremely poor Polish Jewish immigrants. Sol was born in Pekin, Illinois, in 1870. Five years later his family moved to Peoria where he immediately started to sell newspapers on the streets. Then the family moved to San Francisco, where at only eight years of age he worked a twelve-hour day in a brush factory. Time did not permit him to attend school regularly, so Sol's mother supplied as much of his education as could be worked in between his many activities. At thirteen he left this job to join the business office of Mike de Young's *San Francisco Chronicle* and soon found himself in charge of the ticket office of De Young's Alcazar Theater. At seventeen he built his first theater "and later bought willow furniture and other merchandise from the East and distributed it at a handsome profit to San Francisco merchants. 'When I was nineteen,' he says, 'I had so much money invested and so much money coming in that I really didn't know where it was

1. *PM*, Aug. 17, 1942.

or where it was coming from. So I retired to take a trip around the world.' " [2]

At this point the Chicago World's Fair offered him his big chance to leave a heritage to the entertainment world in which he has always taken the greatest of pride, the "Hootchy Kootchy" dance.

As superintendent of construction of the Fair's Midway Plaisance and as general overseer, Bloom showed his gift for bringing in the unusual by importing scorpion eaters and belly dancers from North Africa and sponsoring the dancing sensation, "Little Egypt." He produced the first Dance of All Nations in native costume and aided George Ferris in providing the public with the famous ferris wheel. He remained in Chicago after the Fair and made a fortune out of a chain of music stores and as a publisher of sheet music.

After 1903 he moved his family to New York's Manhattan and added the talking-machine business and sports promotion to his list of enterprises. In 1910 Sol decided to seek new pastures. He sold his music ventures and entered the real estate and apartment construction business. Among other things he built a chain of modernized and improved theater buildings and has received the credit for being the designer of the modern theater seat. In the real estate business he amassed a fortune running into the millions. His resourcefulness here was shown in his practice of buying land, then calling in reporters to tell them of his magnificent "bargain," whereupon he would immediately resell it at a handsome profit.

In 1920 at the age of fifty he announced his retirement from the field of business in order to seek a new field to conquer and "to devote his life to the public service." Sol had contributed to the Tammany Hall purse and sought aid for his political ambitions from the organization. An opportunity soon appeared when he was "drafted" for the Democratic nomination for United States Representative in a special election in 1923 in Manhattan's nineteenth district. This district, which has the reputation of being one of the wealthiest in the country, in-

2. *Current Biography*, IV (May, 1943), 8.

cludes the Columbia University and Morningside Park area, a sizable portion of the northern part of Central Park and adjacent Fifth Avenue, and is bounded on the west by Riverside Park.

Although it had long been a Republican stronghold, Bloom, with the endorsement of Governor Al Smith, conducted a whirlwind campaign which netted him victory by a narrow plurality of 126 votes over an opponent who had been elected by that district for five terms and was considered invulnerable. The Republican nominee charged the election to be fraudulent and a spirited contest of the election was taken to the Committee on Privileges and Elections. After more than a year the Committee recommended that Bloom not be seated, and the matter went to the House, which had a Republican majority of twenty-six. The House overruled the committee and seated Bloom. His comment on this close escape was, "I changed that Republican majority of twenty-six into a Democratic majority of eleven long enough to get my seat."[3]

Since 1920 he has had little trouble being re-elected. In recent years he has had the support of the American Labor Party. However, in 1940 the party ran its own candidate against Bloom. In this election Bloom received 71,000 votes to 32,000 for the Republican nominee and 9,000 for the Labor candidate. Bloom was re-elected in 1942 polling a combined Democratic and American Labor party vote of 41,000 to 20,000 for his Republican opponent; and in 1944 he won, 87,000 to 36,000. The district has always been pro-Roosevelt, but Bloom ran ahead of the President in 1940 and in 1944. The Democratic organization has supported Bloom in every election. He has been endorsed by some prominent Republicans, including President Nicholas Murray Butler of Columbia University.

Sol Bloom's continued success in carrying what was formerly a Republican district is due in a great measure to his service to constituents. He maintains an office just off Times Square to handle requests for those who are unable to come to Wash-

3. *Ibid.,* p. 9.

ington. A check-up shows that between his Washington and New York offices he has handled over 300,000 cases. Requests for service in Bloom's offices run heavy in matters of expediting the issuance of passports and visas, information about customs and internal revenue regulations, foreign trade, and immigration and naturalization service. Nowadays he seldom gets home to his Riverside Drive apartment, but he still sees a large number of constituents who come to him in Washington. The politics of those who come to him for service are not asked, and he has the reputation of serving all who apply. Bloom's campaign literature stresses this "side line." One leaflet asserts, "This service has been perfected by Congressman Bloom to a degree which has stamped him as one of the most useful and willing intermediaries between his constituents and Washington. No proper request for help has ever been refused. No inquiry has ever gone unanswered. Thousands of letters in his office files from grateful constituents bear striking testimony of the value of this side line of Congressman Bloom."

The sociological complexion of the district has undergone many changes since 1924. During the 'twenties business interests were very important and at one time the slogan, "A Businessman for a Business District," was used. This was dropped during the 'thirties. Today there is a great conglomeration of nationalities with sizable numbers of Negroes, Puerto Ricans, Irish, and Jews. The gamut of occupations is included, but there is an above-average number of professional people.

Bloom's various campaign methods for re-election have been fairly traditional such as the use of posters, sound-trucks, doorstep literature, and newspaper advertisements. He addresses the various fraternal, civic, and political clubs in the district but has not held street-corner meetings. His usual technique is to rely on "invitations" to speak to organizations. Once he accidently got into a meeting composed of a group of Communists. Although urged to walk out by his managers he insisted on talking to the group. After the boos died out he addressed the group in forceful terms. When he finished there were no cat calls or hisses, and he retired in silence. His usual manner of speaking is forceful. He condemns the use of demagoguery both in campaigns and on the floor of the House.

Between elections he has made little effort to discuss public issues with his constituents. His district has approved the domestic policies of the New Deal and, with the exception of a group of Irish, the administration's foreign policy. This, of course, has made it less necessary for Bloom to discuss public issues with the voters of his district, and therefore to place more stress on personal service.

A program of militant patriotism and Americanism has constituted one of Sol's most spectacular activities in Washington. He introduced a bill making it compulsory for civilians to salute the American flag whenever and wherever they saw it and recommended government aid to recondition the frigate *Constitution.* In 1926, Bloom made an unsuccessful attempt to secure President Coolidge's endorsement of a bill to appropriate money for the filming of the story of the *Constitution.*

In 1930 he assumed the directorship of the George Washington Bicentennial Commission and was catapulted into national prominence as the "supersalesman of patriotism." Briefly, his plan called for a nine-month celebration from February 22, 1932, to Thanksgiving. For this he obtained $338,000 and with a staff of 125 set up a large establishment to design publicity. Shortly, millions of pieces of printed matter on President Washington were being franked to all corners of the nation. Press releases, radio broadcasts, and speeches by the hundreds swept the nation. Commercial establishments saw a good thing in this and did a land office business with pictures, plaster of Paris busts, and novelties about the Father of Our Country. Schools, churches, and civic clubs were plied with material for pageants, plays, and various other devices for popularizing the history of Washington's era. Bloom established state and local committees all over the country, and utilized the press, the radio, and lecture platforms to spread the gospel of patriotism. He offered twenty to one that pitcher Walter Johnson could not throw a coin across the Rappahannock where Washington was alleged to have done so. Sol's invitations to give addresses and his notoriety caused the charge that he was "cheapening" the first president and that he, Bloom, was receiving as much publicity as George Washington. As a result Congress in 1932 reduced his appropriations for the commission. On the other hand he received many letters of commendation including those from Presidents Hoover and Roosevelt and prominent civic and religious leaders. The celebration was later commemorated by the publication of a five-volume report prepared under the supervision of Sol Bloom.

From success in this venture, in which he earned the reputation of "Washington's press agent" Bloom became the director-general of United States Sesquicentennial Commission, established by Congress in 1935. The commission flooded the country with material on the Constitution and published Sol Bloom's 192-page book, *The Story of the Constitution.* The book was done in popular style with pictures. Among other things it included its author's masterpiece of rhetoric entitled "The Heart and Soul of the Constitution." This excerpt illustrates the feeling of its writer:

I maintain that, next to the Bible, "that holy book by which men live and die," the most precious expression of the human soul is the Constitution. . . . You may ask me, where in the Constitution is there any language that throbs with a human heartbeat? Where is the soul of the Constitution? My answer is, in every paragraph. All its parts are mighty links that bind the people in an unbreakable chain of Union—a chain so beautifully wrought that it reminds us of the mystical golden chain which the poet saw binding earth to God's footstool.

But some of the plans for the distribution of this book and other materials fell through. The House refused funds to supply it free to every naturalized citizen. The *New York World Telegram* published an exposé charging that several of Sol's Tammany friends were profiting handsomely from the commission's materials which were sold to schools and civic organizations. However, no conclusive evidence was made public substantiating these charges.

In spite of these attacks on his "commercialized patriotism," which, outwardly at least, appear to have some merit, he has continued to associate himself with such enterprises. He is thoroughly convinced of the value of his work as a salesman of American history. When the *New York Times* presented its critique of American history teaching in April, 1943, Bloom blamed the lack of knowledge of "real American history" on the educators in the public schools. "The reason teachers do not make American history interesting to their pupils," he said, "is that they do not know enough about it. Although not a college graduate or a professional teacher of history, I have taught more real American history to more students than anyone in the United States, through my chairmanship of the George Washington Bicentennial Commission and the United States Sesquicentennial Commission." [4]

As might be expected, Bloom has maintained an interest in legislation dealing with the entertainment and publishing world. He fought the tax on boxing matches, sponsored the proposal to place baseball under federal control, and spoke against the broadcasting of radio advertising. In 1927, he was appointed by President Coolidge as the American delegate to the International Conference on Copyrights held in Rome, and diplomatically represented the United States at the conference. Bloom's background and religious faith (Orthodox Jewish) has led him to champion the cause of immigrants and aliens and to denounce the Alien Registration and Deportation Act of 1925. He once introduced a resolution calling for a House investigation of Henry Ford's charges of Jewish control of the financial centers of government. In 1943 he was a delegate to the British-American refugee conference in Bermuda.

In his younger days he was not one to eschew debate or even physical encounter. His activities have ranged from a fist fight in the House in 1927 with Representative Blanton over a "blue Sunday" law for the nation's capital to the most heated of verbal exchanges in the Foreign Affairs Committee with the former ranking minority member, Hamilton Fish. Generally speaking, he is mild mannered, courteous in debate, and possesses a pleasant sense of humor.

On domestic issues, Bloom's record in terms of supporting

4. *New York Times,* Apr. 7, 1943.

legislation recommended by the Roosevelt administration has been almost 100 per cent. This includes a consistent pro-labor record coupled with his votes against amending the existing labor laws in wartime and opposition to the anti-strike bill. He voted against the investigation of the National Labor Relations Board and was one of the few representatives opposing the extension of the Dies Committee. It is interesting, however, to observe that he introduced a bill for federal intervention in the hard coal strike of 1926 and urged President Coolidge to intervene in the matter. In 1944 he introduced an amendment to the Pure Food and Drug Act providing for clearer labelling of boric acid products. He has voted to sustain President Roosevelt's vetoes including the highly controversial tax bill veto of February, 1944. Similarly, when the President was widely criticized for seizing the Chicago plant of Montgomery Ward, Bloom rallied to his support and voted against the resolution for a congressional investigation of the matter. However, he did join a Democratic minority and Republican majority in voting against more funds for the rural electrification program in 1943. His record of attendance and voting on roll calls is excelled by few, if any, other members of the House.

Except for his work in promoting the Constitution and the George Washington bicentennial celebration, Bloom's record in leadership and sponsorship of legislation was not particularly impressive until he became chairman of the Foreign Affairs Committee. Bloom was a member of the House Committee on Patents until 1929, when he was moved to the Foreign Affairs Committee.

During the 'twenties, Representative Bloom traveled widely in Europe, had several interviews with Benito Mussolini, and was decorated by several foreign governments. At one time he was treasurer of the Inter-Parliamentary Union. In spite of this he seldom spoke or wrote of world politics. Newspaper reporters attribute his appointment to the Foreign Affairs Committee as a result of his wife's request because she liked Washington parties and his new position "would mean more of them." Bascom Timmons, a newspaperman, took the request to Speaker Garner who was amenable, but remarked, "Why good God! He might be chairman some day!" He gradually worked up in the committee and as ranking Democrat he rendered yeoman's service in furthering the Good Neighbor policy.

Garner's prophesy came true in 1938 when Bloom became acting chairman during Chairman Sam McReynolds' illness. The Tennesee veteran died the following year and Bloom, over the opposition of the isolationists, was elected to the permanent chairmanship. Though rumored that the White House was fearful of Bloom's accession to the chairmanship, the latter soon won the confidence of the administration when he led the fight for revision of the Neutrality Act and sponsored a resolution synthesizing the administration's program for helping the anti-Axis powers in the event of aggression.

Bloom has made a success of his newest job. Because of both his position and his hard work he has become one of the "inner circle" and has attended many of the "midnight conferences" at the White House. He was one of the eleven congressional leaders who was given the confidential war plans mapped at the Casablanca conference. Likewise he was among those on hand to greet the President at the White House late in 1943 when the President returned from the Teheran and Cairo conferences. His relations with the State Department are close, so close in fact that one Capital observer referred to him as the "mouthpiece and stooge of the State Department."

In February, 1941, Viscount Halifax, the British ambassador, paid a courtesy call on Bloom to ask about the "timetable" of the lend-lease bill and the parliamentary procedure to be followed in connection with it. This drew criticism from opponents of the measure, but it illustrates the fact that the British embassy appreciated Bloom's role in Congress.

Generally speaking, the Congressman has been quick to approve and commit himself on proposals of the administration. This has fostered a high degree of party responsibility as far as the House Foreign Affairs Committee is concerned. For example, in May, 1941, Secretary of War Stimson called for the navy to protect shipments to Britain. While Tom Connally, chairman of the Senate Foreign Relation's Committee was slow to commit himself, Bloom immediately praised the Secretary as having "done the country a great service in presenting so clearly the obvious truths which confront us and which many ignore. I stand behind him 100 per cent." Likewise in 1941 he called for a firmer attitude towards Japan than most of his colleagues in the House. Just four months before Pearl Harbor he told the press, "We must let Japan know that we intend to protect our interests in the Far East."

However, Bloom sometimes has been slow to understand the necessity for change. One such example occurred in May, 1941, when the several members of the executive branch were demanding the repeal of the neutrality law. He told reporters, "I have an open mind on it. The way I feel it does not make a particle of difference whether the law is repealed or not. There may be certain parts that should be repealed and others retained. Recent events may have changed the situation so that we should repeal the law." Dynamic leadership requires that the chairman of such an important committee refuse to hedge on such a vital policy as neutrality. A Foreign Affairs chairman must be fully aware of events and the implication of legislation in terms of them.

Because of sharp differences of opinion among the members of the Foreign Affairs Committee, Bloom's job as chairman has not been easy. Several Republican members accused him of limiting hearings of the opposition to expedite passage of amendments to the neutrality bill and boycotted one of the hearings. Bloom was firm in lecturing these members for their action. He works hard at his job and has given up hobbies, most of his vacations, and much of his former social life in order to spend more time in reading and studying the international picture. He often retires early to read in bed on these matters and frequently continues his reading before rising in the morning. Several times a week he calls upon the Legislative Reference Library for material. He does not seek the advice of many persons or experts on foreign affairs but relies primarily on reading, committee discussions, and visits with executive officials to make up his mind. He also relies on the State

Department for much of his information, apparently making as much use of it as of the Legislative Reference Library, if not more. It will be recognized of course that this can work both as an asset and as a liability.

Since Pearl Harbor, the chairman has used several effective techniques in the committee. Formerly the Republican committee members sat at the foot of the table while the majority members gathered around the chairman at the head of the table. Now Bloom has seated the majority members on one side of him and the Republicans on the other. He spends long hours working for unanimous support of all of the committee members on all measures to be reported. From Pearl Harbor to March, 1945, every measure so reported received the approval of all the committee.

In this plan to present a united front, the committee often anticipates the objections which will arise on the floor. After some discussion this leads to the designation of various committee members to answer points raised by the opposition. Again this relieves Bloom of carrying the burden and passes the honors around to others. The Republicans have been cooperative and Bloom's strategy has been remarkably effective in conducting the committee's work in a nonpartisan and cordial atmosphere. Similarly, instead of assuming full command of all committee measures on the floor of the house, Bloom has passed the position around to rank and file members. For example, several statements on post-war collaboration had been in the committee before the one proposed by Mr. Fulbright. Nevertheless, he and the committee agreed on the Fulbright Resolution and let the author present and carry the responsibility for its successful passage in the House.

The chairman has insisted that the House of Representatives should have a greater share in writing the peace. He has asked Republicans and Democrats to pledge themselves that peace treaties be validated as "agreements" by a majority of both Houses, a procedure used in authorizing lend-lease and the creation of the United Nations Relief and Rehabilitation Administration. "It is absurd," he asserts, "that a two-thirds majority of the Senate is required only when the final vote is

taken on approval or disapproval of a treaty. . . . This seems
to me to be placing a dangerous power in the hands of a minority and to be completely contrary to the democratic theory of
government." [5]

Bloom makes but few speeches on the floor of the House;
these are usually only the perfunctory speeches made by many
chairmen when their bills come up for consideration. On foreign affairs his leadership is exerted largely in the committee
room rather than on the House floor. It has been consciously
directed at a co-operative effort to develop policies acceptable
to both parties. He tried without success to have both parties
adopt identical platforms on foreign policy in 1944.

Sol Bloom has praised the military victories of the Soviet
Union and has argued for continued lend-lease to her. On the
course of our post-war relations with Russia he has been silent.
Though befriending the small nations of Europe and pledging
help to them, he inclines to deal in generalities rather than in
specific blueprints. This holds true of his views on many other
problems. For example, in July, 1943, he told a radio audience
that Congress "looks to the creation of appropriate international machinery with power adequate to establish and maintain a just and lasting peace. . . . This resolution is not a commitment in support of any particular peace plan or treaty. The
United States, always free, remains free to pass judgment upon
any plan to achieve world peace . . . we are not bound to any
peace plan, but we will co-operate in drawing up one that we
can approve." [6]

In his office, Bloom will tell you in vigorous, idealistic terms
that peace can be maintained only if there is "justice, equality,
brotherhood, and the sharing of goods among all nations." He
dislikes the word "foreign" and insists that "international"
should be used to describe relationships with other countries.
"Domestic policy," he says, "cannot be separated from our

5. *New York Times*, Apr. 16, 1944. He has also prepared a nineteen-page
pamphlet on the subject entitled, *The Treaty Making Power* (obtainable at his
office).

6. Sol Bloom, *Our Heritage* (New York, 1944), pp. 438-40. His relatively few
pronouncements on international co-operation will be found in this volume
(pp. 396-457).

policy toward other nations." When questioned, the chairman will tell you that he favors trial and punishment of the war criminals, the Dumbarton Oaks proposals, and an international food board. In his judgment, "the peace should not be written by cynical diplomats, and the common man should have a share in planning it."

No one will disagree with the need for ethical values in maintaining the peace. On ways to implement these ideals, however, the Congressman has been inarticulate. Up to the Crimea conference, he had spoken or written but little on the techniques of international organization. Moreover, he appeared desirous of avoiding a stand on specific policies in this connection. After the Declaration of the conference was made public, he issued no critique of it except for a general endorsement. Bloom seems content to rely upon his role of working for harmony in the committee room and following the executive on vital matters of foreign policy.

At the same time this cautious practice has kept him from being classed with such leaders as Senators Vandenberg, Ball, and Fulbright who have exerted far more influence on public opinion. To many, Bloom's failure to speak out is regarded as wisdom; to others, it is a sign of mediocre leadership. Some who share his view on a greater role for the House in writing the peace regard his admittedly good committee work as insufficient and have felt he should make more public pronouncements. It might be noted here that the chairman of the Senate Foreign Relations Committee, Tom Connally, has, like Bloom, made few speeches on post-war problems. Does this not pose the interesting question as to whether chairmen of congressional committees on foreign affairs are expected to be outspoken in the details of international organization and procedure?

By reason of his position, Bloom was named as one of the delegates to the San Francisco conference to prepare the security charter. He rendered valuable service in the committee deliberations of that historic meeting. On returning to Washington, however, he made no outstanding address on the conference as did his fellow delegates, Senators Connally and

Vandenburg. Judging from his past record, it seems doubtful if he will be one of the dynamic leaders in the House and before the bar of public opinion in implementing the decisions reached in San Francisco and subsequent sessions of the United Nations.

15

ALBEN W. BARKLEY

"Reservoir of Energy"

BY J. B. SHANNON

W HEN SENATE MAJORITY LEADER, ALBEN BARKLEY, "broke" with President Franklin D. Roosevelt in 1944 over the latter's ill-advised veto of a new tax bill, the episode created a sensation. A fleeting but embarrassed hero among his erstwhile bitter foes, the Kentuckian emerged from this political tempest in a teapot a larger and more national figure, apparently leader of the Senate in substance as well as in title. Several causes lay back of his new declaration of independence.

Political observers, unmindful of Barkley's long record as a successful vote-getter and because of presidential support, have unfairly described him as a coat-tail rider and have referred to him as a Roosevelt "stooge." The Kentuckian has tasted but one defeat, and then by a small margin in a primary. In 1938, Barkley happened to be the instrument chosen by Democratic conservatives to beat the President. Many local observers are still dubious whether Roosevelt's intervention aided or injured Barkley, who had the support of the largest labor organizations, the powerful Farm Bureau Federation with its large membership in Western Kentucky, where Democrats are most numerous and loyal, and the Louisville Democratic organization. Finally, as the Senator appraised the situation in 1938, Chandler opposed the WPA and Barkley favored it, so why should not workers on WPA support Mr. Barkley? Political pressure was unnecessary. As a matter of fact, the regions in Kentucky where WPA employment was highest, but traditionally and consistently Republican, opposed Barkley both in the primary and the final election. Yet Barkley was labeled a "yes man," or a "rubber stamp." However thick his political skin, he smarted under these repeated accusations. The President's reliance in his tax veto upon the advice of the Treasury instead of that of the Senate leader was the final straw, for Barkley was subject to all the repressed and unrepressed resentment of Congress over growing executive power. Keenly aware that he was neither the real leader of the Senate majority nor the President's trusted representative in the Senate, his position had become intolerable. A disciple of Woodrow Wilson, a firm believer in the parliamentary system, with resignation as a device for party control, it was natural that Barkley should resign.

If the Democrats failed to elect a President in 1944, as seemed not unlikely in February, 1944, but controlled the Senate, as appeared probable at that time, Barkley would be only the personal agent of the defeated candidate or, at most, of a former President. If he foresaw his own re-election to the Senate leadership, as he probably did, his position would be tremendously strengthened in case of a Republican victory. After his *coup* he could speak candidly to the President and let his judgment be unfettered by the accusation of disloyalty or political obligation. Barkley's dramatic break with President Roosevelt without doubt enhanced his standing with voters in his home state, notwithstanding their deep attachment to the Chief Executive, and helped to remove the stigma of dependence.[1] To understand the Kentuckian's contemporary and prospective political behavior it is necessary to probe more deeply into his nature and the social forces that have been the mainsprings in his career.

The life story of Alben W. Barkley epitomizes a familiar pattern of American political folklore and presents an epic of which Abraham Lincoln and James A. Garfield furnish a combined prototype—from log cabin to national fame. Human personality is protectively colored by the environment in which it grows. The character traits of any man reflect the cultural milieu from which he springs. Kentucky has at least six distinct

1. Barkley received 7,500 greater plurality in Kentucky than President Roosevelt in 1944, but 7,500 fewer votes.

geographic and cultural regions. The phosphatic Bluegrass fertilized the political roots of the Breckinridges and Clays; the Pennyroyal and the more fertile South gave Jefferson Davis to the Confederacy; while the stony Knobs bred Abraham Lincoln. It is the Jackson Purchase, the remote western part of the state which has produced Alben Barkley and Irvin Cobb. The last frontier of the state, it formed a core of Jacksonian democracy, the most intensely Southern and Democratic of all sections of the state, hence the local title the "Gibraltar of Democracy." Only once, in 1928, has a Republican presidential nominee carried a single county in the Jackson Purchase. Ordinarily Democratic majorities run from 60 to 85 per cent.

The Barkleys trace the name back to a Burkleigh who crossed the Channel with the Conqueror. Lost in the mists of time, the family reappeared as adherents of John Knox in Scotland and joined the Scotch-Irish Presbyterians who migrated two centuries ago into Pennsylvania. Pioneer nomads, they wandered into North Carolina, where many of the Barkley tribe lingered. One of these was a Presbyterian elder whose ability to pray both loud and long is a family tradition.

The Barkley family has not been devoid of politicians. A cousin of the Senator's father, Adlai Stevenson, was vice-president under Cleveland, while another cousin was a congressman whose chief claim to fame was his success in reducing the tariff on quinine, for which he was rewarded by appointment as minister to Peru. Alben's maternal grandfather lost his life serving under the Confederate raider, John Hunt Morgan. Grandfather Barkley built a log cabin in a remote part of Graves County, still inaccessible in certain seasons because of poor roads. In this rather commodious log house "Dear Alben" was born November 24, 1877, a fact to warm the heart of any campaign publicity agent, but never fully exploited. Alben, the eldest of eight children, is the only one, according to local narrators, who has ever " 'mounted to anything."

Traditionally and culturally this poor farm boy had to be a Democrat. Circumstances pushed him towards the leadership of an agrarian people. The panic of the 1890's forced Alben's father to sell his meager fifty acres to pay an accumulation of debts. Forced into tenancy, the elder Barkley worked inter-mittently as a railroad section hand. It is not strange that Alben Barkley in later years became a leader of a farmer-labor combination, the "New Deal," a twentieth century coalition not unlike Jackson's successful union of the last century. The elder Barkley seems to have been a character strongly re-sembling the Thomas Lincoln model. When interviewed about his prominent son, he observed saltily that "Alben was the smartest s.o.b. to come from that part of the country." How-ever, he was intelligent enough to follow the advice of one of Alben's early school teachers who suggested that the lad pos-sessed marked ability and should be continued in school. The poverty-stricken farmer moved to Clinton, where he entered his promising boy in Marvin College, really a land grant acad-emy, sponsored by the Methodists. In a fashion reminiscent of Garfield, young Alben paid his tuition by service as janitor.

The Barkley boys were not handsome. A local lawyer says a glance at the young Barkleys was sufficient to convince him of the truth of the Darwinian theory. Fellow students and townsmen dubbed the four boys beginning with Alben, "Big Monk," "Baboon," "Ape," and "Little Monk." As a student, Alben was a "plodder" who early displayed a great fondness for declamation and debate. A part of the folk culture of the region included "public speakin's" as well as the old Southern court day. The youthful Barkley developed an aptitude likely to lead to politics. Commencements attracted people for miles around, many arriving before sundown in order to get seats where they could listen to the budding orators. Legend has it that Alben never lost a debate.

His A.B. degree attained, Barkley borrowed $175.00 to enable him to enter Emory University, Georgia. A loan fund was open to "paupers," the Senator remarks, and "I qualified in that respect." After a year, his funds exhausted, young Barkley returned to Kentucky where he became a law clerk, amanuensis, and general "roustabout" in the office of Judge Bishop of Paducah, a character made famous as Judge Priest by Irvin Cobb. Promoted to court reporter at $50.00 a month, he found this job a stepping stone to politics, for his duties included considerable contact with the public, paying off jurors, meeting witnesses, and similar tasks. In future campaigns those acquaintances in every part of the county "pulled" for him. In addition he received an apprenticeship in the law, especially the technique of persuading juries. He saved sufficient funds to attend the University of Virginia Law School for a brief period, after which he was admitted to the bar.

In 1905, at the age of twenty-eight, two years after his marriage, Barkley ran for county attorney, the usual first step on the political ladder. Totally without funds, his cause seemed hopeless, but he made a house-to-house canvass, a considerable portion of it on foot; later an uncle lent him a gray mule to speed up his campaign. Before the end of the contest he swapped the mule for a horse and finished his electioneering in "style." Suffice it to say, he won by a landslide, receiving more votes than his two opponents combined. The county government had been conducted loosely. Barkley successfully prosecuted one or two former officials. With a reputation as a political reformer, the people "asked" him to become county judge. Elected without opposition, this position provided his only executive experience, primarily in building roads.

In 1912, Barkley was elected to Congress. In his primary campaign, he made his youth the basis of his propaganda. He lived in the most populous county in his district, had been born in the next largest, and had attended school in another. An opponent complained bitterly that Barkley carried his school house and his birthplace with him, setting them down on the other side of the road wherever he spoke. The success of his tactic is shown by the fact that Barkley received almost a fourth of his total vote from his native county, and nearly one-half from the counties in which he had lived. For seven successive terms Barkley was returned to the House of Representatives without primary opposition and by top-heavy majorities of approximately two-thirds of the final vote. The country lawyer was established in the "Gibraltar of Democracy."

What were the impelling forces which had pushed young Barkley so rapidly to the fore? During the 1890's, Populism had many adherents in western Kentucky. In some Purchase counties, including the one where Barkley was born, Green-backism and afterwards Populism had outstripped the Republican vote. When Bryan first captured the Democratic nomination for the presidency the Barkley family was delighted. The Senator recalls the hot summer day in 1896 when he was plowing through a stumpy field with a heavy log chain on his plow breaking down the weeds for the next furrow. To quote him, he fell into a "spasm of blasphemy." At this juncture his landlord appeared on a "slick black horse." The sharp contrast between the two struck the tenant farmer's son. His landlord told him of the nomination for the presidency of William Jennings Bryan whose "Cross of Gold" speech charmed Barkley and his family. The school boy and his fellows spent many hours declaiming the famous oration and Bryan tariff speeches from stumps near Marvin College, with the trees as their principal audience. His father was terribly disappointed by Bryan's defeat, while an uncle spent a year in bed sickened by the matchless orator's loss. Bryan like Lincoln, the great martyr folk-god of pioneer agrarian democracy, was a symbol of achievement for the tenant farmer's son born in the persimmon and sassafras "barrens" of the Jackson Purchase.

Arriving in Washington in 1913, the freshman representative of thirty-five fell under the spell of Woodrow Wilson, who, according to the Senator, has been the dominating intellectual influence in his life. Wilson made him a "New Dealer." Always a liberal in thought, he has believed in adapting government to changing circumstances. Wilson he constantly refers to as his political mentor, though the ultimate source of his political philosophy was Thomas Jefferson. It was Wilson who gave him the faith and the ideal. Barkley believes Franklin D. Roosevelt was similarly influenced by the former Princeton Professor of Politics.

With Wilson and Bryan was a third personality who influenced his life—oddly enough, Champ Clark. He found the elder Clark a handsome and lovable man with an inexhaustible fund of stories—legends and anecdotes of the great and near great. Barkley, himself an excellent raconteur, has always been fond of stories. In Clark he found a master of the art of story-telling. From him he acquired the habit of browsing in second-hand book stores and purchasing out-of-print biographies with their half-truthful and half-fictional episodes from the lives of Clay, Webster, Calhoun, and other politicians. A young apprentice in the craft himself, he was an apt pupil at the feet of the great master craftsmen in his chosen profession, politics.

In 1923, Barkley ran for governor. The "organization" of the Democratic Party was controlled by the "interests," in this case horse racing and coal mining. Barkley's platform called for a coal production tax and abolition of pari-mutuel race track gambling. At the age of forty-three, he undertook to challenge the political Goliath of Kentucky, a bipartisan machine, well oiled with campaign funds and reinforced by regional and sectional jealousies.

In his intense campaign, he won the sobriquet of "iron man," on account of his ability to make five or six speeches a day, each lasting from an hour and a half to two hours. He spoke as many as sixteen hours in one day! On one occasion, he actually achieved the feat of fourteen speeches in one day, albeit they were somewhat shorter than his usual order. Driving from one town to another, sleeping in intervals between speeches, Barkley sometimes existed on two or three hours of sleep a day. He was able to sleep in a railway station, a train, or an automobile, strongly resembling Bryan in this characteristic. During the 1938 primary, his snore could be heard outside his room sixty seconds by the watch after he retired. Like Bryan, also, he has an enormous appetite, eats huge quantities of all kinds of food, but he is especially fond of sweets. As a boy he had challenged the admiration of a threshing crew by the tremendous quantities of Irish potatoes which he consumed. During the gubernatorial campaign, Barkley fattened and at the end of the contest seemed in better health than at the beginning.

He lost the 1923 primary contest by nine thousand votes, but some informed persons still believe that he actually won. His campaign established him as a power in Kentucky politics for he swept western Kentucky, receiving 48 per cent of the total vote in the state. He was given the senatorial nomination by default in 1926. Kentucky had two Republican United States senators, a situation without precedent in the state's political history. The Democratic party organization wished to get Barkley out of the state since he was a thorn in their flesh locally. Typically he toured the state from end to end defeating the Republican incumbent by a comfortable majority in one of the two statewide Democratic victories during the Republican twenties. Though he lost Louisville, his vote was heavy enough in western Kentucky to make Barkley the first United States senator from the Jackson Purchase.

In 1932, Barkley had little opposition in the primary, and his prominence on the national scene as the keynote speaker in the Democratic convention, together with the Roosevelt landslide, elected him easily. However, he received sharp criticism in his party for voting for a tariff on coal and a few other Kentucky products. His long record as a personal and political dry was embarrassed by the Democratic platform pledged to the repeal of the Eighteenth Amendment. His advocacy of this platform was consistent with his vigorous support of Alfred E. Smith in 1928, when home folk stood loyally by him, only one county deserting in the Republican avalanche. Keynote speaker in 1936, Barkley was chairman of the Third Term Convention, and in 1944 placed Roosevelt in nomination.

The dramatic events which made him majority floor leader in the fierce battle over the Supreme Court reform measure in 1937 are well known. This occasion won him the title "Dear Alben," even though the President had used it before.

What manner of man is Barkley? He stands five feet, eleven inches and formerly weighed over two hundred pounds. Recently he has systematically reduced. His sturdy, even stocky, appearance has been altered until he looks much taller, more "senatorial." The layers of fat which had gathered around his waist line to give him a typical pyknic shape, have disappeared. Short arms and large, hairy, freckled hands show the effects of early exercise on the plow. His hand clasp is firm but not crushing.

The Barkley chest is broad and masculine, enclosing probably the most powerful lungs in American political life since death silenced the voice of Huey Long. Barkley's feats of oratory are phenomenal. During the 1938 campaign, inspired on one occasion by a huge crowd, he spoke for one hour and thirty-five minutes, shouting all the time. His voice, usually husky at the beginning, soon warms up to become clear and resonant; before a crowd of ten thousand a loud speaker is largely superfluous. Barkley's protruding jaw is his most prominent facial feature. He has a manner of thrusting it out whenever he makes a point 'or reaches a peroration. Frequently he accompanies this gesture by a queer goose-like twisting of his neck. His big ears are not out of proportion on a sizeable square head. A large orator's mouth, filled with well preserved teeth, is buttressed by a broad nose flattish on the bridge, tending to bluntness at the tip. Grayish blue eyes are set under a high receding forehead. Brown hair streaked with gray, usually cut short, covers his head. His temples have whitened, the chief indication of the Senator's sixty-eight years, though the lines around his eyes are evidence of his approaching three score and ten. His skin still glows with life, a clear testimony of a healthy body.

Publicly Barkley impresses onlookers as a man always posing —in the popular stereotype of a distinguished and dignified senator—a too conscious effort to be a Webster or a Clay. On the stump he relaxes his pose to be the true crowd compeller he is. Barkley's chief forte as a political leader is his oratorical ability, but sources of his strength as an orator are hard to analyze. His long speeches are rather pedestrian in nature, frequently alliterative and characterized by a plebeian play on words, or a humorous touch calculated to appeal to rural audiences. Accordingly, an analysis of Barkley's power depends largely upon an exposition of his campaign techniques. How is it possible for him to fill his speeches with figures, sometimes long paragraphs of statistics, and still hold his audience? In a fashion, he is always the prosecuting attorney. The vehemence of his attack, the vituperation of his language, and the vigor of his voice are such that they sway his crowds. In 1923, his opponents were "political pirates and buccaneers."

In 1932, ice water not warm human blood flowed in the veins of Herbert Hoover. Hoover was the great engineer who "ditched and drained the whole damned country in four years." His oratorical vocabulary is ample while his private vocabulary is adequate both in variety and force.

Whether he reasons with his crowd or not, he indulges in the more subtle flattery of making them think he is reasoning with them. He can rouse his listeners to a fever pitch of excitement by raising his voice, flailing his arms and going into a spell of near self-hypnotism. With his rising voice, his words flow more swiftly, his gestures become more forceful, his face reddens, and he seems near a stroke from paroxysms of rage as he assails his opponents. These apoplectic spasms are intermittent, however, for he can talk in a conversational tone, his voice carrying easily to his entire audience. This is his manner on the floor of the Senate.

Barkley is not a typical machine politician. Ordinary patronage seems to bore him, though his immediate family has not been neglected. Sometimes he is embarrassed because of his previous failures to reply to patronage appeals. During the depression, Barkley received as many as a thousand letters a day, most of them asking for jobs. Five hundred persons called at his home within three weeks after the 1938 primary asking for jobs. Patronage he regards as a liability rather than an asset. His first post office selection probably created "eleven enemies and one ingrate." The pressure for jobs leaves too little time for reading or preparation of a legislative program. However, the entire federal bench in Kentucky has really been selected by Barkley. One appointee managed his gubernatorial campaign while another managed his senatorial campaign in 1938. A third is the son of an active district manager in 1923.

In the campaign of 1938, Barkley met his acid test. An older man who had lived in Washington for a quarter century, out of close touch with local politics, he was challenged by a young and vigorous campaigner, acknowledged by most men as the best entertainer on the stump in contemporary Kentucky politics. Seemingly Barkley was on the defensive, although his opponent presented no significant issue. Governor Chandler accused the Senator of traveling too much, criticized him for going to Europe, poked fun at him because his daughters married non-Kentuckians who held federal jobs; called him "Old Alben." The Senator modified his strategy accordingly, though he contends he developed no conscious technique of appeal, save "telling the people the truth." However, he found his listeners wanted him to reply to the personal attacks on himself by making similar accusations against his opponent. The politician must give his crowds what they want—entertainment and conflict.

One of Barkley's platform performances became a campaign classic, a device stumbled upon rather than consciously designed. Repeated in each speech, the Senator requested reporters not to print his masterpiece lest publication would spoil its effect on later audiences. Nor did he tell the "story" on the radio till toward the close of the campaign, because he thought its flavor was such that it might shock some women voters. Illustrative of Barkley's campaign behavior, the story bears a condensed repetition.

Chandler's campaign slogan, printed beneath his picture throughout Kentucky, was: "A man of action not of words!" Barkley began his recital slowly, almost softly: "I have been criticized because I went to Europe twice. The first time I went on a mission of peace. In this troubled world who in the United States but Happy Chandler would criticize me for trying to bring peace on earth?"

"On the second occasion I went to visit my grandchild in Paris, France. My daughter was there with her husband. They were making $2,700 a year, and I had to send them money once in a while so they could make out. I went over to see my grandchild on his second birthday. What mother in this audience will criticize me for going to see my grandchild?"

"But the Governor is a traveling man also. I have never taken a cruise in the Caribbean. I have never been to Trinidad. I have never been to Porto Rico where they make rum. I have never been to Mexico City to watch the dancing senoritas. I have never been to Miami nor to Biloxi—Why Happy has drunk mineral water at Hot Springs, Arkansas, White Sulphur

Springs, West Virginia, Hot Springs, Virginia, and French Lick, Indiana, where Pluto is king." (Pause) "NO WONDER THE GOVERNOR IS A MAN OF ACTION!" The Senator would pause for the first ripple of laughter to roll over his crowd, but as he started to resume his speech a great roar of laughter and applause would burst forth as women nudged each other behind discreet fans. Crowds never failed to approve. Omission of any part of the background lessened its effectiveness and many repetitions were required to perfect his technique until his anecdote became the mordant weapon it was in poking fun at his opponent. The inauspicious illness of the Governor at the climax of the campaign added to the force of the account making its mass effect much greater.

Among the traits which have made Alben Barkley a political leader, his powerful physique can not be overlooked. His opponent in 1938 was a former football player, coach, and all-round athlete, twenty years Barkley's junior, who boasted he would have "Old Alben" in bed within six weeks. Instead, "Old Alben" had Happy in bed, grew stronger all the time, and ended his campaign in fine fettle, calmly sleeping on his lawn while the people voted. Cautious in all respects, Barkley was careful of his diet, ate in smaller quantities than usual, and watched his drinking water, especially after Governor Chandler's illness presumably from drinking ice water. Barkley attributes his stamina to the labors of his early farm life. His father cleared ten or twelve acres of ground every year. The son who helped fell trees and clear debris in winter plowed the cut-over land in the spring. This work toughened his muscles, hardened his frame, and built his lung capacity. The hardships of his youth have proved a reservoir of energy in his mature years. At sixty-seven, he made seven campaign speeches a day.

Alben Barkley possesses political courage. In 1928, he went down the line for Al Smith, fighting vigorously in a losing battle, though his own political future in dry and Protestant Kentucky might be endangered; but he has been a Democrat first, last, and always. It was not easy or popular to compel some of his Southern colleagues to attend Senate sessions to secure a quorum during debate on poll tax repeal. Finally, he denounced Franklin Roosevelt's veto of a tax measure, an action a more timid man would have hesitated to take.

No glamor boy, the Kentucky Senator has in his political armory physical power, a resonant voice, a tenacious memory, a reputation for integrity, for persistence, and for personal democracy. Typical of his profession he is a joiner. His education in a Methodist institution led him to affiliate with that denomination when he was seventeen. He belongs to Rotary and Lions, to a golf club in Washington, and to the Alfalfa Club. Besides he is an Odd Fellow, an Elk, a Moose, and formerly was a Red Man. He returns annually to the little town where he went to school. In the courthouse yard he greets old schoolmates, calling them by their first names; he talks over old threshing experiences with farm hands; he dines with college chums who respect but do not intensely love him. He has not forgotten his friends—the wife of a classmate is postmistress at Clinton, his college town; a close personal friend was head of WPA and later of OPA in Kentucky. A keen sense of humor stands Barkley in good stead not only on the stump but in face-to-face contacts. He does not slap backs too obviously. His face is too grim for magnetic smiles and his features too rugged for glamorous grins—but he can laugh; he is genial, while his voice always carries a friendly tone to his audiences. A gift for the honeyed and flattering phrase has grown with the mellowing years. At a birthday party in his honor, given by a wealthy eighty-year-old Washington hostess, Barkley replied to a toast offered him, in his best and most charming manner; "May she live to look her age."

Barkley's amiability is not of the clownish type. In fact, he is a bit pompous in public and certainly his formal speech-making is frequently both ponderous and verbose. Despite an apparent public dignity, privately he is simplicity itself. There is no assumption of airs, no effort to impress, very little flair for publicity, in striking contrast with his junior colleague from Kentucky.

The love of the countryside is still in Alben Barkley. A few years ago he purchased a small farm on the outskirts of Paducah. The old brick house has been remodeled to be comfortable and commodius but not elaborate or luxurious. This small country estate fills out the stereotype of a squirearchy which an ambitious country boy might have formed of the Henry Clay type of statesman—ante-bellum Southern style. For Senator Barkley is patently serious and evidently sincere in his wish to be a statesman. He feels that it is exceedingly difficult to convince the public that a politician is ever motivated by anything but self-interest, for columnists and newspaper correspondents looking from the galleries develop a cynicism which they attribute to legislators themselves. The Kentuckian does not remain aloof from party or personal alliances. He is a *party leader.* "Loyalty" is the cohesive force which makes American politics function. A long-time associate thinks "loyalty" is Barkley's leading trait. He can make and keep political bargains.

Seniority has brought Barkley membership in some of the most powerful Senate committees, including Foreign Relations, Finance, and Interstate Commerce. Finally, as leader of the Senate majority, he is one of the keystones in the national policy-forming arch. Strategically, he is liaison man between the executive and the upper house of Congress. In a measure, he is the funnel through which presidential ideas flow into the Senate to be processed. Bridging the gap between the executive and legislative branches of government under American conditions is a task beset with pitfalls hazardous enough to daunt the most courageous and skillful political leader. In a limited sense, the majority leader occupies a parliamentary position similar to a British premier, but has neither the power nor prestige of that office. His principal power arises from his control over the time of the Senate; his greatest prestige from direct contact with the President and the administration.

Undoubtedly the increasing sharpness in tone of executive communications to Congress was a factor which brought about Barkley's oratorical outburst against the President. Placed on the defensive in Senate debate, because of his relation to the executive, Barkley's strategy is to puncture the opposition by alert questions, frequently turning a wisecrack, sometimes crudely, at the expense of his more "windy" assailants. In general, however, the Senator is conciliatory and reasonable in attitude, and seeks to reconcile different points of view. This is not a particularly easy task for one whose whole career, before 1932, had been devoted to vigorous opposition.

Barkley's position as leader is an unenviable one. To forge a coherent international policy between ardent internationalist Claude Pepper and equally ardent isolationist Burton Wheeler is not easy. To develop agreement between a rabid pro-labor Senator like Guffey and a labor baiter like "Pappy" O'Daniel is impossible. To keep a semblance of party unity between Negro-hating Bilbo and Senator Wagner, advocate of poll tax repeal and exponent of liberal legislation, is a superhuman task. Barkley lives in a border state where treatment of the Negro has never been as harsh as in the deeper South, for Negro voting is unencumbered by a poll tax in Kentucky. As a matter of fact, for some years a Negro has served in the Kentucky legislature. Barkley was reared in a region with a strong pro-Southern bias and with a relatively high Negro population. Accordingly, he is well equipped by experience to understand the delicate racial issue, one of the chief divisive factors in the Democratic Party.

The Kentuckian has shown growing impatience with wartime regulations. After the Republican victory in the Kentucky gubernatorial contest in 1943, he complained that the people did not understand the necessity for OPA, and were voting against unpleasant, detailed regulations. Later, Barkley put up an intense and successful fight for a higher ceiling for Kentucky's chief cash crop, tobacco. This was undoubtedly an effort to soothe the feelings of farmers who, impatient with high feed costs accentuated by prolonged drought, were boiling up into an "agin it" mood in Kentucky. Previously, despite administration opposition, Barkley supported higher wages for his old friends, the railway workers. In 1933, likewise, he had voted to override President Roosevelt's veteran payment cuts. In other words, the Senator is alert to the pressure of powerful organized groups—labor, farmers, and veterans—but what successful politician is not?

The Majority Leader may be expected to continue his advocacy of legislation favorable to farmers, labor, and veterans. He will oppose poll taxes and vote for a federal anti-lynching bill. He supported a federal ballot for soldiers, arguing that if the Constitution authorized Congress to put soldiers where they could not get state ballots, then Congress could send them the ballots. Congress has constitutional power to restore what it has taken away. Barkley will support a world organization as strong as or stronger than the League of Nations. He staunchly advocated the United States' entrance into the League during the 1920's, when the League issue was very unpopular in America. His loyalty to Woodrow Wilson has never wavered. In the 1944 campaign, he discussed the League more openly than any other national Democratic leader, and his overwhelming re-election on that issue immensely strengthened his position.

Whatever else he may be, Alben Barkley is not a rubber stamp. The agrarian liberalism which is so prominent in the New Deal was bred in the bone of this tenant farmer's son. It was part and parcel of his social heritage. He preached this doctrine long before the presidency of Franklin Roosevelt. If he followed Roosevelt's leadership it was because the interests of his constituents and his philosophy were fashioned in the same pattern as those of the President.

The Kentuckian is now an elder statesman. For a third of a century he has served in the national legislature and has another six-year term. He has had the longest consecutive tenure in the Senate of any Kentuckian. Likewise, Barkley has been majority leader longer than any other man. It is only natural that he should begin to look backward somewhat, and with pride. If he had his life to live over again he would follow much the same course, he declares. The Senator very frankly admires the English system of making politics a professional career. Learning the ways of legislative bodies requires years of study and experience. The Senator feels he could have made more money by working as hard in private life as he has in public. Financially, he says, he is about where he was when he started his political career.

Although Barkley may not be one of the ablest senators of our generation, since he has no creative legislative record like Norris or Wagner, yet he appears a great statesman when compared with patronage hunters like McKellar or demagogues of the Bilbo-O'Daniel-Langer type. The Kentuckian can rouse the rabble too, but his record indicates he uses his demagoguery for purposes other than purely self-aggrandizement. Perhaps this is the acid test of practical political ethics in a representative democracy—to employ the means necessary to achieve political power but to use this power substantially in the general interest rather than exclusively for self interest.

16

CLAUDE D. PEPPER
"Champion of the Belligerent Democracy"

BY FRANCIS P. LOCKE

W HEN HITLER BEGAN HIS WARS OF CONQUEST, THE MOST lurid spreader of the alarm on this side of the Atlantic was Senator Claude Denson Pepper of Florida. To his Catoesque role he brought youth, insight, and a vigor that verged on recklessness. He was served by a forensic equipment seldom seen in the modern day of the United States Senate.

His crusade catapulted him into international fame and assured him a place in history. The exact size of his niche will hardly be known until the war years have settled into perspective.

Before the war issue arose, Senator Pepper already had attained some national note. Near the end of the first Roosevelt administration he came to the Senate and at once established himself as an articulate and, in the main, a dogged and forthright liberal. He gained fresh prominence in 1944 by winning renomination in a primary which was watched by millions as a barometer of national political trends. Shortly thereafter he led the fight for the renomination of Vice-President Wallace at the Democratic national convention. He took an important part in the subsequent presidential campaign. He is now forty-five years old and, barring the accidents that often cut short political careers, he has plenty of time either to add to or detract from his record.

Senator Pepper has built his attainments from small beginnings. He sprang from the semi-sterile red soil of eastern Alabama. Although his parents were of old Southern stock, they were neither wealthy nor aristocratic. Both grandfathers

257

had fought for the Confederacy, a fact which has cushioned the Senator's pursuit of many sectionally unpopular policies.

On September 8, 1900, the date of Claude Pepper's birth, his father was farming 129 acres of cotton in a county (Chambers) which had brought forth Americans of such varied distinction as Tom Heflin and Joe Louis. When Claude was ten, the family moved to Camp Hill, a small town a few miles to the west. Claude graduated from high school as an athlete, editor, and debater. After teaching school a year, he entered the University of Alabama. Although earning most of his own support, he completed the course in three years, winning Phi Beta Kappa honors.

In the fall of 1921 he entered the Harvard Law School and graduated with distinction three years later. His law course represented the investment of a friendly banker in Camp Hill, who naturally did not realize that he was assisting at the birth of a New Dealer. Pepper taught a year in the law school of the University of Arkansas, then went to work for a legal firm in Perry, Florida, in those days a tough frontier town in the cattle country. Within a few months the sign men were called in to redecorate the office door. The lettering now read: "Davis and Pepper." The firm had the largest practice in town and young Pepper became president of the Chamber of Commerce.

At the age of twenty-eight, he took his place on the state Democratic committee and that same year was elected to the lower house of the legislature. In 1930 he was defeated for renomination. He then moved to Tallahassee, the state capital, joining the law firm of Curtis L. Waller, one-time secretary to Pat Harrison. The liaison was helpful to Pepper when he went to Washington six years later as a freshman senator.

From 1930 to 1934 Pepper served on various state boards and developed civic and fraternal alliances. By 1934 the time seemed ripe, and with faithful friends, abundant nerve, a gifted tongue, and a borrowed tuxedo, he plunged into the United States Senate race against Park Trammell. Trammell was a man of small senatorial distinction but of eighteen years seniority. He was invested with a myth of invincibility. Notwithstanding, Pepper ran an amazing race and would have won, had he not been "counted out" in Hillsborough County. He waived a recount and bided his time philosophically.

His sportsmanlike conduct enhanced his popularity, and when both Senators Trammell and Duncan U. Fletcher died in the summer of 1936, Pepper was nominated, without opposition, to the unexpired portion of the latter's term and won with little difficulty against a Republican in November. He was re-elected in 1938 to his first full term in the Senate.

Pepper took his seat on November 4, 1936, while the debris of the Roosevelt landslide was still crashing about the ears of Alfred Landon. At home, recovery was making headway, but Spain was already locked in civil war, and, eight months previously, Hitler had marched into the Rhineland.

Strangely enough, these early challenges to world peace did not arouse the young senator. In his college and law-school days he had developed an abiding reverence for Woodrow Wilson. In 1922, while still at Harvard, he had given his oratorical services to the unsuccessful campaign of the Massachusetts Democrats to unseat Senator Lodge. But in the late 'twenties and early 'thirties, he had been touched by the general post-war disillusionment. Traces of it clung to him when he came to the Senate. In 1937 he voted for the Neutrality Act and the Spanish arms embargo. Of course, these were administration measures and everyone else was voting for them, the count on the former being 62-6 and on the latter 80-0.

Pepper's awakening came in 1938, the autumn of the Munich crisis, when he was a delegate to the Interparliamentary Union at The Hague. He made important contacts in western Europe. He talked to Ambassadors Hugh Wilson, Kennedy, and Bullitt. He heard Hitler harangue the Nazi party congress and later sat within a few feet of him at the House of German Art in Munich. In a subsequent Senate speech, he described his impressions of the Fuehrer: "I looked him in the eye. I looked at the cut of his face. If I ever saw the stare of a man inconsiderate of all sentiment which stood in the way of the realization of his purpose, it was in the eye of Adolf Hitler. I looked at that face, and it seemed to be cut out of stone. . . ."

Pepper returned to the United States with a full appreciation of the menace of German Nazism. Likewise, he was one
of the first to size up the Japanese situation. On June 17, 1940,
he asked the Senate: "When Hitler and his combination . . .
attack Great Britain . . . do you think the Yellow men of the
East are to stay quiet in their territory, or do you not know
that they will raise their sword upon the East Indies?"

When war broke out in Europe, Pepper was the spearhead
of efforts to aid France and Britain. He often proposed steps
which the administration took weeks or months later. Almost
at once, he was accused of being a "trial balloon" for President
Roosevelt. He has always denied this and circumstances seem
to support the disclaimer. Although the President consulted
him now and then, and often expressed appreciation for what
he was doing, Pepper maintains there was no priming or collu-
sion.

A case in point occurred in May of 1940. It was the evening
of the day the Germans reached Abbéville. The lights were
winking out in western Europe, but they burned late that night
in the office of the Senator from Florida. The Senator was
drafting a resolution to authorize the President to transfer
planes from our own air forces to France and Britain. Seated
across the desk from him was Benjamin Cohen. The drafting
done, Cohen insisted that Pepper notify the President. Pepper
agreed and at eleven the next morning he telephoned Miss
Margaret LeHand, the President's secretary. He explained his
plan and asked Miss LeHand to report it to the President. He
said that unless Mr. Roosevelt should directly request him to
withhold the resolution, he would introduce it that day. When
no word had come from the White House by noon, Pepper
arose in the Senate, soon tense when he explained his purpose,
and offered his resolution. The air was heavily charged the
following morning when Pepper strode into the Foreign Relations Committee room. Senator Hiram Johnson was in a state
of great excitement. It would be a "disgrace," he raged, for the
resolution to go "an hour unrepudiated." Pleading for harmony, Senator Barkley asked Pepper to withdraw his resolution. Pepper declined and let it come to a vote. The vote was

12-1 against it. A poll of the absentees was quickly taken. Before the day ended the count was 22-1 against sending our planes to France and Britain.

Three days later Pepper, aided by Cohen and Walter Lippmann, framed an even broader resolution, an authentic forerunner of lend-lease. This time Senator Guffey voted with him. For almost a week Pepper spoke daily on the floor of the Senate. On May 26 he came close to dropping the "short of war" façade in a speech which the late Raymond Clapper described as "the most aggressive call that has echoed from any official source since the last war ended." The day of his first speech, most of Pepper's colleagues walked out on him. The second day a few remained. The third day there was a full-fledged debate. The fourth day, telegrams began coming in. The snowball was rolling. That snowball was the core of the lend-lease movement.

After Paris fell, Pepper offered a seven point program for national defense. His proposals embraced (1) full wartime powers for the president; (2) universal defense service; (3) presidential power to suspend army and navy seniority rules and all laws of Congress that might be found to interfere with maximum production, not excluding labor legislation; (4) power to suspend debt limitation; (5) authority to grant material aid and credit to nations fighting the Axis; (6) a tax program adequate for the national defense; (7) power to arrest dangerous aliens. In this speech Pepper talked in terms of 50,000 airplanes, a two-ocean navy, and a motorized army of between two and three million men. The Senate was not persuaded.

By votes and speeches Pepper supported every administration effort to loosen our neutrality, to aid our friends, and to arm the American nation. Often he was ahead of the administration in strategy, if not in conviction. He was first to propose the transfer of destroyers to Britain. At the Democratic national convention in 1940 he fought a bitter battle against the isolationist plank submitted by the Wheeler sub-committee on resolutions and was instrumental in obtaining a compromise which was barely satisfactory to the President.

Increasingly he took his crusade to the people. He made a long stump tour. He invaded Chicago and drew a crowd of 30,000 in the face of the *Tribune's* editorial challenge: "We warn Pepper against coming out here with his warmongering." He charged into Helena, Montana, and vainly challenged Senator Wheeler to share the platform with him. He carried the fight onto the campus of Harvard, scene of student anti-war demonstrations. Taking the offensive, he accused the non-interventionists of being "the real warmongers." He wrote newspaper and magazine articles and made numerous radio speeches. He derided the invokers of "international law," which, as he pounded home, Hitler had already "murdered." He was intolerant of those who talked as if Roosevelt were the menace to peace rather than Hitler. He charged them with crying out "against the surgeon who would amputate a wounded finger with charges of mayhem and assault, while they ignore the deadly infection that creeps toward the heart."

Through all this time he fought an uphill battle against apathy and indifference. A Miami congressman attacked him publicly. Important newspapers in his state ridiculed him. He stuck to his exposed position. During the debate on the conscription bill a group of war mothers descended on the Capitol lawn and hanged, mauled, and kicked an effigy labelled "Claude 'Benedict Arnold' Pepper." The ladies were in the tow of Mrs. Elizabeth Dilling, author of "The Red Network." Mrs. Dilling was later to be indicted for seditious activity.

Notified of his "death," the Senator made a graceful statement: "Knowing these women, like all other Americans, are sincere in their patriotism, placing America first and Hitler last, I feel that their hanging me in effigy is a splendid demonstration of what we are all trying to preserve, freedom of speech and freedom of action in the American way of doing things. I only hope that the spectators and those who hear about this business will feel that I also love America and that I am sincere in my daily efforts to defend the United States in liberty, the right of free speech and free action."

Raymond Clapper was struck by this "brief gem." It "breathed so deeply of the spirit of our free democracy," he wrote in his column the next day, "that it deserves its place among the classic utterances of our history. Lincoln could not have said it better." The Senator, however, had asked from his critics a greater forbearance than he himself had been willing to extend a fortnight previously to Colonel Charles A. Lindbergh. In an emotional speech on the Senate floor, he had characterized Lindbergh as "the chief of the nation's fifth columnists."

If Pepper was *persona non grata* to the "war mothers," he enjoyed a compensatory popularity with the people of Great Britain. In a transatlantic broadcast, Pepper was told by Ambassador Joseph P. Kennedy that "your name appears in these papers over here almost as much as the President of the United States." The *Chicago Tribune* made due capital of the incident. Pepper also was warmly received in Canada.

After the United States entered the war, Senator Pepper was among the first to call on the people to prepare for an organized, durable peace. His views, while not extremist, went beyond the position taken by President Roosevelt and Cordell Hull. They were more nearly akin to those of Sumner Welles and Wendell Willkie.

Pepper gave dramatic application to his beliefs during the historic debates in the autumn of 1942 on the Connally postwar policy resolution. First in the Foreign Relations Committee, then on the floor, he led the fight to substitute for the Connally draft a more meaningful resolution. In a debate that became so spirited at times that it verged on the unparliamentary, he charged that the committee draft was "impregnated with studied ambiguity" and that "all it will do is to afford an umbrella to those who might like to get out of the rain of political indignation next year or later."

"This great, bold, brave, strong nation," he thundered, "this nation wherein reigns the supremacy of law and not the government of men; this nation, which in theory is supposed to have been a leader in every humane movement on the globe, somehow or other has had its virility, its moral stamina, sapped by some strange apathy, until it dares not utter a decent sentiment worthy of acceptance in the councils of world opinion."

After the debate had raged for days, the issue was settled by publication of the Moscow declarations, which were the product of Secretary of State Hull's conversation with Premier Stalin and Foreign Minister Molotoff. On the suggestion of Pepper and others, a compromise was worked out by which a portion of the Moscow text was inserted in the Connally resolution. The Pepper forces left the field in possession of all they had hoped to gain.

Shortly thereafter, Pepper initiated the movement for a change in the constitutional requirement for the ratification of treaties. His plan, adopted by the House but pigeonholed by the Senate, would make ratification depend on a majority of both houses, sitting in joint session, instead of a two-thirds vote by the Senate. Included was a provision for blocking filibusters. Pending action on the amendment, he proposed that peace pacts be presented to Congress, not as treaties but as executive agreements.

Pepper felt that the United Nations Charter was lacking in strength, but he supported it vigorously in the discussions that preceded its ratification. In an address which occupied the greater part of a day, he also stressed the importance of worldwide economic co-operation. He warned against perversion of colonial trusteeships into "pillars of American empire." Pleading for progressive disarmament, he said: "We cannot do it in a day, we cannot do it without other nations collaborating, but I wish it might be made known to other nations at the council table that America was always ready to put its gun on the table and, if necessary, to take it off entirely when others were ready to do so."

By no means totally overshadowed by his activities in the international field, is Pepper's record of domestic liberalism. Its roots are not easily discerned. His parents, although poor, were substantial members of their little community. The father owned his own farm and, later, small mercantile enterprises in Camp Hill. From time to time he held minor public positions. Although young Claude had to work his way through college as waiter, furnaceman, and helper in a steel mill, he did not acquire the essentially emotional point of view that animates some liberals. His political philosophy was a product of leisurely growth, in the process of which his admiration for Woodrow Wilson was reinforced by an enlarging study of Jeffersonian and Jacksonian principles.

At the age of twenty-eight, as a Florida Democratic committeeman, Pepper wrote a letter to the newly elected Governor of New York state, Franklin D. Roosevelt. In this letter he said:

Our party must proceed not from excitement but from conviction. The smell of battle and the hope of victory will stir men to tremendous effort. But such effort, having its origin in excitement must wane with the emotional reaction. It is deep-rooted, dogged conviction of right that makes men endure and persist. . . . For one, I want the Democratic party genuinely to become the liberal party of this nation. I want it not to compromise upon that matter, because we cannot go to the people with conviction in our eyes unless we are sincere in our own liberalism—in our belief that right in this respect is the conferring of the greatest good upon the greatest number.

The letter was dated December 22, 1928. Roosevelt was four years away from the White House and Pepper was a young party officer in a state which had just cast an overwhelming vote for Herbert Hoover. The circumstances would seem to dispose of the charge that Pepper's principles are shallow and of recent origin, that he has been a "coat-tail rider," and "an expedient friend of the administration."

In this letter, Pepper urged Roosevelt "to furnish to our party its leadership in the coming years," and that flag he never furled. In 1940 he was one of the earliest agitators for a third term. At the convention he made the first speech seconding the nomination. In 1944 he came later into the field, but supported the fourth term with equal ardor.

With a few exceptions, perhaps enough to clear him of the charge of being a "rubber stamp," Pepper has voted with the administration in the Senate chamber. Consistently he supported the humanitarian legislation sponsored by Mr. Roosevelt. He voted for large relief appropriations, although he is not wholly indifferent to the size of the national debt. He resisted efforts to dismantle such agencies as the National

Youth Administration and the Farm Security Administration. He has supported public housing and has been active in the fight for federal aid to the states in education. He has worked for extensions of social security and has supported public health measures. He has introduced bills to extend federal aid to handicapped children and to war veterans. He was the first to introduce a bill providing for the education, at government expense, of returning servicemen. He fought unsuccessfully for the Murray-Kilgore bill with its liberal unemployment benefits.

He sided with the President on the Supreme Court issue and the controversial government reorganization bill of 1938. With noteworthy exceptions, he has supported the reciprocal trade program. Save for his vote for the Smith-Connally bill, both on original passage and on overriding the President's veto, his labor record has been pro-administration. He was a leader in the framing and passage of the original wage-hour legislation. In the summer of 1945, he introduced a bill to raise the floor on wages in interstate commerce from forty cents to sixty-five cents. He has a good record on civil liberties.

He has been a consistent foe of monopoly. He cried out early against railway freight rates which discriminate against the southern and western sections of the country. He refused to support the bill to exempt fire insurance companies from the anti-trust laws. He has fought to obtain for "dirt farmers" a greater share in Florida sugar production, a field occupied almost exclusively by the United States Sugar Corporation. He has been especially active on behalf of small business and has encouraged the growth of farm co-operatives. He has fought Senator McKellar's efforts to wreck the TVA.

Pepper followed President Roosevelt closely on tax policy, and was one of fourteen senators to vote to uphold the veto of the 1944 revenue bill. He is against sales taxes. He opposed the Ruml plan, but voted for the compromise involving 75 per cent forgiveness. He favored the proposed $25,000 salary limit. He has supported wartime price-control measures, including the farm subsidy program. Introducing a nine-point plan for war mobilization in 1942, he urged an equality of sacrifice in forceful and inclusive terms.

One of his significant battles has been his attempt to abolish the poll tax as a prerequisite of voting in federal elections. He introduced his bill on March 31, 1941, and fought for it with great vigor in the Senate. The House passed a companion bill sponsored by Representative Geyer, but the Senate stopped Pepper's measure by a filibuster and it has not come up on the floor again.

Advocating his bill in the Senate on November 1, 1942, Pepper said: "Mr. President, I envisage a South where the feudal system will remain as a beautiful, romantic legend, but where democracy shall practically be a functioning institution. I foresee a South which comes to the bar of the Congress with clean hands asking justice, which will practice democracy and seek it from its Congress and fellow countrymen."

In January, 1943, Pepper introduced a resolution to tighten the Senate rules on debate by putting teeth in the cloture. His purpose was to clear a path for the anti-poll tax bill. If the resolution were passed it would sound the death knell of the filibuster, but so far there has been no action on it.

A great many of Pepper's activities have required courage. The poll-tax crusade caused the Negro issue to be raised against him in the 1944 campaign. Photographs taken in 1942 when he stood in the pulpit of a Negro church in Los Angeles, were resurrected and circulated by the thousand. In the shadow of this hard struggle, he supported Mr. Roosevelt's tax veto against the entreaties of his closest political advisers. On the wage-hour bill he took a stand that was unpopular in the South. In voting to extend the reciprocal trade treaties in 1943 he offended important agricultural interests. In the anti-trust case, the insurance lobby placed heavy pressure on him.

Pepper has made a number of notable speeches in the Senate. His maiden effort, delivered on June 17, 1937, in the midst of a revolt against the administration's relief policy, caused a sensation on the floor. Taking an analogy from the Old Testament, he said:

Mr. President, I do not know what may constitute this thing that we call idealism, but I do know that it is made of very fragile substance, because I know that in no period of history has it long been able to show

consistent duration. . . . I suspect that even here in this body the old
sentiments of conservatism, the old belief that back to the wilderness or
even back in Egypt were the better course are beginning to reassert themselves. . . .
Yet, under the impulse of the social conscience . . .we have gotten where
we are today, transgressing every red flag of danger that has been held
up by every honest reactionary. . . . As for me and my house, I do not like
to wander in the "wilderness," and I shall not return to the bondage of
Egypt.

The next day President Roosevelt commended the speech
to Senator Wagner. Senator Norris described it as the best
maiden speech he had heard in thirty years. Drew Pearson and
Robert Allen wrote in the "Washington Merry-Go-Round":
"The speech was one of the greatest of its kind ever heard in
the chamber. . . . It was extraordinary in brilliance of delivery
and stunning effect. . . . Few paid much attention to him when
he started. Five minutes later all eyes were riveted on him and
the Senate was as still as a tomb. History was being made and
the Senators and press gallery knew it. . . . A new leader was
taking his place. . . . When the speech was over, the Senate for
a moment sat in blinking astonishment. Then from all over the
chamber members broke into applause (which is forbidden)
and rushed from their seats to congratulate him personally."

Pepper made a special flying trip to Washington to vote on
the 1944 tax veto. In his speech, delivered despite two entreaties by Senator Barkley not to take the floor, he declared:
"I believe the issue involved goes far deeper [than the considerations involved in a tax bill]. I believe I can say that the
issue is related to the winning of the war and the future of
America; certainly it is directly related to the future of the
Democratic party." Pepper then read the letter he had written
sixteen years before to Governor-elect Roosevelt, and warned:
"I see a country so divided over detail that if they win the war
they will lose the peace; they will have such lack of harmony in
their action that they will produce an economic chaos which
will condemn more millions to sacrifice and toil and poverty. . . ."

Pepper's usefulness in Congress has not been confined to
casting votes and making addresses. He has a capacity for con-

structive work. He is industrious and effective in committee. He has been among the leaders in breaking ground on such subjects as streamlining the Senate rules, organizing the country's economy for war, and preparing for reconversion. He has given attention to the problems of small business and of the white-collar worker, to public health and to juvenile delinquency. In many of these causes he has worked in close association with such senators as Elbert Thomas of Utah and Harley Kilgore of West Virginia.

Pepper has boundless energy and a facility for getting things accomplished. In addition to his work on the floor and in committee rooms, he is more diligent than the average in doing favors for his constituents. His speeches are based on research. His mail averages 80 to 100 letters a day—sometimes thousands a day in peak periods—and is said to be the heaviest of any senator's. With all this, he finds time for lectures, radio broadcasts, and the writing of newspaper and magazine articles, somehow without impinging too much on the relatively active social life which he and Mrs. Pepper lead in the capital.

There is no question that Pepper is one of the abler senators. He has a gift of fluent and picturesque expression. Most of his speeches are extemporized. Some of his oratory is florid, but more often there is a spontaneous rhythm and color to it. As a speaker, he is physically impressive. He has a strong build and his large, high-cheek-boned head is set solidly into powerful shoulders. He is a faultless, conservative dresser. His voice has a quasi-ministerial intonation. He is quick tempered on occasion and is adept at sarcasm, although he does not resort to it frequently. In a speech in February of 1944, he characterized Governor Dewey as "that gilded, public-relations-advised candidate . . . in his best and most studied pose of the coy maiden who is so diligently sought, the one who says 'No' with her lisping lip, but with the dark lashes of her inviting eyes says, 'Come on.' " He can take care of himself in rough and tumble debate, and senators of considerable parliamentary prestige have come off the floor with second honors after exchanging salvos with him.

Withal, he chooses his words discreetly and most of the time is notably urbane. A Republican senator recently said of him: "A more gentle and kindly opponent I never have had. His courtesy is unfailing, and he has a gift of rich vocabulary which he uses to make his friends happy, instead of to make them suffer." Some say he is too courteous, that overuse of such terms as "the able Senator" and "my distinguished colleague" detract from the force of what he is saying.

The Florida senator is not without weaknesses. When the Supreme Court invalidated the white Democratic primary of Texas, Pepper rushed into print with an assurance that the Florida primaries would be "kept white" and that the South would not "allow matters peculiar to us to be determined by those who do not know and understand our problems." Coming a few weeks before the Florida primary and at the height of the campaign to smear Pepper by circulating the pictures of him in the Los Angeles Negro church, the Supreme Court's decision placed him in a position that was uncomfortable, if not desperate. Senator Hill in Alabama, facing a concurrent test, made the same obeisance. Although the circumstances were extenuating, Pepper's hedging embarrassed his leadership of the anti-poll-tax fight and stirred up a storm among the liberals. Some of the luster of his poll-tax fight and his concomitant effort to abolish the filibuster already had been rubbed off by the discovery that some years earlier he had taken a leading part in the filibuster against the anti-lynching bill, and twice had voted against the cloture. Also the impression gained currency that Pepper had not gone out of his way in the spring of 1944 to bring the anti-poll-tax bill before the Senate.

To placate truck farming constituents, Pepper voted in 1940 against renewal of the reciprocal trade treaties. This was in clear contravention of his internationalist principles. But when the act came up again in 1943, with a war on, he voted for renewal. Many believe his votes in favor of the Smith-Connally law were cast under pressure of public opinion, agitated at that time by the behavior of John L. Lewis. Pepper made no apologies, insisted that Lewis was "the most dangerous man in the nation," and that for its own good, labor must be "defended against some of its own embittered and avaricious leaders by its real friends."

Pepper's anti-monopoly record is marred by a vote to limit the number of cars on freight trains—a restraint of trade practiced by labor unions—and by his refusal to vote for a bill to abolish "block booking" and "blind buying" of motion picture films. He has gone all out for rivers and harbors, and he has given important support to the Townsend Plan.

His record on civil service legislation is spotty. He has fought for the integrity of the TVA but consistently has voted against extending the Hatch Act to forbid political activity by state-employed administrators of federal projects. In the state of Florida, the impression is general that Pepper plays the patronage game with some avidity. He was accused of levying contributions from WPA supervisory personnel in his campaign for renomination in 1938. There is no doubt that he takes good care of his personal friends in the matter of judgeships and other federal appointments. He is not averse to talking down to a political audience. His campaign speeches in backwoods counties are something less than models of light and logic. But as Southern politics go, he is guilty of relatively minor demagoguery.

Pepper's defections from pure statesmanship should not be judged without reference to the factors that govern his chances for political survival. Although Florida in many respects is the most cosmopolitan of the Southern states, feeling is high on the race issue. Even a man with Pepper's moderate approach runs the constant risk of being misunderstood. Like California, Florida is a haven for retired people. The Townsend movement is correspondingly strong. Only one congressman from Florida has had the nerve to oppose it openly, and he was beaten in 1938 when he ran against Pepper for the Senate.

Pepper also has to cope with a complexity of special economic interests. The vegetable growers in the southern end of the state are pressed by Cuban and Mexican competition and are violently opposed to the reciprocal tariff program. There are important citrus, timber, cattle, turpentine and fishery interests. There is no large labor movement in the state, an obvious disadvantage to a liberal.

The Senator is frank about his playing of politics. He hews to three consciously defined objectives:

(1) To do "chores" for his state, seldom letting the administration attitude cut across local interests.

(2) To take an active part in legislation.

(3) To take part in the formulation of public opinion and party leadership.

On points two and three the record speaks for itself. Pepper likes to explain the origin of the first plank. When he was defeated for re-election to the state legislature in 1930, he concluded that his aggressive and liberal record had gained him fewer votes than he had lost by failing to obtain an increase in the fees granted county judges for recording vital statistics. Since then he has not been indifferent to the upkeep of his political fences.

Broadly speaking, Pepper does what he feels he must do to survive and fight another day. He is as faithful to principle as he dares be, and on issues that he feels are vital, he often takes serious risks. A study of his imperfections is a study of the price in compromise which a man of the firmest convictions finds it necessary to pay for his continuation in public life. As such, it offers an insight into the hazards of representative government and the limitations of the general run of citizens.

In Washington, appraisals of Pepper's stature vary. Among the liberal Senators, his ability, courage, and sincerity are not questioned. A good many senators who do not follow his political line think well of him. Others are less laudatory. Some bear the scars of rather sharp senatorial debates with Pepper and occasionally they take their grudges home with them. At the other extreme, there are those who do not take him seriously. His "heaviness" is questioned by a few even among those who regard his courage, character, and principles most favorably.

It is significant that he was held in the warmest esteem by Senator George Norris. In a letter written shortly before his death, the Nebraskan told the author of this chapter:

I did not know Senator Pepper before he came to the Senate, but I was impressed with what I believed to be his ability and his courage soon afterward. I have been associated with him in various matters of national legislation, and my opinion of his ability and his integrity and his courage has increased during that time until I look upon him at the present time with a great deal of admiration. . . . I think his ability and his standing far above that of the ordinary member of Congress. . . . I think Senator Pepper . . . has done very fine work in the Senate.

Among Washington newspapermen the estimates of Pepper also vary. As with the senators, they appear to divide along lines of political or philosophical sympathy. Speaking well for Pepper, in Washington and at home, is the fact that the persons who express the greatest admiration for him are usually those who have known him longest and most intimately. For fifteen years he has retained the loyalty of every living member of a group of a dozen or so who clustered around him in the Florida legislature. Those who know him best vouch for his rectitude, and although there have been whispers about his integrity, these have not been taken seriously by informed persons. In 1941, there was a newspaper flurry about an airfield contract, but Chairman May of the House Military Affairs Committee, after a sub-committee had investigated the matter and made a report, issued a public statement exonerating Pepper.

Politically, in his own state, he is liked by liberals, internationalists, working people, pensioners, and citrus growers. Despite the hardening of conservatism in the South, he enjoys the support of many businessmen, including some bankers, shippers, oil company magnates, and public utilities officials. His campaign organization in 1944 included both the retiring and incoming presidents of the Miami Chamber of Commerce.

Big industry, much of it representing absentee capital, is rather solidly against Pepper. The Associated Industries of Florida, affiliate of the National Association of Manufacturers, was active against him in the 1944 campaign. The DuPont interests opposed him. He is unpopular with vegetable growers in the southern end of the state, many of whom farm on the corporate level.

With this lineup of forces, it was natural that Pepper faced a bitter battle for survival. Big money poured into the state. There is evidence that many Republican voters were advised to enter the Democratic primaries. The race issue was flaunted in the manner previously described, and at times it was hard to tell whether the candidate was Pepper or Mrs. Roosevelt.

Pepper fought back with his customary political and forensic mastery. At one time it looked as if he would be defeated, but in the end he closed out the contest by gaining a clear though narrow majority over four opponents in the first primary. Among the devices that probably saved him was his statement on "white supremacy." As is customary in Southern states, there was no serious contest in the November election.

The primary, on May 2, came shortly after a succession of dreary months, for the Democrats had been broken by an unexpected Republican victory in a congressional by-election in Oklahoma. The fortunes of Pepper and Lister Hill, to be decided on the same day, were looked to as the first real test of the national trend, and the Florida and Alabama primaries engaged the attention of the nation.

Two months after his triumph, Pepper plunged into the fight to save Henry Wallace at Chicago. Although a minor boomlet had developed for himself, he remained loyal to the Vice-President. He carried his fight to the newspapers, and his extemporaneous seconding speech was one of the highlights of the convention. In the course of this speech he said:

> The Democratic Party seeks and honors great political leaders, but there is no place in the Democratic Party for political bosses. . . . Mr. President, this convention is not nominating a politician. Were that the choice to be made, I should not favor Henry A. Wallace. He is shy, he is too sincere to be a manipulator. He is too honest for double dealing. He has not been schooled . . . in the devious ways of politics which would make him supine to political dictation and coercion. He would be, Mr. Chairman, the champion and the unfailing and unfaltering spokesman of the belligerent democracy.

The evening of the same day, Pepper personally touched off the wild demonstration that for a moment appeared likely to stampede the convention into remaining in session throughout the night to conduct the balloting for Vice-President. After shouting vainly for ten minutes for recognition in the seething din, Pepper dashed out into the aisle and raced for the rostrum. At that moment Senator Jackson, permanent chairman of the convention, banged the gavel and announced an adjournment. Pepper had lost his chance of striking for Wallace while the psychological iron was hot enough to provide an outside hope of driving through the nomination.

After the convention, Pepper held several conferences with Wallace, following the first of which they issued a joint statement in aggressive support of the Roosevelt-Truman ticket. In September Pepper opened the Democratic campaign on the Pacific coast with a tour which was timed to bring him into Los Angeles, San Francisco, Portland, Seattle, and other cities shortly in advance of Governor Dewey. Later he toured the East and the Midwest. He was heard often by nationwide radio audiences. In the columns of the *New York Times* he debated the foreign policy issue with Senator Taft. He did likewise with Senator Austin, a fellow internationalist who was supporting Dewey in one of the publications of the Foreign Policy Association. He did specialized work as chairman of the Democratic National Committee's foreign language division.

After the death of President Roosevelt, Pepper did not stand so close to the White House. But President Truman and he were friends in the former's Senate days, and there has been no evidence that ill-feeling resulted from Pepper's belligerent backing of Henry Wallace at Chicago. From their separate ends of Pennsylvania Avenue, they seem, at the moment of this writing, to be supporting common causes.

Whatever the verdict of time may be on Claude Pepper and his services to the nation, it will hardly deny him rank as one of the significant men of his day in Washington. He was the vocal spearhead of our preparation for war. He led the forces in the Senate which insisted on planning for a bold and imaginative peace. He has been, and still is, an articulate and generally courageous and consistent upholder of liberalism as interpreted by Franklin Roosevelt.

There is no question but that Pepper is ambitious politically. As a high school lad he wrote on the wall of a Justice of the Peace office where he worked nights: "Claude Pepper, United States Senator." The idea never strayed far from his consciousness. Do his ambitions now reach beyond the Senate? Pepper told the writer recently: "It may be there is a larger future for me; that is in the lap of the gods. I am not going to resist the current if it should try to pick me up—but I don't spend much time worrying about it."

The record tends to support the statement. Pepper has stood on principle too many times to be regarded primarily as an opportunist.

17

THEODORE G. BILBO

"Shibboleths for Statesmanship"

BY ROMAN J. ZORN

The poll tax brings the entire race question before the American people. . . . It has become necessary for us now to consider and to openly discuss the forces which are today attempting to destroy the color line. . . . We will tell our negro-loving, Yankee friends to "Go Straight to Hell." —Senator T. G. Bilbo, Address to Mississippi Legislature, March 22, 1944.

VISITORS TO THE UNITED STATES CONGRESS, IN MID-NOVEM-ber of 1942, witnessed deliberate sabotage of the legislative process. To casual spectators the Senate might have seemed engaged in routine business, but further observation would have revealed a weazened, be-spectacled little man—Senator Theodore Gilmore ("The Man") Bilbo—lengthily haranguing a sea of green carpets and empty desks. In continuing the filibuster against the anti-poll tax bill, the Mississippian had announced: "Let me say to the Senators now present that if they have any business to transact in their offices, I hope they will feel at liberty to attend to it; because I propose to hold the floor until the Senate adjourns."[1] Accordingly, only a half-dozen somnolent senators remained in attendance while "The Man Bilbo" continued his five-day speaking marathon.

In the galleries, wondering visitors leaned over the railings, trying to understand the proceedings. Instead of watching a legislative mill grind out solutions for wartime problems, they listened to a monologic defense of the Southern "color line" and of anachronistic "States Rights." Instead of statesman-like debate, they heard Bilbonic fulminations against Negroes and

1. *Congressional Record,* LXXXVII (Nov. 13, 1942), 8830.

centralized bureaucracy. Hours on end Bilbo rambled on, now quoting at length from printed committee reports, now commenting on hostile editorials, now reading constituents' letters into the *Congressional Record*. Occasionally the monotonous oratory was varied by the Senator's witticisms, or by helpful interpolations from sympathetic Southern colleagues. Slowly the afternoon wore away, and the filibuster had stalemated the Senate's legislation for another day. The visiting citizenry, partly composed of soldiers and sailors taking time off from the war to see Congress work, had long since withdrawn in disgust.[2]

A similar poll-tax filibuster, likewise successful in thwarting a majority of the Senate, was staged in early May, 1944. Again Senator Bilbo's oratory was directed toward a distant Mississippi audience. Having officially launched his 1946 re-election campaign with announcement of intent to·lead this filibuster,[3] Bilbo was using the Senate forum to arouse Mississippi's seldom latent prejudices on race relations, states rights, communism, and federal bureaucracy. Thereby Theodore G. Bilbo was enhancing his reputation as a political champion of the Deep South, and thus building fences for his re-election to a third term in the United States Senate.

Who is this politician who thrives upon the agitation of racial prejudice and sectional fanaticism? Unknown nationally until his filibustering exploits lifted him to news-weekly notoriety, "The Man Bilbo"[4] is the pre-eminent demagogue of the Magnolia Commonwealth. Indeed, over the span of nearly forty years, his fellow-citizens have heaped upon his shoulders more political honors than have been given any other Mississippian.

2. *Ibid.*, pp. 8830-9026; see also "Washington Notes" in *The New Republic,* Dec. 13, 1943, p. 850.

3. New Orleans *Times-Picayune,* Mar. 23, 1944.

4. Bilbo's sensational career made him a natural target for colorful appellations. He early won state-wide notoriety as the "Poplarville Prophet," "The Pearl of Pearl River County," and as the "Bilbonic Plague"—the nomenclature reflecting the reaction of friends or foes. And Bilbo, never afflicted with the political sin of modesty, had deliberately publicized himself as "The Old Maestro of the Stump," and even more frequently as "The Man Bilbo."

Senator Bilbo, who has survived a series of scandals that would have broken an ordinary politician, ranks as one of the indestructible men in American politics. Early in his public career, once while serving as state senator, and subsequently as lieutenant-governor, Bilbo was charged with acceptance of bribes. In each case he narrowly escaped expulsion from office. In 1923, for refusing to testify in a sensational seduction case, ex-Governor Bilbo was jailed for ten days. A decade later, just as "The Man" was finishing his second gubernatorial term, there occurred a mysterious episode in the governor's office which involved Bilbo, a blonde, and a pistol shot. Shortly thereafter the "Poplarville Prophet" received much unfavorable publicity concerning his marital difficulties. In 1933 Bilbo left his wife, and thereafter Mrs. Linda Gaddy Bilbo obtained a relief job and then aired her claims in court. Again in 1937, when Mrs. Bilbo sued to compel payment of her separate maintenance allowance, Senator Bilbo sought and secured a divorce on grounds of cruel and inhuman treatment.[5]

Bible-Belt Mississippi has generally been intolerant of marital and financial irregularity, but despite Bilbo's role as a major figure in such scandals, "The Man" has remained a potent factor in the political affairs of the Magnolia Commonwealth. Repeatedly the sovereign electorate of Mississippi has bestowed upon him the highest offices within their gift. From 1908 to 1920, Bilbo served successively as state senator, lieutenant-governor, and governor. Then, constitutionally debarred from succeeding himself, Bilbo aspired to a seat in Congress but failed to wrest the Democratic nomination from the incumbent representative. "The Man Bilbo" reappeared in the race for governor in 1923, launching this campaign from a prison cell, and again he narrowly lost the Democratic nomination. Undismayed by these setbacks, the ubiquitous Bilbo campaigned again in 1927 and thereupon became the only governor of Mississippi to serve a second term.

5. For accounts of the early scandals, see H. R. Fraser, "Bilbo: Mississippi Mouthpiece," *American Mercury,* Aug., 1936, pp. 427-30; and J. Beatty, "Mississippi Pearl," *American Magazine,* Feb., 1935, pp. 96-97. Later involvements are chronicled in *Time,* Sept. 2, 1935; Mar. 29, 1937; Aug. 1, 1938; Sept. 9, 1940.

Depression troubles and a deadlock with the legislature embarrassed his second administration, and by 1932 Mississippians generally conceded that "The Pearl of Pearl River County" was hopelessly discredited. Refusing to give up political ambitions, however, Bilbo secured a "lame duck" appointment as "Pastemaster General" of the news clippings files of the A.A.A. Then after two years of conspicuous oblivion in Washington, D. C., Theodore G. Bilbo bounced back into the middle of the 1934 U.S. senatorial election in Mississippi. Ousting the veteran incumbent in the Democratic primary, Bilbo attained the senatorial toga and re-emerged as a power in Mississippi politics. In 1940 Senator Bilbo successfully campaigned for re-election, and now he is entrenched as the senior senator from Mississippi.[6]

The melodramatic career of "The Man Bilbo" can be understood only when it is considered in the light of conditions which characterize the Magnolia Commonwealth.

Perhaps the most significant aspect of Mississippi is the predominance of agrarian poverty. Some 85 per cent of the population is rural, and cotton-growing is the chief occupation of the citizenry. The share-cropping and tenantry evils are both chronic and acute, for less than 30 per cent of Mississippi farmers own the land they till. The combination of long-depressed cotton prices and share-cropping production largely explains the poverty-ridden condition of the state. Indeed, from the economic standpoint, Mississippi is one of the poorest states in the Union. Even in relatively prosperous 1930, only 42 per cent of the population could be described as "gainfully employed"; and when the national average income per capita was a bare $432, in Mississippi it reached only $170.[7]

6. For incidents of Bilbo's political career, see *Congressional Directory*, Jan., 1941, p. 54; *Time*, Oct. 1, 1934; Sept. 17, 1940; *Literary Digest*, Feb. 9, 1935; *Newsweek*, Sept. 29, 1934; Fraser, "Mississippi Mouthpiece," pp. 425-32; and Beatty, "Mississippi Pearl, pp. 53, 96-97.

7. *Mississippi Blue Book* (Jackson, Miss., 1937), pp. 35-36; see also figures quoted by Senator Bilbo from *Report of the President's Committee on Farm Tenancy*, pp. 35-36, appearing in *Congressional Record*, LXXXI (July 2, 1937), 6757-58; also Senator Bilbo's statement in *Congressional Record*, LXXXIV (June 12, 1939), 8922-23.

Religion, race, and illiteracy combine to further complicate the political substratum. Mississippi's 800,000 church-going inhabitants are almost exclusively Protestant, and over two-thirds of these are affiliated with strongly fundamentalist and evangelical sects. Then, too, Mississippi is the only state with a majority of Negro citizens. In a population of two million, Negroes outnumber the whites by about 15,000 persons—50.2 per cent. The white population, too, is unusual, for it is composed of 99.6 per cent of native born stock. Moreover, in terms of literacy, Mississippi ranks as the fourth lowest state in the nation. Approximately 200,000 Mississippians over the age of ten years cannot read and write, and an average of 15.6 per cent of the adult citizenry must be classed as illiterate.[8]

Impoverished and illiterate, long agitated by the tub-thumping bigotry of Bible-Belt preachers, and afflicted with acute racial friction and prejudice, the Mississippi electorate reaches no high level of political maturity. The "red necks" of the bayous and hills do not interest themselves in political abstractions nor in analysis of statesmanlike political conduct. On the contrary, they give generous support to those who pander to local shibboleths—as demonstrated by their long-continued adherence to the Ku Klux Klan. Small wonder that Mississippi should prove a fertile field for the activities of rabble-rousing Theodore G. Bilbo!

The key to Bilbo's success in dominating Mississippi politics is to be found in his skillful exploitation of the peculiarities of the Magnolia State. The pattern of Bilbo's political behavior is clear: He has resoundingly promised economic manna to the discontented rural "red necks"; he has raucously championed "white supremacy" and "100 per cent Americanism"; and he has mastered the demagogic techniques of the argument *ad hominem*. And for colorful showmanship, ingenious political manipulation, and effective rabble-rousing, "The Old Maestro of the Stump" has rarely been equaled. So successfully have Bilbo's opportunistic tactics made him the spokesman of Mis-

8. *Mississippi Blue Book*, XXV, 35, 36; *Statistical Abstract of the United States, 1940* (U.S. Department of Commerce, Washington, D. C., 1941), p. 53.

sissippi's masses that observers estimate "The Man" commands the personal loyalty of at least a third of his electorate. Verily, he is a worthy successor to such notorious prototypes as Tom Heflin and Huey Long.

A basic feature of Bilbo's political strength stems from the fact that he is *of the People*. Like many Mississippians, he is of "poor white" origins, has had to struggle for subsistence on a back-country farm, and has faced recurring financial difficulties. Resembling his constituency in religious and fraternal association, "The Man" is a Baptist, a Mason, and a Shriner. Along with many other white nativists, Bilbo has been active in the Ku Klux Klan. And in political activity, he follows popular stereotypes in vehemently advocating redistribution of wealth, Democratic party regularity, maintenance of the "color line," and Southern sectional traditions.[9] Moreover, he speaks the language cherished by the common man and mingles freely with the ordinary voters of the state. Frequently reminding the masses that he comes from their ranks, "The Man Bilbo" claims support as their spokesman. In the words of Senator Bilbo's secretary, Eve Squire Brooks, "He prides himself on being of the people and ONE of the people ... as being the representative of the plain people, the masses." [10]

In line with this attitude, Bilbo gives extraordinary care to the factor of personal attention in his relations with the Mississippi electorate. In nearly every state election "The Pearl of Pearl River County" engages in extensive personal campaigning. Not only does he stump the state with formal speeches, but he uses every occasion to meet the voters personally, in order to ascertain their views and solicit their support. Such activities reached a peak in 1934, when in a four-month campaign, "The Man" gave over 1,000 speeches and appeared at virtually every city, hamlet, and crossroads in the state.[11] Moreover, Bilbo encourages the voters to write to him, and he carefully arranges that every letter and postcard will receive a

9. "Biographical Sketch," MS furnished the author by Senator Bilbo's secretary; see also Beatty, "Mississippi Pearl," p. 94.

10. MS letter to the author, July 24, 1941.

11. See *Newsweek*, Sept. 29, 1934; *Literary Digest*, Feb. 9, 1935; and Beatty, "Mississippi Pearl," p. 94.

personalized and prompt reply.[12] To further encourage a feeling of personal intimacy, Bilbo invites the citizenry to call at his home, and he frequently arranges mass social functions for them. Thus, at the start of a difficult gubernatorial campaign in 1927, "The Man Bilbo" was host to the public at a tremendous free barbecue. Again in 1935, upon completion of his twenty-five room "Dream House" at Poplarville, Bilbo entertained his electorate at a mammoth "Housewarming" celebration.[18]

Besides maintaining close touch with the masses, the "Poplarville Prophet" exploits all the techniques of demagogic showmanship. Indeed, so important does Bilbo consider this factor that he has been known to say of politics, "Psychology, psychology—all is psychology." [14] Ever mindful of this concept, the "Pearl of Pearl River County" is careful to keep always in the public eye. Even when not himself a candidate, he stumps the state in all elections and he makes every effort to impress his audiences. Not only does he act the role of a flamboyant political leader, but he dresses the part. To impress his hill-country followers, he wears a loud check suit, red suspenders, a roaring red necktie with a diamond horseshoe stickpin, and a rakish snapbrimmed felt hat.[15]

In addition to feasting the eyes of the yokels, "The Man" also provides entertainment and excitement. From the outset of his career, Bilbo has sought favorable consideration by singing hymns while accompanying himself on the melodeon. In another approach to the sympathies of his auditors, "The Man" exploits the scandals in his career by posing as a greatly wronged martyr who needs vindication on election day. More generally, however, Bilbo fills the ears of the "red necks" with

12. Bilbo's secretary comments, "None is so humble or ignorant but that he knows he will have a respectful audience in the Senator. Our mail is simply colossal. It is proverbial in the Senate Building that in relation to the size of the state, Senator Bilbo receives more mail than any other Senator. Each letter is answered—immediately if possible.... He answers them all."—Eve Squire Brooks to author, July 24, 1941.

13. *Time*, Dec. 30, 1935; Beatty, "Mississippi Pearl," pp. 94-96.

14. Eve Squire Brooks, letter to the author, July 24, 1941.

15. Raymond Gram Swing, "Bilbo the Rabble-Rouser," *Nation*, Jan. 30, 1935, p. 124; Fraser, "Mississippi Mouthpiece," pp. 425-26; Walter Davenport, "Brethren and Sisters," *Colliers*, Mar. 16, 1935, pp. 19-20.

anathemas against "the interests" and with promises that give glimpses of the millennium. Bilbo's dramatic rhetoric so sways his audiences that they weep when he weeps, shout when he shouts, and for the most part vote as he urges them. So effective is Bilbo's demagogic showmanship that he has built a blindly loyal following throughout Mississippi.[16]

Senator Bilbo's rabble-rousing oratory is chiefly composed of personal invective. As he explains, "It is always a family fight down here, and a family fight is best of all. We're all Democrats, and we have to deal in personalities because there are no issues—we're all in favor of the same things. So you don't show the other fellow is in favor of this or against that, you just show he's a low-down blankety blank." [17]

Since backwoods folk are not interested in vague generalities, Theodore Bilbo has specialized in dispensing vitriolic and personalized oratory. In one of his earliest campaigns he denounced an opponent as a "cross between a hyena and a mongrel . . . begotten in a nigger graveyard at midnight, suckled by a sow, and educated by a fool." [18] Eventually the target of this abuse caught up with Bilbo and battered him into unconsciousness for twenty-four hours. But this mishap did not deter the oratorical flights of "The Old Maestro of the Stump." Again in the 1915 gubernatorial election, he crushed his opponent under this barrage: "John Armstrong is a vicious, malicious, deliberate, cowardly, pusillanimous, cold-blooded, lopeared, blue-nosed, premeditated, and self-made liar." [19] And as late as the 1934 U.S. senatorial campaign, Bilbo branded the incumbent senator as a "tool of cannibalistic capitalism" and "more reactionary than Herbert Hoover," and after a choice selection of billingsgate concluded, "Hubert Stephens is a . . . plain United States Senatorial liar." [20]

Such rhetorical outbursts are usually leavened with assiduous courting of the sovereign electorate. A prime example of this

16. Davenport, "Brethren and Sisters," pp. 19-20; Fraser, "Mississippi Mouthpiece," pp. 429-30; Beatty, "Mississippi Pearl," p. 96.
17. Quoted in Beatty, "Mississippi Pearl," p. 95.
18. Quoted in Fraser, "Mississippi Mouthpiece," pp. 428-29.
19. *Ibid.*, p. 430.
20. *Newsweek,* Sept. 29, 1934; Swing, "Bilbo the Rabble-Rouser," p. 124.

mob-appealing tactic, taken from a 1934 campaign speech, runs:

Friends, fellow citizens, brothers and sisters—hallelujah.—My oppo-nent—yea, this opponent of mine who has the dastardly, dew-lapped, brazen, sneering, insulting and sinful effrontery to ask you for your votes without telling you the people of this almighty state of Mississippi what he is a-going to do with them if he gets them—this opponent of mine says he don't need a platform. Why does he ask you for your votes? He asks, my dear brethren and sisters, that you vote for him because he is standing by the President. Standing by the President, folks! So am I. But I'm doing better by you, folks, than that. I'm a-standing right smack on his corns, folks, lest he forget the great sovereign Magnolia state of Ole Miss. . . . I shall be the servant and senator of all the people of Missis-sippi, brothers and sisters. I shall know no North, no South, no East, no West. The appeal and petition of the humblest citizen, yea, whether he comes from the black prairie lands of the east or the alluvial lands of the fer-tile delta; whether he comes, yea, from the vermillion hills of north Mississippi or the sun-kissed shores of the Gulf of Mexico, yea, he will be heard by my heart and my feet shall be swift. But listen to fair warn-ing, brethren and sisters: Don't you go a-sending me up there to Wash-ington to be anything but your servant, your voice that will never cease to ring down the great, gray marble corridors of our Capitol, your Sena-tor whose thoughts will not wander from the humble, God-fearing cabins of Vinegar Bend or the lowing sheep-folds of Honeysuckle Creek, your champion who will not lay his head upon his pillow at night before he has asked his Maker for more strength to do more for you in the morrow —don't go a-sending me to those mighty classic halls of government, if you don't want that kind of a man. Brethren and sisters, I pledge. . . .[21]

The "Old Maestro of the Stump" is also adept in the more unscrupulous techniques of demagoguery. Since he does not hesitate to practice deceit and trickery, he is a dangerous man to have for a political foe. For instance, he boasts of his role in the 1928 presidential campaign, when "The Man Bilbo"—a Baptist, a dry, and a Ku Klux Klansman—managed to keep Mississippi as one of the few Southern states to remain loyal to Al Smith. This he accomplished largely by a strategem: In Memphis he announced that during the 1927 flood Herbert Hoover had got off the train at Mound Bayou, Miss., and danced with a Negro woman named Mary Booze. As this ca-

21. Quoted in Davenport, "Brethren and Sisters," p. 53.

nard rapidly spread throughout Mississippi, the Republican managers had a hard time to deny the story without offending either black or white voters. And when confronted with a "wet" Catholic and a "black" Republican, the Mississippi electorate chose Al Smith.[22] Bilbo has applied similar tactics to other opponents, and even in the 1940 campaign he charged that Wendell Willkie's father had once lived in Mississippi under a false name.[23]

Besides showmanship and rabble-rousing, Bilbo also uses the device of promising all things to all men. Since he panders to every vote-getting appeal, his platforms leave little unpledged. Thus, in his 1934 campaign he advocated a 27-point platform calling for the redistribution of wealth, old age pensions, the restoration of agricultural prosperity, both "controlled inflation" and "sound money," the conscription of wealth in wartime, a strong national defense, etc.[24] No panacea for the masses lacked Bilbo's loud endorsement.

Moreover, "The Man Bilbo" has the transcendant political gift of being able to make stupenduous promises to the voters, then fail to deliver results, and still find continued support at the polls. Perhaps the Bilbo masterpiece along this line occurred in a gubernatorial campaign. Noticing that vitrified brick is made from the red clay of Mississippi, "The Man" armed himself with samples of these bricks and stumped the state, promising the rustics that large portions of their farms would be purchased and turned into brick highways. "The roads will be the best roads in the world," he told hundreds of meetings from Yellow Rabbit to Vinegar Bend. "Why my countrymen, we can lay the bricks on one side and run off 'em for a hundred years. We can turn 'em over and run on the other side for a hundred years more, and then we can stand 'em up on end and run them right on into Kingdom Come."[25] The envisioned roads were not forthcoming, but the promise of them

22. *Time*, Oct. 1, 1934; J. C. Petrie, "Bilbo Wins Senatorial Seat," *Christian Century*, Oct. 3, 1934.

23. *Time*, Nov. 4, 1940.

24. For Bilbo's platform, see Davenport, "Brethren and Sisters," pp. 53-54; and *Time*, Oct. 1, 1934.

25. Quoted in the *Saturday Evening Post*, Jan. 1, 1938, p. 7.

certainly enhanced the popularity of "The Man Bilbo" during the campaign. Such incidents have led cynics to declare that Bilbo's main promise is "The voters will always forget," but the "Poplarville Prophet" successfully continues to follow the promissory path.

Thus, at a typical Bilbo rally, the electorate is gorged with promises, entertained by personal abuse of rival candidates, and worked into a near-frenzy by finishing touches of invective against "poor-folks haters," "underhanded bankers," "rich enemies of the public schools," "Communists and pacifists," etc. It is no wonder, therefore, that as the audience disperses they go away reading and believing a typical Bilbo campaign dodger, such as this:

The Man Bilbo! The race for the United States Senate!
A man of titanic energy and of dynamic driving force!
A wonder in sustained power of endurance and a marvel of intellectual brilliance!
He has fought the good fight and henceforth there is laid up for him a seat in the United States Senate!
Neither falsehood nor truth, neither censure nor praise, neither love nor hatred, sunshine nor storm can now deter nor detour him from his destined goal!
Bilbo's hour has arrived! For him victory is writ, yea, in the very stars above as it will be recorded by the ballots here below! [26]

"The Man Bilbo" began his career as a United States senator with the opening of the Seventy-fourth Congress in 1934. Like most neophyte members, he deferred to the custom of the Senate and delivered no major speeches during his first year. But Bilbo was not idle, for he immediately began to consolidate his position. With the assistance of his colleague, the late Pat Harrison, "The Man" successfully secured appointment as the ranking new member of every committee on which he wished to serve—Agriculture and Forestry, Commerce, and District of Columbia. Having thus attained positions from which he could influence legislation affecting his Southern constituency, Bilbo turned his attention to the matter of patronage. And here, because both the administration and Senator Harrison

26. Reprinted in Davenport, "Brethren and Sisters," pp. 53-54.

wished to conciliate him, he was given control over the bulk of new patronage affecting Mississippi.[27]

By 1935 the decks were clear for action, but strangely "The Man Bilbo" did not immediately play a conspicuous role in the Senate. Upon his election he had declared, "When I get to Washington I'll make as much noise for the common people as Huey P. Long and raise as much hell as President Roosevelt!"[28] but once seated in the Senate he lapsed into long-continued and unaccustomed silences. Aside from bills affecting local affairs in Mississippi, Bilbo sponsored little legislation; and his floor activities consisted of periodic endorsements of increased federal appropriations for work-relief projects, old-age pensions, and agricultural subsidies.

But after three years of quiescence, Theodore Bilbo reverted to demagogic tactics. Using the Senate rostrum as his soap-box, he renewed raucous agitation of Mississippi's favorite themes —white supremacy and relief for the cotton farmer. Moreover, mindful that national publicity would improve his standing with the home electorate, Bilbo exploited every opportunity to make sensational news. To this end "The Man" has prominently participated in two Senate filibusters concerning the Negro problem; and since becoming "Mayor of Washington,"[29] he has disturbed the capital city by deliberate irritation of racial issues. These performances have won newspaper headlines such as "BILBO RUNS AMOK," and "BILBO PREACHES RACE HATRED IN RABBLE-ROUSING SPEECH";[30] but they have consolidated Senator Bilbo's political strength in Mississippi.

27. *Time*, Feb. 4, 1935; *Newsweek*, Sept. 5, 1936.

28. Quoted in *Time*, Oct. 1, 1934; see also *Newsweek*, Sept. 29, 1934, June 6, 1938.

29. The Chairman of the Senate District of Columbia Committee is commonly referred to as the "Mayor of Washington." When four senior-ranking Democratic senators side-stepped this assignment, Senator Bilbo was designated as chairman of the committee in February, 1944.

Since the racial question is ever-present in the city, Bilbo finds the position strategically important for his white supremacy publicity overtures. Many Washingtonians, however, are unhappy about the situation; indeed, the Scripps-Howard *Daily News* fumed, "This socially benighted man . . . throw him out!" But Senate seniority gave Bilbo the job, and Senate seniority will keep him in it. See *Time*, Feb. 21, April 23, 1944.

30. Washington *Post*, Mar. 23, 1944; New York *PM*, Mar. 23, 1944.

THEODORE G. BILBO 289

Since Senator Bilbo represents a race-ridden state and personally derives his chief support from negrophobe "poor white" voters, it is not surprising that he should advertise the thesis of white supremacy. Not only does he categorically insist that the Negro race is inferior, but he loudly affirms that the races must be kept separate lest Caucasian civilization decline into ruin. In the light of these premises, he contends that either the Negro population must be repatriated to Africa, or the Southern method of disciplining the Negroes must be left alone.

When the Wagner-Costigan anti-lynching bill was introduced in the Senate in 1938, Theodore Bilbo seized his first opportunity to dramatize a defense of "Southern Rights." Joining in the filibuster against the proposed legislation, he unleashed floods of ranting oratory. Senator Bilbo charged that the bill had been introduced at the behest of "Negro lovers, Negro leaders, and Negro voters," and he declared, "If it becomes necessary to defeat this unthinkable, un-American, and un-democratic piece of legislation, I am ready to speak for 30 or 60 days or longer. To defeat this measure, so help me God, I would be willing to speak every day of the year 1938." Occasionally interpolating abuse of advocates of the bill as negrophilists, miscegenists, and hybrids, Bilbo continued his harangue in these terms:

It has been 73 years since the Civil War closed; and during all these years the South has had to carry the black burden brought about by the emancipation of the black man who resided in our midst. With wisdom, charity, and statesmanship we have handled this problem well. Why is it now, after three-quarters of a century . . . that an attempt is made to cram down the throat of the South this insulting, undemocratic un-American piece of legislation? . . . But I want to tell the advocates of this bill one thing: If you succeed in the passage of this bill, you will open the flood-gates of hell in the South. Raping, mobbing, lynching, race-riots, and crime will be increased a thousandfold; and upon your garments and upon the garments of those who are responsible for the passage of this measure will be the blood of the raped and outraged daughters of Dixie, as well as the blood of the perpetrators of these crimes that the red-blooded Anglo-Saxon white southern men will not tolerate.[31]

31. *Congressional Record,* LXXXIII (Jan. 21, 1938), 873-74; see also pp. 881-92.

Pleased with the notoriety attained through participation in this filibuster, "The Man Bilbo" took steps to further tickle the prejudices of his constituency. Recognizing that the Negro was a serious economic competitor of the Southern "poor white" class, he presented an amendment to the work-relief act of 1938 which proposed to return America's 12,000,000 Negroes to Africa. In a four-hour speech Bilbo reiterated that the Negro was inferior to the white man and that racial equality was impossible in the United States; and he argued that unemployment could be eliminated when white citizens would take over jobs vacated by emigrant Negroes. After recording these views Senator Bilbo tacitly admitted that he was aiming at personal publicity, for he withdrew the amendment—and then mailed 100,000 copies of his speech to Mississippi voters.[32]

A year later, in April of 1939, Bilbo again strove for Southern applause through revival of the same scheme. This time, introducing a specific bill, he sought to have the federal government subsidize a Negro exodus to Africa. This proposal would have the United States acquire 400,000 square miles of African territory from Great Britain and France as a partial payment on their war debts, and it would provide a billion dollar appropriation to help establish the Negro republic. Claiming that a petition signed by 2,500,000 Negro citizens supported this plan, Bilbo estimated that at least 8,000,000 U.S. Negroes would welcome a chance to establish farms and businesses in an African Negro commonwealth. And in support of this project, he asserted that only through such physical separation of colored and white people could miscegenation be prevented and Western civilization be preserved.[33]

Though a Senate committee buried the bill, Bilbo refused to let his colonization proposal die. In 1940 he published an article, "An African Home For Our Negros," in the Living Age magazine;[34] and he has indicated that he will re-introduce

32. *Ibid.* (May 24, 1938), 7348; see also *ibid.*, LXXXVIII (Nov. 19, 1942), 8955.
33. *Ibid.*, LXXXIV (Apr. 24, 1939), 4649-73.
34. Theodore G. Bilbo, "An African Home For Our Negroes," *Living Age*, June, 1940, pp. 327-35.

Negro repatriation legislation in post-war times.[35] Indeed, in a 1944 report to the Mississippi legislature, Senator Bilbo stated, "When this war is over and the two million Negro soldiers whose minds have been poisoned with political and social equality stuff return and 'hell breaks out' all over this country, I think I'll get more help in settling the Negroes in Africa." [36]

The emergence of the anti-poll-tax movement furnished Theodore G. Bilbo with other convenient opportunities for stimulation of Mississippi's racial hypertension. At first Bilbo overlooked local agitation of the issue, but he hastened to repair this omission during his 1940 re-election campaign. Then, in statements echoing from Vinegar Bend to Honeysuckle Creek, he repeatedly declared:

> I am above all a white Mississippi Democrat and have every day of my life fought for white supremacy. No man or woman of the state can question this fact; but these unconscionable maligners have tried to represent to the people that I favor the repeal of the poll tax making it possible for the Negroes to participate in governmental affairs. This is the biggest lie that has been uttered against me in this campaign.... I want to make it absolutely impossible for the Negro to vote in our white primaries and thus guarantee white supremacy and at the same time I want all white Democratic men and women of the state to have a say-so in nominating the party's candidate in our party primaries....[37]

After Senator Bilbo returned to Congress, he carefully watched the progress of federal anti-poll-tax legislation. And when the Geyer bill, H.R. 1046, reached the floor of the Senate in November of 1942, Bilbo joined Senators Connally and McKellar in organizing a Southern bloc for filibustering purposes. Thereupon, while Senator Connally directed parliamentary strategy, the Mississippian gladly carried the chief burden in the oratorical marathon.

With national attention focussed upon the stalemated Senate, "The Man Bilbo" prepared to capitalize upon his strategic

35. *Congressional Record*, LXXXVIII (Nov. 19, 1942), 8955-57.
36. "Senator Bilbo's Address Before the Joint Session of the Mississippi Legislature," Mar. 22, 1944, p. 8. (Mimeographed text of speech supplied author by Mr. Heber Ladner, Clerk of the Mississippi House of Representatives.)
37. 1940 campaign publicity sheet. (Copy provided author by Bilbo's secretary.)

prominence. Appearing with arms overloaded with magazines, papers, and judicial tomes, the filibusterer posed for photographers and then announced that he was "ready to talk until Christmas."[38] And his performance gave emphasis to the threat. Day after day Bilbo erupted colorful bombast about States Rights and White Supremacy, and he plainly labelled his efforts as a defense of "Southern Rights." Then, admitting, "No doubt the majority of the people of the United States are against the poll tax as a qualification for voting," Bilbo baldly claimed:

I feel that today I am as much a soldier fighting the enemies of our American dual system of government as is any marine on Guadalcanal. . . .
I am fighting this bill because I know that if it is possible to remove the poll tax as a prerequisite to voting, it will be possible to pass a bill to remove some of the other qualifications we have in Mississippi. . . . If that is done we will have no way of preventing the Negro from voting. . . . Then as the Negroes get their political power, they will demand social rights, economic rights, and other rights. . . .
The proposed legislation would be the entering wedge. It would open the flood gates. It would prize open Pandora's box . . . that is why I would be willing to speak for 30 days, or 60 days if necessary, in order to prevent passage of this proposed legislation. . . .
I may have little popularity at the other end of Pennsylvania Avenue, but what do I care, when I know that I am fighting to save the American dual system of government? Or, to put it on a political basis, what do I care when 99% of the people of Mississippi are 100% behind me on this question?[39]

Five days of such oratory won Bilbo a lush harvest of publicity. Newscasters described his antics, newspapers chronicled his filibuster, and news magazines prominently displayed his picture. Moreover, Mississippians took notice of his activity and endorsed his work. After a full week of Bilbonic filibustering the Senate still refused imposition of the cloture rule, consequently the majority leadership decided to by-pass the Geyer bill. Thereby the poll-tax bloc won a parliamentary victory and garnered the plaudits of the South.

38. See *Time*, Nov. 23, 30, 1942.
39. *Congressional Record*, LXXXVIII (Nov. 19, 20, 1942), 8953-69, 9020, *passim*.

But when the Seventy-eighth Congress convened, a second round of controversy developed. The House of Representatives again passed the Geyer bill, thus anti-poll tax legislation reappeared off the Senate calendar. Again Bilbo announced that he would "filibuster this damnable bill for 18 months to kill it," [40] and again the poll-tax bloc plotted obstructionism. Ultimately, in May of 1944, the Geyer measure reached the Senate floor. Immediately Southern senators invoked technicalities designed to pigeonhole the legislation, and in the course of two days of parliamentary maneuvering they demonstrated sufficient support to avert cloture. Then Senator Bilbo obtained the floor and indicated his intention to conduct a full-scale filibuster. At this stage, faced with an indefinite impasse in the wartime Congress, the Senate leadership capitulated. The anti-poll-tax measure was sidetracked, and the filibusterers ended their campaign. [41] Once more Bilbo and his allies had won a victory—and again they reaped Southern approbation.

While exploitation of racial friction is his demagogic forte, Theodore G. Bilbo similarly capitalizes upon chronic economic discontent within his electorate. Mississippi ranks as the most poverty-stricken segment of the Union; consequently Bilbo has campaigned for office upon platforms promising the redistribution of wealth. More specifically, speaking from the Senate rostrum, he has consistently endorsed larger federal appropriations for the benefit of cotton farmers, the jobless and destitute, and dependent aged persons. Very few potential voters can charge that their pocketbooks have been ignored, for Senator Bilbo periodically deluges Mississippi with off-prints of the *Congressional Record* which reveal his constant efforts to procure financial aid for his constituents.

Since Mississippi is the second largest cotton-raising state, "The Man Bilbo" naturally champions the interests of King Cotton. Frequently reminding the Senate of the long depressed status of the cotton farmers, he has particularly sponsored three ameliorative measures—extension of federal crop insur-

40. "Bilbo's Address to Mississippi Legislature," Mar. 24, 1944, mimeographed text, p. 7.
41. See *Congressional Record*, XC (May 10-12, 1944), 4327-47, 4383-4405, 4469-4512.

ance to cover cotton, establishment of research laboratories for the investigation of new uses of cotton, and governmental purchase of the annual cotton surpluses. Moreover, Senator Bilbo is always ready to loosen national purse strings for the benefit of cotton producers. In 1937, urging government guarantees of "parity prices," he extravagantly asserted, "We will never reach the ideal price for cotton to give the grower a fair deal until he gets 25¢ a pound for cotton." [42] Similar incessant demands for larger subsidies reached a peak in the election year of 1940, for he then introduced legislation to treble national appropriations for agricultural benefit payments. Even the impact of World War II did not abate Bilbo's zeal for the cotton-growers' profits. Steadfastly opposing price ceilings for agriculture, he has argued, "There are some things worse than inflation. . . . The so-called parity prices are not enough." [43]

Senator Bilbo also remembers the chronic distress of Mississippi's share-croppers. Realizing full well that only 30 per cent of his constituents own the land they till, Bilbo has urged federal assistance to improve the plight of tenant farmers. Not only has he promoted such projects as seed loans, the Resettlement Administration, and the Farm Security Administration, but he advocates more comprehensive action. On this subject the Senator has typically declared, "I speak especially because Mississippi is the banner state when it comes to the number of tenant farmers. . . . We must have laws and policies which will make it possible for these farmers to succeed after we have bought him a farm and equipped him to carry on farming operations." [44]

Moreover, Theodore Bilbo has conspicuously attempted to raid the federal treasury in behalf of other destitute Mississippians. One of these schemes, designed to curry favor with Townsend Club members, concerns the expansion of old age pensions. Pointing out that impoverished Mississippi can provide her elderly citizens with but $10 monthly whereas aged folk in wealthier states are paid $30, Bilbo has attacked the

42. Ibid., LXXXII (Aug. 3, 1937), 8097.
43. Ibid., LXXXVIII (Sept. 23, 1942), 7319.
44. Ibid., LXXXI (July 2, 1937), 6758.

existing federal social security system as discriminatory. He has denounced the "dollar-matching" principle of national contributions as "vicious, inequitable, unfair, unrighteous, almost criminal," [45] and he has agitated for federal financial aid to equalize state old age pensions. Indeed, perennially introducing futile legislation to make old age assistance solely a national responsibility, Senator Bilbo often has taken care to publicize statements such as this:

> For 7 years I have had before the Finance Committee a bill or an amendment to change the miserable and criminal matching law which is now in operation. I hail from a state which is not economically able to match Federal money in order to provide decent compensation for our old citizens who are in need. . . .
> I feel very keenly the need of this legislation. I appreciate the fact that it would cost additional money. . . . But the obligation is a federal responsibility and should be so met. . . . Thirty dollars is not too much; it is not enough.[46]

Senator Bilbo likewise has identified his name with the expansion of federal relief activities in Mississippi. Consistently supporting large congressional appropriations for work-relief purposes, he has always made certain that his constituency received a maximum share of federal largesse. Moreover, when the 1939 curtailment in relief funds foreshadowed the dismissal of thousands of Mississippians from government projects, Bilbo implored Congress to restore $150,000,000 to the WPA program. And to exploit full political credit for these efforts, he has frequently padded the *Congressional Record* with remarks like this:

> Mr. President, I believe in governmental economy, but I do not belong to the so-called economic bloc which is attempting to cut to the bone every appropriation which has a tendency to relieve suffering humanity and contribute to the social uplift of the people of our Nation.
> We boast of the fact that we have the greatest nation on earth, the wealthiest nation on earth. . . . This is no time to get economic hysteria and defeat an appropriation which is very essential to the welfare of 700,000 or 800,000 American citizens. . . .[47]

45. *Ibid.*, LXXXIV (July 12, 1939), 8922-23.
46. *Ibid.*, LXXXVIII (Feb. 19, 1942), 1475.
47. *Ibid.*, LXXXIV (Apr. 11, 1939), 4103-4.

Apart from his demonstrations of economic or racialist demagoguery, "The Man Bilbo" has not played a conspicuous role in Congress. For over ten years he has occupied a seat in the Senate, but his legislative record is still barren of constructive accomplishment. In general, Senator Bilbo's political activities have conformed to a stereotyped Southern pattern. Substituting shibboleths for statesmanship, he has hidden behind the verbiage of States Rights, White Supremacy, and Democratic Solidarity. He has introduced virtually no legislation that transcends local or regional significance, and he has avoided definite commitments on national issues. Even on questions of great consequence—foreign policy, governmental finance, post-war planning, etc.—the Mississippian has usually offered only fragmentary and unconstructive comments. And when voting roll calls have been taken, Bilbo has discreetly followed party directives.

The basic pattern of Theodore Bilbo's demagoguery is far from new. The politicians of ancient Rome courted the masses with "Bread and Circuses," and Bilbo successfully follows the same method in contemporary Mississippi. In his twentieth-century version of the classic Roman formula, "The Man Bilbo" has entertained his electorate with colorful electioneering and filibustering fulminations. And he has lavishly promised financial manna—WPA checks, AAA subsidies, and old age pensions—to his impoverished constituents. Shrewd and wily in his exploitation of the prejudices and chronic poverty of his fellow citizens, the "Poplarville Prophet" has long enjoyed a large personal following among the hill folk of Mississippi. And since he is now firmly entrenched as Mississippi's senior United States senator, "The Man Bilbo" seems destined to remain an indestructible demagogue.

18

JOSEPH H. BALL

"A Liberal Dose of Candor"

BY NAT. S. FINNEY

T HE CAREER OF U. S. SENATOR JOSEPH H. BALL, JUNIOR Republican member from Minnesota, began with an accident. The air liner in which the late Senator Ernest Lundeen flew northward out of Washington in 1940 to keep a speaking appointment before an isolationist audience was caught in an autumn storm and smashed against a hillside. Investigation of the mishap in which Lundeen died indicated he was, in a sense, the victim of an act of God, for the plane's pilot appeared to have blundered into that one cloud in a million in which the stress of conflicting air currents has the power to twist a wing off a strong aircraft or hurl it a thousand feet in either direction like a helpless leaf. At any rate the accident killed perhaps the most recklessly determined isolationist in the U. S. Senate, a man who had not hesitated to invite George Sylvester Viereck, known and avowed German propagandist, to use his offices on Capitol Hill as central point in a determined campaign to confuse an America upon which Germany later declared war.

To replace Senator Lundeen, Governor Harold E. Stassen of Minnesota appointed perhaps the last man Minnesota's Republican old guard would have listed as available. Governor Stassen picked a thirty-five-year-old St. Paul newspaper reporter known to his colleagues as Joe Ball, and it is fair to say that the appointment satisfied no one except Governor Stassen and Joe Ball. The county chairmen from the Lake of the Woods to the Iowa border went around for weeks with bloodshot eyes and apoplectic faces. Some of them grumbled incoherently for print against Stassen, the young Republican Moses who had led them out of an Egypt of Farmer-Laborite state control. Had they known what line Joe Ball was going to take when he got down to Washington the arteries of the old-guardsmen would have popped like so many carnival balloons. And the roar of indignation that would have gone up from the violently anti-war voters who put Lundeen in office less than two years before his death would have been something to hear.

Governor Stassen's selection of Ball to succeed Lundeen, however bitter a pill it may have been to Minnesota's old-line Republicans and to the Farmer-Laborites who had elected Lundeen, was not an accident. Ball had earned a plum. As top political writer for the St. Paul *Pioneer Press and Dispatch* he had effectively sold young "Red" Stassen to his readers, both when Stassen, as leader of the Young Republicans, had demanded and got his chance to lead the party and while Stassen was putting his program through a state legislature long dead-locked with Farmer-Labor governors who had fallen short of mustering working majorities in that branch of government. That Ball's stories were approved by his editors, who also backed Stassen is, of course, true. But Joe was no king's man or publisher's hack around his own city room. He believed his stuff, and that belief had its impact on his readers. Joe Ball meant it across the board. As an individual he sat in the counsels of Stassen's new Republican machine. He put in all the hours he could steal from his own sleep to get "Red" Stassen elected, and to sell his program to the state when he became its first Republican governor in a dozen years.

Ball's first national notice came in Eastern journals, which seized upon his appointment to the Senate as proof that Governor Stassen was the creature of a new Republican boss. Ball was pictured as the boss, and his appointment as emergence of a power from behind the scenes. The Minnesota politicians who heard about that one might have had a belly laugh out of it had they been able to laugh. They weren't able. Their sour observation at the time was that Minnesota's junior senator had never been elected dog catcher under his own steam, and that the 1942 elections would settle his hash. That view strengthened through the summer of 1941 as they watched the course Ball was steering in Washington. It wasn't until the question of American involvement in the war became one of when, rather than one of whether, that Minnesota's political wiseacres began to hedge their bets on Ball. "If we are in it before election day he might make the grade," they conceded.

There is no doubt that Senator Ball's colleagues in Washington were inclined to ignore him as a political accident when he arrived here in late October, 1940. They had the best of reasons for taking that view. The Minnesota delegation of eight Republicans and one Farmer-Laborite in the house, and one ex-Farmer-Laborite Republican in the Senate presented an unbroken front of opposition to the measures by which the country was moving toward declared war. They had given the late Senator William E. Borah unanimous support in defeating President Roosevelt's attempt to amend the Neutrality Act during the spring of 1939. If their formula for winning re-election in Minnesota was right, Joe Ball's freely expressed views were an invitation to political disaster. Furthermore, with but few exceptions, Minnesota's Republicans in Congress hated Governor Harold Stassen's guts. He had not consulted them about his senatorial appointment, nor, in fact, about much of anything else. There was plenty of irony in the little ceremony in which Senator Henrik Shipstead, political beneficiary of the terrific reaction that swept Minnesota after World War I, introduced to the Senate a young man who was to cancel out his vote on many an occasion. Republicans were a scarce article in the U. S. Senate in 1940 and committee appointments for them plentiful, yet it's hard to see how Joe Ball could have been given much less. He was assigned to Banking and Currency, Education and Labor, Immigration, Manufactures, and Printing. Appointment to the Special Committee to Investigate the National Defense Program, the Truman committee, came later. That would have been enough to send a professional politician sore and sulking to his office in the big marble building on Constitution Avenue designated as S. O. B. (Senate Office Building.) Committee assignments are the hard money of senatorial business. They put a member in position to do a lot of little and some big things for his constituents. Any major committee appointment will do, but members from various regions have favorites. It lightens their work to be able to do their trading inside committees to which they belong, rather than between committees. A Minnesota senator works most comfortably on such committees as Agriculture and Forestry, Finance, and Interstate Commerce. Farming, taxes, and transportation are important to a lot of people in Minnesota. If assignments on these committees aren't available, seats on such committees as Claims, Naval and Military Affairs, Appropriations, and Judiciary supply a member with good trading stock. The closest Senator Ball got to a solid fence-building committee was Banking and Currency. In the recondite symbols of senatorial politics, Joseph H. Ball was marked for slaughter in the next election.

Tall, shaggy-haired, somewhat lumbering in gait, Senator Ball has little of the physical magnetism political figures often possess, yet he is a man not difficult to remember. He has some humor, but the dominant note in his personality is sincerity. He believes what he says. The weight of his belief makes him a bit heavy in his public speaking, though as he has gained experience, this heaviness has been to a degree relieved by a better sense of timing. He has a much better than average mind and is more able than most men in politics to grasp conceptual distinctions. Newspaper work has made him what theatrical folk call a "quick study." He is able to get over written information quickly and to grasp its import accurately. His outlook is essentially liberal. It is that of a comparatively young man who has worked hard for his living, making his own way without the assistance of family or any degree of accumulated wealth. He lives on his senatorial salary and such income as comes to him from speaking and writing. He writes clear, well-buttoned-up prose with few trimmings.

Senator Ball's attitude toward his job is a serious attitude. His convictions about that job are strongly held. They are hardly the convictions of the usual professional politician, and it is at least reasonable to doubt whether they would have led Senator Ball back to Washington in 1942 had the circumstances of that campaign been ordinary. He believes, among other things, in a high degree of candor in political relations with his constituents. His handling of two issues, the so-called equal rights-for-women bill and the bill to prohibit sale of liquor in the vicinity of army camps, offers an example of Senator Ball's idea of candor. Both issues were, characteristically, issues on which a member of Congress can lose votes without gaining them. It is customary to follow the Biblical precept that a soft answer turneth away wrath. Senator Ball wrote constituent backers of the measures that he was opposed to them, and why. In an address to a Townsend-Plan-sponsored meeting in southern Minnesota, he frankly stated that he did not believe the plan workable. Joe Ball believes such candor pays political dividends; that it played an important part in his re-election in 1942. He is convinced the voters are ready for a straight answer. He was re-elected by a very substantial majority. Perhaps he is right.

Senator Ball has the deepest convictions about international affairs. He is among the Senate's foremost advocates of international organization, super-government, if you please, as the only feasible way to maintain world peace.

A devotee of the League of Nations in his earlier years, he is convinced it failed because it did not go far enough in the delegation of national sovereignty to an international agency. He believes an international agency should have, and be in a position to wield, military force. Though he has been less vocal in expressing this correlative conviction, he believes an international agency should have power to enforce economic arrangements upon individual nations. He cannot fairly be called a free-trader (if that term has any meaning), but he is strongly hostile to arbitrary trade barriers, erected for the selfish protection of individual states. He not only voted for extension of the Trade Agreements Act in 1942, he actively sought votes for its extension among fellow Republicans in the Senate.

These convictions about the course the United States should follow in international leadership have an important parallel in Senator Ball. He is sharply hostile to the bi-lateral or tri-lateral alliances characteristic of what he calls power politics. The balance-of-power principle which gave Europe its long period of relative peace prior to 1914 is, he feels, inimical to world peace in the twentieth century. In short, Senator Ball's espousal of world organization is accompanied by active hostility to what might be called historic methods of international organization.

The position a member of the Senate takes on such a paramount issue as the peace that is to follow a present war is more than likely to reflect the thinking of his constituents. This fact may be stated without aspersion of servility to the member or cynicism about the legislative function. A legislator is a part of the body of his constituents, just as they are a part of him. To describe the whole it is necessary to study both parts, legislator and constituents. The study is especially interesting in Senator Ball's case, for it poses political riddles which probably cannot be solved without close study of the anatomy of Midwestern isolationism. Minnesota is properly regarded as a strongly isolationist state. Yet it elected, in 1942, both a governor and a senator who boldly advocated delegation of a part of the national sovereign power to an international agency. It has been asserted and in some quarters is believed that the voters of Minnesota remained isolationist but were willing to overlook an aberration in their candidates because of other virtues, compelling ones, seen in them. The assertion is not susceptible of either proof or disproof, but the probabilities are strongly against it. Senator Shipstead, exponent of the opposite view, actively campaigned against Ball in 1942. Light is thrown on the matter by Senator Ball's phenomenal success in winning adherence to the so-called Ball-Burton-Hatch-Hill resolution he and other senators pressed during the summer and autumn of 1943. The campaign for this resolution undoubtedly generated the steam that forced the Fulbright and Connally resolutions through Congress, and it played a major part in winning almost unanimous support for the San Francisco Charter.

In origin the B2-H2 resolution—which would have placed the Senate on record as advising the President it would support an international organization with military power to enforce its determinations—can be traced back to the first unfolding of Senator Ball's career in Congress. Ball's first important contacts developed in the so-called Truman Committee to investigate the national defense program. This committee, when formed early in 1941, was considered of minor consequence. Its chairman, Harry S. Truman, was then a Missouri machine Democrat of unknown quality. Its membership was not, at first, regarded as strong. Actually the committee's strength was in its weakness. Its members were relative newcomers, hence not preoccupied with the game of staying in the Senate through sedulous use of office to erect political fences. They had marks to make and the freshness of approach that often withers out of senior members.

Senator Ball took his assignment to the Truman Committee in the same spirit he had taken important assignments from his editors back in St. Paul. He contributed the skill of a working newspaper reporter at digging out facts and the facility of a sound reporter at writing them down in plain, direct English. His colleagues on the committee liked him. The word got about that however short his stay might be in the Senate, he was all right. His work on the committee commanded respect. He generally kept his mouth shut on the floor. When he did speak he made sense. The Truman Committee developed a good staff and began to attract attention by a sound job of investigation without too much of the ballyhoo that often emanates from such committees. What few realized at the time was that the Truman Committee was more than its name implied. For want of a better word it might be called a coterie of young senators of both parties.

Such a coterie could have developed only in the unusual atmosphere of the Seventy-seventh Congress. An overwhelming Democratic majority and a puny Republican minority made a situation in which party discipline grew lax on the Democratic side of the aisle and well-nigh disappeared on the Republican side. The Democrats did not need all their votes to carry an issue involving a party position. The Republicans had no real hope of successfully opposing the majority. Bipartisan groupings were not discouraged from free-lancing by party leadership. After all, there was no real power question on a showdown. Democrats and Republicans, if so minded, could talk freely with each other. In the Truman Committee coterie they did so. They kicked around all sorts of questions, and among them the question of what sort of a peace the country was fighting for. Actually the B2-H2 resolution was born at an informal luncheon of the Truman Committee members. Three of the four senators who gave their names to the Ball-Burton-Hatch-Hill resolution were members of the Truman coterie. When speakers went out over the country to sponsor the ideas embodied in the resolution, every member of the Truman Committee but Senator Tom Connally of Texas volunteered.

The story of how the resolution developed and its influence upon final Senate action is public property. What should be emphasized in Senator Ball's story is the simple fact that the kernel idea of the resolution caught the public eye and fancy in a way that must convince any thoughtful person that it struck a natural vein of public response. The success of the resolution's central ideas—which are identically Senator Ball's ideas —was due to something more than the vigorous support given those ideas. It was a case of hitting on an acceptable expression for a widespread feeling in the public mind. Senator Ball may be credited with an outstanding act of political divination, no less phenomenal because it was a sincere act. Such political water-witching is rare enough on minor issues. To hit a vein that appears to underlie a major part of the country is indeed an achievement.

A simple reading of the election returns in Minnesota indicates that the vein underlies that state as well as others and that Senator Ball tapped it there in 1942. There remains a fair question whether its existence in Minnesota means that state is not isolationist. Had Senator Ball advocated a strong alliance with the British Empire would the results have been the same? Was it the fact that he advocated strong alliance with a constructive everybody rather than a specific somebody that made his position acceptable? Does this apparent willingness to accept national responsibility through schematic world organization reflect a true disposition to shoulder an obligation in world affairs? These are the questions that must be answered if one wishes to get at the essential character of an apparently changed opinion in Midwest America.

Yet the fact that they are asked should not cast doubt on the sincerity of Senator Ball's willingness to see his country accept a responsible position in world affairs. There is a simple and effective test. It is whether the advocate of international organization for world peace is willing to see the hide of international economic co-operation go along with the political tail. Ball is keenly aware that international co-operation on the political level without parallel co-operation at the economic level is an empty dream. He understands fully that a post-war emulsion of economic nationalism and political internationalism will separate in short order. He is aware that his own constituents are likely to be slower to accept international economic co-operation than international political co-operation. He believes Minnesota voters will accept the idea that towering national tariff barriers are not the way to peace, or, for that matter, to prosperity. It is his conviction they have been hoodwinked on the tariff issue, and that a liberal dose of candor will change their minds. He intends to administer that dose.

Senator Ball's views on a second mammoth issue of his times place him in the liberal camp, but toward the center rather than out on the left. He is advocate of a federal code of labor relations which will provide for systematic settlement of employer-employee disputes in the public interest but without favor to either camp. His views on this issue are by no means illiberal, but they strongly emphasize the element of law and the use of lawful machinery in handling disputes. As a member of the Senate Education and Labor Committee, which had become the burial ground of all legislation to curb labor unions, Ball worked might and main to bring the committee to agreement on some congressional expression that would remove regulation of labor relations from the sphere of presidential executive order. In a measure he succeeded. The committee actually reported out for Senate action a bill bearing Ball's name, despite the fact he is a Republican and was therefore, hardly entitled to see an important act of Congress bear his name. Space is lacking here to examine the bill in detail, but it can be safely asserted it is a sound proposal concealing no tricks to throttle trade unionism. When it was stymied, as was to be expected at the time, Ball voted for passage of the so-called Smith-Connally Act. He says he did so realizing it was bad legislation. He felt he could not vote nay on the one piece of legislation the administration's congressional supporters permitted to come before the Senate—the one chance offered to establish labor-dispute regulation by law. Like other senators, he resented the president's veto.

Nowhere were the contrasts between liberal and conservative viewpoint more difficult to tab with party labels than in the Senate of the United States during the seventy-seventh and seventy-eighth congresses. The atavistic conservatism of a Bilbo on the Democratic side of the aisle could hardly be squared on party principle with the frenetic liberalism of a Pepper. Nor could the Republican escutcheon cover in the differences between Hiram Johnson and Joseph Ball. It was very confusing. One had to ask: What do you mean when you use the word Republican? Senator Ball's answer to that question throws a good deal of light on a part of his record that is puzzling to the citizen who still thinks the word liberal can be defined in fewer than ten thousand well-chosen words. Ball consistently voted to ban consumer subsidies during the fights over that issue. He voted for the Rankin version of the soldier's vote bill. He was opposed to a National Service Act. As a member of the Truman Committee he cast many a sharp harpoon into the flanks of Roosevelt's war administration. In campaigning for convention delegates for the nomination of former Governor Harold Stassen he did not hesitate to belabor the New Deal. While no Roosevelt hater, he concealed no secret admiration for the Democratic chieftain.

How then can one explain Senator Ball's last-minute declaration that he would vote for Roosevelt in 1944? The question cannot be satisfactorily answered solely in terms of Ball's assertion that Roosevelt was in a better position to win a clear and constructive mandate from American voters to proceed with the establishment of a world organization to guarantee future world peace. Some of the political realities in the background must be remembered.

Harold E. Stassen, Ball's political sponsor, aspires to be President of the United States. He resigned the governorship in Minnesota in 1943 to accept a commission in the Navy, and as a commander and flag secretary to Admiral William F. Halsey, was out of direct touch with politics during the 1944 presidential year. Yet Stassen took care not to remove himself from the reach of his party if it saw fit to draft him as its 1944 candidate. The effect of the statement Stassen issued some months before the convention was that he was interested in the pre-convention campaign even though he took no active part in it. Stassen's position saddled Senator Ball with some very complex problems, and it is not surprising that he was unable to solve them all without leaving black marks on his own record.

The first problem Stassen's position presented to his political lieutenant was the problem of Wendell L. Willkie's candidacy. Stassen, who was Willkie's floor leader at the 1940 Republican convention, had been careful to stake out a reservation of his own in foreign policy before he joined the Navy. He had, in poker phraseology, seen Willkie and raised him one. The Willkie-Stassen friendship had, as a result, measurably cooled, and the two men had become competitors for the same wing of the Republican party. But with this important difference: Willkie's bid was for the immediate support of the Republican party at its 1944 convention, while Stassen's bid, on any realistic political terms, was for future support. A Stassen campaign for a favorite son delegation from his own state in 1944 would have made political sense. The pretense of Stassen backers, Senator Ball included, that his campaign for the 1944 nomination was a die-in-the-ditch affair did not make political sense. The chances of a Minnesotan, no matter how outstanding, for the nomination of the Republican party are "peripheral" even when the candidate himself is present to push his claims with the utmost vigor. Stassen was absent; he was unable to direct and lead his own campaign, his claim to the nomination had not, in terms of his own career, matured. His absence in the Navy was, indeed, the most practical sort of admission that he did not consider himself ready to demand the leadership of his party.

Yet Senator Ball was compelled by simple political loyalty to support Stassen for the nomination. And this placed him in a doubly anomalous position. He hàd first to support Stassen for the nomination, which in effect, if not intent, meant that Senator Ball led a stop-Willkie movement. He could not, and it may be asserted, did not avoid the suspicion of the Dewey faction that both he and his sponsor, Stassen, had a stake in seeing the 1944 candidate of the Republican party defeated so that Stassen might have a clearer shot at the Republican nomination and election in 1948. The logic of Senator Ball's position is clear enough, and the action he took proceeds unfalteringly from that logic. He wanted Willkie defeated for the nomination and Dewey defeated in the election, leaving Stassen a clear try in 1948. Yet we are left with two questions that are of interest in a search for the key to the riddle of a public man's motivation. Did Senator Ball have to sacrifice principle to follow the course he followed? Did he handle himself in such a manner as to avoid the charge of having been politically used by the opposition party, and to leave his title clear to membership in his own party?

The answer to the first question depends upon which candidate best served Ball's convictions on the foreign policy issue. It is doubtful whether any such question ever existed in Ball's mind, and if it did it was certainly answered very early in Governor Dewey's campaign. Ball, as a St. Paul political reporter, had watched the launching of Dewey's 1940 campaign for the nomination, and he had first hand information that Dewey's support was the America First organization of that year. This naturally aroused his suspicion of the sincerity of Dewey's professions. And this suspicion was amply confirmed by the persistent unwillingness of Dewey and his associates to consult Ball about the foreign policy issue in the campaign. Without attempting to look into Governor Dewey's mind, it is possible to say Ball was sincerely convinced President Roosevelt's position was preferable to the Republican candidate's.

But Senator Ball did not succeed in handling himself in such a way as to be invulnerable to the charge that he was "used" by Roosevelt. The point at which he was in honor bound to bolt the Republican party was at Chicago, before the convention had agreed upon Governor Dewey as its candidate. This Ball did not do. Instead he resoundingly pledged the Stassen delegates to support Dewey. His bolt to the support of Roosevelt came much later and was timed to serve Roosevelt's vote-getting purposes rather than Ball's convictions. In the Roosevelt camp Ball's bolt was properly regarded as a campaign coup, and nothing the Senator can adduce can change the belief of the Democrats that they "used" him in winning the election. What effect all this may have upon the political futures of Senator Ball and former Governor Stassen remains to be seen. Certainly there is some cloud upon the party regularity of both. Yet so scrambled is the Republican party itself that it seems unlikely either Ball or Stassen might be forced to leave the shelter of the elephant's tent.

Senator Ball's Republicanism is rooted in the conviction that America is in real danger of failing to maintain its economic and political liberties. His alarm is by no means excited solely by dangers to the left. He fears an undiscriminating conservatism as keenly as he does the paternalism-in-government that has been a leitmotif of the New Deal. He feels himself to be representative of a "younger group thinking in terms of the future rather than of the past; asking what part of this system is good and must be preserved, and how we can move forward." He observes that he has no interest in conserving monopoly and exploitation. He notes that old, established businesses of major size adjust themselves readily to government regulation. It is the new outfits that find difficulty in surviving under it. Old industry, he feels, becomes itself bureaucratized and is at home with bureaucratic government. Regulation, he feels, encourages organized economic activity to load up with too much dead wood; and security for this dead wood implies restraint of competition. Sharply competitive industry can't afford dead wood, yet it offers economic opportunity. Ball feels certain that economic opportunity and political freedom walk hand in hand, and he is convinced that the New Deal, in its pursuit of economic security for modern man, trends toward sacrifice of opportunity and freedom. Were Senator Ball well-fixed financially or on the make for money, this view would be understandable enough. He is neither. He does not even exhibit a typically senatorial anxiety to remain in Congress. He knows he is hardly a diligent choreboy for the interests back home, but that self-knowledge does not worry him.

Joe Ball, the political reporter who came to Congress by accident, holds views about staying there so singular they are hard to credit. The belief that rotation of crops of politicians is healthful for the grass roots is not uncommon, especially in election year. Yet rare is the incumbent who feels it would be good political agronomy to plow him under. Heaven knows how Senator Ball will feel about it in 1948, when he again faces the voters, but in 1944 he thought he might well be ripe enough by then to be cut down. New blood and vigor outweigh experience, he feels. The thing that hurts democratic government most is the tendency of politicians to hang onto power long after their usefulness is spent. Health in government can be maintained by booting a man out when he has shot his wad of ideas, and Minnesota's junior senator believes that applies to Joseph H. Ball.

19

TOM CONNALLY
"One of the Senate Gallery's Favorites"

BY OTIS MILLER AND ANITA F. ALPERN

T HE PAST, PRESENT, AND FUTURE FIND A COMMON MEET-
ing ground in American politics; and the future destiny
of the United States and of the world will, to an unknown
extent, be shaped by Tom Connally, senior senator from Texas,
who is the Chairman of the Senate Foreign Relations Committee. Since Senator Lodge prevented the approval of President Wilson's world-embracing peace movement in 1920, no
one has doubted the inherent power of this position. Before the
outbreak of World War II, the Foreign Relations Committee
had acted on the ship-arming bill, lease-lend legislation, the bill
to revise the Neutrality Act, and all other matters pertaining
to our foreign policy. After Pearl Harbor, the difficulties in
dealing with neutral nations, governments in exile, were part
of this committee's work. Important as these matters were,
the committee's role is even more compelling in shaping the
peace, and the willing or unwilling recipient of these huge responsibilities is Tom Connally.

He is big and broad, with blue eyes, and wavy streaked gray
hair curled up at the ends like the curl on the north end of a
south-bound mallard duck. Connally's appearance and garb
have fixed him indelibly in the political mind of the nation. His
black suit cut along political lines, his stiff-bosomed shirts, his
flowing black silk ribbons for his glasses or his watch, his black
string tie—all once led the late Joe Bailey to remark, "Tom
Connally is the only man in the U.S. Senate who could wear a
Roman Toga and not look like a fat man in a nightgown."

His unusual dress, which attracts attention wherever he ventures, is not the only Connally trademark. Development of an individual style of oratory that combines the intensity of a Bryanesque tone with an acrobat's grandstand flare for popular acclaim has made Connally one of the Senate gallery's favorites. Upon first entering the political arena, Tom probably possessed the basic viewpoint that an orator is only as good as his delivery, that an actor is only as good as his gestures and characterizations. Today, he is a favorite of visitors and senators alike when complete with facial expressions, gestures, and even pantomime, he lets go at some opponent or issue. Outstanding in Connally's repertoire are his grimaces and prances which accompany his calling some person "an old woman." When referring to someone as "pompous," he draws in his breath and expands his chest. In building up to a blow-off, Connally first speaks in a low tone; his eyes assume an almost paternal expression; and his glasses, in time to the throbbing of his voice, slowly slide down to the tip of his nose. When the M-moment arrives, Connally jerks his glasses off at the same instant in which his voice assumes its full force. News that certain senators are going to take the floor to speak will often clear the Senate of most of its members. However, word that Connally is going to handle even a mildly hot potato will bring Senators thronging from cloak rooms, offices, and lunchrooms.

Connally might have been awarded a page in America's popular history on these bases alone—but the chairmanship of Foreign Relations in wartime is a sure-fire road to the national archives. His name is to be found on more resolutions declaring war against first-rate powers than that of any other man who has ever been in Congress. This has not been accidental. A few minutes after the President's war message on December 8, Tom introduced a resolution declaring war against Japan. Again, three days later when Germany and Italy declared war against the United States, Tom anticipating a presidential message calling for a declaration of war, scheduled a special morning meeting of his committee. Immediately after President Roosevelt's message, Tom announced that the drafts were already committee approved and could be acted upon without delay. On both occasions, Sol Bloom, House Foreign Affairs Committee chairman, was scooped by Connally and the Senate.

Photographers, present in the White House for the historic pictures of President Roosevelt signing the declarations of war, noticed Tom Connally in the foreground. It was only natural for the people to see these pictures of Roosevelt and Connally side by side in their front page newspapers the next morning. This scene of friendship and co-operation was not always the case. For some, it was a strange sight particularly when one recalled the Connally opposition to certain administration domestic policies in the past. As one of the "Immortal Twelve," Connally tore the fringe off the surrey of President Roosevelt's horse-and-buggy-days argument to pack the U.S. Supreme Court in 1937. This is the same Connally who vociferously attacked the NRA and the first reorganization bill. For this opposition, Connally was stripped of most of his political patronage. He was probably saved from a presidential purge attempt in 1938 only because he was not up for re-election that year. Between the court-bill fight and the autumn of 1939, when the President called Tom to congratulate him on a speech for repeal of the arms embargo, there had been no contact between the two.

After Connally assumed the chairmanship of Foreign Relations, he was rated as one of the "big boys." The President made him a member of the privileged group which he invited to the White House almost weekly to discuss foreign affairs. Tom, although accepting the President's gesture of good will, was still somewhat resentful of FDR's former attitude and didn't thaw out toward him overnight. When the President attempted to wave the olive branch, Tom took advantage of the opportunity to tell him that he had been a better friend to him than many others on Capitol Hill on whom the President had fawned. In fact, those in the "know" say that Tom let the President have some "inside information" on what he and John Nance Garner had done for FDR at some former Democratic national convention. In any event, the President's "kitchen cabinet" meetings were not the pink-tea affairs they had previously been. The Senator from Texas enlivened things somewhat by frequently dropping a bomb among the more docile brethren.

Senator Hiram Johnson of California once told Connally, "You are not afraid of any man or issue." Once, in answer to Senator Nye's statement that Woodrow Wilson had duped the United States into World War I, Connally shouted, "Some checker-playing, beer drinking back room of some low house is the only fit place for the kind of language which the Senator from North Dakota puts into the record about a dead man, a great man, a good man, a man who when alive, had the courage to meet his enemies face to face. . . . This committee [Nye's] comes back like a ghoul, a historical ghoul. . . . It has discovered that some international woman of the streets, lurking at the corner of an alley, enticed Uncle Sam down the alley and got him into the war. . . . When the history of this Republic is written, Woodrow Wilson will tower above the puny pygmies who now bark at his memory as Pike's Peak towers above the fogs of an Arkansas swamp."

In a debate, Connally has one objective—to make his opponent look ridiculous. He reads meaning into their words. He infers arguments which were not intended as such. If an opponent unfortunately makes a verbal slip, Connally dismisses all else and concentrates on building the miscue into a mountain.

In the course of one of these debates with Senator Bridges, Republican senator from New Hampshire, Connally stated: "If the Senator from New Hampshire would approach these matters with an open mind instead of an open mouth, . . ." Laughter put an end to this discussion.

Former Senator Burke of Nebraska took Connally on one day with the following result. Burke began, "Am I correct. . . ." Speaking as he rose to his feet, Tom interrupted, "I don't know, but I doubt it very much." Burke never continued.

Perhaps the most famous of all Connally tiffs occurred when he was a representative in the House. During that period in his political life, Tom was constantly opposing Representative Tincher of Kansas, a "big" gentleman weighing about 300 pounds. One day Tincher said: "The trouble with the gentleman from Texas is that when he gets up in the morning and gets his clothes on, he thinks half the world is dressed." Without a moment's hesitation, Connally shot back: "When the gentleman from Kansas gets dressed, he knows half the world is dressed."

Connally doesn't always get the last word. Senator Danaher of Connecticut once accused Connally of being "guilty of a caustic, jeering, mocking type of approach which has been all too common from him." He added that the Connally "gyrations and acting were all directed toward the gallery to elicit some present, temporary applause. . . . The Senator from Texas must know that that kind of cheap, police-court-lawyer tactics may have a certain appeal in some places, but this is not such a place." Connally did not answer this charge; he listened and then quietly slid from the chamber.

Tom's use of legal tactics is quite in keeping with his early training. From childhood, at his father's urging, he prepared for the bar and for politics. Born on a farm near Waco, Texas, August 19, 1877, he was christened Thomas Terry (his mother's maiden name), which he later shortened to Tom, pronounced "Tawm." At fifteen he entered Baylor University at Waco, Texas, a school which Henry L. Mencken might have referred to as the "Baptist Buckle of the Bible Belt." His college years, in fact, coincided with the activities of a Texas Mencken, one Brann, who published a Waco paper called *Brann's Iconoclast*. Much of the invective and bitter repartee which Senator Connally has used so effectively on his opponents in later years has come from his reading and study of this Texas master of sarcasm and vituperation.

Finishing Baylor, Connally hied himself to Austin, capital of Texas, where law and debating were his two chief interests. While he was a law student, the Spanish-American war broke out and Connally volunteered for service, obtaining his law degree "in absentia." His outfit, the Second Texas Volunteers, never left the U.S.A. and when the war ended, Tom and his Second Texas buddies were still stranded at Jacksonville. He volunteered for the First World War, also, but just after his regiment had been given sailing orders, the armistice was signed and Connally was again left at the gate without having done any fighting. This latter time, however, he rose to the rank of captain and adjutant in the Twenty-second Infantry Brigade. He had only been a sergeant major in the Spanish-American war. Of his war experiences, Connally has said on numerous occasions, "I've been in more wars and done less fighting than any man alive."

Connally returned to his old haunts after the Spanish-American war and opened a law office at Marlin, Falls County, Texas. He wasted no time in getting into state politics. Elected to the Texas legislature, he served two terms and then dropped out to again establish his law practice and to earn a better livelihood for his wife, whom he had married against her parents' wishes. After four years as county prosecutor he gave up public office once again to practice law and to build his political fences. He became a member of many organizations: a Mason, Grand Chancellor of the Texas Knights of Pythias, and even a psalm-singing Baptist. He mastered the old but still effective stunt of stopping in the middle of a speech to hail an old friend in the audience, and then to remark casually to the audience— "You folks will pah'don the interruption. It's jes that I hadn't seen Joe Doe in seven years and I felt I jest had to say howdy." In 1917, Connally went to the House of Representatives.

In 1928, after six terms in the House, Connally filed for the Senate. His opponent, the incumbent Earle B. Mayfield, possessed enormous strength from his association with the Ku Klux Klan, then still a mighty political pressure in the South and growing more powerful at that time because of Al Smith's campaign for the Democratic presidential nomination. Connally made the Klan an issue. He roamed the broad Texas prairies and threaded the winding, rutted, and sandy roads of the deep piney woods of East Texas telling all who would listen that the Klan was a work of the Devil and that he had never worn a sheet and a mask.

It was during this campaign that a rumor circulated asserting that Connally had a daughter in a Catholic Convent School in San Antonio. Tom used a stock answer in reply to this. He would introduce his son, an only child, and remark dryly, "Now this is my daughter who is attending a Catholic Convent school for girls at San Antonio." His gangling son would step up, grinning, and permit his dad to introduce him. The crowd laughed, getting a kick out of the joke, and Connally found himself with more friends. The Klan got a reputation for having started a false rumor and devout Baptists and Methodists went away feeling kindly toward even the Catholic church. The fact of the matter is that no one ever knew whether Connally or Mayfield started the rumor, or whether there ever was such a rumor current. In any event, Tom was elected and has been a senator ever since.

Connally has acquired other tricks of the trade which mark a successful office-seeker. Possessing an amazing memory, he never fails to put it to a test, so that a political legend has grown up about him. There are tall tales in Texas about his having once recognized a man he hadn't seen for over twenty years—a rural justice of the peace who once overruled a motion for default judgment against Connally's absent client when Connally interposed the plea that the opposing attorney's motion had died for want of a second. But Connally's greatest vote-getting power lies in his loyalty to Texas; this despite his loyalty to party. Texas is the blood-stream of his political life, and Connally never forgets it. When the bill to abolish the poll tax came up in the Senate, Tom ran on for hours in a filibuster that covered everything from why nearly every stream in Texas is navigable under state law to why watermelons cannot be grown in certain East Texas river bottoms because of the fertility of the soil, the vines growing so fast as to wear the watermelons out dragging them around over the watermelon patch. Again, when the question came up of abolishing the community property law in Texas and in certain other Southern and Western states where Spanish influence once held sway (an old Spanish custom of which Texans heartily approve), Tom went after the defeat of this bill hammer and tongs. If not the greatest orator in the Senate, Connally is certainly no slouch at the art of filibuster. Connally also goes out of his way to forget battle scars once the fight is over— his method of preventing hatred and grudges. After winning his point on the tax bill he told the administration's supporters that their boast of continuing the fight was "just the Japanese doctrine of saving face," and then he added cheerfully, "but that's all right. I'm trying to save mine too."

One of Connally's greatest faults is tactlessness, and in his official position he has put the administration on the frying pan as a result of it. Up to the present time, he made his outstanding *faux pas* when the Rio De Janeiro conference was in session and President Ramon S. Castillo had been quoted as saying that Argentina would never break with the Axis powers. Connally risked his political shirt-tail being caught in the administration clothes wringer by boldly saying to his press conference newsmen that unless Señor Castillo changed his mind, the Argentine people should change their president. All this coming from the chairman of the Committee on Foreign Relations had a firecracker effect on the sedate Mr. Hull and the State Department, which hastened to assure Argentina that Mr. Connally spoke only as Mr. Connally.

On the night of December 7, 1941, President Roosevelt called his cabinet members and party chieftains to the White House to inform them of the Pearl Harbor events. The President finished with the laconic statement, "And that's about all, Gentlemen," when Connally exploded with the monosyllabic question, "All? All?" He then proceeded to "pour it on" Secretary Knox for being caught with his anchors down and for making public statements in the press and over the radio assuring the people that "the navy is ready." Washington gossip has it that the next day when Senator Connally was attending a session of the U.S. Supreme Court, a certain Justice sent him a note reading, "If you gave Knox hell, I concur."

When the European war first began in 1939, Connally was of the opinion that the United States should remain neutral. With this belief, Connally voiced a good deal of opposition to the administration's program, and was associated with isolationism. With the passage of time, he changed his course and became one of the most aggressive Nazi-haters in the Senate. Isolationists, recalling Connally's former speeches, taunted him about his early views. Connally put a sudden end to these taunts by admitting that "my appetite is being well prepared to eat a lot of words."

Some have thought there was a trace of animosity toward the British in Connally's makeup. The facts seem to indicate that although Tom has always demonstrated a cagy attitude toward the British and never rode on Churchill's coat tails, he was in the front rank of those favoring aid to Britain. Once when a State Department representative brought over a proposal for a reciprocal tax exemption agreement for British war industries operating in the U.S. and American war industries operating in the British Isles, Connally said, "Take your treaty out of here before it gets kicked in the seat of the pants." Nevertheless, Tom has voted a pro-Britain ticket.

This may be a straw in the wind indicating what our foreign policy will be under the leadership of Senator Connally. On his shoulders rests a burden that will bear heavily before he is rid of it. He is one of the key men in the little group that are shaping the world's destiny at the close of this war. Tom Connally is already feeling the weight of this burden. He watched with intense interest the course of our foreign diplomacy with the French National Committee, with Spain, Portugal, Turkey, Italy, Russia, and the Middle East. Much of his time was expended on the attitudes to be taken toward India and the Moslem world, the Jew and Palestine, oil interests in the Middle East, air bases we have built in foreign lands, and islands we have taken from Japan. The winning of the war was the immediate task; the winning of the peace is the ultimate Utopia. As chairman of the Senate Foreign Relations Committee, Connally should find himself under the people's closest scrutiny, the nation's finest microscope. A good deal of what America may expect from this man is to be found in the Connally Resolution, a Declaratory of the War and Peace Aims of the United States, introduced and adopted by the United States Senate on October 25, 1943. Speaking before the Senate, Mr. Connally said:

"Mr. President, the Committee on Foreign Relations has recommended to the Senate the passage of the following resolution:

Resolved, That the war against all our enemies be waged until complete victory is achieved.

That the United States co-operate with its comrades-in-arms in securing a just and honorable peace.

That the United States, acting through its constitutional processes, join with free and sovereign nations in the establishment and maintenance of international authority with power to prevent aggression and to preserve the peace of the world.

"The primary condition upon which the peace of the future may be based is the necessity that the present war shall end in victory. It is therefore provided, 'Resolved that the war against all our enemies be waged until complete victory is achieved.' After victory shall be achieved, the next logical step is the securing of an honorable peace. Therefore it is provided, 'That the United States co-operate with its comrades-in-arms in securing a just and honorable peace.' When these pressing and imperative achievements shall have been accomplished the resolution then looks to the establishment and maintenance of international authority to prevent aggression and preserve the peace of the world. It is therefore provided, 'that the United States, acting through its constitutional processes, join with free and sovereign nations in the establishment and maintenance of international authority with power to prevent aggression and to preserve the peace of the world.'

"It thus gives the widest latitude to nations that may become initially, or later, members of any organization or authority which may be created.

"The Senate of the United States will express the desire of the United States to join in the establishment of a world peace agency to curb international bandits and robbers and to preserve the peace of the world. Such an agency does not necessarily imply that world conditions will be frozen. It does not follow that the status quo in every particular will be preserved. The constitution of such a body could provide the necessary elasticity to meet the needs of the future. It will not be an easy task. Difficulties will be encountered. Obstacles will face us. But we need not despair. We have faced great national and international problems before. American genius and leadership and statesmanship will not be deterred by hardships and struggles.

"From our commanding point of vantage we must declare to the world that our influence and our might will be dedicated to the maintenance of world peace and the suppression of military aggression whenever and wherever it may lift its venomous head."

20

JERRY VOORHIS

"What Is Right Rather Than What Is Expedient"

BY CLAUDIUS O. JOHNSON

M R. SPEAKER, CAN DEMOCRACY SURVIVE? THIS IS THE overshadowing question of this age.... What has destroyed democracy in the nations that have lost it? I am convinced it has been the unsolved economic problems which have produced unemployment, fear, and insecurity for the people of those nations. Can a people solve that problem without loss of liberty? If it cannot, democracy is doomed. If it can, then democracy is sure to win in the long run." [1] Congressman Jerry Voorhis, representing California's Twelfth District, has no doubt that democracy *can* solve the problem. To change "can solve" to "has solved" is the task to which he has dedicated himself. Omnivorously he reads, constantly he studies, gratefully he listens to the suggestions of his friends and co-workers, insistently yet patiently and modestly he proposes and expounds to his colleagues in the House, and fervently he prays to his God. Without drama, without the use of flags or other symbols, without partisan appeals or recriminations, but also without an obvious saving sense of humor, and not without occasional discouragement he serves the people sixteen hours a day.

I

Horace Jeremiah Voorhis, the son of Charles Brown and Ella Smith Voorhis, was born at Ottawa, Kansas, April 6, 1901. His parents, both in their intrinsic worth and in their

1. *Congressional Record,* Seventy-seventh Congress, First Session (Apr. 2, 1941), p. 2944.

influence over Jerry and his sister, Virginia Jean, are entitled to much more than passing reference. The elder Voorhis, only a moderately successful business man in Kansas for twenty years, later acquired a few millions in the automobile business and in investments. Well-educated, keen in mind, and skilled in the conference room, he is a leader of solid ability. For some years he served as chairman of the board of the Los Angeles Federal Reserve Bank. Jerry's mother gave her entire time to the children. She read to them for hours each day, and as they grew up she surrounded them with the best of literature. Both parents are deeply religious (Episcopalians) and most generous. They have given away not much less than three millions, a large part of it going to the Voorhis School for homeless boys. A Republican before 1932, when he became a Democrat, the father may have felt some concern over Jerry's first political experience (1934), his EPIC adventure with Upton Sinclair (presently to be noticed), but he now follows his son's tempered liberalism not only without dismay or misgivings but with pride.

When he had completed his course in the public schools, Jerry went to Yale University. Bearing the unmistakable signs of his background, he may have impressed his fellow-students as a "queer duck" who was not getting much out of his college life, not developing his personality, not making substantial connections which might later pay rich dividends in business deals. As a matter of fact, he was not happy at Yale. But he excelled in his studies, and he was particularly good in history and economics, his chief interests. He was elected to Phi Beta Kappa, and he was an outstanding member of the Yale debating team, meeting the Oxford debaters for a memorable discussion in 1922. But the Yale activity which Jerry mentions first is the Y.M.C.A. This, he says, had a decided influence upon his religious life and substantially changed the course of his career.

Upon his graduation in 1923, he decided to learn more about people, first hand. He worked as a day-laborer at thirty cents an hour in a New Haven factory. After several months, he was laid off with 5,000 others. Then he found a job as freight-handler in the New Haven Railroad Yards at New Haven, Connecticut. In the winter of 1923-24, he sandwiched in a trip to Germany, going as a representative of the Students Friendship Committee of the Y.M.C.A. and entering whole-heartedly into the purpose of the Association to create friendly relations between the youth of the two countries. He lived with the working people. He shivered with them in their poorly-heated homes and ate their scanty fare. And as many of them in that winter of inflation and privation fell victims to pneumonia, so Jerry came down with a serious case. Later, his "mission" concluded, he worked on a cattle ranch in Wyoming.

About the time he entered upon his tour of duty as a rancher, he met Alice Louise Livingston of Washington, Iowa. She was engaged in social work, a fact which, added to her exceptional ability and charm, easily made her Jerry's first selfish interest. Within a few months they were married, and by all accounts their life together has been ideal. Three children do not prevent Mrs. Voorhis from taking an active, intelligent, and sympathetic interest in all her busy husband does.

After the marriage, the young couple went to North Carolina, where Jerry worked a year in a Ford assembly plant. The next year (1925-26), Jerry taught at the Allendale Farm School for homeless boys, Lake Villa, Illinois. In 1926 he was asked to open the boys' unit of the Episcopal Home for Orphan Children at Laramie, Wyoming. This he did. And here he found himself completely. But he wanted a boys' school of his very own, a school for boys who otherwise would have none. He talked to his parents, and it was arranged.

Near San Dimas, California, father and son built the Voorhis School. The site selected is one of great beauty, set among the rolling hills and looking off to the high mountains. The buildings erected and the equipment installed were in every way comparable to those of the best private schools in the country. When the physical plant was ready, Jerry enrolled the boys—boys from homes broken by death, sickness, or divorce. Applicants who had money were referred to one of the excellent boarding schools of California. The Voorhis School admitted only boys without funds who needed a home. Without distinction of race they were entered on the basis of ability to profit by the opportunity and to fill an important place in the life of the whole group of students. Among some sixty boys, the young headmaster and Mrs. Voorhis lived simply as comrades and friends. Jerry found the job exhausting but satisfying beyond anything he had ever experienced. He was with his boys all the time—in the classrooms, at work, and at play. But let the boys tell what they think of the headmaster and his school.

"The first thing I ever learned about Jerry," writes one, "was that he was never called anything else—never 'Mr. Voorhis,' 'Headmaster,' or 'Sir,' never anything but Jerry. Every boy at Jerry's school knew there was at least one person in the world who cared about him—Jerry. Jerry was at the center of everything we did, teaching us, partly by word but largely by example, about something which was referred to in the New Testament as the 'Kingdom of God'—a society in which men would treat each other as brothers."

In this period of his life Jerry was perhaps dogmatic in his stern judgments on his own comfortable class, an attitude which his later political experience has modified.

Election to Congress of course terminated Jerry's career as a teacher, but it did not end his interest in the boys, nor their interest in him. At least eighty former Voorhis School boys were later in the armed forces. "Most of us Vikings are scattered fairly far now," one writes. "Jerry is . . . our special link with democracy." For some time after Pearl Harbor, Jerry tried in every way to get into active military service, to share the lot of the boys, but his age and his lack of military training would simply leave him in a camp in the United States for the duration. Consequently, he gave up the effort. But his boys in the service are ever on his mind and he has been to the Blood Bank more than a dozen times and he will continue to go as often as donations are permitted.

II

All during his teaching days, Voorhis was in great demand as a public speaker. He loved it and so did his audiences. With consuming intensity he spoke on burning issues. One speech usually led to several more invitations, and he almost never declined one. He addressed an audience of half a dozen with as much energy and zeal, in the "where two or three are gathered together" spirit, as he did an assembly of a thousand. He held his audiences by obvious sincerity, his mastery of facts, and his appeals to mind and conscience. They believed him, or believed enough to want to listen to him. As the gray autumn days of 1929 turned into dark winter of want and despair, the speeches of this young liberal became even more popular. His diagnosis of the ills of the economic order had been interesting and his proposed remedies challenging. Now, standing with a program in the midst of chaos, he had a large following ready to follow his leadership.

Then came the New Deal. Jerry watched it with growing interest. His father and his other progressive well-wishers, seeing their opportunity, suggested that the Democratic party offered ample scope for his liberalism. Jerry was convinced when Upton Sinclair entered that party (1934) with the program to "End Poverty in California." Young Voorhis joined this crusade, accepting a place as a member of the Board of Directors of the "End Poverty League." At the request of friends and neighbors (and probably of Sinclair), he announced his candidacy for the Democratic nomination for the State Assembly in the Forty-ninth District. It is well known that Sinclair won the Democratic nomination for governor, not generally known that Voorhis won the nomination for the Assembly. Defeat in the general election seemed to end the novelist's brief political career, but defeat was the beginning of the headmaster's public life. Voorhis had made six speeches a day for three months, meeting thousands of people and winning hundreds of friends. It should be added that he was defeated by only 2,000 votes in a district which had never elected a Democrat to the Assembly. It is significant that Voorhis should have come so near to being elected.

The campaign for the Assembly revealed to one or two of the old-line Democrats the possibilities of the well-educated, earnest, dynamic, but politically naive headmaster. The Twelfth Congressional District, a "rurban" area contiguous to the eastern boundary of the city of Los Angeles, had never taken kindly to Democratic candidates. It is true that the last representative chosen (1934) in the district was a registered Democrat, but he had seen long service in the Republican party and had climbed on the Roosevelt bandwagon just in time. Since his election he had been convicted of selling an appointment to West Point and had been removed from the halls of Congress to the walls of a federal penitentiary. Voorhis, a few of the old-time Democratic leaders thought, might be just the man to redeem the Democratic party in the Twelfth District. They began to cultivate Jerry. He grew upon acquaintance, and, in 1936, these experienced politicians joined with a large body of liberals in boosting him as a candidate.

Voorhis agreed to announce his candidacy only after very anxious thought, for victory would mean giving up his school and "his boys." A rather unorthodox campaigner, he inserted no newspaper advertisements, bought no bill board space. One of his politically mature sponsors saw to it that a little leaflet was printed which carried his picture (doctored up to make him look older, for despite his thirty-five years and his deadly serious manner he looked rather boyish), his life history, and the basic tenets of his program. "What America needs," Voorhis wrote in the leaflet, "is a great moral and essentially religious crusade to establish Christian righteousness as the foundation stone for all governmental policy. Once we start deciding public questions on the basis of what is right rather than what is expedient, we shall be on the road to the solution of our problems. We have just one main question to decide— whether our government has the right to act constructively in defense of the basic rights of the common man or whether it doesn't. I believe our government not only has that right but that duty." He has never receded from this position.

His chief reliance, however, was upon his speeches and personal work. Displaying the physical capacity for speaking that Bryan possessed in his prime, he told audiences, some of them large but most of them small, what his political beliefs were and asked them to support him for Congress if they accepted his views. "His speeches were the sort a first-rate professor makes to an intelligent, alert class," writes Ben O'Brien,[2] once a student at the Voorhis School and later associated with the former headmaster in his political campaigns. "No flag waving, breast beating, pointing with pride or viewing with alarm," continues O'Brien, "just simple, straight, logical discussion. He did not expect to be nominated, but regarded the whole campaign as an unusual opportunity to conduct a huge educational program."

Convinced that Jerry would win if he could get a good hearing, those of his friends who wore long pants, politically speaking, arranged for him to be heard. They organized "Voorhis for Congress" clubs, and they scheduled small house meetings where twenty or twenty-five people would meet in a home and talk informally with Jerry. They held hundreds of such meetings, sometimes two or three a night, and they scheduled many of them for Sunday afternoons when the laboring people could attend. They even succeeded in coaxing one or two of Jerry's opponents to meet him in public debate. These debates drew large crowds, but Jerry made his rivals look pretty silly and soon his challenges found no takers. Then Voorhis and his friends turned to basket picnics for Sunday afternoons in the parks, where the people could have a little relaxation and hear Jerry.

Of newspaper publicity he had practically none, the papers of the district being nearly all Republican. So the "long pants" men, without Jerry's knowledge, started a "throw away" weekly newspaper, styled the *San Gabriel Valley Tribune*. It always carried a snappy column of political gossip which was partial, but not too obviously partial, to Jerry. An interesting publication, it was eagerly read all over the district. The number printed was usually about 20,000, but when necessary more could be provided. One week 52,000 were printed. If local papers would get too nasty, the *San Gabriel Valley Tribune* could be delivered to every home in the community. Jerry's partisans, of whom there were some in every locality, would see to that.

Considering Jerry's own activities, the zeal of his many

2. To the writer, Feb. 5, 1944.

liberal crusaders, and the political astuteness of some of his old-line supporters, it is really not surprising that he won the nomination. It seemed at the time, however, and this is the testimony of one of "his boys," that he had only become "the richest man in the poorhouse" because the Republicans, who dominate the district, had put up as their candidate a very able man, Frederick F. Houser (later, lieutenant-governor of California), a Harvard graduate, son of a state supreme court justice, and seasoned by two terms in the State Assembly. Everybody agreed that Houser, experienced and with a solid organization behind him, would beat Jerry easily. But the regular Democrats now came to Jerry's standard. And Jerry and his backers kept right on with the tactics which had proved so effective in the primary. Their meetings grew in size. There were voters who came to scoff but who remained to pray. The *San Gabriel Valley Tribune,* continued its good work, giving Jerry many a lift in its political gossip column. The November vote was a great triumph for Voorhis and his workers. It was Voorhis, 62,034; Houser, 53,445. And so, in 1936, Voorhis went to Congress, and in Congress he has remained, surviving the Republican trend in 1938 and the same, plus a gerrymander, in 1942. "Give the voters hokum, that's what they want." Do they? Or do they take hokum because that is all they are offered?

III

This freshman congressman had faded brown eyes, a strong, earnest face, thick brown hair, an excellent physique (he is 5 feet 11 inches tall and has weighed 174 pounds, just that, no more no less, for twenty years), robust health, in fact a constitution of iron, but little disposition to play except with his children. He soon became a familiar figure on the floor of the House, for it is quite probable that no more serious, earnest, hard-working, determined young man ever went to Congress than Jerry Voorhis. He was both in an academic sense and by natural ability much better equipped for the place than the average congressman. And he had a goal, a definite goal—it was to make life brighter and happier for the inarticulate and impoverished millions. And Voorhis thought he knew how to attain his goal. Therefore, he was eager, restless, and somewhat impatient. He plunged immediately into many issues.

It is obviously impossible within the compass of this article to give adequate explanations of Voorhis' position on the leading questions of the day. At the time the Selective Training and Service Bill was being discussed, he presented a much broader and more enlightened national training and service program.[3] His interest in and his program for co-operatives has never flagged and he has found in them a partial answer to his question, Can democracy survive?[4] This man, who as a part of his education worked for several years as a common laborer, champions labor, although he is not its blind partisan.[5]

In 1940, while still a member of the Dies Committee, he cautioned that the committee "will miss its mark unless not only our Committee but other people as well make a very careful distinction between a real 'fifth column,' by which I mean people in this nation whose loyalty is elsewhere . . . and people who simply and honestly in their own hearts believe that progressive or even radical economic change would be best for the America they love and for which they would gladly die."[6] Later, he strongly protested as it became obvious to him that the committee was bent upon "missing its mark," was failing in "exposing and combating the work of people who attempt to create confusion in our country and to build up sympathy with the Nazi philosophy of government,"[7] and was spending so much of its effort in running after federal employees who had at one time been on a mailing list of some Communist "front" organization. His patience was exhausted when the chairman handed him the committee's annual report for 1942 to sign on a "take it or leave it" basis. He "left it," and sub-

3. *Congressional Record,* Seventy-sixth Congress, Third Session (Sept. 3, 1940), p. 11,395.
4. *Ibid.,* Seventy-seventh Congress, First Session (Apr. 2, 1941), p. 2944.
5. *Ibid.* (March 31, 1941), p. 2755.
6. *Ibid.,* Seventy-sixth Congress, Third Session (May 17, 1940), p. 6338.
7. *Special Report on Subversive Activities Aimed at Destroying Our Representative Form of Government,* House of Representatives, Seventy-seventh Congress, Second Session, Report No. 2748 (Jan. 3, 1943), p. 14.

mitted a minority report.[8] Shortly thereafter he terminated his services with the committee, thus giving up what to many members of Congress would be a gold mine of publicity.

In pre-war days Voorhis advocated large appropriations for WPA because it meant work instead of a dole for the unemployed and because there could be no recovery without purchasing power in the hands of the people.[9] He regarded WPA as only a makeshift, however, and in 1940, he was the chairman and leading spirit of a nonpartisan group of some seventy members of the House who over a period of three months, and in addition to their regular duties, held weekly meetings to study the causes of unemployment and the fundamental measures necessary to accomplish its solution. *The Report of the House Conference on Unemployment* [10] bears many signs of his work, and it takes its place as one of the serious efforts to grapple with the problem. In May, 1940, Voorhis presented his own long-range, basic plan for ending unemployment. It included tax reform (higher income and inheritance taxes), a broadening of the retirement pensions system, the curbing of monopoly, and last, and all the time, a complete reformation of our monetary system.[11]

On the subject of monetary reform he has labored and studied; on it he has spoken many, many times and doubtless will continue to speak; on it he has written a book, *Out of Debt, Out of Danger.*[12] The heart of his program is that Congress should exercise its constitutional power to regulate money, and that it should begin by depriving the banks of the special privilege they now enjoy to create check-book money by making loans and of destroying that money by the simple expedient of calling those loans. He is most bitter in his criticism of the present system of government borrowing from

8. *Ibid.,* pp. 14-16. It should be stated that Voorhis had not sought a place on the Dies Committee; that he accepted the assignment only when urged by Vice-President Garner to do so in order that the liberal element might be represented on it.
9. *Congressional Record,* Seventy-sixth Congress, Third Session (May 17, 1940), p. 6338.
10. Seventy-sixth Congress, Third Session, House Document No. 850.
11. *Congressional Record,* Seventy-sixth Congress, Third Session (May 7, 1940), p. 5709.
12. Devin-Adair Company, New York, 1943.

banks, the system under which the government presents bonds to the banks in return for which the banks simply give the government a bookkeeping credit against which it is entitled to draw. Behind such loans banks are required to have only a "fractional reserve" (now approximately 20 per cent) in cash or its equivalent. It is possible therefore that a bank may make a loan of $1,000,000 and have only $200,000 behind the loan. In effect, the bank has created $800,000 of new money. Nevertheless, the government will pay the bank interest on the $1,000,000 and, in due time, the principal also. This, says Voorhis, is very good for the banks, but very bad for the government and the people. He would stop this practice. He would have the government borrow money from people who actually have it and from institutions which actually have it. And he would have the government get funds by direct creation of its own money or by borrowing, at no interest, from a national central bank belonging to all the people, thus performing for itself services for which it now makes handsome payments to private banks.

This is an appropriate point to explain that Voorhis, a supporter of many New Deal policies, has never liked what he characterizes as the New Deal refrain on debt: "That the National Debt does not matter, that policies can be pursued indefinitely even though they require a continuous practice of deficit financing... that we owe the debt to ourselves, to our own people, and that, therefore, what is paid in interest is income to some citizen.... That it would even be desirable to have a larger debt than we have yet acquired, since it would offer a safe source of investment for the savings of the people...." A huge national debt is bad, he says, because while it is *owed* by all the people it is *owned* by comparatively few people, and because there is a limit to the proportion of its income that any nation can afford to pay in interest to its bondholders. This "dreamer" is also practical enough to emphasize the point that the size of the national debt is a matter of grave concern for the reason that nine out of ten Americans are troubled about it. "No political party or group can expect to hold the support of the American electorate unless it can furnish that electorate some answer other than oratory to the problem of the public debt. For the people are fundamentally right and the Washington philosophers are fundamentally wrong about this question." [13]

IV

Voorhis joins with many others in the belief that Congress is not adequately discharging its functions. He defends it from unfair attacks, maintaining, for example, that congressmen's use of the X-cards for gasoline was grossly exaggerated in the press and that in like manner the press did not fairly set forth the facts of the so-called pensions-for-congressmen bill. Without a doubt he is right. But the selfless gentleman deplored the fact that, as the nation was frantically girding itself for war, congressmen should have shown any concern whatever for their own welfare. And then he presented a war-time program for Congress.[14]

Congress must prevent waste. He commends the work of the Truman Committee and other committees, but he asks that much more be done. "I suggest that the Appropriations Committee be granted sufficient funds to engage a staff of not less than fifty high-grade men to be given the task of following through Government contracts to be certain that they are carried out with absolutely no unnecessary additions to expense, and no waste of material or manpower that is avoidable."

In the second place, Congress should take a significant part in shaping American foreign policy, particularly in relation to the kind of peace we are going to have, and the kind of world we are seeking to build. And here he expressed the hope that every member would read Henry A. Wallace's speech of May 8, 1942, "The Price of Free World Victory," which the Congressman characterized as "one of the greatest speeches

13. *Out of Debt, Out of Danger*, pp. 224-26.
14. *Congressional Record*, Seventy-seventh Congress, First Session (May 21, 1942), p. 4442. See also Voorhis, "How Can the Democrats Win in 1944?" *Bulletin of America's Town Meeting of the Air*, Jan. 6, 1944.

ever delivered in the annals of American history." [15] Voorhis stated that the good-neighbor policy should be promoted by Congress as well as by the Chief Executive and that it should be a nonpartisan policy.

In the third place, "Congress must show the people of America that it can and will deal effectively with such problems as will arise when the war has been won." It should begin by providing now "for an outstanding national commission, not only in the ranks of Government, but from the people generally, and the important economic groups of the nation and giving this commission the task of working out and building support for four or five basic principles to be followed in assuring our people of a continuance of full employment and full production in the post-war period." And the resourceful gentleman from California had his Post-War Reconstruction Bill (H.J.Res. 291) ready, a resolution which carried the approval of the labor unions, the National Association of Manufacturers, and many other organizations, and which was favorably reported by the House Committee on Labor.[16] But the House, ever hating and fearing executive plans and extremely reluctant to make plans of its own,[17] shelved the Voorhis Resolution. It is but fair to add, however, that, more than a year later, Congress did set up the Committee on Post-War Economic Policy and Planning, a committee of which Voorhis is a member.

In the fourth place, Congress should do everything possible to build up a reserve of buying power in the hands of the people. He suggested the following means of doing this: discharge pay for service men and women, a special type of bond in which corporations should be permitted to invest a certain percentage of their earnings, which bonds should be callable after the war on condition that the proceeds be used to employ labor, and a framework of taxes, to be immediately provided,

15. Wallace spoke of the "Century of the Common Man," of the citizen's duty when the time of peace comes, "the supreme duty of sacrificing the lesser interests for the greater interest of the general welfare," and of an "economic peace that is just, charitable, and enduring." This is exactly what Voorhis was thinking.

16. *Congressional Record*, Seventy-seventh Congress, Second Session (June 5, 1942), p. A2101.

17. See William Hard, "Congress's Biggest Job: A Better Congress," *Reader's Digest*, Oct., 1942, p. 18.

which would make possible, after the war, the installation of a general federal old-age pension system.

Fifth, the most important of all the tasks of Congress is that "of bringing about as nearly as is humanly possible an equality of sacrifice and equalization of the burdens of this war.... The request for an upward pay adjustment of postal clerks and carriers is justified. Supposing that such an increase were granted by an act of Congress and at the same time the salaries of higher-paid federal officials, including ourselves, were somewhat reduced. The effect of such action upon the people of our country and indeed of the entire world would be tremendous."

Congress should prevent a further rise in living costs. "Price control is the easy way to do this," he said, "but not the basic one.... The first thing is to prevent the uncontrolled creation of new money by the banking system." The second thing is to take by taxation surplus dollars from the hands of the people who have them. Taxes should be based on incomes, not on consumption of goods, except on the consumption of luxuries. From reports that came to him he greatly feared that the 1942 tax bill was not going to meet this demand. It did not.

Finally, Congress should require that savings be made by the people through the purchase of nontransferable government bonds. This should be done because the voluntary purchase of bonds, despite all the praise that is being heaped upon it, is entirely inadequate; the bonds are not being sold to the people in anything like sufficient quantities. And why should the people be *compelled* to buy government bonds? Voorhis answers: "The effect of the purchase of war bonds by the people will be exactly the same as the effect of taxes so far as the anti-inflation influence is concerned.... If we had compulsory savings we could then substitute this method for at least part of the tax burden.... Second, I want as much of a reserve of savings to be in the hands of our poorer people when this war is over as possible."

This is a program. One may disagree with some features of it, but it is specific and courageous. And if Congress enacts such a program into law, he concludes, "...we will, I imagine, receive scant credit for doing so. Many of us will probably be defeated. But the Congress, as America's one agency of government which is really close to the people, will have been justified fully and completely." In other words, congressmen may save Congress by losing themselves. This is an ancient truth of general application.

Voorhis might have gone further. He might have said that when each congressman is thinking primarily of his own district and his own seat in Congress, we have no Congress—only congressional districts and congressmen; that we have a Congress only when members put aside local and personal interests and think and act nationally. He might have suggested that many electors would be pleased to vote for the continuance in office of congressmen who courageously voted for the heroic measures demanded by the times. Does any serious observer of the activities on Capitol Hill believe that the turn-over in Congress which took place in November, 1942, would have been greater had that body previously enacted comprehensive measures to finance the war and control inflation? Is it not at least arguable that the congressional reverses of that year may be found in the failure of Congress to take effective and courageous action?

V

Voorhis himself serves as an excellent example of the political effectiveness of courageous, independent action. He does not ignore his district; quite the contrary. His people claim his unremitting attention. And he represents them, not by complying with each demand of the day, but with foresight as to what their interests should be five or ten years from now. Much as he hates to do it, he not infrequently "votes against his mail." He softens the blow by giving his constituents detailed reasons for his action. For this purpose he uses news releases, the radio, and letters.

Voorhis receives very satisfactory publicity in the newspapers of his district. This represents a distinct achievement on his part, for only one is Democratic, two or three nonpartisan, and all the others are Republican. When he first ran for Congress the papers gave him no support and practically no publicity. They continued to give him the quiet treatment after he took his seat in the House, ignoring his releases and otherwise withholding publicity to which he was fairly entitled. Voorhis met this challenge. He built up a mailing list which many "bread and butter" letter-writing congressmen would envy. He sent his constituents reprints of his speeches, mimeographed letters, and a weekly leaflet. This technique proved so effective that the citizens insisted that the local press give space for his material. Papers in his district are still silent during campaign months, but between campaigns, they publish his weekly column, "The People's Business," in which he gives a frank discussion of the leading issues of the day.

Representative Voorhis has yet another means of reaching his people from the Capitol. For the past two years he has been a guest speaker (by transcription) over radio station KPAS, located in the Huntington Hotel in Pasadena, "Where the sunshine spends the winter." These weekly speeches are nonpartisan and are designed to give accurate information to the people concerning national affairs.

Effective in reaching the people of the Twelfth District by long distance methods, he is most convincing as he meets them face to face. Jerry meets and talks with everybody, individually and in small groups. He listens to their troubles with infinite patience and with obvious sympathy and understanding. He explains to them the problem of government and outlines his plans. The voters are not always convinced, but they believe in him, and they are willing to allow him to use his own judgment and conscience. Thus he communicates with the people. He thinks of it as reporting to them. It is good politics, too; mighty good politics. Of this there is rather convincing proof. First elected to Congress by a margin of 8,589 votes out of 115,504 cast, he was re-elected in 1938 by a 26,539 majority and in 1940 by a 43,567 majority. By a conservative estimate 10,000 Republicans supported him in 1940 for his third term. Before the next election, reapportionment gave California three more seats in the House. And this gave the Republican state legislature an opportunity to gerrymander Jerry out of

Congress. The East Los Angeles part of his district containing a Democratic majority of 20,000 was carved off, leaving him the Republican eastern portion of his old Twelfth District. Nevertheless, in 1942 (a bad year for Democrats), he was sent back to Congress by a 13,000 majority. In 1944, despite the powerful opposition of certain corporations, his majority was approximately the same.

VI

Certain other techniques of Voorhis call for brief analysis. Considerable space has already been devoted to his speeches, and it has been made clear that his ability as a speaker was the chief factor in electing him to Congress. His speeches in the House are invariably well prepared, but he freely admits a feeling of nervousness and concern as to whether or not he will succeed in putting his point over to his colleagues. To some observers he appears to be in the position of a professor who, accustomed to delivering fifty-minute lectures, is cramped and hurried when called upon to cover the same ground in fifteen minutes. More often than they think possible the professors could eliminate the detail and perform their function rather satisfactorily in the shorter period. Perhaps Voorhis (long a teacher) might do the same. Surviving from the academic days is Voorhis' apparent determination to omit no point. Also surviving is a great deal of the academic language, although this is less obvious in his later speeches. Consequently, he sometimes gives his colleagues the impression that he is talking down to them, an impression which even his critics admit has little or no basis in fact.

He speaks eagerly, earnestly, almost pleadingly—with his whole body, using his hands, his arms, his shoulders, as well as his voice. His face is singularly expressive, showing intense sincerity with every change of mood and feeling. Himself convinced, he speaks to convince others by setting forth his position in the most direct manner possible. He makes no attempt to be eloquent or flowery, preferring figures, charts, and maps to oratory. A man of the deepest human sympathies and religious convictions, he nevertheless makes his appeal primarily to the head and only incidentally to the heart and soul. When interrupted by an honest question or pertinent observation from a colleague, he yields graciously unless the time is running out. But if a member is simply baiting him, Voorhis can cut him off in a hurry. A large number of congressmen listen to him with great interest, nearly all of them with respect. Without a doubt an effective speaker, he might increase his power if he reserved his efforts for a few of the most urgent topics.

"Voorhis is probably one of the hardest working members of Congress," says one of his Democratic colleagues and friends, John M. Coffee of Washington,[18] "putting in long hours at thankless tasks. From many a meeting which concludes at 10 o'clock, he returns to his office, unobtrusively, and works alone until 1 : 00 A.M., after which he takes a streetcar or bus to his home in Alexandria." All the testimony is of a piece with this. He probably works too hard. "Sometimes I can see written in his face the heavy marks of a very tired spirit," commented another colleague. On occasion, when he is exhausted, he makes less than effective answers to comments and questions, but he plunges ahead giving himself little rest. Somehow, though, he manages to keep in good physical shape. He seems to have a remarkably efficient digestive system, and the little sleep he gets is as sound and undisturbed as that of his romping, six-year-old son, Jerry Livingston.

The ever active young statesman does have some social life, some recreation. He relaxes and plays with his three children. The father has never abdicated to the statesman. Fixing Jerry Junior's train or taking Charles to a stamp shop are important —things that must be done. He enjoys the movies and baseball, he dearly loves to climb a mountain, and he is completely "nuts" about railroads, having at his finger tips such intriguingly useless information as the time the westbound "Chief" is due at Emporia, Kansas, and the eastbound "Sportsman" at Waynesboro, Virginia. He spends some time with his stamp collection, but more time with American history and any kind of geography. "A visit to his home is always a special treat,"

18. To the writer, Nov. 12, 1943.

writes a friend of the family,[19] "because one is made to feel at home. Mrs. Voorhis is gracious and charming *and* capable, and together they make one feel genuinely welcome."

Congressman and Mrs. Voorhis have many friends among the more liberal element in the nation's public life. Often Jerry is the life of the party, at which times he may display his mimetic talent. Representatives who know Voorhis only as they have seen him in the House and at committee meetings would hardly believe their eyes and ears if they should be present when he imitates (profanity deleted) his good friend, former Representative Maury Maverick; or Ted Lewis singing "When My Baby Smiles at Me"; or when Jerry gives a purely Voorhis version of "The Dark Town Strutters' Ball." Those who sing Jerry's praises as well as those who grudgingly admit that he has many excellent qualities join in testifying that he will not tell or listen to a "dirty story," testimony to which the latter group adds "not even a good one."

Voorhis has some weaknesses, some handicaps which experience may enable him to overcome. He is now rather successful in avoiding the academic approach, which, as already noted, was a disadvantage during his first years in Congress. He has been less successful in overcoming the temptation to master all issues, great and small. Without a doubt he would be more effective if he would limit his efforts to, say, half a dozen major issues. This would probably strengthen his position as an authority and it certainly would conserve his physical and mental energy.[20]

There are those who maintain that Voorhis is not a man of action. They suggest that he should be a better "mixer," more skilled in congressional mechanics. Voorhis elucidates—and stops—they say. He analyzes—then just files the papers away somewhere. His, the charge continues, is only the scholarly approach. It is a fact that legislators who are in advance of majority opinion do not write their record in the statute books.

19. Floy Hendricks (formerly a secretary to Voorhis), to the writer, Feb. 5, 1944.
20. In *Beyond Victory* (Farrar and Rinehart Inc., New York, 1944), his latest book, Voorhis writes, as always, interestingly and with conviction, but he again seems to lose some of his punch by striking in too many directions.

It is more likely to be found in the journals of proceedings. For example, Voorhis offered an amendment, "That all obligations of the United States bought directly from the Treasury by any Federal Reserve Bank shall be non-interest-bearing obligations." And the verdict of the House: "The amendment was rejected." [21] This does not mean that the Californian is not a man of action. It would seem rather to indicate simply that he stands by his principles. His day of action may come (as it did in 1933 for former Senator George Norris) when majority opinion catches up with him.

Voorhis "is subject to innumerable worries about the foibles of mankind, and he always has a harried or worried look," comments a discerning friend.[22] Maury Maverick, observing that Jerry always carried a great burden, named him "Atlas." Yet Jerry is not "hopeless," for he thoroughly enjoys a gift from Maverick which hangs in his office, a framed cartoon of poor old Atlas carrying the world on his back. Perhaps, with added experience, Jerry will assume a more philosophic attitude toward his task and the world. Men with no less zeal and as broad sympathies have often achieved emotional poise and serenity.

Perhaps one of his greatest handicaps, one which objective critics believe he is overcoming, has been his gullibility at the hands of liberals who urge him to champion this or that worthy cause or issue. This is one reason why he has been active in so many (too many) fields. He is learning, though. He never has buckled on his armor just because a liberal he liked or an organization he sponsored urged him to do it. He is still more cautious now, more inclined to judge each proposition entirely on its merits. On June 30, 1940, the Communists of his district denounced him, and he has lost some other radical support because he cannot be relied upon to make an issue of every cause which these elements may urge upon him. He is an advanced liberal, yes, but he will make his own independent decision concerning an old-age-pension proposal. He is a champion

21. *Congressional Record*. Seventy-seventh Congress, Second Session (Feb. 26, 1942), p. 1761.
22. Representative John M. Coffee, letter to the writer, Nov. 12, 1943.

of labor beyond a doubt, but he will present labor's cause in his own way. He wears the collar of no group or organization. His liberalism is based upon what he conceives to be fundamentals, not upon the tenets of any particular movement, faction, or organization.

Most fortunate in his parents, above the average in physical health and stamina, well equipped by natural endowment and training, serene and happy in his family life, and utterly selfless, Jerry Voorhis studiously, earnestly, indefatigably, persistently, and courageously serves the people. The mainspring of his action is his consciousness of the sufferings of men and of his obligation to do something about it. He would say that his motivating power is religion. It is a religion which contains no element of bigotry, none of the gaudy trappings of evangelism, and which finds its expression in compassion for and life with the underprivileged. "Sell all that thou hast, and distribute unto the poor... and come, follow me." He has read these words many times, and he believes them. He is happy that his parents have given away several million dollars, a large part of which would otherwise have been his. His own contribution is himself. This is a key, almost certainly the principal one, to an understanding of Jerry Voorhis. To ignore it because one might not, like him, feel the power of spiritual forces, or because others no less concerned about humanity have been guided by other influences is to miss the secret of this particular man.

Whether we agree or disagree with Jerry Voorhis' views on how to solve our national problems we are impelled to recognize that he represents a type of congressman of which democracy can be proud. His nobility of mind, his unflinching courage, his unquestioned integrity, and his sincerity of purpose are qualities sorely needed, but alas, too seldom found among those upon whom rests the responsibility of guiding the nation. This is not to say that all congressmen should be like Voorhis; but it is to assert that, given the qualities mentioned in combination with the varying backgrounds, beliefs, interests, and skills which they do and should possess, they would find the question, "What is the matter with Congress?" less frequently asked and less discouragingly answered. And if incumbent senators and representatives could only be brought to realize that courageous, independent action might be the best practical politics, Congress would renew its strength as a democratic institution and the people would revive their faith in representative government.

21

ELLISON DURANT SMITH
"A Politician from the Old South"

BY LEONARD NIEL PLUMMER

THE BRASS SENATORIAL CUSPIDOR VIBRATED UNDER THE impact of a bull's eye, scored by Senator Ellison Durant (Cotton Ed) Smith, who then turned and smiled benignly into the face of the Gentleman from Texas [1] who was speaking in opposition to a bill favored by the Gentleman from South Carolina. The Gentleman from Texas had just faltered in his factual exposition, and the unerring discharge of ambeer had marked the mistake with an emphatic sound effect which, of course, could not be noted in *The Congressional Record*.

The Gentleman from Texas resumed his narrative. Again he erred, and again the cuspidor received a baptism from the fount fed by an ample quid rolling comfortably within the South Carolinian's jaws. A smile again lighted the heavy jowls and flickered around a closely clipped mustache. The Gentleman from Texas, in due time, could endure no more of this:

"Mr. President, the Gentleman's grimaces break my chain of thought and I object to them," he complained to the presiding officer.

"If my smiles interrupt the Gentleman's thought processes," interjected Senator Smith, with a low bow, "I shudder to think what would happen if I laughed right out loud, as I feel constrained to do."

Cotton Ed, a member of the Senate for thirty-six years and last of the "spittoon Senators" [2] had scored again, emphasizing his facility in rough and tumble political debate. A winner

1. Senator Tom Connally.
2. Heywood Broun, in the *New Republic*, XCVI (Sept. 14, 1938), 157.

every six years between 1908 and 1944, Cotton Ed proved himself one to be reckoned with whether on the floor of the Senate or on the platform of a time-worn county courthouse of his native state. His long string of victories at the polls finally came to an end in the Democratic primary in the summer of 1944. A few months later he died. Bulky, ponderous, grumpy, grizzled, baggy-faced, and crusty,[3] he was the veteran of many political wars, and his victories were thoroughly personal, since South Carolinians prefer most of the time to take their politics straight without benefit of machines or organizations.

Ellison Durant Smith was a politician from the Old South.[4] Cotton was his first and foremost love. State's rights, white supremacy, and tariff for revenue only were his principles. That the will of God is somehow involved in these, that the lost cause of the veterans in the tattered grey uniforms of the Confederacy is nearly always pertinent in any discussion, and that the sanctity of a good woman's virtue cannot be measured in worldly terms were among the trappings with which he dazzled his constituency and bedeviled the "nigger-loving Yankees." With these he was well accoutered for the political wars of his section, a fact overlooked by New Deal leaders who sought unsuccessfully to purge him in 1938.

And as for cotton: Let no one be surprised that Ellison Durant Smith was devoted to the South's great crop. Cotton put Cotton Ed in politics and gave him his nickname; Cotton Ed kept cotton in politics and won for it recognition as a national economic problem. When he came to the Senate he came with a mission. The government "ought to do enough for cotton to put it up to 15 cents and keep it there."[5] He was one of the first to demand national action for the economic relief of the agriculture of the South, and he specialized in periodic investigations of cotton and the cotton markets. He told the

---

3. Appellations given Senator Smith in reports of *Time Magazine* which also described him as a whittler, a storyteller, and a bird hunter.

4. In a letter to the author, Senator Smith emphasized that he did not consider himself a politician "in the ordinary manner in which the term is used." Neither did he consider himself a statesman, but he had "never played politics."

5. *News Week*, XIX (June 15, 1942), 33.

Senate that a cotton shirt cost him two dollars, which was paying for cotton at the rate of seven dollars a pound. This price he compared to seven cents a pound he received from the product of his ancestral acres near Lynchburg.

"Between the $7 a pound I pay for cotton to go on my back and the 7 cents a pound I get there is a tremendous spread somewhere," he concluded. Somewhere in a cotton patch in the Deep South a one-gallused farmer paused and nodded vigorous approval, satisfied that Ellison D. Smith was indeed the cotton grower's friend.

The son, grandson, and great grandson of farmers,[6] Cotton Ed was deeply rooted in the soil of South Carolina. The broad fields of his 2,000-acre plantation have been in the Smith family since the eighteenth century, when title was obtained by grant of George III. When he spoke he was sure in his own mind that he spoke the language of the practical, hard-working dirt farmer. He had very little use for the theorists—the "window-box agriculturists"—who prepared reports on farm problems. He did not want to see what they wrote, either. Questioned once as to whether he was acquainted with a certain report, he declared flatly, "I do not care to be familiar with it, and I do not want to know anything about it. I have some other ways of getting facts. . . . The making of these reports is in many instances disturbing to the morale of our people."

Cotton Ed was born on the home plantation, then in Sumter county but now in Lee, on August 1, 1866, His childhood was that of any normally active boy except for one fact: "Ellie" Smith, even as a child, had an unusual capacity for throwing his playmates into confusion. He was never content to let the stream of life glide by without tossing in a few stones to ripple its surface or churn mud from its bottom. In due time he was sent to Stewart's School in Charleston, S. C., where he prepared for college. After spending his freshman year at the University of South Carolina he transferred to Wofford College at Spartanburg, S. C., from which he was graduated in 1889, incidentally carrying off all the oratorical prizes in sight.

6. Senator Smith's father was also a Methodist minister.

From 1896 to 1900 he was a state legislator, after which he returned to the family plantation.

In 1905 he answered the call for a meeting of cotton growers in Louisiana to discuss the boll weevil problem. Obtaining the floor, he departed from the topic and launched into a denunciation of manipulation of the cotton markets. His listeners heard him with enthusiasm and accepted his proposal that they organize for self-protection. Out of this decision came the Cotton Association, with Smith named the field agent and general organizer. From January, 1905, to June, 1908, he served in this capacity. He met the slow-moving, slow-talking planter in the low country; he journeyed into the Piedmont and he talked farming with the taciturn hillman. Everywhere he preached the gospel of more money for the farmer. When the primary election came in 1908 Ellison Durant Smith was ready to participate in that political extravaganza so peculiar to South Carolina. His entry into national politics was an overwhelming success, and he carried off the Democratic nomination by the largest majority ever received by a South Carolina senatorial candidate. Nomination, of course, meant election.

Many persons, especially those residing in the North, observed with amazement Cotton Ed's regular trips back to his native state to receive again the blessings of his constituency. They made no pretense of understanding Cotton Ed—or South Carolina, for that matter. It was simply bewildering that this man should be in the Senate, returning for term after term. But great was the error of these observers, for they forgot that what they regarded as weaknesses were, in reality, citadels of strength in South Carolina. They overlooked local prejudices, local habits, local problems, and local principles. They failed to see that Cotton Ed, in his prime, was South Carolina from the low country to the Piedmont, and they passed over the fact that the South has always liked a rough and ready wit, a good story-telling technique—a dash of whoop and holler—in its political leaders. But there can be no doubt that Cotton Ed fully understood his people as well as himself. He had no sudden whim when he stalked angrily out of the Democratic national convention in 1936 as a Negro arose to deliver the invocation. Cotton Ed's snort of disgust, "Hell, he's as black as melted midnight," did not hurt his popularity in South Carolina, and that is where the votes are counted. As a matter of fact, Cotton Ed made good use of the Philadelphia incident in the bitterly fought primary of 1938.

"The Negro minister was not put there to invoke divine blessing," he told his constituents. "He was there to invoke Negro votes. He was not asking divine blessing, but *primary* blessing." [7]

The truth is that Cotton Ed, who learned his people so thoroughly in the years when he met and talked with them in their own localities, knew all the arts of appealing to voters in South Carolina. He could lave them with the Constitution flavored with state's rights, the Bible, and Shakespeare, if they were in the mood for this type of oratory, or he could shift to a roaring, fighting technique which could be punctuated satisfactorily only by appreciative and blood curdling "rebel yells."

"Every audience is different," he explained. "You've got to feel your way along until you strike the chord and sense the response."

Cotton Ed often put his own advice to good use. In the 1938 primary he had been advised to meet the New Deal's attempt to purge him by going to his people with a calm discussion of the issues. The campaign must be kept on a high plane, he was told. He was almost convinced.

"Yes, sireee, bob!" he exclaimed. "In that first speech I got away up there in the clouds, and began it. I started off with the Magna Charta on the plains of Runnymede, I came down through the Battle of King's Mountain, and was warming up to the constitutional issues which led to the first shots fired at Sumter, with a lot about the immortal John C. Calhoun, when I felt somebody was watching me.

7. On February 29, 1944, the House of Representatives of South Carolina adopted the following resolution: "We indignantly and vehemently denounce the intentions...of all organizations seeking the amalgamation of the White and Negro races by commingling of the races upon any basis of equality.... (We) demand that henceforth the damned agitators of the North leave the South alone."

"Of a sudden I looked down. There, hunkered up near the platform, was an old farmer with a torn black hat on his head and tobacco juice running down both sides of his mouth. I looked at him. I heard him croak, 'Aw, hell, Ed! Tell us about Philadeffy.'

"And, by God, I did!" [8]

The Circus, as the primary in South Carolina is sometimes called, was made to order for Cotton Ed, and for telling his constituents about "Philadeffy." In the primary—which is to say, the Democratic primary—all the candidates for the Senate and House, the latter changing according to districts, assemble and tour the state together for ten long sticky hot weeks. Each county seat is visited, sometimes two or more a day, all the candidates appearing on the platform together. Each takes his turn at addressing the voters, varying the order of appearance from day to day.

Pointed references to one another are permissible, even expected, if the campaign is heated. Cotton Ed thrived under these conditions. In 1938 his opponents were Edgar Brown and Governor Olin D. Johnston. It was not long before Cotton Ed was referring to Brown as "Bacon" Brown because this opponent was promising to bring the bacon home from Washington if elected. Governor Johnston drew the appellation of "Brother Oleander" for no particular reason except that it evoked a laugh from the crowd.

"Brother Oleander tries pitifully to imitate my actions and voice," roared Cotton Ed. "But he can't imitate my brains—because he ain't got any!" He said a lot of other things about "Brother Oleander" and "Mr. Bacon Brown," and he heard a lot of things said about himself. But he bided his time and assured his delighted listeners that his opponents were merely "buzzards, searching for one speck in a glorious career."

Six years later it was "Brother Oleander" who finally defeated Cotton Ed for the Democratic nomination, and he did it convincingly. Cotton Ed, at the age of seventy-eight, simply was not physically able to meet the challenge, and he had nothing to match the fact that Governor Johnston had been in the

8. Beverly Smith, in the *American Magazine*, CXXVII (Jan., 1939), 146 ff.

forefront of the drive to make legislative changes to meet the threat of Negro votes in the Democratic primary.

Observers will tell you that the primaries in South Carolina are quieter now than in the old days. Crowds are not as large, and it is possible to hold most of the meetings indoors in courtrooms, schools, or halls. Fisticuffs, which once were not infrequent, are more rare, and all in all the decorum of candidates and crowds alike has improved. But with Cotton Ed in action, a primary could not escape being colorful, for he was a "rarin', rattling campaign speaker, though his words may not parse." [9] He required plenty of room, too, for he flailed his arms and shot out his fists to drive home his points. In the Senate his fellow-legislators gladly made room for him by retreating to safer positions when he went into action. "A roving explosion," one observer has remarked. Another said simply, "His name is Ellison Durant—and he sure do."

Cotton Ed was not happy in recent years as he watched the Democratic party under the leadership of the New Deal. And it should be added, in all fairness, that the New Deal leadership was not happy with Cotton Ed. That purge primary which fizzled was a matter of deep chagrin to many in high places, for it returned the Gentleman from South Carolina to the strategic position of chairman of the Senate Committee on Agriculture and Forestry through which flowed much of the legislation dear to New Deal philosophy.

On the topic of agriculture Cotton Ed was never inclined to hide his views under the bushel, and though he went along in general with the New Deal's principal farm measures, his way was marked by rumblings of revolt and snorts of disgust. "Am I to be asked to come into this body and subordinate my convictions to the theories of those who do not know a cotton stalk from a Jimson weed?" he once asked his senatorial colleagues. Later he was greatly surprised to learn that the "one-gallus farmer" wanted crop controls, whereupon despite his previous convictions, he pushed a cotton control bill through the Agriculture Committee. In addition, he helped sponsor the

9. Characterization given by a South Carolina newspaperman in a letter to the author.

Smith-Kerr Act for tobacco control. Later he asked the press not to use his name as co-author. But whether or not the New Deal agriculture theories were rank heresy, Cotton Ed was sure of one thing: the farmer ought to be helped. "I think it necessary and essential for the Federal government, so far as it can legitimately do so, to see to it that the farmers of this country have consideration pre-eminently above and over those engaged in every other vocation, avocation, profession, or business...." [10] And that was that!

Sinful, in the view of New Deal leaders, were other of his senatorial decisions. He opposed processing taxes, he kicked over the traces on the Supreme Court plan, he arose with a roar to flay wages and hours legislation,[11] he soughed old-school eloquence through his mustache against passage of a housing measure, and he unlimbered every weapon in his oratorical armory against the anti-lynching bill.

That anti-lynching proposal hit Cotton Ed in his ideological solar plexus. A two-pronged assault upon his trinity of principles, it left only a tariff for revenue unassailed. It outraged him personally, insulted the fair womanhood of the South, recalled the bitter days of Reconstruction under the carpetbaggers in South Carolina, and vilely and insidiously attacked his constituency. In righteous indignation he joined with other Southern senators to talk the proposal to death. He told the Senate that the proponents of the measure did not appreciate the Gethsemane through which the South had passed. He heaped burning scorn upon the carpetbaggers, the scalawags, the camp followers who had enthroned the Negro in the South and had raped the finest civilization America had ever seen. A deliberate attack was being made upon the South, he opined, by a "so-called Democratic party." It was unbelievable that the loyalty of the South to the party would be repaid by such treachery. And as for the womanhood of the South:

"Nothing to us is more dear than the purity and sanctity of our womanhood, and, so help us God, no one shall violate it

10. *Congressional Digest,* XV (March, 1936), 82.
11. "Jeeze Chris', you ain't going to pay no nigger $15 a week, are you?" demanded one outraged Southerner who joined Cotton Ed in opposition to the bill.

without paying the just penalty which should be inflicted upon the beast who invades the sanctity of our womanhood. ... Certain acts committed are beyond the reach of any court or jury. ... The virtue of a woman is a thing which should not be displayed in courts when the criminal is known."

What if the measure should pass? Well, that would mean secession—personal secession—from the Democratic party for him, Cotton Ed assured the Senate. "I, for one, here today declare that if this proposal involving the destruction of State rights and the usurpation of local self-government, becomes a part and parcel of Democratic doctrine, I shall pay no further allegiance to such a party." This was in 1935 during the Seventy-fourth Congress. The years that followed did little to mollify him, but for the most part Cotton Ed managed to keep his resentment safely checked by his party regularity. Then in December, 1943, came a dispute growing out of the soldier vote issue, and he could restrain himself no longer. Climaxing the outraged cries of Southern senators who had heard themselves accused of conspiring with Republicans to deprive members of the armed services of the right to vote, he called upon the Southern states to organize a new Democratic party. "I have been here for six Presidents," he declared, "and I have enjoyed being a Senator until this miserable thing came along—I mean this miserable party." Cotton Ed was on the warpath. He had left the political reservation and was ready for a scalping party. Two months later, in a moment of reflection, he revealed the abysmal depths of his convictions. He had fallen so low "in the political cesspool," he told his colleagues, that the Republican party had begun to look good to him. That admission from a South Carolinian can immediately be classified among the superlatives.

Throughout his opposition to New Deal leadership in recent years, Cotton Ed continually stressed two points: The legislative branch ought to reassert itself and brace itself against executive domination, and anything that tends to usurp State's Rights should be rejected speedily and completely. These pleas for legislative independence carried with them declarations of personal independence. "There is no man or set of men, no administration, or anyone in power that will ever influence me in casting a vote or performing my duty as a United States Senator," he told his colleagues in discussing a measure which, if passed, faced possible veto by the President. As for that possible veto, he had no fear. "Thank God, we also have the veto power. . . . We can veto a veto," he thundered. Was he making this speech for votes? Not at all. "God made me a man before South Carolina made me a Senator," he explained. "God bless my soul, my forebears lived on parched corn and sweet potatoes to give me a crown of individual rights, and I'm going to wear my crown if it kills me." Under New Deal leadership Congress had become a clearing house and the Supreme Court had vanished. "The entire government has gone to hell." Certain administrative leaders were, in Cotton Ed's words, the "Lords of America," and, of course, objects of suspicion. As for administrative boards, "We ought to take back every bit of power we have delegated to those rascals." Finally, even the rationing program felt his scorn. "You can't win a war by rationing away state and individual rights. And who the hell expects to win one by taking the ruffles off ladies' lingerie?" he growled. Well, then, what was the remedy, what should Congress do? The answer: "Get back to the fundamental principles of the Constitution and think and act here in accordance with what we know are the best interests of the American people."

There have been those who sought to embarrass Cotton Ed by pointed references to his lusty language. How was it that his constituents countenanced his salty rhetoric? Were not they offended by such language from one whose father wore the cloth of the Methodist church, whose brothers numbered two ministers, one a bishop, whose sisters included two who chose ministers for husbands? Apparently this was a matter that never bothered Cotton Ed to any considerable degree. The election returns were perfectly satisfactory to him. But if you insisted on a statement he pointed out that the closeness of his family ties with the ministry is within itself explanation of his choice of expletives. "I've got the cussin' to do for the whole family," he declared, "I'll never catch up in a lifetime."

Other attempts to embarrass him generally were equally as unsuccessful. For example, there was the matter of nepotism. Many public men who believe that the placing of relatives on the public payroll is a personal privilege have found themselves hard pressed to justify themselves before their constituents. Not Cotton Ed! For example, he was once taken to task by an opponent for landing a federal job for an elderly aunt. It was claimed that the respected lady was seventy-six years old. Cotton Ed strode to the front of the platform, livid with indignation. "It's a lie," he roared. "It's a base and infamous lie. She's 80 years of age, not 76!" And anyhow, he continued, she had more energy than many federal workers he knew, and who he hired was nobody's business. Early in 1944 a national columnist revealed that the Smith family was well represented on the federal payroll, especially as employes of the Senate Agriculture and Forestry Committee.[12] Cotton Ed simply ignored this report on his political life, and nothing else was written about the Smiths' annual pay check of $18,300. But Cotton Ed was perfectly capable of lashing back at his critics. There are many South Carolinians who remember the time when an aspiring opponent assailed him with apparent success for the high prices the Army was said to be paying for mules and harness. Replied Cotton Ed, "I don't know how much the Army is spending for mules or how many harnesses it is buying. But for goodness sakes, folks, don't you go and pay $10,000 a year for a jackass like my opponent." And they didn't.

At the age of seventy-eight Cotton Ed reached the end of six consecutive terms in the Senate. He passed the record of the late William E. Borah who served thirty-three of the thirty-six years for which he was elected. That he was at last defeated was cheering to those who viewed with little approbation Cotton Ed's crusade for his principles. They are cheered too easily, for while Cotton Ed has gone, the South remains— with its memories, its unsolved problems, and its traditions.

12. Drew Pearson in his "The Merry-Go-Round," dated Feb. 23, listed among others, the following: son-in-law, secretary to the Senator and committee clerk, $3,900; daughter, assistant clerk, $2,200; daughter, assistant clerk, $2,200, these in addition to the Senator's salary. Mr. Pearson included two of Senator Smith's sons in his list, stating that they drew a total of $5,080 in salaries. These, however, are not federal employes, according to Senator Smith.

III

IN CITY AND IN STATE

22

HAROLD EDWARD STASSEN
"Candidate in Absentia"

BY ROBERT THOMPSON

THE JURY OF AMERICAN VOTERS HAD COME IN ONLY THREE days before. Thomes E. Dewey lost out in his prosecution of the New Deal, by which he sought to gain the presidency of the United States and to put the Republican party back in the leadership of the nation.

Washington political writers cast about for a likely candidate to retrieve the GOP fortunes in 1948. Almost unanimously, they picked out Commander Harold Edward Stassen of the United States Navy, the youthful former governor of Minnesota who quit his office to fight the war with his own generation.

True, Stassen had been an unsuccessful candidate in absentia in the Republican pre-convention presidential race in 1944. True also, Stassen's principal protege and representative at home, Senator Joseph H. Ball, had gone off the Republican reservation and plumped for President Roosevelt against Mr. Dewey.

Nevertheless, the political writers felt that Commander Stassen's stature still qualified him to be a Republican Moses who might lead his party's return to the political promised land.

All of this was no surprise to the voters of Minnesota. Since 1937, they have been conditioned to accept as the usual thing almost any precedent-shattering accomplishment by their young leader from South St. Paul.

Since leaving the governorship, Stassen has added the political appeal of a war record, including a decoration, to his other attractions as a public figure. Further, President Roosevelt chose him as one of the eight delegates and the only military man on our panel of representatives to the first large United Nations conference.

Some of Stassen's attractions are very solid and obvious. Others are almost intangible. But added together, they have filled out a record of astonishing success for the almost juvenile leader. In any study of Stassen, or prophecies about his career, it must be remembered that he was born well within the twentieth century, April 13, 1907.

Three or four years before Stassen traded the governor's chair for a warship's bridge, toastmasters in Minnesota gave forth with free-wheeling and knee-action predictions that the presidency was his certain destination. With some, it was a dinner-time pleasantry. Others wanted to be right on the record, just in case. With many, it was a clear sign of the political and personal enthusiasm which Harold Stassen generates. This induced enthusiasm makes him a political phenomenon of the day. Time may very possibly add the rank of statesman.

The word phenomenon is well advised. Stassen was elected public prosecutor of his home county at twenty-two, and served eight years. At thirty-one he became governor of Minnesota by a landslide vote. This vote, incidentally, might be a precedent for things to come. It not only seated him but also returned the Republican party to power in the state after eight years, or four state terms of office. It wrecked the previously dominant Farmer-Labor party.

Twice Stassen was re-elected, the last time with as heavy a campaign burden as any candidate could carry. He was Republican national convention keynoter at Philadelphia at the age of thirty-three. After his speech there, he declared for the late Wendell Willkie, and floor-managed that outsider's drive for the 1940 nomination.

At thirty-six, while he was serving as flag secretary to Admiral William Halsey in the distant Pacific, Stassen's friends placed him in the race for the Republican nomination. That he lost out in the campaign seems to have cost him no loss of political face. While his friends electioneered unsuccessfully, he was seeing plenty of battle action.

That action absorbed him entirely. Navy scuttlebutt relates that he was so closemouthed on politics, even in the informality of the mess and wardroom, that Halsey upbraided him for his silence. In fact, he was so far removed that he was probably the last interested person to learn of Senator Ball's defection to Roosevelt.

Then, while he was still only thirty-seven, President Roosevelt recalled him from battle duty to assume one of the eight distinguished places as delegate of the United States to the United Nations conference.

In the past, wiseacre predictions about the young man's course and his personal future have usually been inaccurate. He made them so. Any forecasts short of his fiftieth birthday would probably be just as wide of the mark. There is a record on him, though—a complete one. It must be the basis for judgment of what may happen to him, as well as of what he is and what he has done.

His early history is much the same as that of thousands of other successful young men. He was born of Scandinavian-German-Czech ancestry on a small farm in West St. Paul. His parents homesteaded the farm and live there yet, operating a market garden business.

The father, William Stassen, through the period of his son's governorship and Navy career, beat the summer sunrise to the St. Paul city market to sell his produce. A revealing sidelight here is that the elder Stassen bought his first tractor in 1944, the year his son was being put forward as a presidential candidate.

Harold's brothers and sisters are substantial, normal, and unpretentious folks. They go about their jobs and pleasures, accept their responsibilities as thousands of other Americans do. Stassen married Esther Glewwe, a high school sweetheart. They and their two children now live in a modest, comfortable home he built for them on a high bluff overlooking the Mississippi and their community of South St. Paul.

The former governor is tall and big-boned, with reddish blond hair and complexion, and not an ounce of spare flesh since his Navy indoctrination. He has a round, friendly, open face, with a high forehead and a smile that bespeaks sincerity.

As a boy, Stassen went across fields to a country school, then commuted to St. Paul and back to high school. He graduated from high school at fifteen, an age when many boys enter it.

After a year helping on the farm, he entered the University of Minnesota. Like many others there, he worked and earned while he studied. One job occupied him two full nights and several evenings a week as a grease-boy in a bakery. Later, he clerked in a store. For two years, he worked nights and weekends as an extra-list sleeping-car conductor.

Graduating from the University law school, he was admitted to the bar in 1929, and set up a law practice in South St. Paul.

In addition to his jobs and his academic and law studies, the young man took the ROTC course. Becoming cadet colonel, he made himself one of the best rifle marksmen in the unit. With another cadet, he once scared the daylights out of a University president. At the preview of a campus military circus, the president saw Stassen and his partner shoot the blouse buttons from a comrade's uniform. Student audiences never got to enjoy that act. The president ordered it out of the show.

Stassen's political knack showed up in his student days. He was at first disregarded by the prominent fraternities. They woke up after a typical Stassen blitz of organization. In the law school, he banded together the non-fraternity men and made trades with some of the lesser fraternity groups who had been outsiders in choosing candidates for student offices. Stassen was elected law-school representative on the University student council before the overconfident old-line fraternity men knew what had happened. Later, he became president of the council.

A Stassen characteristic is to remember his friends. Shortly after he became governor, the Milwaukee railroad inaugurated a new streamliner train. It was on this road that the sleeping-car-conductor job had paid his school expenses for two years.

Frank Newell, the Milwaukee's publicity man, asked Stassen

to be guest conductor on the train's first run. Stassen didn't forget his past. When the train loaded at Minneapolis, the blue-uniformed and brass-buttoned governor put down a step box. He checked passengers and swung aboard as the train pulled out.

The thirty-one-year-old chief executive lost no prestige by this courtesy to his old employer. But Newell developed high blood pressure hunting up a uniform cap size 7¾. Stassen is a big man.

When Stassen had practiced law for a year, he ran for Dakota County attorney, or state's attorney, and was elected. When he stood for a second four-year term, he got an all-time record vote in the county.

This was not because he was a great prosecutor or put on a dramatic show, Tom Dewey style. He did a competent job, but any young attorney against older lawyers in a rural community will take a trouncing now and then. Stassen occasionally took one.

In contrast to his trial record is a story told by Edward J. Thye, the man who succeeded Stassen as governor. At the time of the incident, Thye was a Dakota County farmer.

"It was back in the nineteen-thirties," Thye said, "during the worst of the depression. The price of milk was down to 68 cents a hundred pounds. Many of us couldn't meet our obligations and provide for our families. A big group met at Farmington, in the county, at the call of the Farm Holiday Association.

"Excitement was high. Speakers urged the farmers to dump their milk and block highways toward the Twin Cities market to force a price increase. Someone said, 'Suppose the sheriff and the county attorney stop you?' The speaker replied, 'We will run them down or club them out of the way.'

"Just then, Harold Stassen elbowed to the front of the meeting. He faced the crowd and said, 'Men, I appreciate your situation and I want to help you. But I must tell you as county attorney that if you break the law, I will have to prosecute you. I think there is a better way out of this situation.'

"Stassen urged that a committee be appointed to seek a

better price by negotiation. He offered to be the committee's attorney without charge. The plan was accepted and the committee got a substantial increase in the price of milk. The farmers, much older than Stassen, swear by him yet, because he kept his head while they were losing theirs."

Soon after he succeeded in county politics, Stassen was bound to think of larger fields. By inclination and family background, he was a Republican. His father had been Republican county chairman. The youngster became active and then prominent in affairs of the state Young Republican League. (County officials in Minnesota are elected without party designation.)

Meanwhile, he watched the inside of a political campaign in another party. His law partner and University classmate, Elmer J. Ryan, was a Democrat of sorts. Dakota County is in a congressional district made up of rural and smaller city and town areas. Ryan filed for Congress in that district in 1934 as a Democrat.

Stassen will not admit taking part in Ryan's campaign. Some members of both the Republican and Democratic parties still give him credit for the brains behind the election of his law partner. Whatever the facts are, Stassen certainly could not avoid the strategy discussions and campaign planning in his own office. Whether or not he took any part in them, he is one who would benefit by and file for the future any lessons learned by the Ryan organization.

The eight years Stassen spent as Dakota County attorney and as a comer among the Young Republican group included the worst of the depression period. They also bridged the heyday of the Farmer-Labor party in Minnesota. The late Floyd B. Olson was governor from 1931 until late 1936, and Elmer A. Benson through 1937 and 1938.

Before Benson had sat long in the governor's chair, it became evident that Minnesota voters were ready to make a party change. Even the Old Guard Republicans felt the upheaval coming, but Stassen apparently sensed it long before they did. Through the years he worked among the Young Republicans, he was developing two qualities which served him well then and have come to successful maturity since.

One is his ability to form and wield an effective organization of workers for his projects and programs. At political meetings he can trade, negotiate, and sell others on the Stassen objectives. His best performance at this took place at the 1940 Republican convention, when he floor-managed Willkie to the party nomination.

The other quality is his magnetism for a close circle of devoted friends. They were and are convinced that Stassen's political sights remain as true and accurate as his rifle sights the day he pinged off a cadet's blouse buttons.

In the middle nineteen-thirties, dinner presiders began to predict that Stassen would become governor, the same way they now prophesy the presidency for him. Polite disbelief met the predictions at first. Then, listeners were not so sure. One of the first to accept certainty of Stassen's important political future was a St. Paul newspaper political writer, Joe Ball. He is now Senator Ball, first placed in his job by a Stassen appointment.

During Governor Benson's term, Stassen and his friends began active organization for the 1938 campaign. Victor Johnston, another newspaperman, allied himself with the inner group of Stassen enthusiasts. He circulated campaign material for his friend.

In the 1938 Republican primary, Martin Nelson filed as a third-time candidate. Twice before, Farmer-Laborites had licked him. Stassen filed also. At the start, all the wise money was on Nelson for the nomination. He had the Old Guard backing. When the primary votes were counted, Stassen had soundly beaten Nelson. As nominee, Stassen had seized leadership of his party in Minnesota from the Old Guard control of traditional standing.

After a bitter final campaign, Stassen drew 678,000 votes to 387,000 for Elmer Benson. The Farmer-Labor party never recovered from the impact of that defeat.

His election meant a new and searching test for Stassen. Could he measure up as a leader and administrator to the mark he set as a candidate? The record answers. It also spotlights his stand on questions that are national issues yet, just as much as they were 1938 problems in Minnesota.

Efficient and economical operation of government versus a political spoils system, public expenditures and debt, legal control of organized labor—all these were explosive questions in Minnesota at the time. They were particularly volatile and potent because of the Farmer-Labor administration's performance through the preceding eight years.

Though he was cautioned to tread softly around all of these questions, Stassen jumped into them resoundingly. He understood public desire for a drastic change. In his first inaugural address, he demanded a reorganization of the state government's budgeting, spending, and purchasing controls. He asked an effective civil service for state employes. He called for a labor relations law to enforce a "cooling off" period of negotiations before any strike or lockout could take place. He asked amendment of tax laws and cessation of business badgering by state government.

To the intense surprise of many, the legislators made Stassen's major program into law.

The enactment was through no miracle of mesmerism by the young governor. He spent long hours, both daylight and dark, in conference with committees and leaders of the state senate and house of representatives. They worked, debated, traded, and wrangled. Finally, they managed to emerge with bills that were passable in the legislature and workable after the lawmakers went home.

During that first legislative session, Stassen started a series of radio addresses which he called "Capitol Conferences." They were not modelled exactly on the FDR fireside chats, but they carried much the same effect. The big youth reported progress to the people. When the going was tough, with opposition from balky legislators and special interest lobbies, he told the public about it. Mr. and Mrs. John W. Citizen listened. If they got the idea that their representative or senator wasn't doing right by his job and his state, they said so. As a result, Stassen didn't have to be hard-boiled or crack down on the lawmakers. He was still able to negotiate in his office.

When the session ended, he had a reorganization law, a state civil service law, and a labor relations act.

The reorganization bill substituted a commissioner of administration, or state business manager, for the previous "big three" control. That "big three," originally dreamed up by a previous Republican governor, had functioned pretty nearly as they saw fit by dividing up authority over major state business functions. The new act said that the business manager must allow or disallow advance budgets for every state department every three months, for ordinary operations. Every nickel must be not only available, but also earmarked. In other words, no got, no spend.

Leslie Gravlin, Stassen's first appointee on the new job, found after he took office that state revenues would run about 10 per cent under earlier estimates. He summarily ordered a 10 per cent cutback in all state outlays, including salaries. Stassen and Gravlin took the cut, along with the rest. There was a howl from employees and from some department heads. But the state economized and dispensed with red ink.

The Farmer-Laborites had played fast and loose with state purchases. The green eyes of avarice, and the mellifluous behind-hand whispers of politics dictated in too many instances who was to sell what to the state, and for how much. Reorganization put an end to that and replaced it with strict competitive bidding.

The civil service system was installed, with competitive examinations and merit ratings. It must be said that not all the state workers are happy about it. There is a sizable volume of complaint, even after some years of operation. But the main objections seem to be on details rather than the principle of the system. It is certain that the Farmer-Laborite practice of levying a 3 per cent "contribution" against the salaries of all state employees is out the window. Each employee knows he can get a hearing on charges before being ousted instead of depending on politics or the whim of his department head for job tenure.

The Labor Relations Act is also important on the Stassen dossier. For a primarily agricultural state, Minnesota had a bad record of labor strife. Two violent truck strikes in Minneapolis, and a walkout of WPA workers cost lives, tens of thousands of lost work days, and martial law. Blood ran in the streets in these conflicts. There were other injurious strikes.

Let it be said here that labor and its leaders were not alone to blame. Reactionary management, in many instances, was just as bull-headed and responsible as union business agents. Both sides were guilty. Extremes bred new extremes.

Stassen proposed a law embodying the best practices in the Scandinavian countries plus successful features of the Railroad Retirement Act. Union labor fought bitterly against any bill to circumscribe use of its strike weapon. Employer groups were less than lukewarm about any compulsion on them to negotiate disputes except in just the way they alone saw fit.

Nevertheless, a law was passed. It created a state labor conciliator. Before any strike or lockout could be called, ten days written notice to employer and conciliator was required. During that period, it is in his power and is his duty to summon in all parties to the dispute, seat them around a table, and take up the issues. He may not compel anyone to agree to anything. He is not an arbitrator. Neither can he prevent a strike or lockout if one or both sides continue adamant. He can and does force them to meet and talk things over.

If he determines that a strike would affect the public interest such as a walkout of bus drivers, he certifies that fact to the governor. This action automatically stays the strike for another thirty days. The governor appoints a fact-finding commission to inquire into the merits of the dispute. It has power to subpoena necessary persons, books, and records. The fact-finding commission also is powerless to force the parties into agreement. But it reports findings and recommendations to the governor and the public. The resulting weight of public opinion is usually effective toward settlement if conciliation has failed.

Much as both labor and some elements of management feared the law, they were doomed to happy disappointment. At succeeding sessions of the legislature, AFL, CIO, and independent unions have opposed every attempt to amend the procedure.

In his last inaugural address, in January, 1943, Stassen was able to boast that while he spoke not a single labor picket walked anywhere in Minnesota. One practice followed by Stassen and his successor, Ed Thye, is to appoint every conciliator from the ranks of organized labor.

Stassen had the good fortune to serve as governor when general business conditions were on the up-grade. Tax collections rose and delinquency declined. Demands for relief money dropped. War plants and profits and rising prices of farm products brought much more money into the state than had come in during depression years.

Even counting this advantage, the fiscal record of his administration is startling. While Stassen was in office, the state debt went down by $39,000,000; state payrolls were reduced from 17,000 to 10,000 employees; state tax rates on real estate dropped; the so-called "moneys and credits" tax, always an obnoxious levy, was suspended; $15,000,000 were nesting in government bonds for post-war highway construction; state aid to schools had been increased; and several million dollars of unexpended balances lay in the state treasury.

This is the administrative record of the farmboy-lawyer-prosecutor-governor, most of whose state incumbency passed before he was thirty-five. It shows clearly what attitude he would take in national office.

All was not beer and skittles for the young governor, though. There were difficulties, critics, and criticisms.

In passing the Labor Relations Act, the legislature failed to include disputes between state or local government units and their employees. As a result, the conciliator was powerless when a long wrangle between the University of Minnesota board of regents and building service employees led to two serious strikes at that institution. Incidentally, more than two years after Stassen went to war, that dispute was still in progress, though the employees were at work. The conciliator also was helpless when state grain weighers walked out and thus plugged Minneapolis railroad yards with unweighed cars of wheat. He could do nothing about a strike of city utility em-

ployees at Moorhead which shut down all water and light
service for hours.

Stassen had other troubles. One grew from the antiquated,
patchwork city government and school administration in Minneapolis. The City Council and Board of Education there
became little better than back-fence squabblers. Taxes, expenditure, and debt are up. Municipal service is down.

Stassen stepped into the mess from the statehouse. He ordered a survey of Minneapolis' school system at state expense.
His idea was that the school administration must be changed or
state financial aids would be curtailed. He also asked the legislature to overhaul the city's governmental structure, whether
Minneapolis liked it or not.

Deep resentment sprang up in that city. The legislature did
nothing. A few minor changes came in the school system and
a superintendent was dismissed with fireworks. The state aids
were paid as usual. After Stassen left for the Navy, the resentment remained. It backfired against the Stassen-for-President
organization in a congressional-district Republican convention
in Minneapolis. The mayor and some aldermen were the ones
who touched off the backfire.

When World War II first came on, Stassen launched an unprecedented state defense setup. There were more than 5,000
uniformed and equipped state guardsmen, complete even with
a nurse corps. A complete panel of emergency civilian services
was organized in line with the paper plans of OCD at
Washington. There were even a physical fitness program and
a gliding and soaring training layout. There was a statewide
phalanx of women known as "Victory Aides," and a group of
"Labor Volunteers for Victory" with three cushy top jobs for
labor leaders paid by the state. All told, 330,000 civilians
enrolled.

The cost was paid through emergency financing powers set
up originally to meet emergency needs. It amounted to well
over a million dollars before the legislature met in regular
1943 biennial session. The lawmakers resented what they
deemed a heavy, unauthorized, and possibly unnecessary interim expenditure. Stassen asked for $800,000 more for the

next biennium. All he got was $160,000, and later this was clipped down by a legislative interim group. He also asked a broad emergency war powers bill. He got one, but it was far different from the original that was drafted for him.

The merit of Stassen's civilian defense program is a moot question, inasmuch as even federal authorities agreed in 1944 that the need for it had passed. Among his enemies there were suspicions that he intended to add the organization to his political setup. His friends deny this, asserting with considerable evidence to support them that the Stassen organization did very well as it was, thank you.

And—there is Joe Ball.

When in 1940, the young chief executive placed his friend in the vacant United States Senate seat, he went over the heads of many of the party faithful who aspired to the job. Ball, by the nature of his work as a political writer, never could join in Republican party activity. He had no party record at all, and this made life-long Republicans furious at Stassen.

Stassen had faith in the bone-deep sincerity of Ball's conviction. Furthermore, the newsman subscribed vigorously to Stassen's program on internationalism. In the 1942 election, this was not an issue for state office candidates. In Ball's case, it was decidedly an issue because he sought return to the Senate from a supposedly isolationist state. Because Ball had been Stassen's appointee, the issue enveloped the governor.

Added to this was the Stassen announcement early in the campaign that he asked election for a third term but intended to serve only through the four months of the legislative session. After that, he said, he would resign to enter the Navy. He wanted a direct part in the war along with the men of his generation.

Ball, meanwhile, overcame much of the initial prejudice against him. His work in the Senate, his forthrightness on public questions, and his leadership in the Stassen-for-President group before the Chicago convention were impressive. Until the last minute at Chicago, he intended to nominate Stassen. Then the crushing progress of the Dewey steamroller flattened any hope for the Navy commander out in the far Pacific.

All through the campaign up to convention time, Ball had privately expressed his dislike, if not his contempt, of Dewey as a presidential candidate. This was not so bad as long as he kept it to himself. But it did not square with the strategy of the Stassen group. They made it a rigid policy not to make deals with other candidates, or to antagonize them. The Stassenites assured everyone that they would support the convention nominee, whoever he might be.

Then Ball popped off. First he said he could not support Dewey "at this time." Later he came out for Roosevelt on the issue of internationalism. Reaction of Minnesota Republicans was profane and thunderous. The fury of a woman scorned was deep affection compared with the attitude of the state's GOP toward Ball. Naturally, much of the anger turned against the absent Stassen. There was nothing he could do. It may be said categorically here that not only Stassen but also his friends and supporters were completely ignorant of Ball's intentions until after the Senator issued his first statement. Things got worse when Ball took to the air and the platform in the Roosevelt campaign.

This, like dozens of other occurrences in the Stassen political career, ought to sink him. In the eyes of the Washington writers, it didn't. Stassen's record of surmounting political disaster is remarkable. It parallels the skill, audacity, and luck that his boss, Admiral Halsey, showed in the Philippine campaign.

Consider again the governorship campaign of 1942. Partnership with Ball that year and early resignation from office would be handicaps enough for any ordinary candidate. But not for Stassen. He also decided to toss overboard C. Elmer Anderson, the young lieutenant-governor who had been elected with him twice before. In Anderson's stead, the governor asked the voters to elect Edward J. Thye, the Dakota County farmer whom Stassen had appointed his dairy and food commissioner. Up to Stassen's first term as governor, Thye had never held higher public office than township and school-board memberships. Thye, Stassen told the voters, was the man who ought to step into the governorship when he left it. Stassen, Ball, and

Thye were elected handily. Two years later, Thye went back into the governor's office with the greatest majority of votes even given a candidate for that place. Yet at the same time, C. Elmer Anderson returned to the lieutenant governorship.

Thye seems to have justified Stassen's decision. He has become popular in every part of the state. Were he like Stassen, it is conceivable that the two might some time be opponents. But the qualities which make Thye popular are different from those which brought state and national recognition to the younger man.

Stassen's honors came not alone in the political field. While he was a prosecutor, he served two terms as president of the Minnesota County Attorneys Association. He was given special awards by the United States Junior Chamber of Commerce and the World Christian Endeavor Union. He served either as vice-president or president of the Northern Baptist Convention, the Governors Conference and Council of State Governments, and the International Council of Religious Education.

President Roosevelt's choice of Stassen as an United States delegate to the United Nations conference started the Washington oracles to columning a whole new speculation as to the Commander's future, politically and otherwise. Some kept to purely political horoscopes. A few went to another part of Stassen's record.

That is the part he spoke and wrote for two years before entering military service, his views on international co-operation for peace in the post-war world. It is impossible to tell how the watches and battle stations out near Asia strengthened or changed his beliefs. After he donned the uniform, he outclammed any clam. Here again, the record must speak.

Campaigning across the country for a post-war United Nations government of the world, Stassen always insisted that he was trying to promote serious, intelligent discussion rather than to sell a settled plan. What he said thrilled some of his hearers, frightened others, but left almost none of them indifferent.

He advocated this United Nations government of the world working through a single house parliament. Member nations would be represented proportionately, not only as to population, but also on fulfillment of international obligations, contributions to the world government, and literacy of their citizens.

The parliament would fix definite policies. To carry them out, an administration something like the English cabinet system would function. The parliament would elect a chairman, in reality a premier of the world. The premier would appoint a council, or cabinet, of seven ministers with approval of the parliament. Each council member, or minister, would have charge of one of the seven undertakings which Stassen charted for his international government.

The initial task would be to establish temporary governments over thoroughly defeated Axis nations. The temporary governments, Stassen insisted, must assure complete disarmament and punish "criminal leadership for acts of horror and betrayal of civilization." He would, however, permit no wholesale reprisals against "innocent civilian populations."

Second on his job list is administration of great international airways and airports of the future. Even before he entered the Navy and flew to duty in the Pacific, Stassen wasn't day-dreaming about air commerce. When the war began, St. Paul and Minneapolis became a jumping off place for a gigantic Army air transport line to Alaska and Russia.

Function three, as Stassen saw it, brought breathless objections from many quarters. Nevertheless, he supported his proposition that the United Nations government could "administer gateways to the seven seas." By his own interpretation, this would mean the surrender of such facilities as the Panama and Suez canals, Gibraltar, and Singapore, to international control.

International commerce came next. Stassen urged both the need and possibility of a world exchange of goods and services multiplied past peacetime levels many times over. He did not ask universal free trade but called for certain guarantees. Stifling tariff walls and choking barriers of nationalism would be banned, but so would heavy dumping of goods. There would be no boom days for international carpetbaggers, freebooters, and imperialists. No country's natural resources could be despoiled, or even exploited, without just payment. Wealthy nations would increase capital investments in undeveloped regions. Necessary checks and balances would be maintained by co-operation of individual governments.

Education was fifth on the list. He said that if men and women everywhere could know how to read and write, then improvements in health, living standards, local government, and world ideals must naturally follow.

Any government to be successful must have a code of justice. There must be a world code and a court to administer it, Stassen said. The code would protect minorities, prevent religious persecution, and abolish slavery of every kind. The United Nations court would be chosen by supreme courts of member nations, and the cabinet minister for justice would be a sort of world attorney-general.

Finally, Stassen would have a world police force, an United Nations legion. This military force would have air strength, modern naval contingents, and highly mobile, mechanized land divisions. It would be backed up by military power of member nations. As immediate jobs, in addition to enforcing peace, the legion would police airways and sea gateways, keep a constant watch over points of international friction.

The world government would be set up, at the start, by the United Nations. Other countries would be admitted as they showed good faith, desire for peace, and ability to meet obligations.

In the domestic field, Stassen has a broad view on policy beyond that mirrored in his administrative record. He pins his faith for a solvent and prosperous future on an economy of productivity. This, he is convinced, can come only through natural play of free enterprise and initiative. He would inhibit free enterprise only by such regulation as will prevent economic monsters of the types of restrictive monopoly, dishonest or coercive financial structures, or abuse of patent rights.

An entirely new weather belt must be set up between government and business, he believes, with benign warmth replacing cold hostility. Revision of the tax structure and of SEC controls are two important, necessary steps, according to the Stassen conception. Change of the tax structure is required, he thinks, both to encourage productivity of present business and industry, and to encourage venture capital into new fields.

In a *Saturday Evening Post* article, he wrote:

Most of our leading productive enterprises have been developed through plowing back into the companies a large share of the earnings, using this capital for expansion, for modernization, and for experiment. When peace returns, there will be many new opportunities opened up by science and invention under forced pressure of war. Properly encouraged, they should usher in a period of progress, worthwhile jobs, and new wealth. There should be no tax that throttles this process.

Government must also permit the free flow of venture capital. Without it, a free, healthy economy is impossible. This means, of course, that the Securities and Exchange laws must be modified.

The encouragement of production does not lessen the responsibility for preventing abuses. Government must insist on real competition by capital seeking investment. It is undesirable to permit special interest tie-ups between enterprise and capital through an exclusive favored-banker arrangement.

Stassen advocates a flexible program, or rather a safety backlog, of public works enterprises to take up unemployment, but only when private enterprise is unable to provide enough jobs. These public works, he believes, should be conducted by state and local levels of government, with grants in aid from the federal level where necessary.

For agriculture, he recommends price floors as needed because farmers are unable to exert proper control over the prices of their own products in a free economy. Above these floors, Stassen says, prices should fluctuate according to supply and demand, in order that production may be adjusted from year to year according to public needs and demands.

Returning veterans of the present war, too, concern him. He asked the Minnesota legislature to set up a fund of several millions of dollars for their benefit, half to be used for scholarships, the other half for small loans or grants to help veterans get established in business or professions. This was months before the GI Bill of Rights was enacted by Congress. The

Minnesota lawmakers complied substantially with his suggestion.

This is the picture of Harold Edward Stassen, and the things he has thought, said, and done. The prisoning anonymity of a battleship's bridge, though it did silence him, never submerged him. In his quasi-diplomatic status at the United Nations conferences he may be well on the way back to the broad land highway of his public career. If not, he will resume it in peacetime. Where that highway may lead is impossible to say. But he has unquestionably fashioned for himself a vehicle of personality and ability, performance and opinion, to speed him on the way.

23

THOMAS EDMUND DEWEY

"Political Resiliency"

BY S. BURTON HEATH

BY ALL THE RULES OF POLITICAL LOGIC, THOMAS EDMUND
Dewey was a gone goose at three o'clock the morning of
November 8, 1944, when he strode into the Hotel Roosevelt
ballroom in New York and conceded his defeat for the presidency.

At that time the full extent of his disaster was not yet
apparent. A number of key states, including New York, still
remained technically in doubt. It was not until considerably
later that Governor Dewey's native state of Michigan swung
over to the Roosevelt column, as the count was completed, and
left the young man from Owosso with a bare ninety-nine electoral votes out of 531.

When all the returns were in, it developed that Governor
Dewey had lost thirty-six of the forty-eight states, including all
of the most important electoral blocs except Ohio's. He
couldn't carry either the state of which he was governor or
even the normally Republican state in which he was born,
reared, and educated. He had failed to please entirely the inter-
nationally-minded elements of his party and had seriously
offended its isolationists.

By virtue of his candidacy, Mr. Dewey had become titular
leader of the GOP. But so, for that matter, was Alf Landon
when he sank into political nonentity after 1936. So was Wendell Willkie, who found after 1940 that his title meant little
in a showdown. Moreover, Mr. Dewey faced a party tradition
that never in its history had the GOP taken a second chance

with a losing candidate for the presidency, however great his prestige or however good the contest he had waged.

It seemed, then, that Tom Dewey was singing his swan song as a presidential possibility when he read his concession of defeat into the group of radio network microphones in front of the Roosevelt ballroom stage—and then, swinging a leg nonchalantly as he assumed his favorite press conference posture on the corner of a table, spelled out that swan song meticulously, phrase by phrase and word by word, until every newspaperman present had copied its text accurately.

But before you accept the somewhat labored attempts of some of Governor Dewey's more vitriolic critics to toss him into the political ash can along with Hoover, Landon, John Garner, and Jim Farley, let's look at the record.

One of the most striking characteristics of Mr. Dewey is his political resiliency, or bounce—his ability to absorb reverses that would destroy most political figures and to come back, after each defeat, stronger than ever before. Three times, during what seemed the most crucial thirty months of his spectacular early career, the young Michigander was knocked down almost brutally. Any one of those failures should have frightened away political realists to whom nothing succeeds but uninterrupted success. Yet each time he came back, and on each second attempt he has succeeded in attaining a coveted goal.

If Tom Dewey does not run again for the presidency, or if, trying, he is beaten again, it will be the first time in his public career that he will have lost permanently a major prize on which his heart was set.

Mr. Dewey's early fame was made as a public prosecutor. For seven years he built up a reputation for something approaching invincibility. It seemed that he couldn't lose in anything important. That astounding string of successes as a prosecutor was, actually, his only claim upon the public's confidence or support. Then he arrested Jimmy Hines, the most powerful political figure Tammany Hall has known since Boss Murphy, occasional house guest in the White House, dispenser of federal patronage in New York for the Roosevelt administration. He indicted Hines for acting as political protector and court fixer for a lottery racket headed by the notorious gangster known as Dutch Schultz.

That was the climax in Prosecutor Dewey's career, the goal toward which he had been pointing since first he was appointed by Governor Herbert H. Lehman to investigate the alliance between crime and politics in Manhattan, which is, for most outlanders, New York—the island of Wall Street, skyscrapers, subways, Fifth Avenue and Forty-second Street, the Great White Way.

The ensuing trial was conducted under the brightest spotlight of nation-wide publicity. Day by day it was front-page news in every newspaper in the country. Everything seemed to be going well. Mr. Dewey was riding high when suddenly, sensationally, the presiding judge declared a mistrial because, he ruled, District Attorney Dewey had pulled a legal boner in cross-examination.

That was disaster where it hurt most—failure in the field in which, if in any, Dewey claimed supremacy—a mortifying cropper in his most important, most widely publicized case. It should have laid him low, but it did not. Most newspapers and much of the public felt that Mr. Dewey had received an outrageous deal. He became something of a martyr. His friends stood by. Nobody was surprised in the slightest when, early the next year, District Attorney Dewey tried Hines before a different judge, in another court, and sent him "up the river" for from four to eight years.

After the first Hines trial fiasco, and before he had redeemed himself by success, the Republican party in New York nominated Mr. Dewey for governor almost without opposition. His candidacy apparently terrified the Democrats, who had controlled the state government uninterruptedly for fifteen years under three governors. Herbert Lehman, the best votegetter the Democrats ever had in New York, wanted to retire. But his party leaders took him into a convention hotel bedroom and verbally bludgeoned him, at the last moment, into running again to save the Democratic party from Tom Dewey.

Mr. Dewey campaigned vigorously, spectacularly and effectively. Large, enthusiastic crowds greeted him everywhere. He received more votes than any Republican candidate before him in a non-presidential year; more Republican votes than Governor Lehman received Democratic votes. But Governor Lehman's 420,000 on the American Labor party line re-elected him by the skinny margin of 64,394.

Dewey had failed to carry his state, on top of having to try Jimmy Hines twice to convict him. The GOP in New York, as nationally, had a tradition against renominating a loser. That tradition was strong and well established. But it failed to stop Dewey. When 1942 rolled around nobody even suggested that the Republicans might possibly consider any other candidate. He was nominated without discussion and was elected by a majority of 245,000 votes above the combined score of his Democratic and American Labor party opponents.

But once more, in an interval between defeat and comeback, Mr. Dewey had suffered a mortifying experience. After campaigning from coast to coast, he had gone to Philadelphia in 1940 with the biggest bloc of pledged delegates and the party's presidential nomination seemingly in his vest pocket, only to have Wendell Willkie, arriving without a single pledge, grab the prize on a wave of almost evangelistic popular fervor.

Coming on top of everything else, that catastrophe might have seemed evidence that young Dewey lacked some final spark that is needed to carry a man to the greatest heights. Left at the altar three times running, it would seem to demand a foolhardy party to woo him once more, or even to succumb to his own courtship.

Yet while Governor Dewey sat back, insisted that he was not a candidate for the 1944 nomination, requested his friends not to put him into state primaries, strongly repudiated those who insisted on running in his name, declined to discuss national or international issues, his strength constantly built up until, two months before the party convention, stalwarts in other camps began flocking to the Dewey bandwagon. He was nominated for President without even the pretense of a convention fight.

The beating that Challenger Dewey took from Champ

Roosevelt in the election was conclusive. Clearly the electorate wanted President Roosevelt to finish the war and make the peace. Nevertheless, it would seem premature at this time to write off a candidate for whom more than twenty-one million Americans voted in the midst of total war; a candidate who, in the opinion of many top political experts of both parties, would have won hands down if the war had been over or its near end had seemed more certain; a candidate who, unlike Herbert Hoover, was not tarred with the blame for a terrible depression—unlike Alf Landon, had not been beaten ignominiously—unlike Wendell Willkie, had not deliberately antagonized the working politicians in his party, but had led them into at least lip service to domestic liberality and international co-operation; a candidate who, up to now, always has risen from defeat to victory.

For two years, at least, Mr. Dewey was assured of the New York governorship as a forum for demonstrating capacity and keeping legitimately in the public eye. No expert has doubt that until 1948 he will exercise his leadership of and spokesmanship for the rejuvenescent Republican party and the millions of independents who voted for him in 1944.

Therefore it is by no means raking over old ashes, or naively seeking to record definitively a political episode still in the making, if we examine the record of Tom Dewey at this time to ascertain who he is; what he is; what he has done; what he has stood for; what more than twenty-one million Americans approved and twenty-four millions disapproved in the election; what, as Republican leader, he may be expected to favor or oppose until he either becomes President himself or gives way to another party chieftain.

When young Mr. Dewey first began running for public office, one of his strongest supporters was the now late Kenneth Simpson, aggressive red-headed county chairman who revivified the moribund GOP in New York county and later became national committeeman and congressman.

In 1940 Mr. Simpson and Mr. Dewey quarreled. The county chairman lined up convention votes for Wendell Willkie and split the New York delegation. Whereupon Mr. Dewey ousted

Mr. Simpson from the national committee and replaced him with a Dewey protagonist, Russell Sprague. Mrs. Simpson, aggrieved for her husband, is credited with the bitter *bon mot* frequently quoted: "You have to know Tom Dewey well to hate him."

Over a period of years his critics pictured Dewey as a very unpleasant young upstart by continually reiterating a barrage of disparaging adjectives supported anecdotally—arbitrary, arrogant, autocratic, intolerant; cold, suspicious, vain, egotistical, selfish, theatrical; ambitious, opportunistic, unscrupulous.

To those who have studied Mr. Dewey and his career closely, two things about this picture are significant. One, that it was repudiated and disputed by virtually everybody who worked closely with him. The other, that such criticism now comes largely from those who knew him more intimately in the past. Among newer acquaintances there is much expressed wonder as to how the Dewey temperament could have got so bad a reputation. Probably one answer is that Mr. Dewey never was as bad as he seemed, and another answer is that he has either outgrown or learned to control some of his more annoying faults. He is not a man who makes many really intimate friendships. Probably the persons could be counted on one's fingers with whom he is capable of relaxing completely, letting down his hair and forgetting appearances. He tries, often, to be just a good fellow, but the effort sometimes seems forced and the effect unreal.

One of Mr. Dewey's most aggravating traits is that he thinks faster and straighter than most of those with whom he comes in contact. He can't understand why they lag mentally. He is impatient with their mental tardiness or slovenliness and anxious to move ahead. This is not an adult development. An early teacher, C. C. Tuck, told newspapermen that young Tom "was the smartest boy I ever saw. He was brilliant—actually better informed on subjects than his teachers. But this boy was also the most disagreeable, cantankerous little devil I ever encountered. He couldn't understand why people did not grasp things as quickly as he did. He was as disliked by his classmates as he was by his instructors."

It can reasonably be assumed that then, as in his earlier political career, Dewey expressed his disgust and disdain sometimes in supercilious sarcasm, for which he had a flair, and at other times by withdrawing physically or spiritually from contacts that had lost interest or value to him. Neither course tended to make or cement friendships.

Increasingly Mr. Dewey either has reconciled himself to the slower pickup of associates or has schooled himself to disguise his displeasure or disinterest. Combined with this flaw is a deep-seated theatricalism which is effective with large gatherings, where the personal touch could not be expected, but which often impresses individual or more intimate gatherings as egotism, insincerity, or both. To this theatricalism many things contribute.

Actually Mr. Dewey is of average height, but somehow he gives an impression of shortness. He is well built, erect, vigorous, alert, and has an air of cockiness. He is meticulous about his appearance. He has a fine baritone voice, trained first as a professional singer and later as a courtroom lawyer. With typical Dewey thoroughness, he has cultivated that voice as an instrument of persuasion—and cultivated the supplementary oratorical use of eyes, brows, mouth, hands, and body, until oratory no longer is an affectation to be picked up as he takes the rostrum and laid aside when he has thanked his audience. It is his natural mode of expression, almost as much with a lone friend in his office as before thousands in Madison Square Garden. He is, indeed, like a veteran actor who has strode the stage in a part so often that he has become the character he portrays.

Nor has Mr. Dewey neglected his mind. His entire life has been devoted to developing inquisitiveness, retentiveness, logic, incisiveness. He never uses half his mind, or listens with one ear. When one talks with him, it is apparent that he is absorbing every word, weighing it, noting every nuance of voice and manner, digesting everything as he goes along. The slightest ambiguity must be cleared up. He listens to a perfectly respectable acquaintance, discussing affairs of state, with the same critical objectivity with which he used to listen to criminals and court witnesses, always seeking the last grain of information, explicit or implicit, upon which to formulate a sound opinion or base a sound decision. Unfortunately, though usually it is not so intended, this makes many visitors feel that Mr. Dewey is suspicious and unfriendly; that he is watching for them to make some misstep. Wherefor, only the brash, until they have become accustomed to the manner, manage to feel at ease with Mr. Dewey and regard him as a comfortable companion.

He seldom acts on impulse. He weighs pros and cons thoroughly before committing himself on even a seemingly unimportant matter. This would seem to be a desirable trait in one holding high office. But it leads one often, justly or unjustly, to wonder whether Mr. Dewey, while he is pondering the merits of an argument, is also considering its possible effect upon his own political fortunes.

I have discussed the controversial Dewey personality at some length, in advance of his record and his views, because that personality has been widely publicized and its less pleasant aspects sometimes have distracted attention from his intellect and his achievement.

Mr. Dewey has been accused of being reactionary. Many think of him as conservative. Surely he is not radical. I think that probably he is what, prior to perhaps 1934-35, would have been called a liberal.

He believes that government has an obligation to serve all of the people, and not merely some; that government must protect the weak against the strong, must regulate and control the ruthlessly powerful, must provide for victims of circumstance—but that government can not do everything for everybody, must not create new victims in rescuing old ones, and should not use its obligation to stop abuses as a screen behind which to seize power for itself.

His philosophy seems to be not that the world owes everybody a living, but that it is government's duty to see that everybody is given a chance to earn his own living.

He considers unemployment insurance "a necessary safeguard for those who may be unemployed, not a substitute for allowing the country to go back to work." He wants "adequate and non-political relief for jobless not protected by unemployment insurance" and a system of old age insurance that will "provide a reasonable standard of living after the years of active work have passed."

In the field of social security he feels that "we have barely made a start." He urges that both old age insurance and unemployment compensation be extended to the tens of millions now unprotected by them, including farm workers, domestics, the self-employed, government employes and those who work for non-profit institutions. He wants statutory provision to fill the gap in social security coverage for the men and women in the armed forces. He advocates medical and hospital insurance, but demands that the system shall preserve the absolute independence of the medical profession and the patient's right to select his own doctor.

When public relief is required, he believes that it should be channeled through public works rather than leaf-raking, boondoggling and handout charity.

He is convinced that no fundamental cure had been found, up to 1940, for the depression—that the national economy had merely been kept alive by continuous injection of stimulant—that, but for the artificial boom created by war, we should still be living by drinking our own life blood. This, and the enormous national debt created first by depression relief and later by the war, makes it inevitable in his opinion that government shall continue to play a vital role after the war.

But, he says, "government intervention need not be destructive of an honest system of free enterprise." It is his contention that the New Deal regarded all business as "the enemy" and deliberately harassed it with bureaucratic interferences that go beyond the requirements of proper regulation.

If what he thinks of as the federal war against business, good as well as bad, is abandoned, if the tax structure is revised to encourage capital to come out of the bomb shelters, if credit facilities are improved for small businesses, if the federal payroll is pruned by eliminating duplicating, overlapping and conflicting agencies, and the budget is balanced as soon as demobilization permits, if, to quote him, "American industry is given a chance, it can produce employment, can generate new purchasing power and set in motion once more the surging flow of commercial venture."

Against his appeal for a chance for good business Mr. Dewey states firmly his belief that the "good old days" of laissez faire have gone forever, and good riddance. He approves the Securities and Exchange Act, the Wage and Hour Law, government protection of the workers' right to collective bargaining, and calls for more vigorous, more sensible enforcement of the anti-trust laws.

Mr. Dewey fancies himself as a practical farmer. In 1939 he paid $3,000 down on a 300-acre farm in Pawling, N. Y., which involved a $27,000 mortgage. Every time he can get a few hours together, he goes to his farm. What luck he would have running it for a living is anybody's guess, but there is no doubt of his sincere interest in it and, therefore, in the problems of farmers.

He has confessed that he knows of no single scheme that will solve the farm problem overnight. It is, he says, completely tied in with the nation's general economy. "We can not have a prosperous agriculture and a prostrate America; we can not have a prosperous America and a prostrate agriculture."

None of his concrete suggestions are novel or startling. He advocates that farmers be given parity with industry as to the prices of their products; that government crop loans should be provided at reasonable levels; that there should be a direct program of soil conservation; that sub-marginal lands should be converted to other uses; that the farm co-operative movement should be extended, the program of marketing agreements widened, and research into new uses for agricultural products broadened.

There is so little difference between these ideas, broadly stated, and those espoused by the late President Roosevelt, that Democratic spokesmen chaffed Mr. Dewey for adopting the New Deal virtually *in toto,* and scoffed that he was seeking to oust President Roosevelt by loudly shouting "me too," to most of the Roosevelt program.

On the record Mr. Dewey, in common with a substantial

majority of Americans, does accept the social goals of the New Deal and the broad principles of much of the machinery installed to further those goals. Even the flaws which he points out, in detail, are admitted by New Dealers. But many of those flaws have been recognized for years, and nothing done to remedy them. In many instances the Roosevelt administration gave lip service to items enumerated above and then, in the opinion of many, did exactly the opposite. The hectic days of war's end and the beginnings of demobilization and reconversion have given no firm evidence, as this is written, what President Truman will do in this respect. Conservative Democrats hope and Republicans fear that he will take much of the wind out of Governor Dewey's sails by plugging the economic holes in the New Deal program.

When Mr. Dewey became governor of New York he found social, economic, and administrative reforms to which his predecessors had given support but had never accomplished. Governor Dewey put them into effect. Very little of the improvement that Governor Dewey has made in state administration rests upon new ventures. What he has done there was to overhaul a mass of good but neglected machinery and make it function better than new.

In the field of foreign affairs, which many objective observers believe is where Mr. Dewey lost the presidency, he has been accused of trying to carry water on both shoulders, to be all things to all potential Republican voters, to hold the Nye-*Chicago Tribune* isolationists while seducing the Willkie-Stassen internationalists.

To those who had decided that he was a wolf in sheep's clothing, an isolationist pretending to be an internationalist, some of his statements were capable of double meaning. To isolationists he was a traitor, by specific denunciation of the *Chicago Tribune* editorially. To many it seemed that he was a sincere convert to international co-operation for peace.

The *New York Times,* for example, found fault because he did not repudiate Senator Wiley of Wisconsin, an isolationist. The *Times* neglected to mention that he had specifically and vigorously called for the defeat of isolationist Ham Fish in his own state of New York; nor did the *Times* think to mention that President Roosevelt, far from repudiating isolationist Senator Walsh in the doubtful state of Massachusetts, was at that moment seeking desperately to persuade Walsh, who had been offended by vice-presidential candidate Truman, to sit with the President on the platform at a major rally.

Politics being what they are, such criticisms as these probably would not have injured Governor Dewey much except for the unfortunate record of his party while the war in Europe was building up to engulf us, and except for the fact that in 1940 Mr. Dewey made publicly the mistake that a majority of Americans made privately.

"If there is one thing upon which we are all agreed," he told the Women's National Republican Club in January of 1940, "it is that we shall send no American to die on the battlefields of Europe."

The next May, in Iowa, he urged that this country make certain that it should not be drawn into "the European war."

When President Roosevelt submitted his "Aid to Britain" bill to Congress in January of 1940, Mr. Dewey blasted it in a formal statement contending that the proposed law would empower the President "to commit acts of war without the approval of Congress in any conflict, present or future, anywhere in the world."

On the basis of that statement it has been said that Mr. Dewey opposed lend-lease, which we now know saved Great Britain and thereby saved the United States and civilization.

But, as a matter of fact, the draft bill did just what Mr. Dewey said it would. In the same speech containing this denunciation, Mr. Dewey said: "I strongly favor every possible aid to Britain short of war." He declined an invitation to appear before a congressional committee in opposition to the bill. The House made some modifications in the President's draft and sent it to the Senate. At that time Mr. Dewey told a GOP Lincoln's Birthday gathering in Washington: "With some necessary further reservations of power to the people through the Congress, I am satisfied that the House bill will be adopted. Speaking for myself alone, I hope it will be."

In the same speech Mr. Dewey described what he conceived to be his party's international policy in that respect. I doubt that he was correct as to the party's leaders, but I believe that he did speak for the rank and file when he said: "We stand for the strongest military and naval forces our nation can produce. With equal firmness, I believe our party stands almost unanimously for all out aid to the heroic people of Britain."

Throughout the period between the invasion of Poland and Pearl Harbor Mr. Dewey criticized the President for not having armed this country to defend itself, and urged that rearmament be pushed to the limit.

By itself this sequence, in the light of history, might seem equivocal. It does not stand by itself. This was the period when Mr. Roosevelt, whose sincere internationalism nobody questions, was telling the people regularly that by supplying England with armament and munitions we could defeat Germany without having to send our soldiers and sailors to war. This was the period when, with lend-lease, he was committing acts of hostility against Germany—acts of undeclared, non-shooting warfare that, before the end, involved shooting. This was the period, indeed, when—as it developed later notwithstanding vehement denials from the White House—American warships were committing acts of war against the submarines of a nation with which, technically, we were at peace—a nation that our Commander-in-Chief was solemnly telling us we could avoid fighting.

Today few Americans remember, or care to admit, how averse they were to getting into a "shooting war"—how sympathetic they were to the viewpoint expressed by Mr. Dewey. But he can't forget. As a public figure, he spoke for the record, and his mistakes are embalmed in the files of every public library and newspaper morgue in the land.

Such half-measures as both President Roosevelt and Mr. Dewey advocated did not work. We know now they couldn't have succeeded. We are glad that we helped Great Britain to save herself, and us. We criticize the President not for what he did, but for not taking us into his confidence and waking

us up—with the inside knowledge that his position gave him—
to do more, more quickly.

"Certainly I have changed my views on foreign policy," said
Mr. Dewey. "Everybody has." And he added, wistfully and a
bit naively: "I suppose at heart I am really a pacifist."

Since early 1940 Mr. Dewey's stand, taken at face value, is
as far from isolationism as any but advocates of a United
States of the World could desire. Only former Governor Harold Stassen of Minnesota, among significant national figures,
has gone beyond him.

President Roosevelt, being in office, did things to create
co-operation among peace-loving nations for the prevention of
future wars. Governor Dewey, being out of national office, was
in no position to do anything except talk. That he did.

He points with pride to the 1942 New York State Republican platform, which he largely wrote and wholly approved,
which said:

"Out of the suffering and horror of this war there must
arise, with God's help, the foundation of a lasting peace, a
peace which will give to all peoples of the world the right to
live and worship as they please without fear of persecution, and
to minorities the fullest protection of inalienable rights as free
human beings.

"To that end the United States must be prepared to undertake new obligations and responsibilities in the community of
nations. We must join with other nations to secure the peace of
the world, by force if necessary, against any further outbreak
of international gangsterism."

In September of 1943 he drew upon himself the wrath of
the *Chicago Tribune* when he told newspapermen at Mackinac
Island:

"We now have had a de facto military alliance with Great
Britain practically ever since the war of 1812."

"Do we understand you to think it likely," they asked, "that
the United States and Great Britain will continue that alliance,
and on a more formal basis, after this war?"

"I should think that would be very likely and would be in
our interest," said Governor Dewey.

"Would you include Russia and China in such an alliance?"

"It would be hoped that in the working out of the peace, Russia and China might be included," he replied.

As a candidate for the presidency Governor Dewey sought to eliminate any fundamental arguments which might seem to the outside world to cast doubt upon American unity in the war and the coming peace. He put himself squarely behind the broad Roosevelt approach to international organization for peace. This might have been from conviction, or from smart politics. In any event, the record is clear.

Many expected that he might criticize when the Dumbarton Oaks conference broke up with complete absence of agreement on the fundamental question whether one Great Power, sitting in judgment on its own act of aggression, could freeze the entire machinery of peace preservation. He did not, but on the contrary counseled patience on the part of critics.

It is utterly impossible to know, even now, whether Mr. Dewey differed with President Roosevelt on any important aspect of the preparations for peace. He did criticize what he felt to be the handling of certain matters, but most of their background still remains a secret shared only by Messrs. Roosevelt, Churchill, and Stalin.

There was, for instance, the Polish question. England and France went to war because Poland's integrity was violated. At that time Russia was Hitler's ally. Yet it appeared very early that this country and Great Britain, actively or tacitly, had given complaisance to Stalin's arbitrary decision to take over much of Poland in violation of the principles of the Atlantic Charter. Mr. Dewey criticized the one-man diplomacy that he felt was involved and went further to hit at the indications that Stalin, having taunted Polish General Bor to revolt in Warsaw, stood by on the outskirts of the city while the Nazis liquidated Bor's patriot forces, which were a menace to the pro-Soviet Polish cabinet.

Governor Dewey put himself on record in strong opposition to any peace and world organization formulated by the Great Powers and then handed to the smaller nations to be accepted

—or else. That is, of course, exactly what happened at San Francisco.

He stuck his neck out with what appears to have been hasty and ill-advised criticism of the mechanics by which the armistice with Roumania was handled. He took the popular, but to many minds unsound side of the argument over recognition of the De Gaulle regime in France—and soon after, De Gaulle was recognized. He exaggerated, in the opinion of at least some military experts, the effect which Treasury Secretary Morgenthau's harsh-peace proposals had on German military morale.

These really are details, and controversial. To the extent that any or all of these criticisms were in error, the error was not one of isolationism, of unwillingness to co-operate wholeheartedly with friendly nations to preserve peace.

He did, however, commit two errors which he did not rectify and which, in the opinion of many, reflected upon either his good judgment or his information.

The first had to do with the armed forces. "I believe," he said, "that the occupation of Germany and Japan should very soon (after the war) be confined to those who voluntarily choose to remain in the army when peace comes." And when asked about compulsory post-war military training he quibbled: "I would certainly not put anyone in the Army unless we need a force for the defense of the United States, which is a decision to be made based on all circumstances after the war."

He stirred up justifiable criticism when, after praising General MacArthur's strategic brilliance, he remarked that "adequate recognition and supply commensurate with General MacArthur's great talents are long overdue." General MacArthur's talents had been very generally recognized—officially, by his command and his then title of full General. The policy of beating Hitler first, accepted and approved by most professional fighters and laymen, obviously controlled the quantity of war materiel that could be sent to MacArthur.

In general, Governor Dewey's political and economic philosophies, his approach to international affairs, his attitudes toward peace and war, are about what one would expect from a man of his mental characteristics and his slightly Horatio Algerish personal career.

When offered a place on the Southern District Attorney's staff, the average youngster of Dewey's age and inexperience would either have declined, on the ground that he could make more money in private practice, or have accepted in hope that he could profit from the publicity and acquaintanceships to be picked up. Dewey did neither. He merely held out for all or nothing, and got all. He was made chief assistant in that very busy, very important law office.

There followed, for nine years, a successsion of notable convictions that made the name of Tom Dewey a byword throughout the country. Some were obtained as chief assistant to Mr. Medalie; some as Medalie's temporary successor, by unanimous choice of the district's judges; some as special rackets prosecutor for New York County; some as district attorney.

Notorious criminals who attested to the Dewey vigor and efficiency included the gambler Jack "Legs" Diamond, the big banker Charles E. Mitchell, the beer baron Irving "Waxey Gordon" Wexler, the vice and narcotics overlord Charles "Lucky" Luciano, the gang mouthpiece J. Richard "Dixie" Davis.

Arthur (Dutch Schultz) Flegenheimer was murdered by other gangsters before Dewey could indict him. Municipal Court Justice Harold L. Kunstler resigned while Dewey was prosecuting him for removal for financial irregularities, and later was disbarred. Circuit Court Judge Martin T. Manton resigned from the federal bench after Dewey had publicized results of an inquiry into his sales of justice and while the *New York World-Telegram* was running articles reporting its inquiries, and later was sent to a federal penitentiary.

Out of these and other successes, including the Hines conviction, came Mr. Dewey's two candidacies for the governorship, the second successful; his two candidacies for the presidential nomination, the second successful; his first race for the White House.

His story is not one of rags to riches. He never wore rags, and he never has achieved riches. His family, as an American institution, only slightly postdates the Mayflower. The first American Thomas Dewey arrived in Dorchester, Massachusetts, in 1634. George Martin Dewey helped found the GOP at Jackson, Michigan, in 1854; his son, George Martin Dewey, published a weekly newspaper in Owosso, Michigan, and was postmaster; his son is Thomas Edmund Dewey. A fifth cousin, George Dewey, was the hero of Manila Bay in the Spanish-American war.

Although George Martin Dewey, publisher, was a man of moderate means, his son Tom did not go in for loafing. During school days he worked as a "devil" in his father's printing plant, clerked briefly in a local drug store, worked one summer as a hired hand on a farm, and at the age of ten organized boy friends into a newspaper-distributing, magazine-selling company which he headed until he went to college.

At the University of Michigan he majored in economics and political science, and made a name for himself with his singing. His voice won for him a scholarship in a New York music school, where he studied while attending the Columbia University law school. As a sideline to completing three years' work in two, he earned part of his living singing in the choirs of the Church of St. Matthew and St. Timothy and a synogogue.

After graduation he clerked successively with two good but not highly publicized New York law firms. In connection with one case on which Dewey was working, the noted attorney George Z. Medalie was brought in. Medalie was so impressed with Dewey that, when he was appointed United States Attorney for the Southern District, he asked Dewey to join his staff.

Critics in both parties have contended that Mr. Dewey still is nothing more than a successful prosecutor who is seeking to capitalize on his success in a highly specialized field that has nothing to do with either politics or public administration. That is disputed by the private laments of Democratic party workers who, off the record, say that he has done a job as governor of New York that does not suffer by comparison with the regimes of his three illustrious predecessors—Al Smith, Franklin Roosevelt, and Herbert Lehman.

Before he became governor, many who admired his intelligence and conceded his administrative ability believed that he would fail because of inability to work with legislators and political leaders and others who could not be treated as subordinates. Those fears, or hopes in the case of political opponents, have proven false. There have been, naturally, differences of opinion, some of them resulting in argument. But on the whole his relations with both subordinates and associates have appeared to be remarkably equable and frictionless.

There is ample evidence that Tom Dewey has changed greatly since 1940, has grown in stature, and still is growing. Whether or not he seeks and gets the 1948 nomination of his party for President, he has much to contribute in the difficult years of post-war readjustment, domestic and international. And unless those who know him best are greatly deceived, he will not be reluctant or reticent about offering his contributions.

24

JOHN W. BRICKER
"Personally Honest"

BY MURRAY SEASONGOOD

A "POLITICIANS' CANDIDATE": THAT IS HOW WALTER LIPP-
mann characterized John W. Bricker, the governor of
Ohio. Lippmann's characterization was veracious. Bricker, preceding the Chicago convention, was the only avowed candidate
for the Republican nomination for president. He toured the
country extensively in behalf of his candidacy and made wide
contacts with delegates and "the boys." At the convention he
was more popular than Dewey. Ollie James, a political writer,
said it was no secret by the time the Republican convention was
two days old Bricker was the personal choice of the majority
of the delegates.[1] But the managers of the convention preferred
Dewey. Almost to the last, Bricker had insisted he was not
interested in anything less than the presidency, and stated categorically he would not accept the vice-presidential nomination
if that were offered to him.[2] However, when Governor Warren
refused a vice-presidential nomination, Bricker behaved like the
lady in Don Juan, who swearing she would never consent, consented. When he came to the speaker's platform to second the
nomination of Dewey, the delegates gave him a tremendous
ovation: he was their kind.

The late William Allen White referred to Bricker as "an
honest Harding," and other detractors have dubbed him vice-
presidential timber of the Throttlebottom variety, and ascribed
to him the slogan, "Back to sub-normalcy." This is unfair char-

1. *Cincinnati Enquirer,* Oct. 15, 1944.
2. *Cincinnati Times Star,* June 23, 1944.

acterization; Bricker, however, is not an exceptionally able man.[3]

He is a little over fifty years old, large, somewhat pudgy, friendly, likable with a loud voice, hearty handshake, and pronounced double chin; goodlooking, healthy, with thick silvery hair which he wears a little too long. He is personally honest.

Current interest in John Bricker arises from his 1944 candidacy for the Republican nomination for president and then as nominee for the vice-presidency. In connection with his aspirations, factors that may be considered are his background and his qualifications, his record as a vote getter, his action in matters calling for the exercise of judgment and character, his administrative ability, and his influence while governor on the legislative branch.

3. Bricker's partisanship, machine politics, and imperfect sense of fitness are illustrated by the following incident:

The Hamilton county Republican machine desired X to be appointed as director of the Cincinnati office of the Bureau of Unemployment Compensation. Mr. X had so little qualification for the position that he passed sixth in the civil service examination. But the organization extracted waivers from those ahead of him on the list and he was brought within the first three and appointed. Later, on complaint of the Hamilton County Good Government League to the United States Civil Service Commission that X had participated, contrary to the provisions of the Hatch Act "to prevent pernicious political activities," in obtaining campaign contributions from civil service employees, the commission instituted an inquiry with a view to his removal from office if the charges were valid. The governor emitted a terrific roar against the "New Deal Politicians" and caused the attorney general of the state to defend X at all costs. The Hatch Act, he asserted, was unconstitutional.

The commission's examiner sustained the charges and ordered X's removal from office. The governor made such an outcry that the commission sent its Republican member into Ohio to re-examine the evidence, and again sustained the charges. Thereupon, in March, 1942, the governor appointed X, whose salary had been $3,000 to the position of Sugar and Automobile Rationer at a salary of $3,600. The United States Civil Service Commission retaliated by levying a fine against the state of Ohio, as permitted by the Hatch Act, of $7,200, or double the amount of the salary. When the OPA succeeded to X's position, X was made State Salvage Administrator and Finance Officer from which position he has recently resigned.

Not only did Bricker show his lack of sense or fitness in this matter, but when invited to make an address at a section of the American Bar Association, he was guilty of the impropriety of giving a partisan speech in which he inveighed against the "outrage" that had been perpetrated by "New Deal Politicians" in the above incident.

Incidentally, the Hatch Act has been sustained as constitutional.—*Neustein* v. *Mitchell et al.*, 52 F.S., 531 (1943), S.D.N.Y. *Stewart* v. *U. S. C. S. C.* 45 F.S., 697 (1942), N.D.Ga. *U. Fed. Workers of America C.I.O.* v. *Mitchell et al.*, 56 F.S., 621 (1944). *State of Oklahoma* v. *U.S.C.S.C.*, 51 F.S., 355 (June 18, 1945.

Born on a farm and educated in the public schools, Bricker has been holding public office, almost without interruption, since he graduated in 1920 from the Law School of Ohio State University. From 1920 to 1928, he was solicitor of a small place known as Grandview Heights, and from 1923 to 1927 served as assistant attorney-general of the state of Ohio. Supporters have stated, in his favor, that he was elected three times in succession, by large majorities, as governor of Ohio and twice previously as attorney general. But he has not had unvarying success in elections. Thus, in 1928, when he competed for the Republican nomination for attorney-general, he was defeated in the Republican primaries.[4]

Bricker was elected attorney-general in 1932 by luck and with a bare 10,000 plurality. As a member of the Ohio Public Utilities Commission from 1929 to 1933, he had voted in the bitterly contested Columbus gas rate case in 1932 to sustain the Columbus ordinance which had established a 48-cent rate, while his two colleagues voted against him and fixed a 55-cent rate. Thus, in the election that followed in November, 1932, Bricker was hailed as the people's friend. The U. S. Supreme Court in 1934, however, decided that the Columbus Gas Company had been deprived of substantial rights even in the fixing of a 55-cent rate.[5]

In 1936, Bricker met defeat by Martin Davey, a tree surgeon and the Democratic adversary for the governorship, by a more than 125,000 majority. Although Bricker was elected governor in 1938, 1940, and 1942, and in the first of these contests won by a slightly less than 120,000 majority, in 1940 by about 265,000, and in 1942 by about 380,000, these impressive majorities require explanation.

A sycophant English lawyer dedicated his book to the in-

4. In connection with this primary, Bricker sought, and obtained, by an appearance of favoring their movement, support from the Independent Republicans, known as the "Good Government," or "Citizens" group in Hamilton county, whose candidates were opposing the regular Republican organization in the primaries. (For more concerning this movement, see, Seasongood, *Local Government in the United States*, Harvard Univ. Press, Lecture II, pp. 38 *et seq.*) Since then, Bricker has treated this group as pariahs or Ishmaels.

5. *Columbus Gas etc. Co.* v. *P.U.C. of Ohio*, 292 U.S. 398, decided May 21, 1934.

cumbent Lord Chancellor, with his Lordship's permission. Before the book appeared the government fell. Whereupon the author added to the dedication, "who is most happy in his successor." Bricker was "most happy in his predecessor." Davey was governor for two terms, four years in all, beginning with 1934. His regime was marked by serious strikes and labor controversies in connection with which he in 1937 called out the militia and incurred the undying ill-will of labor groups. There were also notorious extravagances and scandals in his administration concerning, *inter alia,* road contracting and liquor trucking.

Not only were the Davey administrations under a cloud, but a severe schism developed in the Democratic ranks resulting from an exceptionally bitter party primary contest in 1938.[6] The Democratic candidate for governor who in that primary defeated Davey did not gain Davey's support and that of his followers in the election. The schism was still present in the elections of 1940 and 1942, and in 1942, Bricker ran against a practically unknown and very weak opponent. Moreover, in 1942 there was a pronounced swing to the Republican side throughout the nation and the Ohio vote was extremely light. In this election Bricker received fewer votes than any successful candidate since 1930 and the smallest number he had received in any of his gubernatorial contests, successful or unsuccessful. Hence, his record of successes is not so impressive as a mere recital of results and majorities might make it appear to be.

Feature writers favoring the candidacy of Governor Bricker asserted that he entered the executive mansion of the state of Ohio with a terrifying deficit of $40,000,000, which, by economies and the discharge of useless employees, he changed into a whacking surplus. That there were too many Davey office-holders is an understatement. But Bricker, in his enthusiastic purge, did away with many employees who were of opposite political faith, and the methods used for the deracination of

6. "It may be recalled that the famous 1938 primary contest between Charles Sawyer and Martin L. Davey actually turned into a battle royal between American Federation of Labor and C.I.O., with C.I.O. the winner with Sawyer, a situation which made his election utterly impossible."—*Cincinnati Enquirer,* Apr. 9, 1944.

many civil service provisional appointees, were declared illegal.[7] The Davey administration was, to use no harsher term, grossly extravagant. Ordinary honesty and ability were bound to bring about millions of dollars' reduction in highway and other department costs. In 1935, Governor Davey, always unpredictable,[8] for some reason requested C. O. Sherrill, then city manager of Cincinnati, to make a survey of the state departments with a view to their improvement. Colonel Sherrill, with the voluntary aid of 130 business executives and professional men of Ohio, made an intimate study of some 143 different bureaus and departments and reported that the most readily feasible economies would total more than $5,000,000 a year and subsequent economies of many millions of dollars could be made, contingent on empowering legislation and recommended departmental consolidations. Governor Davey put into effect very few of the recommendations, and fewer still have been utilized by Governor Bricker.[9]

Joseph T. Ferguson, veteran Democratic state auditor of Ohio, re-elected in November, 1944, has always maintained Bricker did not inherit a deficit, but that there was a deficit in some earmarked funds and a surplus in others; that Bricker removed the earmarking, threw all monies into a general fund, and since the surplus funds exceeded the deficit funds, the result was the showing of an immediate over-all surplus; but that the situation when Bricker got through was no different from what

7. *State ex rel Conway* v. *Taylor, Director Department Liquor Control,* 136 O.S., 174, decided Dec. 30, 1939, reaffirming, *State ex rel Solvensky* v. *Taylor, Director Department Liquor Control,* 135 O.S., 601, and *State ex rel Langedrost* v. *Beightler, Director of Highways,* 135 O.S., 624, both decided July 5, 1939.

8. The irreverent said of him, paraphrasing the poem, "Trees," "Only God can make a he like me."

9. "The sad part of the story is that while the aim of the inquirers and investigators was to reduce the cost of government, the state is now spending far more money than was spent when the Sherrill committee began. And the rate of increase continues and is bound to continue when the state takes care of its welfare problem. The increase is today at least $10,000,000 a year."—*Cincinnati Enquirer,* Jan. 2, 1944.

The Sherrill Survey recommendations for a new setup and increased appropriations for the State Civil Service Commission remained unheeded. The governor's Republican appointee was an active organization worker who seems to have little interest in improvement or anything but lip service to operations of the merit system. The Democratic member, also appointed by him, appears to have been accommodatingly quiescent.

it was in the beginning except in name. An article from the *Columbus Citizen* of April 15, 1943, is headlined:

FIGURES SHOW BRICKER ADMINISTRATION, DESPITE
STATE SURPLUS HAS SPENT 124 MILLION MORE THAN
ANY OTHER IN OHIO HISTORY
Receipts for both terms exceed revenue collected in Davey regime by
171 million
Little change in State's tax setup
But war boom has vastly raised income

After the election of November, 1944, ex-Governor Davey sent to the voters copies of a letter he had written to the editor of *Cosmopolitan Magazine* taking issue with the article in its May, 1944, number about Bricker, and "disproving Governor Bricker's false claims." Governor Davey stated he held the letter until after election in order to avoid any suspicion of politics, but resented misrepresentation of his services as governor. A reading of this "Challenge" and "An Earnest Appeal to the Thoughtful and Fair-minded Citizens of Ohio" pretty effectually disproves the claims by and on behalf of Bricker that he inherited a debt of $40,000,000, unpaid bills totalling $22,-000,000 and a state facing bankruptcy and that he had created a surplus instead.

Bricker, during his campaign inveighed vehemently against the Kelly-Nash and other Democratic local political machines. He has had, however, no such hostility to political machines of his own party. For example, Bricker in his appointments has played ball with the powerful Hamilton County Republican machine and its Columbus representative, the state Republican committee chairman, a Cincinnatian who grew up in that machine and participated in some of its worst practices before and after moving to the capital. Judicial appointments from Hamilton County have been completely political. Thus the governor appointed to the common pleas bench, a former chairman of the executive committee of the local machine who had been defeated, when running on its ticket, for Cincinnati council. The governor appointed as a Cincinnati municipal court judge another politician so lacking that he announced, in advance of his turn on the traffic court bench, he would not convict any person against whom speed-check evidence was adduced; and following this declaration, he actually released without hearing evidence, about two hundred violators, of whom some were third or fourth time offenders for speeding, and some were those against whom the evidence indicated a rate of speed of over sixty miles an hour. Following agitation by outraged citizens for his removal, the judge receded from this shameful position.

The governor, before filling a vacancy on the court of appeals of the Cincinnati district, waited several months until the various Republican governing committees of the counties included reached a choice. As soon as this and other choices of the Republican governing committees were certified to the governor, he at once appointed their nominees.[10] Appointments other than judicial from the Cincinnati region are usually traceable to "recommendations" of the local machine. For example: a member of the State Liquor Commission was formerly the organization county auditor. A law was passed calling for the dishing out, by regional agents, of automobile licenses at 25 cents each. As there were some half million of these, this gave a little perquisite of approximately $125,000 a year to recommended party regulars.

The following are examples of how party patronage was worked with the assistance of the subject of this sketch. The original statute creating the Municipal Court of Cincinnati provided that its bailiffs and clerks should be under the merit system. For some reason, however, this requirement was not complied with and these positions were plums for party work-

10. Governor Bricker was asked by a good-government agency not to appoint, or to defer appointment of, a judge for a vacancy in the Hamilton County common pleas court, on the ground that litigation had fallen off and there was no need for the full number of judges so a substantial saving would be effected. The governor replied (although he had waited many months in filling similar vacancies until the machine could make up its mind), that it was his duty to make the appointment immediately, and he did. Governor Bricker's attitude in connection with the appointments to judicial vacancies is in contrast to the fine attitude of his successor, Governor Lausche. The latter inquired if the state of the docket in the locality required immediate appointment, and upon being informed it did not, has not made appointments, stating, however, when he does make appointments, he will request recommendations from the bar associations. Where he has made judicial and legal appointments, he has made them from lists recommended by the appropriate bar association.

ers, many of very inferior character and quality. After it was sought to place these party workers under civil service, the local organization, avid for their campaign contributions and work in the precincts, caused a special act to be passed in Columbus amending the original act and expressly taking these employees out of the merit system. The proponent of this legislation, which is known by his name, received an appointment as an important assistant to the then attorney-general, later governor. Also, in appointments to the board of Ohio State University, the governor denied merit and made some poor appointments for purely partisan reasons.[11] Governor Bricker appointed as a "nonpartisan" member of the Ohio Development and Publicity Commission [12] a Cincinnati contributor to the Republican machine who was to have been named by the machine mayor as a director of the University of Cincinnati. But the directors were so incensed at the prospect of this wholly unsuitable appointment that some threatened to resign. So the city appointment was not made and the mayor's intended appointee was solaced by the governor with an appointment to the state position.[12a]

Governor Bricker, in his campaign for the Republican nomination for the presidency, inveighed mightily against more than one or two terms for a president. However he was not averse himself, quip the political writers, to a go at a fourth term as governor, but was jostled out of this ambition by impatient contestors. It seems a legitimate subject for adverse

11. The governor appointed to a Postwar Program Commission, several organization legislators who would thus have authority in acquiring sites, etc. This was not only unbecoming, but so plainly unconstitutional (as held by the Ohio Supreme Court, *State ex rel Herbert* v. *Ferguson, Auditor,* 142 O.S. 496) that a first-year law student would have known it.

"Simultaneously with the questioning of the validity of the Postwar Program Commission, Governor John W. Bricker's action in appointing four legislators to a commission to spend almost $6,000,000 in erecting new institutions for the blind and deaf, also was questioned. The Governor promptly acknowledged the invalidity of such appointments and named private citizens in their stead."—*Cincinnati Enquirer,* Feb. 3, 1944.

12. Created June 2, 1939, G.C. Sec. 368 *et seq,* 118 O.L. 578.

12a. For improvident or worse purchases of excessive amounts of unsalable brandy at excessive prices by Governor Bricker's administration and exposure of these and refusal to pay purchase price in full by the present governor, Frank J. Lausche, see the *Ohio Magazine* for April, 1945.

criticism of him, which was made by a Republican candidate for the governorship nomination that he promoted his presidential candidacy with long absences from the state and, therefore, on the public's time and money. After the Chicago convention he was absent from the state on a four-week, 10,000-mile trip in the West and then on a 2,500 mile trip east.

Bricker's speeches have been pedestrian and not very intelligent.[13] Admittedly he has little familiarity with foreign

13. Dorothy Thompson said of him after his Lincoln Day speech in Washington:

"In not one single point does Governor Bricker indicate awareness of any postwar problem at all ... except the problem of taxation, and the restoration of complete sovereignty of the businessman's view of life.... On the primary question, upon which the future of our society will rest ... whether we can bring about, in peace, as effective a use of our man power and materials as we have done for war ... on these questions Governor Bricker is as silent as Lincoln's tomb."—*Cincinnati Enquirer*, Feb. 14, 1944.

"His speeches have started no prairie fires. He has dutifully damned bureaucrats, high government payrolls, has praised individualism, sound local government and the state of Ohio. His speeches sound as if they were ghosted by Calvin Coolidge. He has often repeated: 'Public money is trust money.' On international relations, he repeats: 'We want to live and let live ... live and help live.' "—*Time*, Apr. 26, 1943.

"The Pews, the duPonts and Cleveland's powerful Hanna interests (which are affiliated in business with Ernie Weir's National Steel), the mighty and stormy Columbia Gas and Electric, and all the rest are for him as hard as they can be. Not only does Bricker make no secret of this; he is proud of it."—*Fortune*, Feb., 1943.

"... Bricker is not a political phenomenon ... general handshaker, gifted with the art of avoiding issues and an uncanny knack of making friends without influencing people. He is like a country boy in a big city of forces he doesn't understand. His political philosophy is contemporaneous with the hoopskirt and high bicycle. 'Honest John' fits him well, for he is honest, sincere, balanced the budget and has a surplus....

"The cost of government has risen constantly since he has been in office. Latest budget was $375,723,921 some $23,000,000 more than it was the year before; it is slightly higher than that of New York state, which has nearly twice the population. The per capita cost of the government in Ohio is nearly twice what it is in New York. Is that economy? This is significant when it is remembered that most states having surplus reduced their budgets in recent years.

"His shortcomings are, perhaps best illustrated by his singular indifference to the plight of the feeble-minded in Ohio. If conditions are worse in any other state in the union, then the fact must be a well-kept secret. Ohio has three institutions ... one in Columbus erected before the gay nineties contains two thousand people and sleep two in a bed. The others at Orient and Apple Creek are just as crowded....

"He has not interfered in the liquor muddle in Ohio. Long queues of citizens often waited hours while favored characters entered back doors of state-owned stores and bought liquor by the case. This was proved.... Ohioans have become bootleggers."—*New Republic*, June 28, 1943, p. 860.

affairs, regarding which he says he has not fully informed himself. His iteration, "We want co-operation with other countries, but no superstate," is enigmatic. The effort to discover what he believes about post-war problems developed into a national "reportorial contest." [14] He declared: "America is not, never has been, and will never be an isolationist nation"; and, "she must deal with other nations of the world and must and will assume leadership." [15] The Delphic oracle was lucid in comparison. Republican Senator Ball of Minnesota declared, October 26, 1944, that Bricker was talking America First and the isolationist doctrines of the McCormick-Patterson press. Bricker's often repeated protestation that he would rather smash the New Deal than succeed in his candidacy appeared, after a while, to be a bit disingenuous, and his iterated references to "Hillman and his alien philosophy" were somewhat crude attempts to interject prejudices in the campaign. When Gerald L. K. Smith came out for Bricker, Bricker, very stupidly, at a press conference in Albany, in July, 1944, stated "that the support of all elements willing to vote for the Republican ticket would be welcome as far as he was concerned." A staff correspondent of the *Chicago Sun* traveling on Dewey's campaign train (issue of September 12, 1944) reported that Governor Dewey was "directing not only his own personal drive for the presidency but also the political maneuvers of his running mate, Gov. John W. Bricker of Ohio." The connection was so direct that he had one of the Ohio governor's secretaries accompanying him on the transcontinental campaign tour, adding, "This arrangement, it was reported, was in part the outgrowth of Bricker's unfortunate statement which enabled Gerald L. K. Smith and this America First party to embrace the Ohio governor—a maneuver which finally compelled Dewey to intervene and disclaim any connection with America Firsters."

On October 23, 1944, at Denver, Bricker found fault with the President for having admitted temporarily one thousand refugees from Italy, stating, in effect, that it was not true, as

14. *American Mercury,* May, 1943, p. 1.
15. *New York Times.* April 8, 1943.

the President had promised, that a majority of these would be women and children, but that, in fact, they were principally intellectuals; and he did not know if this group "was cleared with Sidney or not." In making this petty and ugly statement, Bricker threw a boomerang because the War Refugee Board made a public answer [16] that actually most of those admitted were women and children and, moreover, Bricker was among others who had petitioned the President, in the previous May, for their admission. In many of his speeches, Bricker would work himself up and go berserk to an extent that might have caused a radio listener to say, like Desdemona, "I understand a fury in the words, but not the words."

When asked to comment on certain English newspapers appearing to espouse the candidacy of Roosevelt for a fourth term, the governor, instead of passing the matter off lightly with something like, "We think we know more about our affairs than anyone, no matter how intelligent, in a foreign country," showed bad temper and an attitude of hostility something like that displayed towards a former king of England by the late Big Bill Thompson of Chicago. Also, Bricker, as a Republican presidential aspirant, did not act wisely in having himself photographed arm around shoulder with James A. Farley, onetime chairman of the Democratic national committee.[17]

Before the 1940 national convention, Bricker, heading the Ohio delegation, was so hostile to Willkie that, although they had been long-time friends, Bricker would not speak with him. When however, at the convention, it became evident Willkie was to prevail, Bricker in the midst of the roll-call, making a parliamentary error, leapt to the platform to move Willkie's nomination be made unanimous. Under the rules, Chairman Martin could not entertain such a motion, but said he would recognize the Ohio governor after the roll-call was completed if he desired to change Ohio's vote from Taft to Willkie.[18]

Bricker gave no public indication that he disapproved the brutal treatment of Willkie by the managers of the Republican

16. *Cincinnati Times Star*, Oct. 25, 1944.
17. *Time*, March 29, 1943, p. 13.
18. *The Cincinnati Enquirer*, June 28, 1940, p. 1.

party. Aside from this treatment of Willkie being almost sadistic it was foolish and alienated a great mass of independent voters who profoundly admired and would have been glad to follow Mr. Willkie. After Willkie's death, however, Bricker mentioned for the first time his old-time friendship with Willkie in the latter's Ohio days and how Bricker had moved in 1940 to make his nomination unanimous.

Bricker was pledged to Taft in 1940 and, in recompense, Taft in 1944 announced being pledged to him. To be for a man for president as *quid pro quo* does not seem an especially good recommendation. But it is about all Taft had to say in behalf of his protege.[19]

Governor Bricker, in his three terms, did not show leadership so far as the legislative branch was concerned. Practically no legislation of substantial value was enacted and much that is retrogressive or vicious was passed with his express approval or without protest by him. He has not evinced support for the merit system, aspirations for good local government, or improved election machinery.

And while Ohio had not adjusted its salaries of state employees for a long time, with resulting hardships and injustices, the governor did nothing to bring about a revision. Mengert, the *Cincinnati Enquirer* political writer at Columbus said (November 26, 1944):

It is now generally conceded that one of the political mistakes made by the Bricker administration was in being tardy two years ago in considering the wage issue in connection with the state service. There are many members of the General Assembly who say that they sought to have the issue treated comprehensively then. They might have succeeded if they had been bold enough to stage some sort of revolt, but they accepted rather tamely the decision of the high command to be satisfied with the substitute proposal for a commission to study the question....

This commission recommended a partial readjustment to be enacted at a special session in December, 1944, in order that those assuming positions January 1, 1945, would not run afoul of the constitution providing against changing compensation of officers during their term. The governor finally declined to call

19. *The Cincinnati Enquirer*, Dec. 9, 1943.

such special session and there is much grumbling among state employees. The president of the Ohio Civil Service Employees Association asserts that the governor had promised a special session would be called after the election. The governor denies having made such a promise.[20]

On the matter of facilitating the soldiers' vote for the presidential election, the Governor at first stated flatly he would not consider legislation relaxing the requirement of pencil mark for vote. But upon insistence and a mounting dissatisfaction with the possibility of soldiers losing their vote because of this requirement, he reversed his position and accepted, at the special session he called, a bill sanctioning marking ballots in the presidential election otherwise than by ordinary lead pencil. Some other examples of legislative ineptitude or worse may be adduced.

The first of these is somewhat amusing. In 1930, the Republican politicians, reasoning from previous elections of seven Republican presidents, figured that Ohio would always vote Republican presidentially and that lesser candidates would ride in with the president on a comprehensive ballot. Hence they changed the form of the party column ballot, which previously had separated national from state and local candidates, so as to provide that all, from president down to coroner, should be on the same ballot, and so that a cross mark under the national emblem of eagle or rooster would be a vote for all national, state, and county offices. They also provided that independents should not be entitled to the advantage of such single cross-mark, straight-ticket voting. But, in 1932, the politicians were "hoist with their own petard." The cross mark under the rooster for President Franklin D. Roosevelt swept into office with him many Democratic state and county officers. The same thing happened in 1936, and, to prevent a recurrence in 1940, the governor, in June, called a special session of the General Assembly to provide for a separate ballot for the presidency. Such legislation was enacted, with an emergency clause attached so as to prevent a referendum. The emergency clause stated that it was necessary that state and national issues should be

20. *Cincinnati Times Star*, Nov. 30, 1944.

separated [21] so that the voters of Ohio should have "full and independent opportunity" of expressing "their judgment on vital issues affecting the state and the union," at the approaching election.[22] But the law enacted did not completely separate state and national candidates. It was merely a clumsy expedient to get Roosevelt off on a separate ballot. It left United States senators and congressmen on the state ballot and in 1944 was one of the causes which almost defeated Taft for senator, since Lausche, the successful Democratic candidate for governor, at the top of the state ballot, almost carried in with him a somewhat weak Democratic candidate only about 17,000 votes behind Taft for United States senator on the same ballot.

Another example: with the growth of outlying territories resulting from better means of transportation, annexation has become a matter of increasing consequence to the larger cities of the state. Cincinnati for example, totally surrounds Norwood, a city of approximately 50,000 population, and encircles much of St. Bernard with about 10,000 residents. These and similar satellite or parasite cities have much important Cincinnati industry within their boundaries and make policing, health protection, zoning, transportation, water, sewer, utilities regulation, and other problems more difficult of solution. The separate municipalities get many of the big city services on an unduly favorable basis, and so compete unfairly with their benefactor by being able to offer an attractively lower tax rate. But they are officered in the main by active members of the local Republican machine which, for that reason, abets them in their effort to fight off annexation, although union would be to the advantage of their citizens as well as of Cincinnati. Legislation making annexation more difficult was enacted with the governor's approval.[23]

The cities of Ohio also suffer from over-all taxation and bond limitations inserted in the constitution by the pressure groups of large utilities and other real estate owners interested

21. 118 O.L. 737.
22. Under Ohio law a declaration of emergency made by the legislative body is conclusive, no matter how absurd, and is not a justiceable matter reviewable by the courts.—*State ex rel Schorr* v. *Kennedy,* 132 O.S. 510 (1937).
23. 119 O.L., 853, Ohio C.G. Sec. 3561-1 (1941).

in keeping down real estate taxes on their property, no matter how serious may be the consequences from insufficient funds for the maintenance of county, city, and school plants and the proper functioning of government. The constitutional over-all tax limit was compressed first to one and one-half mills and is now one mill, with resulting great distress to local subdivisions.[24]

The state statutes require the approval of 65 per cent of those voting for the passage of an extra tax outside of this limitation, for extra levies on real estate (save for schools), and for bond issues. To obtain the approval of the required almost two-thirds is an obstacle that has resulted in the defeat of numerous thoroughly meritorious and urgently needed bond and tax submissions. Efforts have been made to relieve this obvious hardship by the introduction of legislation which would permit passage by a majority or 55 per cent. But efforts have failed completely because of the dominance of the rural element and the real estate owners, combined with the safety brake of the Republican state committeeman who is the boss of the General Assembly. Governor Bricker did not show any interest in relieving this serious plight of the local subdivisions, many of whose plants are progressively deteriorating.

So, too, the Governor failed to help with legislation intended to permit the cities of Ohio to join and pay dues to an Ohio league of municipalities and thus to overcome an unfortunate decision that Cleveland had no such power.[25] About half the states of the Union have leagues of municipalities which are of great value to them in utility regulation, keeping abreast of the best practice, helping to obtain desirable legislation and otherwise.

Rate regulation in Ohio is archaic, indecently expensive, and

24. This distress was intensified by an Act approved Jan. 27, 1939, 118 O.L. 1, amending G.C. Sec. 5546-18, and diminishing the proportionate amount of the sales taxes collected by the state which had gone to local subdivisions, in favor of the State's General Revenue Fund. The relief situation in Cleveland, Toledo, and other cities of the state became most serious; but the Governor remained adamant against calling a special session to undo the injustices perpetrated by the General Assembly and himself against those cities.

25. *State ex rel Thomas* v. *Semple, Dir.,* 112 O.S. 559 *Contra City of Roseville* v. *Tulley,* Cal. app., 131 Pac. (2) 395. App. dismissed by Cal. S. Ct. Jan. 15, 1943.

ridiculously favorable to the utilities concerned.[26] Cities have been called on to pay hundreds of thousands of dollars to experts and special counsel in a single rate controversy. The utility incurs similar expenses, which, however, are treated as capital expenditures and earnings allowed thereon, so that the utility's costs are borne by the consumer. This grotesque situation stems from the Ohio statute calling for a rate base to be fixed on the basis of reproduction cost of the original plant, less depreciation,[27] following the rule established many years ago in the United States Supreme Court.[28] But, since then, that court has stated that such method of valuation is not required and the prudent investment theory is not an unfair basis for the fixing of rates, nor is computing earnings thereon a denial of due process.[29] At the 1943 session of the General Assembly, legislation was introduced to bring about the same most desirable result in Ohio, but it developed no momentum in a sympathetic-to-utilities General Assembly. Here, again, and this time in a matter concerning which he had full information by reason of his having been a member of the Public Utilities Commission of Ohio, Governor Bricker displayed no leadership and made no effort on behalf of the public.

As respects the merit system which is written into the constitution of the state of Ohio, former Governor Bricker showed complete lack of interest. On the contrary, he countenanced flagrant violations and permitted the passage of laws which have dealt it almost mortal blows. The appropriations for the State Civil Service Commission have been so inadequate as to disclose intention to wreck proper enforcement of the law. For years the appropriation for the whole state of Ohio and its eighty-eight counties has been approximately $78,000, or only about twice the amount a single city, Cincinnati, appropriates

26. See Seasongood, "Those Old Age Rate Cases," *Public Utilities Fortnightly,* XV (June 6, 1935), 702.

27. Sec. 499-9 Ohio Genl. Code and see, *East Ohio Gas Co., Appellant* v. *Public Utilities Commission of Ohio, Appellee,* 133, O. S. 212 (1938) first paragraph of syllabus and p. 218.

28. *Smyth* v. *Ames,* 169, U.S. 466 (1898).

29. *Federal Power Commission* v. *Natural Gas Pipe Line Co.,* 315 U.S. 575, *Power Commission* v. *Hope Gas Co.,* 320 U.S. 591.

for its commission. The General Assembly in Bricker's regime passed laws prohibiting use of educational qualifications (except in limited professional instances) [30] and oral examinations,[31] and restricting police and firemen promotional examinations to members of the existing forces.[32] The impairment of the civil service law in the first two of these respects led to curtailment of the grant of federal funds.

Election machinery in Ohio is rigged to give to so-called Republican and Democratic parties an unconscionable advantage over the nonprofessionals, to permit the election machinery to be in the hands of the party organizations, to give opportunities for the grossest election frauds, and to make it extremely difficult for independents to guard against these malpractices. For example, independents are frequently unable to have witnesses and challengers admitted to precinct polling places. By some strange accident, a bill was passed in 1939 permitting, not requiring, a central count. Then the machine woke up and in 1941 caused repeal, over the protests of numerous good-government agencies, of this salutary permissive legislation.[33] Regarding this, the voice of the Governor was not heard. An attempt to substitute the "Massachusetts ballot" for the long, emblem, party-column ballot was laughed out of the General Assembly.

Home rule for cities was written into the constitution of Ohio in 1912 and for counties in 1934. The Supreme Court has whittled down these grants to the strength of broken reeds. Some of the effect of the court decisions could be remedied by legislation; but none such has been suggested by the Governor or enacted.

30. Amending G.C. Sec. 486-9a, 120 O.L. 469 (1943).

31. Amending and supplementing G.C. Sec. 486-10, approved June 5, 1941, 119 O.L. 743.

32. Amending and supplementing G.C. Sec. 486-15a and 486-17, 118 O.L. 215, approved April 24, 1939.

33. G.C. 4785—143a *et seq.* repealed, 119 O.L. 17, approved March 20, 1941. Six Cincinnati good-government agencies importuned, to no avail, the General Assembly not to repeal the Central Count law; the Hamilton County Good Government League, The League of Women Voters, The Women's City Club, the Civic Club, The Bureau of Governmental Research, and the Cincinnatus Association.

Use of the initiative and referendum, also accorded Ohio by the constitution, has been curtailed by obstructive legislation.[34]

Ohio has statutory provisions for a nonpartisan judicial ballot. In practice, however, the political machines often enter their judicial candidate at their party primary. The prospective judge thus runs in the primary as a Republican or Democrat, but is supposed to be a nonpartisan at and after the judicial election. As a condition of standing for election in the party primary, he is obliged by statute to make a declaration under oath that he is a member of the particular party and will abide by the platform, national and state, of that party.[35] Think of a judge being pledged in advance of election! This is an obvious impropriety. Efforts have been made to provide that a judicial candidate shall not run in party primaries, or, at least, shall not be obliged to subscribe such an oath. If Governor Bricker, a member of the bar and a former attorney-general, had an interest in doing away with this undignified and improper procedure, he did not demonstrate it.

Lotteries "for any purpose whatever," are prohibited in the Ohio constitution.[36] Nevertheless, there are strong pressure groups interested in obtaining for charitable or religious purposes financial benefits from the playing of bingo. There has also prevailed in Ohio to a serious degree, a widespread form of gambling known as the "numbers racket." A bill was introduced in the last General Assembly to help overcome some of the difficulties of conviction in this latter form of gambling. But, those interested in bingo caused to be inserted in some of the amendatory gambling statutes the words, "for his own profit." Thus the difficulties of law enforcement have been made incalculably greater. A defendant need not take the stand. How then is it to be proved, besides the difficulty of showing that there is gambling, that it was "for his own profit"? Governor Bricker approved this bill.[37] He should have vetoed it, with an incisive, explanatory denunciation.

34. 119 O.L. 140, approved May 1, 1941, amending G.C. 4785-176 *et seq.* and adding 4785-175a *et seq.*
35. G.C. 4785-71.
36. Art. XV, Sec. 6.
37. Amending G.C. 13063-13064, 120 O.L. 663. Approved Sept. 21, 1943.

In an effort to improve the administration of county welfare a bill was passed at the 1943 General Assembly which is so involved and so confusing and such a mixture of good and evil, that it, too, should have been, but was not, vetoed by the Governor.[38]

The governor announced in one instance, as a soundoff for his presidential aspiration, that he was going to have a part of the Ohio sales tax on medical prescriptions and food consumed in hotels and restaurants repealed. He made this pronouncement without having first consulted the General Assembly, which took a childish, unconcealed pleasure in refusing to pass what he had declared would be enacted.

Bricker in his candidacy for the presidential nomination, trumpeted boldly that there should be no strikes in wartime. But, especially in the 1943 session of the Ohio General Assembly, various bills such as have been passed in other states and, have so far, been usually held constitutional, regulating unions and requiring reports from them, were introduced and made no progress toward passage. Regarding them, the governor maintained silence.

It may therefore be said on the whole, that the former governor's record with legislation and the law-making body did not set the Scioto River aflame. Procedural methods of the General Assembly are very bad and lend themselves readily to boss control and the stifling of efforts to improve legislation. The governor did not attempt amelioration, even by suggestion.

In sum, one wonders, did the former governor ever read Lowell's "The Present Crisis," written just about a century ago, with its inspiring words,

> New occasions teach new duties;
> Time makes ancient good uncouth.

38. G.C. 2511-1 to id.——11 (Sept. 9, 1943). The deficiencies of this act are detailed in XVIV *Greater Cleveland*, No. 23, Feb. 17, 1944, the excellent bulletin of the Citizens' League of Cleveland, under the heading,
"Postpone County Welfare Department,
League's Committee Holds Law Defective
Drafting Better Bill"

Did the Republicans in stirring and critical times nominate a vice-presidential candidate who exemplified Dean Inge's gloomy dictum, "I suppose politics consists in choosing always the second best," and one who, had he been elected and might, by chance, have become chief executive, would have afforded one more example in support of Bryce's chapter in his *The American Commonwealth*, "Why Great Men are not Chosen Presidents"?

25

ROBERT S. KERR

"Realist in Politics"

BY OTIS SULLIVANT

A PEACEFUL, BUSINESS-LIKE ADMINISTRATION OF STATE government came to Oklahoma under Governor Robert S. Kerr, a big, genial man, who carried his philosophy of life into the executive office. It took Oklahomans some time to become accustomed to the conservative, oilman governor whose attitude was exactly opposite to that of two of his pugnacious predecessors in a state in which politics is taken seriously and the governor must be ever on the alert to avoid political pitfalls which bring discredit upon an administration. Kerr is a study in sharp contrast to such governors as Leon C. (Red) Phillips and William H. (Alfalfa Bill) Murray who were quick to fire withering criticism at all persons who crossed their paths and use the power of political patronage and favors to force members of the legislature to follow their wishes. Without use of the political club, Kerr won support for his program in quiet, congenial conferences at a time when economic prosperity reduced both the power of patronage and the influence of a state administration over the legislature.

Bob Kerr fits into the American tradition. He was born in a log cabin, the first native Oklahoman to reach the governor's office. His father, Sam Kerr, an Oklahoma pioneer, never doubted Bob would be governor of the new state. He instilled the ambition in the boy and told him repeatedly he could reach any goal in life if he worked hard enough. Sam Kerr was farmer, rancher, rural school teacher, merchant, and cotton buyer. He served the first term as county clerk of Pontotoc County after Oklahoma's admission to statehood in 1907. He had the good sense to advise his son about the facts of politics. He told him to become financially independent and successful in a business or profession before launching a political career. It was sound advice which the son followed.

America is steeped in the tradition of the rise from a log-cabin birth to the governorship of a state or the presidency of the United States. It is more remarkable in Oklahoma for a man to step from a prosperous oil company and the presidency of a conservative oil trade association to the governorship. Kerr traveled the route from log cabin to wealth and then to the high office of governor. Kerr is president of Kerlyn Oil Company, Oklahoma City, an exploration, drilling, and producing company with a net worth between $7,000,000 and $10,000,000. Kerr and his wife own more than 60 per cent of the company. It has operated with little attention from him since he became governor and in 1944 sold extensive holdings in the West Edmond Oil Field, near Oklahoma City. Kerr resigned the position he held for six years as president of the Kansas-Oklahoma division of Mid-Continent Oil and Gas Association to become a candidate for governor. A combination of circumstances astutely foreseen enabled him to win the governor's race in a state where the great majority of the voters are suspicious of and prejudiced against men of wealth, especially oilmen.

A conservative in administration of state government, Kerr is a liberal in his views on national issues. He has been a supporter of the New Deal, the national administration, and President Roosevelt. He vigorously supported Roosevelt for a fourth term and the Democratic sweep to victory in Oklahoma on November 7, 1944, left him the undisputed leader of his party in the state. It is a precarious position in turbulent Oklahoma politics. No one knows better than Kerr the fickleness of public favor and the probability of losing his dominant position by blunders in a legislative program or the rise of a new favorite in the governor's race in 1946.

Kerr, a conservative, successful governor in a border state emerged as a figure in national politics by his early support of President Roosevelt for a fourth term. His work with the

Democratic national committee won respect of the party leaders and put him in favor with the White House. Kerr was selected as the keynote speaker of the Democratic national convention in Chicago in July. It was a splendid opportunity for an ambitious young governor and a newcomer in national politics. He laid down the challenge of the 1944 campaign to the Republican party on domestic and foreign issues. Kerr was backed by his own state delegation for vice-president and was among the first to join support with Senator Harry S. Truman when the balloting started to assure nomination of the Missourian for vice-president on the second ballot. Kerr performed faithful service for his party in Oklahoma and the nation in the campaign. His ringing speech at Chicago placed him in the limelight as a political orator. He was the speaker most in demand with the national committee. He keynoted several Democratic state conventions and was forced to reject many other invitations. He campaigned his own state and spoke in nine Midwestern and Southern states in the general election campaign.

Kerr was the first Oklahoman ever to win a keynote spot in a national convention. It strengthened him at home, and even his enemies credited the governor with a good job of selling Oklahoma in contrast to abortive efforts of other governors in national conventions. Kerr's fidelity and service put him in line for consideration in Washington. It brought suggestions at home of important appointment and that the governor was capable of filling a cabinet position. Kerr expected nothing of the sort and announced his intention of completing his term as governor which expires in January, 1947. He anticipated aid for Oklahoma in the post-war program of reconversion of industries and road building through his contacts. Kerr privately expressed his intention of becoming a candidate for the Democratic nomination for U. S. senator in 1948. Senator E. H. Moore, Republican, will be up for re-election in 1948 if he chooses to run again. Moore, a Democrat who ran on the Republican ticket in 1942 and won a surprising victory over Josh Lee, a New Deal senator, is the leading spokesman against the New Deal in Oklahoma.

A few of the independent oilmen in Oklahoma followed the lead of Kerr in backing the national administration. They helped finance the 1944 Democratic campaign. Over all, the oil industry opposed the president and supported Governor Thomas E. Dewey, giving great financial backing to the anti-New Deal campaign.

"A program that gives opportunity for economic progress to the greatest number of citizens is the essence of democracy," said Kerr, in explaining support of the national administration by a conservative governor who concentrated upon payment of the state debt. "I am in the oil business. The greatest security the oil business can have is the widespread ability of the average citizen to purchase the production of the oil industry. I think the opportunity for the individual to prosper is the greatest in a society where general prosperity exists. Therefore, I believe in providing general prosperity on the theory I will do better as an individual than if I devote all my energies to my individual prosperity."

Kerr won the respect of friend and foe by keeping his word in business and politics. He is proud of Oklahoma and endeared himself to thousands by that pride. He is astute in politics and has demonstrated an uncanny ability to keep his feet on the ground and to land on his feet. He has operated on the basis of humility in office. His enemies assert it is pretended, but whether real or a mask, Kerr is a pleasant, affable person. His enemies have attempted to dub him "Bumbling Bob" and his friends pay the play on "Smiling Bob."

A big, strapping man, Kerr's genial personality is one of his big assets. He is six feet and three inches tall, and weighs 245 pounds. He makes friends in all ranks and is at home in any company. He can talk the language of the farmer, the laborer, the banker, the business executive. He has a genuine enthusiasm for people, a friendliness that is real, and people like him. Kerr enjoys a good story as well as anyone. He swaps yarns at a political meeting, with ministers, or in a fishing boat.

Kerr loves the fanfare of politics. Some of his friends marvel at his patience, the long hours in office, the long drives and train rides, the more than 300 speeches in one year to every

type of crowd from eighth grade graduates and church con-
gregations to the national convention. He is a great admirer of
Bob and Alf Taylor, brother governors of Tennessee, and the
war of the roses between the brothers for the governorship of
Tennessee was an inspiration for his own campaigning.

Kerr's hobby is fishing. It is his recreation, something to look
forward to for vacationing. He owns a fishing lodge on Pelican
Lake, near Nisswa, Minnesota, and manages to get there each
year. He loves to still fish for wall-eyed pike in the cold northern waters. The love for fishing dates back nearly forty years
when, after the crops were laid by, Sam Kerr would load the
entire family into a wagon for a long trip to Sandy Creek, Blue
River, Little River or Canadian River. Kerr likes to play
games, including chess, bridge, cribbage, poker, and all other
card games.

He is a dry, personally and politically. Being dry is important politically in Oklahoma, one of the three remaining
states with prohibition. Kerr believes a leader in government,
education or the church should abstain from the use of intoxi-
cants because of the responsibility of position. However, he is
not a prude about the other fellow drinking.

The office of governor is more than an administrative job.
The governor is part of a great show, a sort of three ring
circus. In Oklahoma, it is a sort of game for the public to
watch to see how long the governor can stay on top. None of
them has retained popularity to the end of the administration.
Two of the ten elected governors have been impeached and
ousted. It is a great game, and the governor is sometimes compared with a rider mounting a "bronc." He is good if he can
stay in the saddle, but it is not too disappointing if he hits the
dust. The greatest difficulty for the governor is the task of
working with the legislature and persuading it to enact a program. Kerr well realizes the vicissitudes of the game. He is a
realist in politics and showman enough to meet the extra requirements of the executive position.

He won most of his program with the first legislature immediately after he took office. It was based on rigid economy
and a determination to pay off the state debt. Funds were ear-

marked by July 1, 1945, to pay the debt as the bonds became due, and a tidy sum was on hand to supplement the highway funds. Anticipating post-war problems, Kerr reversed his policy during the second legislature in January, 1945. He recommended and finally drove through the legislature, a program of liberal appropriations and some increases in taxation. It meant increased appropriations for aid of common schools, for state institutions of higher education, and for a public health program and funds to match the federal post-war highway construction program. For the last eighteen months of his term, Kerr pointed his efforts to carry out the program of the legislature and to promote industrial development in the state in the post-war era.

Kerr was inaugurated governor January 11, 1943, the second wartime governor in the history of Oklahoma. His announced objectives were a sound fiscal program, retirement of the state debt, a business-like administration, curbing the power of the governor, a minimum of political squabbling and a friendly governor in the executive office. He keyed his administration for maximum aid in the war effort and co-operation with the national government in Washington. Co-operation with Washington was directly opposite to the policy of his immediate predecessor, New Deal-hating Governor Phillips.

Kerr faced a battle from the outset of his administration. He was elected governor by a 16,500 majority, the smallest given any Democratic governor since statehood, with the exception of R. L. Williams in 1914. He barely escaped Republican control of the lower house of the legislature his first year. The Republicans had not dreamed of the 1942 Republican trend which carried into Oklahoma. There were no Republican candidates for the legislature in many of the northern counties which voted Republican. If the party had filed candidates it might have controlled the lower house. Senator Moore, the anti-New Deal Democrat running as the Republican nominee, had been elected to the United States senate over Josh Lee. The small majority and the uphill fight from the start was to help prove the Governor's mettle and astuteness as a political leader. It appeared that Oklahoma was about to emerge from the ranks of the one-party states for a two party system, at least for the period of resurgency of the Republican party nationally. The prospect was wholesome for both parties in the state.

The retiring governor, Leon C. Phillips, was the arch political foe of Governor Kerr. Phillips had been an able governor in dealing with the legislature. He forced through a program that broke the power of the state senate oligarchy, eliminated waste and squandering, and forced a balanced state budget. Phillips, a fiery red-haired lawyer, who rose from obscurity to be speaker of the house and governor in six years, lost his popularity and prestige by bickering over relatively unimportant matters, denouncing all who crossed his path, and by showing a disposition to rule or ruin while in power. Kerr had emphasized his desire to be a friendly, business-like governor in contrast to Phillips.

Kerr and Phillips were once warm personal and political friends. Ironically, each was responsible in a large measure for electing the other governor. Kerr was a leading backer of Phillips in 1938 when he was elected governor. Kerr had arranged most of his financial support. The two men broke relations and Phillips' bitter opposition was one of the principal factors contributing to the election of Kerr. Phillips bolted the Democratic ticket to support Moore for senator and the Republican candidate, William J. Otjen, against Kerr for governor.

At the outset, Phillips succeeded in creating the suspicion that Kerr's administration would be an extravagant one, a repetition of the care-free days in state government of the late E. W. Marland, who preceded Phillips as governor. Many of the legislators were close friends of Phillips and luke-warm to Kerr. Kerr set out to win them by friendly conferences and without using the power of the executive office. He succeeded— and he won confidence of the public as his program progressed. The legislature completed its work in the shortest session in twenty years. The main points of Kerr's program were written into law.

In his inaugural address, Kerr assured both houses of the

legislature that the governor's office would be open at all times to members in order "that we may reason together what is good for the state." He said: "Members of the legislature may expect from the executive office no threats, no domineering, and no bad faith.

"We intend to humanize the governor's office," he added. "I know that it is difficult for one man to see everyone, and I have no illusions about the pressure of time upon the chief executive. But this I know can be done: provision can be made for the fair and courteous treatment of all. Even the humblest shall have a channel of communication with the governor, and his cause will receive full and fair consideration. No matter how crowded the governor's office may be, there can and will be adequate provision made for the courteous treatment of all who come."

It meant long hours in the executive office for a ceaseless stream of visitors, but Kerr kept his promise. The governor was accessible to high and low, and courteous treatment was received in the executive office and by those who approached the governor outside.

Kerr proved he wasn't a "spending" governor. His administration was conservative. Appropriations were reduced below the figure of the previous biennium. This caused some reaction and Dr. Joseph A. Brandt, president of the University of Oklahoma, criticized the policy for causing loss of faculty members at the University. Over all, the reduction in enrollment in educational institutions justified the cuts. Kerr insisted upon applying the surplus upon the state debt. When he took office, the state debt was $40,669,764, but revenues exceeded appropriations and money was piling up. He sponsored legislation to ear mark all accumulating surplus for investment in war bonds to retire state bonds as they became due. Kerr blocked all efforts in his first legislature to reduce taxes because he wanted the tax structure maintained until sufficient funds accumulated to pay the debt. He insisted a debt-free government would be the best inducement for agricultural and industrial development after World War II.

Upon his recommendation, the legislature submitted to the

people three proposed constitutional amendments to curb power of the governor and they were adopted at the primary election, July 11, 1944. In the same election, a law was voted to restore the run-off primary system for nomination of candidates by majority vote. Two of the constitutional amendments dealt with boards of controls for educational institutions. One replaced the state board of agriculture with a nine-member board of regents for Oklahoma A. and M. College at Stillwater and for other agricultural colleges. The other amendment made the statutory board of regents for the state university a constitutional board. The objective was to remove the institutions from control of any governor, as the chief executive cannot remove members of the boards. The third amendment lifted from the governor complete power of executive clemency. It provided a pardon and parole board of five members, three named by the governor and one each by the chief justice of the supreme court and presiding judge of the criminal court of appeals. A majority recommendation of the board is necessary before the governor can grant a pardon or parole. He is limited to arbitrary power of leaves, stays and reprieves of not to exceed sixty days. It is intended to eliminate abuse of clemency power by governors and prevent repetition of past pay-off scandals.

A number of measures recommended by Kerr were passed in the first legislature, including an act vitalizing a constitutional amendment for a teachers' retirement system and increases in salaries for teachers in state-aid schools. Several proposals such as one for a home guard, a free textbook bill, and a measure submitting an amendment for a graduated land tax were defeated.

Kerr emphasized planning for agricultural and industrial development and soil conservation. He sponsored a tree-planting program calling for 2,500,000 trees to be planted in the state in 1944 and twice the number in 1945. He chose a $75,000 a year executive to head one of his administrative boards and tried to build his administration with men of qualifications. He surprised other elective officials on the school land commission by opposing sale of land taken in by mortgage foreclosure, saying the price would rise and the state was on the verge of the greatest drilling and exploration for oil in history. The price of land increased and bonuses from oil leases on foreclosed land added materially to the trust fund for school children of the state. The governor also endeavored to put the vast school land department on a business basis in handling farm loans.

Kerr encountered his greatest difficulty over investigation of textbook scandals of 1937 under the Marland administration.

Two men associated with the preceding administration were arrested, convicted and sentenced to two years in a federal penitentiary. They were charged with having received $60,000 for influencing textbook adoptions.

When Kerr became governor the legislature followed his suggestion in creating a joint committee to continue the investigation of textbook scandals. The investigating committee failed to accomplish anything. Some people charged that it did not want to—that the guilty ones were too near the present legislature. Kerr, however, urged it to act. A majority of the state newspapers supported Kerr in this matter. But nothing was accomplished except the stirring up of public interest in the question of fraud.

The metropolitan newspapers opposed the New Deal and were not in sympathy with Kerr in his efforts to bring about the fourth term nomination and election of President Roosevelt. The *Tulsa World* was one newspaper opposing Kerr from the outset on his state program. The newspaper's opposition was intensified by Kerr's support of the New Deal. The newspaper had supported Phillips to the end, and, with Phillips, had attempted to nominate Gomer Smith, an Oklahoma City attorney and former Townsend-plan old-age-pension advocate, over Kerr for governor in the primary race.

Robert Samuel Kerr was born in a log cabin, 60 miles and three days in a wagon from the nearest railroad station, near Ada in Indian Territory, September 11, 1896. His parents, of Scotch-Irish and English descent, were William Samuel Kerr and Margaret Wright Kerr. They had seven children, Bob being the second and the oldest boy. When their first child was six weeks old, the Kerrs drove north from Texas across Red River in a covered wagon into Indian territory and leased 160 acres of restricted Indian land in a heavily timbered valley in what is now South Central Oklahoma. They lived in a tent the first winter and until Sam Kerr built a log cabin, fourteen feet square, which still stands and is still in use.

Sam Kerr was a man of little formal education, but he was by nature a student, and he was a staunch Southern Democrat. He encouraged these characteristics in his first-born son.

Young Robert was educated in the common schools at Ada, at that time a town of less than 2,500 population, and was serving as an officer in the Baptist Sunday School when he was ten years old. Almost as tall as his father and nearly as strong, Bob, at fifteen, picked 396 pounds of cotton in a day. He thought he had done well, but the elder Kerr said it should have been 400 pounds. Bob attended the Oklahoma Baptist University at Shawnee, the Ada normal, taught school two years and entered the University of Oklahoma for the autumn term in 1915. When the summer of 1916 came he started out as a magazine salesman and got as far as Webb City, Missouri. There he made a sales talk to B. Robert Elliott, a lawyer. After a half hour of strenuous argument, the lawyer said, "I don't give a damn about your magazine, young man, but I'll give you $100 a month to work for me." Kerr accepted the proposal after Elliott agreed to buy a magazine subscription. The association lasted nearly a year—until the United States entered World War I.

Kerr entered the first officers' training camp at Fort Logan H. Roots, near Little Rock, Ark. He was commissioned a second lieutenant, and went overseas in August, 1918, and his division was preparing to go to the front when the Armistice was signed. He returned to America in the spring of 1919.

Back at Ada, Kerr borrowed capital and entered the produce business. After fire destroyed his produce house, he began the study of law and passed the bar examination. In 1924, Kerr was a member of a group of veterans who elected Jim Hatcher, Chickasha attorney, state commander of the American Legion, and in 1925 Kerr became the state commander, the youngest in the nation.

One day in the summer of 1925 he noticed a tall, blonde visitor on the Ada tennis courts. He obtained an introduction to Grayce Breene of Tulsa, and asked for a date. They went horseback riding and she rode well. They played tennis, and she played a good game. On the third date, he informed her they were going to get married and inquired of her whether she had any specific preference as to the date. After a few weeks of this kind of courtship, she consented. They were married December 26, 1925, in Tulsa.

Kerr was a struggling lawyer earning about $1,500 a year when he married. It was not long before he became interested in drilling oil wells. A brother-in-law, James L. Anderson, was in the business, and they formed a partnership.

Wealth came to Bob Kerr as the rest of the nation was plunging into depression. His drilling firm was active in the fabulous, mile and a quarter deep Oklahoma City oil field. The wells were costly and the drilling contractor often had to take an interest in a well in order to get his pay. Kerr's firm did this frequently and almost every well hit oil. Organization of the present oil company followed.

Kerr moved to Oklahoma City in 1932. He plunged vigorously into church and civic life. For five years he was a trophy winner in Y.M.C.A. membership drives. He took the lead in Red Cross drives and other civic activities. It became a habit to ask Kerr to head difficult campaigns. He directed a successful campaign for bonds for additional city water supply.

Kerr became interested in politics. He aided in financing campaigns. He was a supporter of the late E. W. Marland and became a member of Marland's pardon and parole board.

Kerr was interested in legislation as the president of the oil and gas trade association. In 1938, he played the major role in nomination of Phillips. He helped direct Phillips' campaign and arranged the finances for it. The friendship was short-lived. Phillips became cool to him immediately after the primary. However, Phillips was largely responsible for Kerr being named national committeeman in 1940 by giving approval. At the national convention, Phillips opposed the third term nomination of Roosevelt. Kerr supported it and headed the campaign in the state.

Kerr had pitched his fortunes with Roosevelt's cause in Oklahoma. He astutely foresaw it was the chance of a wealthy oil man to be elected governor, especially if America were near to war or in war. His success in winning the nomination because of the alliance partially explains his support of the New Deal, the President, and the fourth term. Kerr's political fortune was staked in part on Roosevelt. He was benefited by opposition of Phillips, the support of party organization, the followers of the New Deal, the Baptists—the largest domination in Oklahoma—the American Legion, the Negroes, and small town merchants. Kerr's own personality was an important factor in his nomination and he began to show promise as a campaign orator.

A large part of Kerr's balance in political affairs and his ability to meet people day in and day out with a friendly disposition may be attributed to a happy family life. Mrs. Kerr is intensely interested with her husband in politics and state affairs. Their family consists of four children, Robert S. Jr., eighteen, Breene, sixteen, Kay, fourteen, and William, seven. All the Kerrs are large in size. Mrs. Kerr is five feet, ten and one-half inches, and Robert Jr., six feet, four inches. The other children are correspondingly large for their ages. Kerr enjoys being with his family and his brothers and sisters.

The governor accepted all invitations to aid in war bond drives. He traveled much, in the state and out, filling speaking engagements. He took it that speech making and appearance of the governor in the state helped build morale in wartime and also laid the groundwork for his own success with the legislature. Some of his critics quipped about his paying occasional visits to the capitol, and publicity about his carrying a jar of sorghum molasses to a New York woman on one of his trips there resulted in jibes about "the sorghum packing governor." All in all, however, Oklahomans took it that their personable governor is an excellent showman, doing a good job of selling the state and trying hard to make a success of his administration.

26

EARL WARREN

"So-called Nonpartisan"

BY THOMAS S. BARCLAY

IT HAS LONG BEEN COMMONPLACE THAT CERTAIN FACTORS in the American political system make exceedingly difficult the development of recognized, nation-wide leaders. The national government operates with irresponsible political parties and diffused controls. This is particularly true so far as the minority party is concerned. The leadership of the party in power at Washington is monopolized by the President himself; he is leader because he is President and not President because he is leader. The methods and conditions which control the procedure of Congress are hardly adapted to produce a unitary national leadership for the opposition. Our constitutional practices result in the nomination of "available" men and in the rather complete elimination of the defeated candidate from a position of acknowledged party leadership.

Among the several advantages of the federal system, however, is the fact that the states constitute "reservoirs from which national leadership may be drawn." The successful governor of a doubtful and strategic state attracts attention and interest in other parts of the nation; his record and qualifications are meticulously examined; he frequently becomes "available" as a presidential possibility.

Thus, of the twelve successful candidates for the presidency since 1876, seven have been governors of their respective commonwealths, while six of the defeated opponents have likewise held that office. To designate California as an important state is not merely to appeal to local pride and sentiment. The state ranks high in population and has twenty-five electoral votes. If

California is "the land of perpetual summer, of orange groves in sight of snowy peaks, of oil wells spouting wealth, of real estate promising fortunes, of cinema stars and bathing beauties," it is also a domain of great wealth, economic power, and votes, all important weapons in political warfare. The governor of the commonwealth frequently becomes a national figure of some significance.

The political annals of California are not dull. Since the turn of the century, reform movements against corruption in municipal politics and government, the long, spectacular, and ultimately successful struggle in state politics to break the control of railroad and corporation domination, the economic conflicts and sectional cleavages between the northern and southern parts of the state, an ineffective, loosely organized, and undisciplined party system, progressive movements, the various forms of anti-Oriental hostility, have provided almost continuous agitation and sharp differences of opinion.

Successfully to combine enough elements to formulate and to put into effect a policy for the state requires executive leadership of very high order, an unusual combination of political acumen, and a large amount of good fortune. The political sagacity, the qualities of leadership, and the accomplishments of a California governor are certain to arouse curiosity and interest in many sections and among those whose business it is to designate the nominees for public office.

Earl Warren was elected governor of California in November, 1942. He was then fifty-one years of age, a large, calm, friendly man who had occupied with reasonable success the office of attorney-general and who had convinced the electorate of the state of his capacity to administer its affairs during a critical period, without the reciprocal antagonism between the chief executive and many important elements both within and without his party which had so unhappily characterized the administration of the Democrat, Culbert L. Olson, in the years 1939-43.

The career of Warren is a typical story of political life in the United States, and in the same patterns which are familiar throughout the country. He was born in Los Angeles in 1891, the son of a car builder of the Southern Pacific Railroad. Warren spent his boyhood in Bakersfield, attending the public schools, doing odd jobs for the neighbors, playing the clarinet in the local band, and living in the simplicity and economy of the average American town in the days before the First World War. At the University of California, his record, both in college and in law school, was that of a steady and dependable student. Subsequent to his graduation, he was admitted to the bar in 1914 and practiced in Oakland for three years. His army experience was gained in 1917-18, when he served acceptably as a lieutenant in the infantry. His military career ending in 1919, as he was not sent overseas, Warren was relieved from duty.

His public career commenced very modestly when he was appointed clerk of the judiciary committee of the state senate. He then held for a short period the office of deputy city attorney of Oakland. The next year, 1920, he became deputy district attorney of Alameda County and thus began a long service of eighteen years as a prosecuting official, serving three terms, 1925-38, as district attorney of Alameda County. This county ranks third in population in the state and includes the city of Oakland. The times called for a prosecutor with legitimate zeal for public order and with adequate legal knowledge. The administration of the law under the proud American tradition of local self-government was rendered exceedingly difficult by the problems of prohibition enforcement, of racketeering, and of the notorious unholy alliance between crime and politics.

During his almost perennial tenure as district attorney of Alameda County, Warren's attitude toward law enforcement was one of orthodox regularity. Prosecutions were rigorously and successfully conducted and victories were won. Although on occasion, Warren, as with other efficient prosecuting officials, was criticized for ruthless methods in obtaining convictions, his conduct of the office was known and approved in substance, if not always in detail, by the voters in his successive re-elections by large majorities. Nor were his influence and interest confined to one local area of government, as Warren was also a leading advocate of simplified criminal procedure, of increasing the powers and authority of local law-enforcing authorities, and of organizing them into regional groups. Meanwhile, he had attracted the interest and support of several powerful Republican leaders who saw in the hardworking and cautious Warren an available man for political preferment.

During the decade following the First World War, certain far-reaching changes occurred in the politics of California. Although the Republicans continued to control the state, the progressive movement had run its course. Despite this fact, there were many progressive Republicans who were dissatisfied with the reactionary labor and other policies of the large financial, industrial, and agricultural interests of the state. The undisciplined Democratic party had neither the organization nor the voting strength successfully to challenge the Republicans; in many counties and cities it was almost non-existent. There was a dangerous widening of the cleavage between employer and employee, both in industry and in large-scale agriculture. There were in the late 'twenties indications that the long-dominant conflict between the northern and southern parts of the state was assuming in the politics of the commonwealth a secondary position.

The depression and the New Deal altered basically the course of politics in California, especially in the southern portion of the commonwealth. In the years 1930-40, from a meager 20 per cent of the total registration of voters the Democratic strength increased to 60 per cent. A Democratic United States senator was elected in 1932 and in 1938, respectively; the party won seats in Congress and in both houses of the state legislature. The constituent elements of the California Democracy included the traditional partisans of the San Francisco area, the supporters of the New Deal, and many others who were drawn into the party fold because of opposition to Republican policies and candidates. The political situation in the state was further complicated by the development, during the 'thirties, of several powerful pension-plan movements, of the Upton Sinclair EPIC plan, and of a great increase in the power of organized labor. Even the conservative Republicans came reluctantly to realize that the restoration of their party to power depended, in part, upon a program and a leadership that had at least the appearance of liberalism.

An able student of politics has accurately characterized party tradition and discipline in California as "almost chaotic." Under the provisions of the California direct primary law, a candidate is not limited to the nomination of his own party; he may, also, seek the nomination of other parties, which means that many candidates file for both the Republican and the Democratic nomination. The person receiving the highest number of votes at the direct primary election becomes the nominee of his party. If he is likewise successful in the other party, his election is thus assured without a contest. A candidate who does not win the nomination of his own party, however, cannot be the choice of any other party regardless of how many of its votes he secures. This "double filing" practice has long been widespread in California, so far as the two major parties are concerned, and has made party designation frequently meaningless and unreliable.

In the state election of 1938, Warren became a candidate for attorney-general. He was supported by some of the largest newspapers in the state, by the business interests, both industrial and agricultural, and by a limited number of labor organizations. He filed for the nomination on the Republican, the Democratic, and the Progressive tickets, respectively, and in the primary won an easy victory, securing a large majority of the Republican vote, of the Progressive vote, and the necessary plurality to win the Democratic nomination. His election was a formality. The Democrats, for the first time in nearly half a century, won the governorship and other state elective offices, and had a nominal control of the lower house of the legislature. Warren conducted with a reasonable degree of competence the affairs of his first state office. It was not to be expected, of course, that his attitude and policies would be satisfactory to all. Despite Warren's professed determination strongly to uphold civil liberties, his administration was criticized for its support of the mass evacuation of Japanese and of Japanese-Americans from the state and for its failure to intervene in an important strike. In 1940-42, he was active and effective in organizing state and local councils of defense, in bringing together in numerous conferences state and local law-enforcement officials, and in organizing training for civilian defense work and welding it into units of control co-operating with the United States authorities.

Meanwhile, the Olson administration had become involved in a series of difficulties. The discipline and unity of the Democratic party in 1938 were more apparent than real, and the first Democratic governor in more than forty years was unable effectively to control the diversified and often antagonistic groups which bore the party label. Clashes in personality as well as in policy were clearly evident. Despite many commendable achievements, the Olson administration was regarded by many as inept, quarrelsome, and "radical." Its press support was very weak, and the attacks upon it were frequently unfair. Warren, too, disliked the Olson regime, and his relations with the governor were formal. As the only Republican holding an elective administrative position, he was not directly involved in the wrangles among the Democrats.

His campaign strategy in 1942 for the governorship was shrewdly devised, and he was assisted materially by the unusual provisions of the California direct primary. Realizing, no doubt, that he would have in his campaign for the nomination the almost complete support of the California Republicans, Warren desired also to secure the votes of the anti-Olson and anti-New Deal Democrats in the primary and in the general election. By the method of double filing the attorney-general was enabled to present himself as the so-called nonpartisan candidate for the gubernatorial nomination. The results of the primary election revealed clearly the party demoralization among the Democrats. With far less than one-half of the registered Democratic voters participating, Warren secured about four-ninths of the total votes cast in that party. He won easily, of course, the Republican nomination.

During the election campaign, Warren, supported by an almost united and partisan press, attacked consistently the Olson administration because of its mistakes, political ineptitude, and quarrels. He was careful, however, to emphasize daily that the war demanded unity and co-operation in state affairs and that these desired results could best be achieved by placing Warren in the governorship. In a conciliatory and friendly manner, he promised to be the nonpartisan executive of a nonpartisan administration. However, he was careful to indicate that in the so-called nonpartisan regime, the qualified members of both major parties would be recognized. His type of campaigning was unusual, but highly effective. He relied only to a limited degree upon the regular Republican organization, conducting a thorough, state-wide campaign that seemed largely personal, with no other Republican candidates participating. Competent observers of his methods believed that the candidate wished to convince the voters that he was not a symbol of economic depression and of reactionary labor attitude which many correctly associated with Republican policies and former leadership. Although in respect of many matters Warren maintained that vague attitude so characteristic of practical politicians, he recommended specifically a program of four parts. These were tax reduction, increased old age pensions, a reorganization of the state guard, and a post-war planning program. Although Democratic registration throughout the state was approximately one million in excess of the Republican, Warren's election was assured. For better or for worse, the unpredictable California voters elected him by a majority of over 300,000. The Republicans also controlled both houses of the legislature.

Warren's administration during the first two years of his term has been a popular one. He is regarded as a "good governor." He entered office at a most propitious time; many of the difficult and pressing problems of the past decade, including labor, unemployment, taxation, and even the perennial pension agitation have been temporarily solved by the prevailing war prosperity which has been so pervasive a factor throughout the state. The governor and his advisers have made few mistakes. His relations with the legislature have been far more effective than those of his predecessor.

Specifically, Warren sponsored with success legislation which reduced the income tax, the bank and corporation franchise taxes, and the sales tax. Old age pensions were increased 25 per cent. Agencies to consider post-war planning, re-employment, and reconstruction were established. Before consideration by the legislature, these laws were discussed by nonpartisan committees composed of members of both houses and spokesmen for agricultural, business, labor, and other representative groups. Although organized labor was not friendly, a truce was arranged to prevent for the duration of the war conflicts between labor and capital.

As attorney-general, Warren's attitude and expressions concerning the Japanese-Americans seemed definitely political in character and designed for the latitude of southern California. Later, as governor, he and some of his appointees talked vaguely of the "menace" and the "threat" with which the state was confronted, and dilated upon the necessity of preventing the return of all evacuees during the duration. Unfortunately, similar opinions were held by many others and were daily reiterated with the embellishments of certain of the notorious California newspapers. However, when the federal government recently announced a drastic change in its policy toward the Japanese-Americans, Warren was constrained to declare for law enforcement and for the full recognition of the civic rights of these returned American citizens.

It was inevitable that Warren's success and prestige as governor of a great commonwealth should attract the favorable attention of Republican leaders elsewhere. He was available, of course, as a "favorite son," but he had other valid claims for their consideration.

During 1943 and 1944, Warren was frequently mentioned by many as a qualified nominee for the vice-presidency. If Dewey were to receive the Republican nomination for president, the choice of Warren as his running mate would present a perfectly "balanced ticket," with due recognition of the political and sectional claims of the West. This situation was embarrassing to the cautious, "nonpartisan," wartime governor of California. If, as alleged, he was flattered and pleased by his sudden rise to national prominence, he may have thought that either he had not acquired sufficient experience for high national office or that 1944 was not the proper time to seek preferment. There was also a hard fact of practical politics, namely, that Roosevelt retained great strength in California and in many other parts of the nation; it would be very difficult, therefore, to defeat him for re-election. Warren had, also, declared his intention of completing his term as governor, which does not expire until 1947. Formally, he stated repeatedly that he was not a candidate for either the presidential or the vice-presidential nominations.

Despite this, however, the "nonpartisan" governor agreed to permit his name to be used in the California presidential primaries in May, 1944, as a Republican candidate for president, and a list of fifty delegates nominally pledged to support him was subsequently elected. Warren soon released his delegation, and became its leader, thus assuring California of substantial recognition in the convention while relieving the governor of any commitments. Thus, the presidential primary, designed primarily to afford the voters an opportunity to express their respective choices for the nomination for president, was made a weapon in the great game of politics.

As temporary chairman of the Republican national convention of 1944, Warren's long and partisan address was above the average for such occasions, but was quickly forgotten in the more important matters of platform and of candidates. In declining to be considered for the nomination for vice-president, he probably incurred the ill will of prominent Republican politicians. His support of the party nominees during the campaign at times seemed nominal although he campaigned in several strategic states and was prevented by illness from being more active. As to the governor's real motives in 1944, there has been considerable speculation. Granted that he felt certain of Roosevelt's re-election, his obligation to serve out his term as governor was also a factor in his decision.

Under the impact of the war, meanwhile, many matters of vital concern to the future of California have crowded forward. Post-war re-employment, reconversion of the huge industrial plants financed largely by the federal government, and the restoration of some proper and adequate balance in the economic life of the state are of far greater importance than the machinations of politicians and the struggles for partisan advantage.

Warren is fully aware of the gravity of the situation. With the end of the war in Europe, the East and Middle West will be placed in an advantageous position as compared to the states of the Pacific slope. To continue in time of peace the industrialism caused by the war, to provide jobs for the hundreds of thousands who now are in airplane factories, shipyards, and war plants, and to maintain decent living standards will require extensive planning and skillful execution by the state government of California. Warren has long realized that no elective public official can evade these and other responsibilities.

Prior to 1945, evidence of the state's concern in the post-war years is found in the creation by the legislature of the State Reconstruction and Re-employment Commission, which is a fact-finding and planning agency for the assistance of business, industry, and employment problems. The unprecedented surplus now accumulating in the state treasury will, under executive recommendation and legislative approval, be used for a state-wide building program, for aiding employment conditions during conversion, and, later, for probable unemployment relief.

Such was the situation when, early in January, 1945, this "typical Republican" but "nonpartisan" governor of a state overwhelmingly Democratic in registration and in voting power presented to a Republican legislature a comprehensive and progressive program. Bewildered Republicans and astonished Democrats alike listened to recommendations for compulsory, prepaid medical care, expanded unemployment insurance, improved workmen's compensation, a new department of mental hygiene, a commission to study the problems of racial minorities, and housing and urban redevelopment. To many Republicans, long interested in state government almost exclusively from the point of view of tax problems, of budget matters, and of routine administrative affairs the proposed program seems a frank surrender to political expediency for the purpose of assisting Warren's future ambitions. Veteran independent Republican legislators, secure in their districts, regard with skepticism or disapproval the far-reaching recommendations. Democrats complain that many features of their own program have been appropriated by a Republican governor, but many will support the measures. The CIO, whose demands Warren now presents in modified form, may decide to oppose his recommendations as only a weak compromise. Powerful pressure groups of varied character will fight to the end to prevent the measures they oppose from becoming law. Truly, the "nonpartisan" governor has caused a paradoxical display of partisanship.

Tentatively, it would seem accurate to suggest that Warren has learned the facts of political life. Admitting that the adoption of the bold program now before the legislature will enhance his chances for re-election in 1946, it is also true that it will be of great benefit to the people of the entire state rather than to a group of special interests. If Warren wins, it would seem to make certain his re-election in 1946 and his possible emergence as a candidate for the presidency in 1948. If he loses, his political future will be endangered, and more important, the failure of a progressive program under Republican leadership will be demonstrated. Warren faces a fight to the finish with the result in doubt.[1] At all events, the new and vigor-

1. The long and controversial legislative session ended on June 16, 1945. Warren's legislative program was the most comprehensive offered by a Republican governor since the first administration of Hiram Johnson, 1911-1915. Although a number of bills embodying important parts of his recommendations were adopted, opinion is divided as to whether the governor's victory was not more apparent than real. The legislature, largely dominated by conservative Republican politicians, failed to enact the respective proposals for compulsory, prepaid medical care, for hospitalization insurance, for the extension of unemployment insurance benefits for workers, and for a commission to study the economic and political aspects of racial equality. Party discipline was weak, Warren not being able to hold in line many Republicans, especially those from southern California who were either largely indifferent or openly hostile. The Democrats supported Warren in several significant matters but lacked effective leadership and party cohesion. On the other hand, the organized lobbies of private interests, primarily concerned with preventive action, were ubiquitous, powerful, pervasive, and, therefore, dangerously effective throughout the entire session. Organized labor seemed content to protect its earlier gains, but was not successful in advancing its cause in other matters. Organized business adopted a similar protective attitude.

ous industrial energy, the incredible growth in population, and the imminent struggles involving the political, the economic, and the social future of the state make certain the prophecy that California will be "no land of quiet dreams which the future will bring into being behind those surf-pounded beaches and in the valleys shadowed by majestic mountains."

It is ironical that, although the most important parts of Warren's legislative program had been advocated in the Republican national platform of 1944, the chief opposition to their enactment into law in California came from the regular Republican organization, both in and out of the legislature. Thus, the session ended with the Republicans divided and with Warren determined to seek re-election in 1946. The contest for the nomination has commenced, and the governor is an experienced and shrewd campaigner. If he receives the support of the Republican rank and file in the party primary and is renominated, a sufficient number of registered Democrats may support him in the election, thus making Earl Warren the only governor since the late Hiram Johnson to succeed himself in office.

27

FRANK HAGUE

"Belligerent Suspicion"

BY DAYTON DAVID MC KEAN

W HEN MAYOR FRANK HAGUE HOLDS HIS ANNUAL NEW Year's Day reception in City Hall, Jersey City, his ordinarily sour face glows with pride at the demonstration of fealty shown by the assembled Democratic politicians of New Jersey. There are usually two or more congressmen present, and at times he has had a United States senator and a governor. One or more federal and a dozen state judges who owe their robes to his favor will come to the reception to show that they are not forgetful of the man who made them.

If a United States senator or a governor is to be elected during the year, the nominee-to-be usually stands at the mayor's right hand at the reception to greet the Democratic politicians, large and small, who have come to the one annual meeting of the Hague organization. New Jersey has, of course, a direct primary, but since Frank Hague's rise to power it has been, as far as the Democrats have been concerned, only an elaborate—and to the taxpayers—an expensive formality. As the mayor once said in another connection, "I decide—I do—me!"

At the reception there are also ex-congressmen and would-be congressmen. There are local lawyer-politicians who would be happy to receive the mayor's blessing the next time a vacancy occurs among the judges on the federal bench for New Jersey or in the United States district attorney's office. Others would be glad to exchange their real estate offices for those of United States marshal or collector of internal revenue.

This crowd of politicians represents the officers of Hague's political army. They and their subordinates are the men who see that the voters really vote. They were shocked at the front-page news in December, 1943, that because the mayor had had the flu he was going to Florida at his doctor's orders, and the reception was cancelled. He had always gone to Florida in the winter—without requiring doctor's orders—and come back for the reception, even if he had to return on the next Miami train. To call off the annual event seemed to the faithful most portentous, and it was revived the following year.

Most of the people present at the reception are men, but among all the male politicians might be seen a large, heavy woman about sixty-five years of age, whose general appearance is somewhat like that of a policewoman, or like that of a warden of a woman's prison. She is Mrs. Mary T. Norton, since 1924 a member of Congress from one of Mayor Hague's pocket boroughs. She is chairman of the House Committee on Labor, formerly chairman of the Committee on the District of Columbia. From 1934 to 1944 she was chairman of the Democratic State Committee, that is, she was nominally the leader of the Democratic Party in New Jersey; but never by word or action did she betray any doubt as to who she thought the real leader was.

Mrs. Norton's rise shows one way that some members of Congress are made. In 1920, the year that women gained the vote, she was appointed to represent Hudson County (Mayor Hague's domain) on the Democratic State Committee. Three years later she got a job with a salary: member of the Hudson County Board of Freeholders.[1] She was a delegate to the Democratic convention of 1924, and she has been a delegate to every Democratic national convention since. That same year she went to Congress, and she has been elected every succeeding two years. Since the defeat of Senator Smathers in 1942, she has been Mayor Hague's dispenser of federal patronage for New Jersey. It is not necessary for her to campaign; as long as she does what Mayor Hague wants, her election is automatic; but if she should decide to think for herself, she would not survive the next election.

1. The equivalent in New Jersey of the board of county commissioners in most states.

For many years a handsome, smiling, handshaking figure at all the New Year receptions was A. Harry Moore, a United States senator from 1935 to 1938 and three times governor of New Jersey. The case of Harry Moore shows what happens to a Hague man who gets notions of independence.

In his nine years as governor of New Jersey, Harry Moore had appointed hundreds of Hague men to public jobs and to jobs in the most strategic places from which to protect the mayor, such as chief justice of the Supreme Court, chancellor, attorney-general, county prosecutor, common pleas judge. He had even appointed in 1939 the inexperienced and briefless barrister, Frank Hague, Jr., to the Court of Errors and Appeals, the state's highest court, "in order," he said, "to make his dad happy."

As United States senator, Harry Moore had been a faithful Washington agent for the federal patronage that had come to the Hague machine after 1932. He had ordinarily followed the White House line in his votes, though he had voted against the Social Security Act because, he said, it would "take the romance out of old age."

After a score of years of service to his boss, he desired to retire from public life to his lucrative law practice, when his third term as governor ended in 1940. The mayor allowed him three years of retirement but demanded at the New Year's reception of 1943 that Moore run for governor for a fourth time in the election of that year. After a summer's attempt to persuade Hague to find some one else, Moore flatly refused to run. Perhaps he foresaw that 1943 was a Republican year; perhaps he felt that the burden of being a Hague candidate had become greater than any man—even an experienced campaigner like himself—could bear; perhaps he felt his advancing years. At any rate, he defied the boss.

The mayor in a blistering public statement immediately denounced his old friend and associate as an ingrate to the Democratic party. The former governor and senator did not reply. All the little dogs in the pack immediately barked at him. From being an honored elder statesman in the Hague organization, Moore was at once brought down to being an outcast.

He was no longer invited to be the orator of the day at the mayor's rallies, parades, and public meetings. He was not asked to be honorary chairman of charity drives. More important, perhaps, the word went out from City Hall that Moore was to be kicked around by Hague judges and prosecutors when he appeared in court.

If the instances of Norton and Moore illustrate how Hague congressmen, senators, and governors must behave to retain the boss's favor, the case of Thomas F. Meaney, United States district judge for the northern district of New Jersey, shows how one may rise in the judiciary within the Hague organization.

When Governor Moore wanted to put Frank Hague, Jr., on the New Jersey Court of Errors and Appeals, a considerable amount of maneuvering was necessary to create a vacancy for the young man, and Thomas F. Meaney was the key to the moves that had to be made. He was then a common pleas (county) judge in Hudson County. He was induced to resign. Then a Judge Thomas G. Walker, formerly Hague's leader in the Assembly, was persuaded to step down from the Court of Errors to take Meaney's place on the county bench. Frank Junior was then appointed to the seat Walker had vacated.

This series of moves left Meaney, for the first time in a score of years, without a seat on some bench. But he was soon taken care of by being appointed at $20,000 a year as special counsel to the liquidator of the New Jersey Title Guarantee and Trust Company, a big Jersey City bank which closed at about the same time. The New Jersey Commissioner of Banking and Insurance at that time was a member of the Hague organization, and Meaney's appointment was easily arranged. It was rumored then, but not for three years was it proved, that in the last days before the bank closed in February, 1939, some of its officers and many of its depositors with connections in the Hague organization had withdrawn their money.[2]

2. For a list of those who made withdrawals just before the collapse of the bank and for a statement of their relationships with the Hague organization see *Hearings before a Subcommittee of the Committee on the Judiciary*, Seventy-seventh Congress, Second Session, on the nomination of Thomas F. Meaney, 1942, pp. 69-84, 120-28.

A. Harry Moore was a director until a few weeks before the bank closed.

It should have been possible to recover on behalf of the less fortunate depositors a pro rata share of the funds withdrawn in anticipation of the failure of the bank, but Meaney as counsel never took any steps to do so. But he did obtain for himself an extra fee of $10,000 for representing the holders of the first mortgage participation certificates (which had been guaranteed by the bankrupt company) when the holders of these certificates brought an action to establish their claims ahead of the claims of other creditors. This extra fee was allowed by a vice-chancellor, but a new commissioner of banking and insurance had been appointed by Governor Charles Edison, and he did not like Mr. Meaney's behavior. As he testified before the Senate committee, "Whether it [the fee] was legal or not, I felt it was certainly against the interest of the trust, and it was on that basis that I severed the connection between Mr. Meaney and the trust." [3]

Meaney was out of a job again, and there was no immediate vacancy for this jurist who, as Governor Edison said, had moved "here and there, up and down, in and out, off and on, at his boss's command." Having earned some $70,000 and expenses in three years, however, he should not have been eligible for the WPA. He had to remain available for two years.

A vacancy occurred on the federal bench for New Jersey in 1941, and the Hague forces moved to put Meaney back on the bench. The Department of Justice had no enthusiasm for him, but Mary Norton and A. Harry Moore did their best. There is a story that Mrs. Norton got to the President and told him what a wonderful man Tom Meaney was, and that he was just misunderstood by such reformers as Charles Edison. At any rate he was nominated, and after a fight led by Governor Edison that was, among other factors, to cost Senator Smathers his seat in 1942, Meaney was barely confirmed by the Senate. It took all the pressure the White House could provide

3. *Ibid.*, p. 65.

to get the votes, and not one senator answered Senator Norris' attack upon the nomination.

Mayor Frank Hague, the man behind Mary Norton, Congressman Edward Hart, Senator Moore, Judge Meaney, and all the others, was born January 17, 1876, in a slum section of Jersey City called the Horseshoe because of a gerrymander of the Republican legislature of 1871. Though Frank Hague has moved uptown, the Horseshoe is still a slum. But so is most of Jersey City.

When he was fourteen he was expelled from the sixth grade, and he never returned to school. His mind was and is intensely practical, with no ability to grasp abstractions. Unlike Al Smith and many other men of limited schooling, he never made up by self-education what he missed of formal education; but probably he would not admit, or even understand, that he had missed anything. His command of the English language is no better than that of a Horseshoe saloonkeeper, and his knowledge of public affairs is only what he has picked up from conversation and from reading newspapers.

At sixty-nine years of age he is a tall, erect figure, in appearance far from the traditional fat, slouching, cigar-smoking political boss. He is always neatly and expensively dressed. His characteristic facial expression is a kind of sour, belligerent suspicion. He neither drinks nor smokes. He has always enjoyed good health, which he has taken care of like a hypochondriac. He has taken regular exercise, and at the slightest sniffle or ache he has run to the Medical Center. He goes to Florida in the winter and to his home at Deal, New Jersey, in the summer; or he travels.

Beyond doubt he is the best traveled boss America has produced, for he has been all over the world. When he is on his travels he governs by telephone; he never leaves to a subordinate any important degree of discretion. His faithful deputy, John Malone, cares for details or carries out orders; or his nephew, City Commissioner Frank Hague Eggers (the heir apparent) represents his uncle at public occasions. But neither of them exercises any independent authority.

He is humorless, vindictive, and unimaginative. For all his

travelling, he does not understand America. When he has been off on a Red hunt, or when he has been keeping labor organizers or speakers from the Civil Liberties Union out of Jersey City, he has never been able to understand why the press of the country attacked him. Because of this lack of imagination, his associates find it difficult, often impossible, to dissuade him from some ill-considered action, such as his campaign against civil liberties from 1937 to 1939.[4] When his old foes, the Communists, unexpectedly endorsed him in 1943 he was speechless; no appropriate comment on their unwelcome support came to his humorless mind.

He is notable among American bosses for the length of time he has preserved himself in power. In 1897, in his twenty-first year, Hague was elected constable; in 1906 he was appointed sergeant-at-arms of the New Jersey House of Assembly; by 1907 he was the leader of his ward, and the following year he was appointed custodian (chief janitor) of the City Hall. In this position he made the political friendships that enabled him to be elected street and water commissioner in 1911. When Jersey City adopted the commission form of government in 1913, he was elected as one of the new commissioners. He was put in charge of the police, and he used his powers to perfect an organization that made him mayor in 1917. He has been mayor since that time and has steadily improved the organization.

In 1919 he became state leader of the Democratic party when his candidate for governor, Edward I. Edwards—who said he would make New Jersey wetter than the Atlantic Ocean —was elected. Edwards was followed by Silzer, and Silzer by A. Harry Moore, who served three nonconsecutive terms. The appointments these governors made in their fifteen years of office filled the state courts, departments, and commissions with Hague men, either Hague Democrats or Hague Republicans, members of that strange species of politician indigenous to New Jersey.

4. For a more complete account of his campaign against civil liberties see Dayton David McKean, *The Boss* (Houghton Mifflin Co., 1940, pp. 183-200; 227-48.

Any leader of a party in a state is bound to be interested in national politics. Since 1920 Frank Hague has been leader of the New Jersey delegation to every national convention. He rose to be vice-chairman of the Democratic National Committee. From 1920 through 1932 he followed Alfred E. Smith in national Democratic politics; he and Smith became firm personal as well as political friends. He was Smith's floor manager at the Chicago convention of 1932, and before the convention opened issued his famous statement that Franklin D. Roosevelt, the candidate "who is weakest in the eyes of the rank and file" could not "carry a single state east of the Mississippi and very few in the far west."

But when Roosevelt was nominated, Hague parted with Smith and followed the party candidate. He worked hard for him, and Roosevelt carried New Jersey. Hague produced again in 1936 and in 1940, when to his other responsibilities was added that of being floor manager for the President at the convention. Though the New Dealers have never liked Frank Hague, he was accepted by the President, who had him as his guest at the White House and at Hyde Park. Hague was enthusiastic for a fourth term. He should have been, because not only has his organization controlled all federal patronage for New Jersey since 1932, but the largesse of the national government in the days of the FERA, CWA, PWA, and WPA saved Jersey City from otherwise certain bankruptcy.

The Hague machine has the characteristics of most urban political organizations: an enormous payroll, provision for charities, the use of the police and the machinery of the law against opponents, and until recently the control of election machinery. These devices it has carried to a greater perfection, perhaps, than have other organizations, as, for example, in providing free hospital and medical care; but it is notable because it has been able to do what others have not.

The organization, for example, controls the newspapers of Hudson County. Nothing unfavorable about the mayor or his policies is ever published; every policy of his, no matter how absurd, whether he is saving Jersey City from a mythical Red invasion or from a mythical railroad lobby, is lavishly praised; and news that he wants suppressed does not appear. When in 1942 a city official was arrested and held in jail for embezzlement, the Hudson County press completely suppressed the information. If Hague's policies change, editorial policies change. It seems safe to say that no other American boss has ever obtained such complete control of the press in his territory or held it so long.

The Hague organization is notable for its infiltration into all the institutions of the community. It has taken over labor unions, the Chamber of Commerce, the veterans' organizations, the medical society, the bar association, and even lodges and clubs. If other political organizations may be said to be horizontal—to be superimposed upon their communities—the Hague organization is vertical: it exists within every institution in Jersey City. The bar association, which in most corrupt cities can serve as a rallying point for opposition forces, is in Jersey City as completely Hague-controlled as is the First Ward Democratic Club. Judge Louis N. Paladeau, who is Hague's personal representative to transmit his orders to friendly legislators, was until recently president of the bar association. The association praises Hague judges and threatens anti-Hague lawyers with disbarment. Even the state bar association has come under his control; it favored a new state constitution until he opposed it, and then it meekly reversed its position. In the same way, the State Federation of Labor is on its way to becoming controlled by Hague; and the New Jersey CIO, which once fought him bitterly, in 1943 endorsed him at its annual convention.

Among the institutions in Hague's domain the Roman Catholic Church is unique in that about 75 per cent of the population belongs to it. The mayor himself and the great majority of his lieutenants are members. Obviously he and his organization could not have lasted as long as they have without the support of the local Catholic hierarchy, and if that support were withdrawn Hague would not survive the next election. Although his policies have been attacked outside of Jersey City by influential Catholics, there is no record of any public opposition by any member of the local hierarchy to any act of his. On the contrary, his anti-Communist and anti-CIO crusades have been praised and his suppressions of civil liberties have been defended. For his part, his police have prevented the sale of printed matter to which the Catholic Church objected, while they have never suppressed gambling games sponsored by the Church; the school board has on it always a majority of Catholics; and the political organization has been used to collect funds for Catholic enterprises. If the Hague organization can be compared with that of any European dictator, the best comparison is with that of Franco in Spain, for both Hague and Franco have had the support of the Catholic Church and either would fall the moment the Church should withdraw its favor. Hague was opposed to the proposed new constitution for New Jersey for many reasons, chief among them, perhaps, that it would have deprived him of his influence on the state courts and would have ended his immunity from legislative investigations. The constitution would not have affected the Catholic Church one way or another; but the hierarchy sent out last-minute instructions for all Catholics to vote against it; and it was defeated in 1944.

Hague is also notable among American bosses for the ruthlessness with which he crushes little opponents. He will make terms with the big and powerful, as he did with the CIO in the free-speech fight; but an individual who actively opposes him runs every risk, from physical violence to a long term in the penitentiary. Of the many examples that might be cited, the case of John Longo is recent and typical. Since he came of voting age, John Longo has taken seriously his school education about democracy, and he has therefore opposed Hague actively, working and speaking against him and his machine. As a result he has been beaten and jailed. No private employer in Hudson County has dared to give him a job. He finally got one in the office of the County Superintendent of Elections—a Republican elected by the legislature. But in 1943 he was arrested, charged with altering voting records in that he had changed his designation on the books from *Republican* to *Democrat*. This charge he stoutly denied.

He was tried, nevertheless, and convicted. Before he was sentenced, an expert on questioned documents testified in an investigation conducted by Governor Edison that before Longo's trial he had been hired by Hague's county prosecutor, Daniel O'Reagen, to examine the record, and further that he had informed O'Reagen as a result of his examination that in his judgment the record had never been altered as charged. This testimony O'Reagen never presented to the court. When Longo's lawyer appealed to Judge Thomas H. Brown, a Republican judge long friendly to the Hague organization, for a new trial based upon this evidence, the judge not only denied the motion but sentenced Longo to eighteen months to three years in jail. Even if he had been guilty as charged, he had committed no very serious offense, and a year and a half to three years in jail was out of all proportion to it. But the gravest doubts existed as to whether he was guilty at all; indeed, there was expert testimony that no crime had ever been committed by anybody in the case.

This is what happens to opponents of the vice-chairman of the Democratic National Committee in his home town. But through all the years that he has been in power in Jersey City, no adherent of his has ever been convicted of any kind of election fraud, although thousands of pages of testimony of their existence have been presented to any number of grand juries. Any known type of election fraud may be illustrated from this mass of testimony.

The Hague organization is notable as well for the extent to which it has imposed the financial burden of an enormous public payroll upon a community. When Hague became mayor the tax rate was $2.10, but the residents of Jersey City paid in 1944 a tax rate of $6.16 on each $100 of assessed valuation of their property. Assessments are now as nearly as humanly possible 100 per cent of true value as required by law; they were brought to this level by a new county tax board, appointed by Governor Edison. Until his action, assessments ran as low as 10 per cent or as high as 1500 per cent of true value, depending upon how the taxpayer stood with the organization. But the total burden of taxes imposed upon Jersey City is the heaviest for any city of its size in the country, is so heavy, in fact, that the last census showed a loss of population to surrounding cities and counties. The Hague organization in recent years has been eating into the capital of the community. Jersey City and Hudson County, long bankrupt in fact, would have been legally bankrupt when the assessments were reduced except for the war prosperity. When that passes, collapse appears to be inevitable.

Frank Hague's public career has been a series of crises, but he has survived them all and accumulated a fortune of around four millions of dollars. The crises of the Edison administration have shaken him, however, as no others ever did, and may very well have prepared the way for his eventual downfall.

When in 1940 he induced Charles Edison, then Secretary of the Navy, to run for governor, he may have thought from Edison's mild manner that he would be as easy to manage as other governors. He may have thought that, because Edison until 1932 had been entirely absorbed in the business his father founded, he would be so politically naïve that he would allow Hague to do his thinking for him. The boss was never more mistaken in his life.

During the campaign, at a meeting at Sea Girt with Hague on the platform, Edison announced that if elected, he would be a yes-man only to his own conscience. He took no campaign expense money from Hague and little advice. He ran his own campaign. When the poll books of Jersey City were burned to prevent an investigation, he denounced the action in unmistakable language.

A break between Edison and Hague was inevitable, for Charles Edison felt that he had been elected by all of the people of the state and not alone by Frank Hague. He was thoroughly honest, and he did not seek office for its emoluments. He was determined, moreover, to be governor in fact. He was not used to being bossed, and his will was just as strong as Hague's.

Shortly after he became governor, a vacancy occurred on the Supreme Court, and Edison appointed Frederic R. Colie, one of the most respected members of the New Jersey bar. But

Colie had denounced the appointment of Frank Hague, Jr., at the time it was made, and Hague was mortally offended. He resolved to fight the governor at every opportunity.

The first chance came when Edison sought to revise New Jersey's antiquated laws taxing railroads. The taxes were so heavy and so inflexible that they were driving the smaller railroads into bankruptcy. A committee of experts, at the governor's direction, drafted a plan for a new system of taxation that would take account of the railroads' income.[5] Hague fought the plan with every means at his command. At the expense of the taxpayers of Jersey City, he published full-page advertisements in every daily newspaper in the state. Time was when all of Hague's opponents were Reds, or communists; now he conjured up a railroad lobby, and all opponents from Governor Edison to the *Newark Evening News* were called "tools of the railroad lobby." The most palpably false charges were made, and the most weird arithmetic was used to show what revenues the new scheme would bring in. Hague lined up all his legislators against the bills, but they were not enough. The bills passed substantially in the form recommended by the governor's committee. Hague induced the Attorney-General, David T. Wilentz, to bring a court action to declare the acts unconstitutional. Since they have gone into effect they have produced far more revenue than the old laws ever did, both for the state and for the municipalities, including Hague's. Though this extra money has helped to postpone the bankruptcy of Jersey City, the mayor has been so embarrassed by the fact that his city has received hundreds of thousands of dollars more, when he predicted less, that his city budgets do not anticipate the amount that the State Comptroller says is available. The city takes the money and spends it, nonetheless.

The second phase of the Hague-Edison struggle occurred over the revision of the New Jersey constitution. Edison had campaigned for a constitutional convention, and Hague had raised no objections, probably assuming that because constitu-

5. A full account of the new taxes was published by the governor, *The New Taxes on Railroads in New Jersey, by Governor Charles Edison* (pamphlet, Trenton, N. J., 1943).

tional reform had been urged by almost every governor since the Civil War and since nothing had ever come of it, nothing would come of it at this late date. But he underestimated the governor's dogged persistence. Edison attacked the defects of the constitution in speeches all over the state; at every opportunity he urged the legislature to act; and at his inspiration a nonpartisan organization was established to promote constitutional reform. In the last year of his administration, the legislature passed a bill to refer to the people at the election of 1943 the question whether the legislature of 1944 should be empowered to act as a constitutional convention. Hague, of course, fought the referendum through his agents and with another series of full-page advertisements. His allied Republican organizations likewise opposed it. The governor, however, toured the state and published in pamphlet form a series of his speeches on the constitution. To the consternation of Hague, the referendum carried by 154,000 majority. As the mayor has become a symbol of democracy at its worst, Edison has become to the people of his state a symbol of what democracy ought to be. No governor of New Jersey, at least since Woodrow Wilson, so captured the confidence and good will of the people.

In spite of his popular following, however, the governor could not get at Hague in his most vital spot—his control of the judiciary of his county. The common pleas judges in New Jersey have wide, common law powers; a majority of a panel of them can purge grand juries and jury lists, and they can conduct criminal trials with considerable discretion. They are appointed by the governor for terms of five years. Hudson County has four common pleas judges, and during Edison's term three vacancies occurred among them. He nominated three honest and independent lawyers; but the state senate, Republican by seventeen to three, confirmed only one of them, so that there was no majority possible. What means Hague used to obtain this co-operation from his nominal political opponents has not been revealed, and never may be. But in view of the extremely grave danger that an independent judiciary would present to him and to his organization, it may be imagined that he used every available means of persuasion.

In his old age Frank Hague must feel some sense of frustration, in spite of the fact that he rose from the slums of the Horseshoe to become Jersey City's first citizen. He must regret that, being known not only all over America but all over the world, he is everywhere most unfavorably known. He must feel disappointed that, in spite of his millions, he cannot, like a successful businessman, retire to enjoy them; he must, as long as he lives, maintain his control to keep covered up the ways in which he obtained them. It may not bother him, but he must know that when he goes he will leave the city of his birth bankrupt, and the life of the community corrupted beyond anything ever seen in the Republic.

IV

INTERPRETATION

28

THE VOTER'S POLITICIAN
"The Voter's Other Self"

BY J. T. SALTER

THE POLITICIANS (OR PUBLIC MEN, I USED THE TERM interchangeably) are the men who govern through suasion, talk, discussion, jobs, and all that sort of thing. Here the emphasis is on wit, the reasonable position, or a flair for presenting a compromise acceptable to conflicting groups. "Finality is not the language of politics," and neither is force. The politician does not in normal times take a stand on a controversial issue. And who does? The individuals who do, stand alone, and a politician cannot afford to stand alone. Neither can he afford the luxury of love and hate, for numbers are important to him. He is necessarily a tolerant man because his success depends on the favorable response of his constituents, and they may be of every race, creed, and color. He lives outside of himself; he is interested in the life around him. He has got to be. He has been called the symbol of the last best hope of earth. And he is a symbol of ourselves too. A modern bible might put it, *By your politicians are ye known.* He is as he is because his constituents—a controlling number—are as they are. A people that cannot pick the right politician will perish, or, rather, self government among such people will perish.

"The most important task confronting the people in a democracy is that of picking the right politicians."[1] This was

[1] "Some of these politicians are leaders and others are just symbols of the status quo. They are men elected to the 800,000 or so elective offices in the United States, and the authentic politicians among them are elected not once, but many times. They—and in some cases their sponsors, who send them rather than hold office themselves—are the government—national, state, and local. They chart the public policies which, in this day of the positive-service state—will largely

true one hundred years ago, but it is even more true today. For we have passed through total war and are trying to find creative peace, security, and prosperity in a reconverted world. The need for positive and constructive help of the government during the days, and, we hope, generations, of peace to come in fostering conditions where human initiative will be most likely to seek and find its own expression and fulfillment, is no less great than it was on December 8, 1941, after the massacre of Pearl Harbor.

For just as 12,000,000 men fighting independently against this nation's enemies but without regard to central supervision or organization of any sort, would be fantastic and futile, so it would be shortsighted folly for our 135,000,000 people, our thousands of industrial, commercial, and agricultural enterprises to follow their own devices without any regard at all to co-ordination and to the outer society of which they are an integral part. In peace we live in a social-service state. The role of the government is positive. It touches and modifies our lives in a myriad ways, not only everyday, but every minute

---

set the conditions under which life is to be carried on in this country."—*The American Politician*, J. T. Salter, ed. (Chapel Hill, 1938), p. vii.

"A leader is one who leads, and knows the ropes; a politician is one who knows the ropes."—J. T. Salter, *The Pattern of Politics* (New York, 1940), p. 112.

"The politician is usually a specialist in the art of governing, either in a neighborhood or in a nation. He is a person who takes a hand in nominating and electing himself or someone else to public office and who spends his time between elections in exercising and maintaining whatever political power he has cornered. He usually campaigns because he definitely wants to direct the course of local, state, or national government. In the majority of cases, however, the politician is as much interested in getting public recognition and in the excitement of political life as he is in the job itself; and his interest is neither casual nor spasmodic. Politics with him not only amounts to a profession, but actually *is* one.

"It is a profession whose subject matter is human nature, whose data, like the lore of the medicine man among the Indians, is retained only in the minds of the living. Sometimes it is passed from father to son, or from friend to friend; but much is irretrievably lost whenever a politician dies. This body of knowledge that *is* politics, is the folklore of all the city halls of the land; it is the living language of the county court houses, the vivid and real talk in the corridors of state legislatures, and the personal conversations on the fringe of Congress. Much of it is as evanescent as smoke or as plum blossoms in spring, but sometimes a word, an expression or an idea is permanently fixed in the annals of the craft." J. T. Salter, "The Politician and the Voter," *The American Political Scene*, Edward B. Logan, ed. (New York, 1936), p. 89.

of every day. And the human expression of the government is the politician.

Why? What good does he do for the people? What is the nature of this indispensable service that he renders the public? Readers may ask these questions. Some will doubtless say, "The Politician—isn't he the fellow who steals your pot to cook your goose?" Or Wendell Phillips: "Politicians are like the bones of a horse's foreshoulder—not a straight one in it." Yet the discerning individual knows that the public does untold harm to itself—to the very cause of free government—when it unfairly criticizes its own servants, the elected politicians, or when it fails to reward the meritorious ones with commendations, with a smile, with the equivalent of such words as, "Well done."

This matter is of first importance because people tend to be what we expect them to be. And what gets our attention gets us. If the public cannot quite give its attention to its politician, save to speak of him as a fool or a crook, how can the politician be expected to do his best in the public service? The answer is, he cannot. And neither could the rest of us. Man works for social approbation as well as for money, but if the former is denied and the latter minimized, the conditions under which the politician's work (that is, the public's work) is done are unnecessarily bad. Wastefully bad, and at a cost, according to Merriam, of billions of dollars each year.[2]

Burke spoke most eloquently and wisely on the subject one hundred and sixty-five years ago. We seem as much in need of his words of advice today as were the voters in Bristol in 1780. (Substitute the words "private interest" for the word "court" in the following):

Gentlemen, we must not be peevish with those who serve the people: for none will serve us, whilst there is a court to serve, but those who are of a nice and jealous honour.... We shall either drive such men from the public stage, or we shall send them to the court for protection: where, if they may sacrifice their reputation, they will at least secure their interest.[3]

2. "Boycott of Government Costly," *Public Management*, XIV (April, 1932), 115.

3. Works of Burke, Speech at Bristol, The World's Classics edition, III, 4.

Ten years earlier Burke had said: "Men are in public life as in private, some good, some evil. The elevation of the one, and the depression of the other, are the first objects of all true policy." [4]

And incidentally, this is the reason why a free government is the most difficult of all governments to maintain, requiring more initiative and nervous energy on the part of the people generally than does any other type. For here the voter must pay attention to what is going on; otherwise he will not know whose hands to uphold. A politician cannot serve the people all alone—the people must help; they must know whom to elevate and whom to depress. That is the crux of the people's function in a democracy.

The politician works out the acceptable compromise. And the principle of compromise is to democracy what imagination is to poetry or precision is to physics or sympathy is to preaching. It is the crux of the matter, the thing without which the subject could not exist or could not exist in anything like its present state.

Roosevelt on March 28, 1945, wrote a letter to Senator Elbert Thomas urging the Senate to adopt the conference re-

4. *Ibid.*, II, 33. The little politicians whose names appear on ballots wherever men are elected to office, by the people, are condemned so widely that one might conclude either that one does not like to look searchingly at himself in a mirror or that a universal campaign of defamation is being waged against the garden variety of politicians, from the President down. Appointive centers of control and power like our State Department seem more apt to work with a Petain than a De Gaulle, with a Badoglio than a Salvemini, with a Hapsburg than an Austrian republican, with a Franco than a Spanish Loyalist. And there seems to be a tendency to speak of that more remote politics as "statesmanship" in deliberate contrast with the activities of the elected men immediately responsible to the people. The fact that this kind of politics *is* "remote" may even partially explain its prestige; for possibly the voter is sometimes more impressed with figures he cannot clearly see than with those he meets face to face. We believe that the State Department's argument for dealing with the Darlans, Petains, Badoglios, and The Emperor, Son of Heaven, is that these are the people that are in office, and that it would be more difficult to deal with a liberal out of office. Our rejoinder to that argument is that this war was fought, first to save our own hides, but secondly to destroy the power of the authoritarian governments that produced the war, and to foster the liberal forces in any country where presumably those forces would have the support of the people in a free vote.

port on the manpower bill. The President said that the compromise was not all that the Army and Navy or he wanted, but, "in a controversial matter of this kind, legislation can be enacted only as a result of a compromise." Congress may be described as the institution that resolves the conflicts of a nation into workable compromises.

A great speech by Edmund Burke is called *Conciliation* with America. Conciliation is a synonym for compromise. If Burke's ideas had been followed there would have been no war—but that is not important now; however, part of Burke's great discussion is pertinent here and will be important as long as men discuss a free society.

All government, indeed every human benefit and enjoyment, every virtue, and every prudent act, is founded on compromise and barter. We balance inconveniences; we give and take; We remit some rights, that we may enjoy others; and we choose rather to be happy citizens, than subtle disputants.[5]

T. V. Smith has more recently written about the subject:

A man is not a good man who will compromise the core of himself—that is, the final principles by which he lives. But a man is not a good citizen who does not meet other citizens halfway.[6]

Any way it's put, the truth stands out that the politician is performing an indispensable service (the zig zag path of his compromises in the past we call civilization).[7]

President Truman's report on the Potsdam conference shows that world politics is like ward politics on this basic matter of compromise. In speaking of what was done about Poland the President said: "Nearly every international agreement has in it the element of compromise. The agreement on Poland is no exception. No one nation can expect to get everything that it

5. *Ibid.*, p. 226.
6. T. V. Smith, *The Legislative Way of Life* (Chicago, 1940), pp. 77-78.
7. Leonard D. White and T. V. Smith, *Politics and Public Service* (New York, 1939), p. 245.

wants. It is a question of give and take—of being willing to meet your neighbor half-way."

The merest glance at our history shows the presence of compromise at every turn, and at minor ones too. Our constitution, the institution of which we are most proud, is a "bundle of compromises." Henry Clay called it "a magnificent compromise." It was created out of the life and experiences of a people, by politicians who knew that finality was not for them, and neither was perfection—nor the precise choice of any. These remarkable fifty-five delegates took the second, third, maybe the sixth best thing, and created a constitution that has endured.

One needs only to examine a law passed by a town meeting, or by Congress or by any other legislative body to find examples of compromise. The peaceful way involves compromise. Only war and death ignore it. And the fact that the voter accepts it rather than insisting on his own first extreme demands indicates that he has a kind of political maturity, and that is the stuff a democracy is built on. It suggests the reason why we have two parties instead of thirty or forty.

A recent example of compromise may be seen by examining the Social Security Act:

A survey of the one-hundred and eight amendments made to the original bill shows that each legislator was willing to support the act as long as his constituents' interests were included. For in each amendment one can discover benefits for one particular group of people: the aged, the crippled, the returning service men, the people connected with the preparation of fruits and vegetables for market, the blind, certain states, the individuals operating homes for children and indigent or aged persons, the husbands and widowers of insured wives, certain nurses, domestic servants, the Indians, and certain dependent children. Each amendment was a part of a great compromise and therefore was representative of the democratic way of life.[8]

The politician is the one in the democratic process that brings about the acceptable solution that is a compromise. That is the principle upon which his elective office is based. For people

8. E. Wilson, "Compromise and Democracy." An unpublished Stanford University student research paper, 1943.

of divergent and diverging viewpoints must vote for him for many different reasons. The familiar expression, "What strange bedfellows politics makes," suggests this. Therefore it is not odd that the politician is useful in suggesting the acceptable compromise and concession for others.

The politician approximates the majority and familiarizes the issue. He is very much like the rest of us—not the best, not the worst either, although there are examples of each in our politics. But on the whole the men we elect again and again are like the great majority of the people. They are like the people, only more so. Some other writer, I think it was Mark Twain, remarked that Americans are most characteristically themselves at election time. They do not pick strangers or foreigners when they go to the polls. They pick themselves.[9] In selecting a surgeon or a musician they may aim at getting the best professional man or artist they can find. But who knows what the "best" in politics is? And a smile or some minor benefit in the hand today can be recognized on the spot as something good. These, however, offer no clue to "the best." When voters mark the ballot they are thinking of someone like themselves—or as they imagine that they would like to be. The words "blood of my blood, and bone of my bone" seem applicable, so applicable that when many politicians are criticized, when the breed is condemned, an entire socio-political process is involved. It is an indictment against the whole people, or those who elected them, and those who failed to vote, or to vote for better ones. It furthermore raises the question of self-government itself: Are the people capable of governing themselves? They are not if they cannot pick candidates devoted to the public interest. Our history shows that we can

9. Strickland Gillilan, the fine American humorist, has made a most interesting comment in this connection: "No misfit in an elective office should be blamed for being there. It isn't his fault. He didn't put himself there. He didn't hide his weaknesses and he didn't elect himself. For every crackpot or incompetent noodlehead in Congress—either branch—there are from 10,000 to 50,000 crackpots, incompetent noodleheaded voters in his electorate who put him there with full knowledge of what they were doing to themselves and to the rest of the country. When you find a belt buckle or a side comb in the soup, you don't cuss that belt buckle or side comb do you? No. You say, "How come that fool cook uses the soup pot for a trash basket?""

do this, not unfailingly but usually; and this is democracy's strength.

The politician is the voter's alter ego. He is the representative of a thousand, a million, or 135,000,000 little politicians—for each of us has a smack of the politician in us. We believe in peaceful persuasion instead of brute force, in a compromise that recognizes all interests involved rather than in the exact point of anyone. We are interested more in the spirit of the law than in its liberal observance. Our loyalty is likely to be to a friend instead of a principle, yet we believe in "fair play" and that honesty actually is the best policy. The politician believes this too, or he would not be re-elected. Our politician may be wrong, but he is not out of step for long; the voter takes care of that. The voter's public man is his other self—at the court of St. James's, in Congress, in the governor's mansion, or in the county board. The voter has a stake in what goes on in these places, and the politician is the physical embodiment of this psychic stake.

The politicians are the government that runs the government. They are the government; they are the President and the members of Congress and the other elected people in this country. One may think that the President, or the Congress, or the Constitution are fixed immutable institutions beyond the reach of human passions, whims, and fancies. Actually, of course the government is the men who run the government. And these men are politicians, or they are put in office by politicians. They are necessary to democracy because the people, 135,000,000 or more of us, cannot act directly on the myriad problems that make up the work of the government—all the governments. For the most part the sovereign citizen from time to time delegates his authority to elected persons: mayors, town chairmen, aldermen, sheriffs, assemblymen, governors, senators—the executives and legislators who formulate and execute the governmental policies of the people.

A contemporary who says that one woman will do just as well as a wife as any other woman, is no more idiotic than old Samuel Johnson would be today if he were to repeat his comment made in 1772: "I would not give half a guinea to live under one form of government rather than another. It is no moment to the happiness of an individual." The statement was not true then; much less is it true now. Government is important to the individual because correct decisions on issues of life and death, are important. The politicians are the government. They are something more, too. They are indispensable to our democratic society.

They are the ones who make the incomprehensible state meaningful to the voter. Or if this does not always happen, if the politician doesn't always make the issue clear (and all of us know that he doesn't) he does what he can to stand in the spotlight himself. His success at staying in office—in all cases where party organization is not strong—depends on it. And if he makes himself positively visible to the voter, some great good is done in our democracy. For the citizen has in that ubiquitous individual, the perennial politician, someone that can be personally and privately, or socially and publicly, kicked or applauded, opposed or supported. The right to do this, and better still the actual doing it—voting and speaking for or against—is a psychic stake that more than 50,000,000 adults have in American democracy. It is one step in the process that we call self-government. It is not an inconsequential step either; in taking it the voter reaches out beyond himself and participates in the managing of public affairs.

The world is so big it is like a thousand billion dollars; it is beyond comprehension. An incident in war or peace may bring it home to us, but, for the most part, it is the politician that cuts the world down to our size, or helps bring us up to its size. And that is the permanent need now—to see the world realistically, to see it as an interdependent whole, and to help voters see it that way rather than through the fatal spectacles of isolationism. Actually democracy is a process that weaves back and forth. The people tell the politician and he tells the people.

An outstanding vote-getter in Wisconsin, when once asked how he knew what the people wanted, answered: "I listen." and Mr. Fred Zimmerman received more votes in Wisconsin in 1944 than did Mr. Dewey. This was partly because he was a candidate for the comparatively unimportant and unexciting office of Secretary of State, for in 1945 he was overwhelmingly defeated for a place on the Supreme Court. His victories at the polls, however, were—and are—most definitely won because this candidate, like the great majority of candidates, naturally and inevitably lives according to the minor formulae of Burke: "Let us identify, let us incorporate ourselves with the people—'War with the world, and peace with our constituents.' . . ." [10] Other politicians act according to this principle too. Senator Bilbo for example recently said in his anti-poll tax filibuster, "What do I care (what the President or any one else thinks) when 99% of the people of Mississippi are 100% behind me on this question." [11]

Burke would naturally be entirely opposed to Bilbo's reasoning and he most brilliantly told why he was. He said, in speaking of the legislator, "But his unbiased opinion, his mature judgment, his enlightened conscience, he ought not to sacrifice to you: to any man, or to any set of men living. These he does not derive from your pleasure; no, nor from the law and the constitution. They are a trust from Providence, for the abuse of which he is deeply answerable. Your representative owes you, not his industry only, but his judgment; and he betrays, instead of serving you, if he sacrifices it to your opinion. . . ."

"My worthy colleague says, his will ought to be subservient to yours. If that be all, the thing is innocent. If government were a matter of will upon any side, yours, without question, ought to be superior. But government and legislation are matters of reason and judgment, and not of inclination; and what sort of reason is that, in which the determination precedes the discussion, in which one set of men deliberate, and another decide; and where those who form the conclusion are perhaps three hundred miles distant from those who hear the arguments." [12]

Logically the position stated by Burke is unanswerable, but voters are not always logical. And the voter sets the standard

10. Burke, *op. cit.,* II, 383.
11. Cf. p. 292, above.
12. *Ibid.,* pp. 164-65.

in our democracy. But the voter can be educated. The people tell the public man and he tells the people. What he tells them is the measure of his value to the democratic process. But even the greatest public man must talk guardedly in public. Some subjects are not to be mentioned lest support be alienated. What is said must be in accord with what the people think. A Borah, a La Follette, or a Norris may seem to champion a novel idea for a time—a brief time. Usually, however, the viewpoint of the legislator is the known (or unknown) viewpoint of the generality of the people in his district. Sometimes a public man achieves a position so secure in the minds and hearts of his people that he might even on certain great occasions voice opinions different from the run-of-the-mine views of his constituency. This is done sparingly, however, and only after long years of service. In 1942 Senator Norris told me that in the later years of his life he enjoyed a freedom in discussing differences of opinion with his Nebraska constituents that he dared not avail himself of as a young man in politics.

Some politicians do more telling than listening. The reformers, the Horace Greeleys in politics, are examples of this sort. Others, like the machine type of individual in politics "just listen." They do not educate anybody even as an afterthought. President Harding was such a man, and so is Frank Hague of New Jersey. Men of this caliber are living off the public—the public is a means to their private end. The reformer is of varying social value, but a large number of the most publicized ones are more interested in their favorite reform than in the wishes of the people. Their canary may be a beautiful idea, not the wants of flesh and blood humans. They do not live off the public, neither do they live for the public, save the special kind of public that they are working to create.

The politician is the hardiest fellow of all. I do not mean the machine version like Hague, but the voter's politician, or public man. He can look at life as it is, and he can do something about it. Abraham Lincoln is the classic example, but there are uncounted thousands of the breed today in rural towns, in cities, in state and national legislatures and in the presidency. These men know that democracy is not an unilateral affair. It is a give and take process. In the language of radio there are both sending and receiving stations here; voters have a positive role to play, and so do politicians.

President Roosevelt listened too, but he also spoke. A man who merely listens may be a thriving earth worm but it takes a talker who knows the issue to guide the destiny of a people. Roosevelt illustrated the nature of the valuable talker in politics when, in the course of his fourth inaugural address, he said, "Today in this year of war, 1945, we have learned lessons —at a fearful cost—and we shall profit by them. We have learned that we cannot live alone, at peace; that our own well-being is dependent on the well-being of other nations, far away. We have learned that we must live as men, not as ostriches, nor as dogs in the manger. We have learned to be citizens of the world, members of the human community."

In the case of some politician, either national or local, that is identified with views and practices that cause enlightened people to feel disgust and despair, when reading about this "Honorable Simon Pure," we should remember that the public man in question, if he has held office for a lifetime, as some of them have, is only partially responsible for his deplorable political existence. The mere fact that he is elected and re-elected means that there are thousands or millions of little Simon Pures in his constituency. These "public men" in miniature are the reason for the Public Man being as he is.

This does not mean, however, that the public man from a backward district should get off scot free in our discussion, even though he has been elected and re-elected for term after term. For the politician should never merely confirm a voter in his filth; he should help clean him up. Possibly there are one or two sketches in this volume which inadequately recognize this latter political fact.

A clergyman told me: "You take all of those men in politics, and put them under the hardest pressure that man is under in civilized life. The man who is sandstone crumbles; the man of putty is shaped by the business interests or by some other pressure groups; the man of granite breaks the mold of the pressures." This is an attractive theory and a false one. It suggests that everything depends on the individual politician; and that is not true. It depends on the individual politician plus the other politicians, living and dead, plus the people. Furthermore, if the mold of the pressures are changed, they will be changed not by a granite man, but by an accommodating individual who is also an artist in explaining his viewpoint to the other fellow or to the public.

Our educators, clergymen, movies, radios, newspapers, magazines, and books may join in a concerted drive to shape a specific opinion (it's not so public as it is preponderent) to create a situation that the politician must act upon. An excellent example of this sort of thing is the 202-203 House vote to keep an army at all, right on the eve of Pearl Harbor. It seems that a free discussion of the question might have saved the army by more than the margin of one vote. That one vote was not secured by public discussion. Men that could not see the issue were buttonholed by members of the House and persuaded to vote the right way for friendship's sake.

Oscar Wilde once said that all wives are the same, but all women are different. In somewhat the same sense, all politicians are the same politician, but all men are different. Of course, neither statement is entirely true, but each statement approaches the truth. Not all men are different in all ways, but individual men, or men *qua* men can act in a greater variety of ways than can politicians act in their role as politicians.

A bright young man from a New York publishing house told me that he had worked to help elect the highly educated Congressman XYZ the first time he ran, but he added, "I will not work for him again." I inquired why he had lost his enthusiasm for the brilliant Honorable XYZ. I was told, "Because he acts just like every other congressman." I suggested that the institution known as Congress or as politician in its own peculiar way creates a pattern or orbit according to, or within which, the congressman, as politician, works, and lives, and dies. Everyone in politics is influenced by everyone else in politics. No congressman can live unto himself alone. What he does in Congress invariably depends not only on what other members of the legislative body do, but on what his predecessors through uncounted sessions have done. There is no substitute for brains, either in Congress or in life; but brains alone are not enough. Chairman Sabath of the Rules Committee, in his thirty-ninth year in Congress, told me that experience is the thing that counts most. "We go on seniority in Congress because a man must be here a few terms before he can be informed on his duties." John M. Robsion, Kentucky Republican serving his twenty-fourth year in the House, remarked: "Take it by and large, seniority is a pretty fair thing." A. S. Mike Monroney, Democrat from Oklahoma serving his fourth term in Congress, said while vice-chairman of the Joint Committee on the Organization of Congress that "seniority is of great value up to a point. But if it is to work, it must be made to progress. Maybe a man should be chosen for committee chairman according to the seniority principle, but after he has held that place for about six years, a change should be made. The next man should be moved up. He would have all of the advantages of the preceding chairman in experience; he should also have the opportunity for leadership. Make the line move." Robert M. LaFollette, senator since 1925 and chairman of the Joint Committee, very largely agrees with Monroney, and he adds: "It is easier to criticize seniority than to find a substitute for it. Probably the best change that could be made is to prevent a man from serving indefinitely; maybe the next man in line should be moved up after six years."

III

A news story early in 1945 about a soldier and a medal of honor interests me very much. It makes me wonder what a politician would have to do to have a medal conferred on him. Actually politicians are not awarded medals—they are apt to receive unsavory epithets, not epaulets. This is very strange, or at least regrettably unfortunate, for our soldiers fight for democracy and that democracy cannot exist without politicians; at least it has never managed to do so as yet.

While the politician does his work well we do not need soldiers on any battle field. It is only when government by politicians breaks down that millions of our soldiers face suffering and death in war. It must be obvious to the dullest that all of us should do what can reasonably and effectively be done to maintain and strengthen the politician and the government. I suggest that there are just as compelling and unanswerable arguments for giving an appropriate medal of honor to a politician as to a soldier. The ego of the former is as certain to respond to public recognition as is the morale of the armed warrior. America must give effective recognition to both, and she will too, when we become as wise in our politics and politicians as we are in our armies and fighting men.

Major Richard I. Bong is the soldier in the news item. He shot down thirty-eight Japanese planes and has been awarded the Congressional Medal of Honor. The medal was given for "Conspicuous gallantry and intrepedity in action above and beyond the call of duty in the southwest Pacific area from October 10 to November 15, 1944." The item adds that Major Bong was assigned to duty as a gunnery instructor and was not expected to enter into combat service, but he did. Major Bong voluntarily and at his own urgent request engaged in repeated combat missions and shot down eight enemy air planes during this period.

I cannot imagine any person objecting to the distinguished recognition given to this most valuable and intrepid warrior. Yet a soldier has in a sense a more favored time than a public man. The former risks his life, but the latter may place his immortal soul in jeopardy not once, but many times. The soldier has arduous, maybe bitter days and nights living out of doors, sleeping on the ground—getting shot at too. The politician may work late into the night, every night, on a more perfect piece of legislation and then see it defeated or amended beyond recognition. He may serve the people faithfully every waking minute of every day for two years, or four or more years and then suffer defeat at the polls right in the first blush of his most creative period. He may begin to construct a super-highway, or a new city plan, or in a totally different field, he might work to reorganize the administrative side of our government, and just before he accomplishes his great objective, he is defeated. In the months following his defeat he may see the work of a lifetime overturned, come to naught. Winston Churchill tried to arouse the conscience, the mind, of England to the positive danger of war, but he failed; and yet in the months and years of his failure he saw war coming on just as he had predicted it would. The horror of that vision must be as awful as anything witnessed by soldiers in actual warfare.

The soldier has a decided advantage in that he can most definitely recognize the enemy, his enemy and his country's enemy. But how can the politician recognize the people's enemy? Sometimes it can easily be done, but on other occasions the detection of truth and error, good or evil, and their protagonists, is not easy. It may be impossible until it is too late. It was in France.

The soldier works in the field of absolutes, but the politician, like Einstein, is forever concerned with relativity. If the soldier shoots a man the man stays shot; but the politician may make a great speech today, and later feel that he must make an even better speech a week from today or the situation is lost. A president or governor may have a working majority in the legislature during the first part of his term but not the last. There are no absolutes in politics. Everything is relative and everything is constantly changing. A favorable majority in the legislature or at the polls may change overnight into an unfavorable minority. The politician must forever strive for the objective; only in war is the battle won once and for all.

The politician may hear the truth he has spoken "twisted by knaves to make a trap for fools," or he may see it unheeded or ignored as though he had never lived—never uttered a word. Yet he may know, and later the history books might record and verify, his truth. In fact the history books do verify and celebrate the politicians' truth more often than that of the soldier. Yet the politician of all men must be recognized on the instant, on the day that the ballots are marked, or he will be denied official place; he will be defeated if he does not have this positive approval on election day. A million votes after the polls close are not worth as much as one single ballot vote before the polling ceases. As I have said before, the politician is contemporaneous. And to be that he must get attention; more than that he must have favorable response. He must get the voter to act, and to act according to the politician's interpretation of the facts.

This means that his life is one of action, dramatization, and contact with people. He must feel the passion of the day, he must be part of it, he must express it; I mean he must express the nature and significance of the issue or problem that confronts the people so that the people will better know the truth or the facts, and consequently be in a better position to work out their own salvation. For we now know, if we know anything, that if any good is achieved by the people, the people themselves will have to do it. There is no one to do it for them. The politician is an agent or tool that they use in governing themselves; the soldier is a warrior-agent that they use in defending themselves. However, it is important to remember that either in case of the politician or the soldier we have the citizen too—the citizen as politician or as a soldier, always the citizen. But the citizen takes more naturally to politics than he does to armed warfare. He volunteers for politics, but he is drafted for war. And that is right and proper, for America has achieved its greatness under politicians, not generals. Of course we are what we are because of both our politicians and our soldiers. (And they are what they are because of us.) But the primary importance of the civil authorities, the politicians, was recognized as early as 1787 when the Constitution was drafted. It provides that the military shall be subject to the non-military or civil. The President is to be commander-in-chief of the Army and Navy and not the other way around. Congress declares war, not the Army. Yet we give the army medals, but have none for Congress.

The army likes its medals. In Ernie Pyle's *Brave Men* there is the remark that no matter how a soldier may joke about a medal, he never misses the ceremony at which a medal is to be conferred on him. He wants it. I think a politician might want it too if the people ever got interested in the idea, if some institution were established to award a medal now and then for some great service to a great cause. There might even be the counterpart of the Purple Heart for one who labored mightily and failed. I am not now concerned with how the committee would award the medal or how often or on what occasion or with the method of selecting the committee or its personnel. Here I merely want to point out the incontestable fact that the politician deserves credit as well as censure. His cup is running over with criticism. Friends of democracy should also give him praise.

I say this because I want to direct attention to the political function in our democracy, and more particularly to the voter and *his* politician. I say the voter too, because the voter sets the standard and the politician comes up to it.

It is important to know that the awarding of the palm instead of the boot to the politician will work both ways. It will help the politician's morale; he will feel more pride in his work. This will happen because the voter's attention will encourage it. People will see their politicians or public men as individuals valuable to our democracy. Physicians and dentists are recognized as useful and necessary members of our society now; so are plumbers, ditch diggers, and undertakers. Politicians are useful and necessary too, but often we fail to realize this simple fact. Our neglect costs us, the people, untold millions of dollars, for any servant that is not adequately appreciated is not able to do his best. We should come more and more to see that politics is not only one of the most strenuous arts that men follow, but it is also one of the noblest.

A George W. Norris might faithfully and effectively serve his state and his nation for a life time, he might bring about the creation of a giant public electric system, TVA, a system that revolutionizes the life of a region; and near the end of his life he is defeated at the polls and goes home after a long day well spent, with great sorrow in his heart, and shortly thereafter dies.

How much more fitting for America and for all public men, as well as for Senator Norris and his family in particular, if he had been awarded a medal of some sort—a medal comparable to the concrete recognition a gallant soldier receives for conspicuous service to his country. It might be a Carnegie Medal or a Nobel Prize or a Pulitzer Prize. Better still I think it should be something entirely new. It might be called *The People's Medal* or *The American Prize*. It might be awarded to an elected person for service of extraordinary value to his country. Who will do the awarding and who will receive the award are problems to be worked out in the future. And such problems can be. The existence of innumerable prizes or medals or honorary degrees in this country today indicates that the awarding of distinctions in any number of fields can be done with great, if not unanimous approval.

The words "conspicuous gallantry" are words beyond comparison in war or in peace. But in times of tranquility people are likely to associate those royal words with warlike deeds. I suggest the need for symbols or royal words for the politician doing the work of the citizen—the citizen *qua* citizen. The public man cannot live by words alone, and neither can he live without them. In the days of peace ahead we might come to realize that the sympathetic understanding of the politician, in neighborhood and nation, is of public value to us and our country as truly as is our appreciation of the gallantry of the soldier or the honor and virtue of men and women. For we agree that "the enduring institutions of a people are not made by cavalry charges. The victories of peace 'are to be won not in days but in centuries, and by the energy not of feeling but of thought.' " [13]

IV

A congressman in a world at war who refuses to look at the lesson of history unfolding before him, or one who looks and not seeing, votes against such measures as the repeal of the arms embargo in 1939, the conscription bill in 1940, the extension of the period of draft in 1941, the lend lease bill of 1941, the Fulbright Resolution in 1943, and the United Nations Relief and Rehabilitation Act of 1944 is some day likely to strike many voters as not good enough. And even if these voters do not say to him what Henry IV of France once said to a soldier who was not present on the day of battle: "Hang yourself,

13. Works of T. H. Green, III, 354. Cited by D. W. Morrow, Introductory essay, in Anson D. Morse, *Parties and Party Leaders* (Boston, 1923), p. xx.

brave Crillon; we fought at Arques today, and you were not there," yet they will at least think that their congressman has outlived his usefulness. (I assume that there are two sides to political questions. I also assume that the findings of history may or may not verify the validity of the opinions that we hold today. My thesis here—to cite one example—is that this world war involved the United States whether Congress passed lend-lease or not. The passage of this measure made it possible for the United States and the other United Nations to win the war against the Axis. If I am in error in holding these conclusions, my argument that follows for *discussing the issue* is still valid; even more valid, for in the latter case, the voters in 425 districts, not merely the ten mentioned above, need the winnowing of truth from error that comes with two-way discussion. I would not be so sure of the value of discussion if a fact were ever enough to change an opinion. It seems that a fact cannot explain itself; discussion of the fact, or issue, is necessary.)

The elections of 1944 probably revealed the American electorate educated by the impact of war to a new interest in world affairs. Not completely educated, however, for ten out of twelve congressmen who voted against all of the above measures were re-elected. In many constituencies, however, back in 1939-41, the controlling electorate was no more, or not much more, interested in voting favorably on the above measures than were their representatives; and that is the reason why their representatives voted as they did—because they were the people's representatives. The question is: If the people do not know the issue, who will tell them?

V

I have a suggestion. It is based on the incontestable fact that civic education is the only secure basis for a democracy. I am here interested in the probable idea that effective knowledge was lacking in the ten districts that support congressmen who voted against all the foreign-relations measures that have been mentioned; measures that seemed necessary to Bricker and Dewey, as well as to Truman and Roosevelt and millions of other Americans. The significant thing here is, not merely to know a fact, but to realize the implication of that fact. This means discussion. How can discussion of the issue in the ten congressional districts and in the other districts be implemented? My answer is, to require official newspaper publication in each county in the United States, of an *official roll call plus*.

First, the smallest city cannot vote on the adoption or rejection of a new charter until the proposed charter is first published in a newspaper or distributed in pamphlet form among the voters. The same publication requirement applies to the submission of charter amendments. Or, before a bond issue for the construction of a school house, a sewer, or anything else that involves more than five hundred dollars can be voted on by the people, a descriptive statement about the bond issue must usually first be advertised in a newspaper. Or, if the people of the state vote on a constitutional amendment, newspaper publication of the proposed amendment must precede the election, and, of course, this is true in case of an initiative or referendum measure. Newspaper publication is invariably required by law.

In each case, the purpose of publication of the pertinent facts before voting is to do at least this much to insure an informed vote. The idea is, that if the charter is published in a newspaper or made easily available in pamphlet form, the voter is more likely to inform himself before voting than would otherwise be the case. It is true that some voters will not read the charter, or the amendment, or the description of the bond issue, no matter how widely it is published before the election. It is also true that some people do not vote, but we do not consider voting useless for that reason. In many elections the majority of people do vote, and a controlling number among them are interested in knowing what the question is on which they are voting. This required publication helps them find out.

If it is recognized public policy throughout the United States to require the publication of charters and charter amendments before the people can vote on them, and it is, why would it not be equally valuable to require the publication of the congressman's voting record? That really is the *evidence* on which the voter should judge the worth of his representative in Congress.

How does he vote on the great issues? How did *he vote on the greatest issue of all?* If the citizen cannot answer this question, no matter in which one of the 435 districts he lives, he is not a valuable voter. He not only fails himself and his country, but he fails his politician too. For just as the congressman should educate the district, so should the people in the district educate their representative in Congress. Our national legislative body formulates our national policies or ratifies policies initiated by the executive. In either case the responsibility for what Congress does is basically the people's. It belongs only secondarily to Congress. It is held accountable every two years in the lower house, every six years in the Senate. I propose that each state shall require one or two newspapers in each county to publish the pertinent voting record in Congress of the representative for that county and the United States Senator for that state. If it is important to advertise a charter or a bond issue in a newspaper, I submit that it is no less important to advertise the pertinent legislative record of congressmen and senators.

The basic idea as I see it, involves the use of an official roll call record and statement in one or two newspapers in each county on several different days preceding the primary, and on several different days at least three weeks before the congressional election. The official notice will contain a chart, showing, by the most descriptive brief title, what (1) the party in power, the administration, and (2) the party out of power, the opposition, consider to be the several most significant measures passed in the present term of Congress and the voting record of the congressman and senator on each of the measures.

Adjoining the chart will be a brief description of each measure listed on the chart. This description will be prepared by the Clerk of the House and the Secretary of the Senate, or as the administration may determine. There will also be a brief statement opposing the measure. The administration or the legislator in question will prepare one statement and the legislator or opposition party, or the Chamber of Commerce or trade union or Farm Bureau or some other group or representative individual will prepare the contrary view. In every case each statement of opinion is to be plainly identified as to author or source. It is only a device, but I think it will improve the quality of thinking and the voting of constituent and representative. It is a useful device for the voter who wants to know.

The thing that is new about my suggestion is the kind of roll call that I am urging—*an official one,* not merely another roll call, for there are many excellent ones now. Labor, agriculture, civic, and religious organizations often prepare and circulate their versions of the pertinent issues and roll call; magazines and newspapers do too. The *Capital Times* of Madison, Wisconsin, is particularly active in this connection. It publishes roll calls on the city council, the state legislature, and the representatives in Congress—enlightening editorials accompany the roll calls. The *New Republic* for May 8, 1944, published a most useful roll call on the way each Congressman voted on twenty most vital foreign and domestic measures.

The state of Oregon sends each registered voter an official voters' pamphlet before the regular general election, and before any special election at which any proposed law is to be submitted to the people. The pamphlet that I have before me looks like a full-fledged encyclopaedia of political measures and men. It is the most comprehensive document of this sort that I have seen. It contains 104 pages, the first 32 of which are devoted to initiative and referendum measures, in addition to signed arguments for and against each measure. The remaining pages carry statements and arguments in behalf of political party nominees and independent and nonpartisan candidates for the federal, state, and district offices. The candidate's picture as well as his chosen words are here, also the platforms of the Republican and Democratic parties, plus statements of recommendation for individual candidates by the state central committee of their respective parties.

The pamphlet has an attractive format and is intelligently prepared, but is very, very long. Yet in spite of its formidable size, it contains no official roll call. An official roll call is the new political device about which I am thinking. It can be given in several paragraphs in a newspaper, but if it contains the right data it might be more persuasive than a hundred-page almanac of other material.

In talking to my very good friends about one of the ten congressmen who voted against all the preparedness measures mentioned above, I was told in all sincerity and kindness, "I would suggest that you get his record from Washington, and the full record, not the one prepared by his enemies or some New Deal opponent." The *New Republic* is not either widely known or favorably known in this congressman's district, but the *Chicago Tribune* and Westbrook Pegler are. The latter are not likely to mention the pertinent record, and if the *New Republic* does, it will not count. This is where an official roll call may come in. It will be as available as the daily newspaper, as easy to read as a sales letter from *Time Magazine* and as authoritative as the government of the United States.

John Dewey said: "'The new age of human relationships' has no political agencies worthy of it. The democratic public is still largely inchoate and unorganized." [14] Later, in his chapter on "The Eclipse of the Public" he wrote:

Man, as has been often remarked, has difficulty in getting on either with or without his fellows, even in neighborhoods. He is not more successful in getting on with them when they act at a great distance in ways invisible to him. An inchoate public is capable of organization only when widest consequences are perceived, and when it is possible to project agencies which order their occurrence. At present, many consequences are felt rather than perceived; they are suffered, but they cannot be said to be known, for they are not, by those who experience them, referred to their origins. [15]

Dewey concludes his analysis of the unarticulate public with the statement that the new age in which we now live has no symbols descriptive of its activities. "Communication can alone create a great community." [16] We have the physical tools of communication—the newspaper, radio, motion picture, pamphlet, poster, the letter—but we do not have the communica-

14. John Dewey, *The Public and Its Problems* (New York, 1927), p. 109.
15. *Ibid.*, p. 131.
16. *Ibid.*, p. 142.

tions worthy of the ideals and problems of our time. The presence of a pertinent roll call will improve the value of communications.

Such a roll call might implement the new world in which we live. It points in the right direction. It says, and not only before the primary and the election, but at other times: *Here is the issue.* Your congressman says this about it. The administration, or the Farmers Union, or the Chamber of Commerce, or the P.A.C. or some other leading voice in opposition expresses this opinion. What do you—the voter, the king pin in our democratic plan—think of it? What, you say you have never heard of it? Well you are hearing of it now! And some of these issues you will continue to hear about. Hearing about them this way may be the first step in your training in the evaluation of issues. Unless you live like an ostrich with your head in the sand, you will see these issues subjected to a running fire of criticism. Before you can express a valid opinion about them you must know something about them. The roll call tells you what to study; what you must know. It points out the issue. Keep your mind on it. Democracy deserves your best opinion. Your informed opinion. Your modern opinion.

Then when you learn that your congressman voted against the public interest—as of today—you will be less likely to accept as satisfactory such inadequate answers as, "I am fearless." "I am honest." "I make the same kind of mistakes you would have made had you been here in my place." "I am against Roosevelt." "I am against the New Deal." "I am against war." "I am against Walter Winchell and international bankers." "I am against the grasping Labor." "I am against foreigners." "I am against school lunches." "I am patriotic and loyal." "I love the Constitution."

Instead of these general statements you will want to know whether or not the candidate is intelligently aware of the issue, and to know his position thereon. A thousand smiles will not negate one error. Doing errands all day long and half of the night for the constituents will not make up for the sum of the congressman's lack if he does not know—as well as he knows his own name—that future peace and security depend upon having the United States thoughtfully and incessantly working with other countries for peace.

Walter Lippmann tells the story of the absent-minded professor who while walking through the woods at twilight, accidentally bumped into a tree. He stopped, removed his hat, bowed and in a most pleasing voice said, "Excuse me, sir, I thought you were a tree." [17]

The professor's manners were very nice, but his knowledge of his environment was very bad. It really doesn't matter in this case, but suppose we have a congressman and not a mere professor. Suppose the congressman has no valid idea of his environment, of America's interdependence on the rest of the world. In this crucial present, we must understand how tragic and costly this might be for all of us. The alert electorate, the voters making up their own minds, will want to know how they voted on the issue.

One time I was riding in a big grey bus in the San Bernardino Valley. I asked the husky good-looking driver if he had read the proposition in the official pamphlet that the State of California sent to its registered voters. The driver was surprised at my question, although the election had just passed, and he frowningly said, "Say, if you were driving a bus like I am you wouldn't have time for reading anything." There are voters of this sort in every electorate, but the strength of democracy depends on other people. Not certainly on the earthworm type of patriot who can't quite see beyond the next minute, and can't get interested in anything that is not in his belly or within reach of his hands. He couldn't quite know that we were at war because no bomb had yet destroyed his bed, and his son was a daughter. Such a person cannot take his voting obligation seriously because he cannot get interested in anything beyond his own skin and bones. His neighbor's good is not his problem. He is not a politician, but merely a mean, unenlightened citizen trying to get along. He happens to live in a democracy, but that is an accident of birth rather than the result of his own effort and planning.

There are few people of this sort among us. The great ma-

17. *The Phantom Public* (New York, 1925), p. 28.

jority have achieved an outgoing interest in community affairs. And if their community is now the great society and the great society is an integral part of the world community, they are interested in knowing that fact and living up to their added responsibilities. America was not made by people who did not believe in helping one another. Shared experience was common then; it need not be impossible in this new world of today and tomorrow.

One time Abraham Lincoln was asked, "Do you know who Douglas is?" "Why, yes, he's a man with tens of thousands of *blind* followers," said Lincoln, and he continued "It's my business to make some of those blind followers *see.*" [18]

There were presumably no effective opponents in the ten congressional districts to make the voters who were unaware of the implications of their representatives' voting record, see. That is not always the case. Congressman Day was defeated in Illinois because an intelligent woman discussed the issue with the electorate. Another case is that of Howard McMurray who in 1942, though he was a newcomer both to politics and to the Milwaukee district in which he ran, defeated an isolationist congressman. The significant thing about McMurray's victory over Congressman Thill is the more basic fact that it is the victory of a man who believes in international co-operation over an isolationist congressman in a congenitally isolationist district. It is a spectacular example of what an educational campaign in politics can do.

Congressman McMurray thinks he won because he carried his message directly to the voter. I quote excerpts from his letter of December 22, 1944:

I operate politically on the basic assumption that political leadership is essentially an educational job and that people are educable....

We won because we organized a force which would take the issues directly to the people. We used almost everything imaginable—that is, every means to reach the people, including the press (publicity and advertising), the radio, distribution of literature, and speakers. Our most important work, however, in my opinion, was done by individuals organized into teams who punched doorbells and told a story about the candi-

18. Carl Sandburg, *Abraham Lincoln. The Prairie Years* (New York, 1926), II, 294.

date and the issues. This work was done primarily by women and I think we won because we punched every doorbell in the Fifth District at least once.

McMurray and the women's clubs did help former Congressman Thill's followers *see*. The McMurray forces gave the facts to the people of Milwaukee, and the people rose to the occasion. In each case, though, someone must give the facts to the people—a fact alone is not enough. It must be discussed to be understood. And the individual in any self-governing society must practice being articulate, in word and print, if he is to retain his ability to govern himself. And we need not comment on what such lethal devices as the poll tax, for example, do to the body politic. Their effect on the community is similar to the action of a sniff of chloroform on the body human.

The question may well be asked, do voters want a candidate with an issue? Since Civil War days they have invariably voted for men, not issues. These exceptions come to mind. Prohibition was an issue in American politics. Al Smith's religion determined the voters' choice in many instances in 1928, and the Great Depression and the New Deal attitude toward government and life and the war since then have called the turn. An issue might bring death, not life, to a political party or a candidate. I heard the Honorable Fred Zimmerman, Wisconsin Secretary of State say: "A candidate in Milwaukee declared that he did not want any wet voters. Well, he didn't get any wet voters, and he got very few dry ones. Now I want all of the wet votes and all of the dry votes. I want all of the votes just so they are marked for Fred Zimmerman." This is the platform of a candidate who in seven state-wide elections received more votes than any other candidate in Wisconsin. This is partly because he holds a non-policy-forming office. A part of his process in wooing the voter depends on the Honorable Secretary's listening to what the voter is saying and then repeating it back to him pleasantly, embellished with a smile and a warm hand clasp. (A Wisconsin congressman told me that when he met the Secretary on the Square in Madison and Mr. Zimmerman took his hand in both of his and said in a mellow, low voice, "Hello, Tom! How are you, Tom? How's Mary?" he felt so good that he almost wanted to vote for him himself.)

But these are days filled with great problems—great problems now and great problems ahead. This means that personalities will count for less and issues will be in the forefront of the voters' thinking. During the bitterest days of the Depression the following happened in what had only the day before been a highly organized Philadelphia division. When the very popular leader, Tony Nicollo, asked his people to vote Republican some of them cried, and said, "Tony, we will do anything for you but give you our vote. It is now important to us." They wanted the kind of relief and benefits that the Roosevelt administration gave them.

The congressman cannot go beyond the ideas and opinions of his constituents. That is why a congressman must be a teacher —a teacher who can dramatize the issue. The issue must be made real. When it is, the leader is invincible. Take the congruous examples of Willkie, Dewey, and Lincoln.

Willkie took a stand in 1944 and did not win a single delegate in Wisconsin. In 1940, however, he was not a candidate in a single state primary, but he was nominated for the presidency by the Republican Party in their national convention. Dewey had the opposite experience. He was nominated in 1944 although he did no public campaigning. He said nothing to clarify the public mind or to identify himself with any issue. He was a candidate, but he acted privately. In 1940, however, he publicly campaigned for delegates and lost the nomination to Willkie, a man who did not publicly campaign for delegates. Dewey in the pre-convention campaign of 1944 was not concerned with educating the public. He cleared it with somebody other than the voter.

There are two observations that come to my mind. One is that in each case the candidate who was nominated said nothing publicly before his nomination; but the other comment is more interesting. Each of these candidates was defeated by Franklin D. Roosevelt, a man who, by the very nature of his office and the circumstances that surrounded it, spoke out again and again. The truth in politics is never simple because politics is life, and life is complex and mysterious.

Maybe, therefore, Governor Dewey did not size up the people so well after all. In an earlier day another public man, or politician, Abraham Lincoln, the greatest of the breed that America has produced, had a relevant experience. He believed that if a man stood by a cause the cause would stand by him.[19] And he stood by a most important cause. He wrote a speech that began with an honest, forthright paragraph that contains the unequivocal lines now so well known, so startling in their clarity and force then. "A house divided against itself cannot stand. I believe this government cannot endure permanently half slave and half free. I do not expect the Union to be dissolved. I do not expect the house to fall, but I do expect it will cease to be divided. It will become all one thing, or all the other." [20]

Lincoln's picked political friends said that he had gone too far. Democratic newspapers called him, "Agitator" and "blatherskite." But Lincoln himself never hesitated. He did not change a word. He thought it was his greatest speech.

But the telling thing is that Lincoln was nominated. He was elected President of the United States. He has been given a place never given to any other man. He is the people's own. He made them feel at home. But he told them something worth knowing too. A politician, but he was more than a weathercock. He not only listened to what the voters were saying, but he was concerned with what they ought to say. He told them what he believed. He helped them see the truth as he saw it. We now know that his truth is the truth of history.

A final comment: In a period of uncertainty the people want a leader who leads—someone who knows them and knows not only their needs but their wishes, too, and is prepared to do something about them. Lincoln met this test, and so did Roosevelt. Dewey does not, and neither did Willkie—but for a different reason. Willkie did not know the people whose support he asked, and they did not know what he was talking about. He could not tell them. To have done so would have required more time, patience, understanding, dramatic ability and channels of

19. *Ibid.,* p. 84.
20. *Ibid.,* p. 103.

communication than he possessed. It was here, however, as teachers who could dramatize great ideas—who could present pertinent truth as theater—that Lincoln and Roosevelt stood out as the public men, or politicians, of their day. Each spoke on the issue in a voice that was recognized as the people's own even though there was also the magic accent of the individual speaker. And it is this new, individual accent added to the known voice—the atypical plus the typical—that fashions an appeal which most effectively compels attention. The importance of the question or issue to which attention is directed can be judged only by the people themselves. And it can be judged effectively only by a public that is informed. It is for this reason that I think the frequent publication of an official roll call herein described would be a device that would prove helpful in this democratic task.

THE CONTRIBUTORS

ANITA F. ALPERN was born in New York City, was graduated from the University of Wisconsin in 1941 and from Columbia University in 1942. Since that time she has worked as an economic analyst in Washington, D. C. Miss Alpern is particularly interested in increasing the number of University people who look upon government as a career.

THOMAS S. BARCLAY is professor of Political Science at Stanford University. He is a native of Missouri and a graduate of the University of Missouri with the class of 1915. After graduation he became a fellow at the University of Chicago and in 1919 served with the Department of State at Paris, where he was for some months private secretary to the late Henry White. On completion of his graduate work at Columbia University in 1924, he joined the faculty of the University of Missouri. He has been at Stanford since 1928. Professor Barclay has served as a consulting fellow at the Brookings Institution and as visiting professor at several leading universities. He has been vice-president of the American Political Science Association and is a member of the Board of Editors of the *American Political Science Review*. In addition to articles and reviews in various journals, he is author of *The Liberal Republican Movement* and *The Movement for Municipal Home Rule*. Professor Barclay has long been active in politics, serving as delegate to the Democratic national conventions of 1936 and 1944, as assistant to the chairman of the Democratic National Committee in the convention of 1940, and as a presidential elector for California in 1944.

JOHN R. BEAL joined the Washington Bureau of *Newsweek* as associate editor in 1942 and is now *Time*'s Washington correspondent. Previously he attended Ohio Wesleyan University and has been a reporter for the Elmyra, Ohio, *Chronicle Telegram* and for the Paterson, New Jersey, *Press Guardian*. In 1929 he joined the staff of the United Press in New York. He was transferred to Washington in 1934 as head of the House and later of the Senate staff of the United Press.

WILFRED E. BINKLEY was born in Allen County, Ohio, in 1883, took the B.A. degree at Ohio Northern University, the A.B. at Antioch College, and the A.M. and Ph.D. degrees at Ohio State University. He has been a high school teacher at Lima, Ohio, and visiting professor at Ohio and Bowling Green State Universities. Since 1929 he has been professor of Political Science at Ohio Northern University. He is author of books on aspects of government, among which is his *American Political Parties, Their Natural History,* for which he was awarded the Alfred A. Knopf fellowship in history.

HUGH A. BONE holds degrees from North Central College (B.A., 1931), the University of Wisconsin (M.A., 1935), and Northwestern University (Ph.D., 1937), and has held appointments in the political science departments of Northwestern University, the University of Maryland, and Queens College, where he is now an assistant professor. His non-academic activities include association with the U. S. Senate Campaign Expenditures Committee (1940) and with the Queens County Committee for Economic Development (1944-45), and membership on the Legislative Committee of the Citizens' Union of New York (1943-44). He was a course compiler for the U. S. Army Education Branch (1944-45) and is now Research Advisor to Representative Henry J. Latham, Ninth Congressional District, New York. He is author of two books, *Smear Politics: An Analysis of 1940 Campaign Literature* (1941) and *Current American Government* (with L. V. Howard, 1943), and is a contributor to *Amerasia, American City, National Municipal Review, Social Studies,* and other periodicals.

RICHARD NELSON CURRENT, now on the faculty of Lawrence College, was born in Colorado Springs in 1912. He holds degrees from Oberlin College, the Fletcher School of Law and Diplomacy, and the University of Wisconsin. He is the author of *Old Thad Stevens*.

NAT. S. FINNEY was born in Stewartville, Minnesota, in 1903 and was graduated from the University of Minnesota. He has been reporter, special writer, city editor, and feature editor for the *Minneapolis Star,* the *Minneapolis Star Journal,* and the *Minneapolis Star Journal and Tribune,* for which he is now serving as Washington correspondent.

MAX HALL, thirty-four years old, is on the Washington staff of the Associated Press. Born in Atlanta, Georgia, a Phi Beta Kappa and a graduate of Emory University, he taught school for a year and then worked on the *Atlanta Constitution* and the *Atlanta Georgian*. He joined the *New York Mirror* in 1937 and resigned as night editor of the paper in 1942 to go to Washington. He covers Treasury and Commerce departments and foreign economic administration for the Associated Press.

EDWARD A. HARRIS, Washington correspondent of the *St. Louis Post-Dispatch,* has contributed articles to the *New Republic,* the *Nation, Liberty,* and other publications. Born in St. Louis thirty-five years ago, he graduated with scholastic honors from Washington University there, learned political reporting on the rugged, hard-swinging *St. Louis Star-Times,* where he wrote a special column, and in 1940 moved over to the *Post-Dispatch.* Sent to Washington on trial during the temporary absence from the bureau of Marquis W. Childs, he "clicked" with a series of beats, and the Washington assignment was made permanent. At the Democratic national convention in Chicago in July, 1944, he was the first correspondent to disclose that President Roosevelt had given the nod behind the scenes to Truman as running mate. He lives within commuting distance of the capital at a place called Buffalo Hill, site of old Fort Buffalo of Civil War days, near Falls Church, Virginia.

S. BURTON HEATH has been manager of two political campaigns and publicity consultant for others. He began his career as apprentice printer. Born in Massachusetts in 1898, he was editor and later owner of the *Groton Times*, reporter of the Associated Press and the *New York Telegram*, and is now staff writer for the Newspaper Enterprise Association.

CLAUDIUS O. JOHNSON, a native of Virginia, served in the A.E.F. in the First World War. He received the Ph.D. degree at the University of Chicago in 1927 and is now Professor of Political Science and Head of the Department of History and Political Science at the State College of Washington. He is author of *Carter Henry Harrison: Political Leader; Government in the United States; Borah of Idaho; George William Norris, American Politician; George Turner: A Character from Plutarch;* and four other articles on Turner published in various professional journals of the Pacific Northwest. He has served the state of Washington as a member of the Governor's Advisory Constitutional Revision Commission, 1934-35, and as member of the Board of Sponsors for the Merit System, Department of Social Security, 1937; and he was Public Panel Chairman, National War Labor Board, Twelfth Region, 1943. He belongs to the American Political Science Association, the American Society of International Law, the American Society for Public Administration, the Academy of Political Science, and the American Academy of Political and Social Science.

FRANCIS P. LOCKE was born into a newspaper family on May 1, 1912, in Lincoln, Nebraska. His father, Walter Locke, was at that time associate editor of the *Nebraska State Journal*. As a youth he moved with his parents to Ohio, where his father became editor of the *Dayton Daily News* and editorial columnist for the James M. Cox papers. After graduating from Harvard in 1933, the junior Locke joined the staff of the *Miami Daily News*, Florida, as a cub reporter. Three years later he became an editorial writer. After a turn on the *St. Louis Post-Dispatch* editorial page in 1941, Locke returned to Miami as editor of the *News* editorial page. He is the junior member of what is reported to be the only father-and-son combination in the American Society of Newspaper Editors.

DAYTON DAVID McKEAN is Professor of Political Science at Dartmouth College. He is author of *"The Boss,"* a book about Mayor Hague.

CHARLES E. MARTIN, Head of the Political Science Department at the University of Washington, has been visiting professor at the University of Hawaii and at various Far Eastern Universities. As member and delegate of such associations as the Institute of Pacific Relations and the Institute of World Affairs, he has attended conferences all over the world, including Kyoto, Japan, and many European capitals. He studied at the universities of California and Southern California and at Columbia University, and has written books on the foreign policy of the United States, the Constitution, and the organization of peace.

OTIS MILLER was born in Texas in 1894, and studied at the University of Texas, where he received the A.B., the M.J., and the LL.B. degrees. He has taught journalism at Baylor University and the University of Wisconsin. He has been county attorney, county judge, and district attorney of Jones County, Texas, and has worked on numerous Texas newspapers, including the *El Paso Herald* and the *Austin Statesman*. He is now editor of the *Jones County Observer*, Anson, Texas.

MONTELL OGDON has been chief of the foreign trade policies and programs section of the Office of Foreign Agricultural Relations in the U. S. Department of Agriculture since 1943. He has been a research assistant for the international law and agriculture committees and is a member of the U. S. Inter-Department Committee on Post-War Commercial Policy and International Organization. A former member of the International Joint Food Committee of the Combined Food Board, he is the author of *Juridical Bases of Diplomatic Immunity* and a regular contributor to professional periodicals.

LEONARD NIEL PLUMMER, Kentucky newspaper man, is the head of the Journalism Department of the University of Kentucky. He received two degrees from the University of Kentucky and the Ph.D. degree from the University of Wisconsin, where he was on the staff of the School of Journalism. He is the author of *The Political Leadership of Henry Watterson* and has contributed articles to professional, legal, and popular publications.

ROBERT S. RANKIN, Professor of Political Science at Duke University, is a Tennessean by birth. He received his undergraduate training at Tusculum College and did his graduate work at Princeton. He is a past president of the Southern Political Science Association and is the author of *When Civil Law Fails* and *Readings in American Government*. Having lived in North Carolina since 1927, he has had an exceptional opportunity to follow the political career of Robert L. Doughton.

FLOYD M. RIDDICK is the legislative analyst of the U. S. Chamber of Commerce. He was a statistical analyst for the federal government, did research in public law and government at Columbia University, and received the Von Humbold Stiftung award for study in Germany. He was editor of the *Congressional Intelligence* and now edits the legislative daily of the U. S. Chamber of Commerce. He is the author of *Congressional Procedure* and has contributed articles to the *American Political Science Review*.

J. T. SALTER is a political scientist who is interested in presenting the politician and the voter to the public. A native of Michigan, he was educated at Oberlin College (A.B., 1921) and the University of Pennsylvania (Ph.D., 1928). As holder of Social Science Research Council fellowships in 1930 and

1931, he made first-hand investigations of political leaders, methods, and voters in Philadelphia. His books, *Boss Rule: Portraits in City Politics* and *The Pattern of Politics*, and articles in various journals represent part of his findings. He edited and contributed sketches to *The American Politician* and has been assistant editor of the *Annals* of the American Academy of Political and Social Science, has taught at the universities of Pennsylvania and Oklahoma and at Stanford University, and was one-time secretary of the Oklahoma Municipal League and editor of the *Oklahoma Municipal Review.* He has taught political science at the University of Wisconsin since 1930. Now temporarily attached to the War Department, he, like much of the rest of the world, is proud to call Washington his headquarters.

J. L. SAYRE is Professor and Head of the Department of Political Science at the University of North Dakota. He received the Ph.D. degree from the University of Michigan in 1938. His special interest is in the field of political parties and elections.

MURRAY SEASONGOOD is a native of Cincinnati. He took the A.B., A.M., and LL.B. degrees at Harvard University and in 1903 was admitted to the Ohio Bar. He has been part-time Professor of Law at the University of Cincinnati since 1925, mayor of Cincinnati for two terms, chairman of the City Planning Commission, president of the Hamilton County Good Government League, and is now president of the Cincinnati Bar Association. He holds a number of important trusteeships and has served on numerous civic, state, and national commissions and committees. He is the author of *Local Government in the United States* and other books and articles.

J. B. SHANNON was born and educated in Kentucky, was graduated from Transylvania College, and took advanced degrees at the University of Wisconsin. In 1935 he was appointed first Henry Clay Professor of History and Political Science at Transylvania. He was a research associate in Public Administration, Tennessee Valley Authority. He is now Professor of Political Science at the University of Kentucky and has written, among other books, *Henry Clay as a Political Leader*.

PAUL SIFTON is a newspaper man and a playwright. After service during the First World War with the A.E.F., he worked on newspapers in New York, Washington, Chicago, Des Moines, and Kansas City, covering aspects of the 1922 coal and rail strikes in Washington and the Herrin massacre in 1923. His play, *The Belt*, was produced in 1927. Other plays include *Midnight, Blood on the Moon*, and *The Girdle of Venus*. In 1934 he was appointed to the New York State Department of Labor, where he became assistant and then deputy industrial commissioner and administrator of unemployment insurance. In 1938 he became first deputy wage-hour administrator; in 1939, assistant director of the Consumers Counsel Division, Department of the Interior; and in 1942, labor and public relations director of the National Farmers Union. He is now director of the Washington office of the Union for Democratic Action. With his wife, Claire, he gets out the UDA Congressional Newsletter.

JULIAN SNOW was born in Wyoming and attended the university of that state. As city editor of the *Wyoming Eagle*, he began following the activities of Senator O'Mahoney and has served as the Senator's secretary since 1934.

GRAHAM STUART has taught political science at a number of universities, including Stanford, Chicago, and Washington. He has served as visiting professor at Toulouse, Poitiers, and Montpelier and at the University of Hawaii. He was analyst and consultant of the Board of Economic Warfare, 1942-43, and is active in the Institute of International Relations. He is the author of *Latin America and the United States, American Diplomatic and Consular Practices*, and other books.

OTIS SULLIVANT has been State Capitol reporter and political writer for the *Daily Oklahoman* for nearly eighteen years. A native Oklahoman, he was born at Norman, November 24,

1902. A graduate of Castle Heights Military Academy in 1920, he attended the University of Oklahoma for three years. He was a reporter for the *Fort Worth Press*, Texas, from 1925 to 1927, when he joined the *Oklahoman* staff. He served a brief turn in Washington as *Oklahoman* correspondent during the special session of Congress in 1939.

ROBERT THOMPSON has been a Midwest newspaperman for the past twenty-two years, and a news correspondent for *Collier's* magazine for the past ten. He is now political writer for the *St. Paul Pioneer Press and Dispatch*. He was born in Minneapolis and attended the University of Minnesota.

ROMAN J. ZORN is a native Wisconsin, born at River Falls in 1916. He was reared and educated within the borders of the Badger State. Upon his discharge from the U.S.N.R. in 1943, he was made Acting Instructor in History at the University of Wisconsin, where he had formerly been a graduate student in American history and political science. In 1945 he became Instructor in American History at the University of Arkansas. He was attracted as an eight-year-old boy by "Fighting Bob" LaFollette's campaign oratory, and attention thus aroused developed into a long-sustained interest in political leadership and public service. He is currently working on a biography of Wendell Phillips and upon a study of Garrisonian anti-slavery leadership.

INDEX

INDEX

ADAMS, Charles Francis, 23
Adams, John, 23
Aid to Britain, Dewey's attitude, 387
Allen, Leo E., 206
Allen, Robert. See Pearson, Drew
Amau, Mr., chief of Japanese Intelligence, 41
America First, spokesmen for, 215; supported Dewey, 308
America-Japan Society, addressed by Grew, 46; by Matsuoka, 47
American Legion, on munitions investigation, 138; Fish an organizer of, 214
American Liberty League, against Roosevelt, 211
Anderson, C. Elmer, 370, 371
Anderson, James L., partner of Kerr, 426
Anti-lynching bill, Fish supported, 211; Bilbo filibuster, 289; E. D. Smith denounced, 351
Anti-poll-tax legislation, Pepper favored, 267, 270; Bilbo filibustered, 277, 291; Connally filibustered, 317. See also Geyer bill
Araki, General (of Japan), 39
Arita, Foreign Minister (Japanese), 47
Arnold, Thurman, member TNEC, 121
Ashurst, Henry F., 118
Austin, W. R., 117, 275

BAHAROFF, Sir Basil, before munitions investigating committee, 136

Bailey, Joseph W., of Texas, 311
Bailey, Josiah W., of North Carolina, conducted Commerce committee hearing, 93-96
Ball, Joseph H., appointment to Senate, 297-98, 369; early backer of Stassen, 298, 363; Old-Guard resentment of, 298-99; Senate committee assignments, 299-300; character and personality, 300-1; on international issues, 301-2, 304-5; on domestic issues, 305-6; appointment to Truman committee, 302-3; support of Roosevelt, motives behind, 306-9, 370; at 1944 convention, 307-8, 369; concept of government, 309; probable future, 310; a handicap for Stassen, 357; criticism of Bricker, 404; mentioned, 238, 359
Ball-Burton-Hill Hatch peace resolution, Fulbright and, 188-89; substance of, 302; how originated, 304; public's response to, 304-5
Bankhead, William B., former speaker, 155, 161
Baptista, Colonel, president of Cuba, 33
Barkley, Alben W., break with FDR over tax-bill veto, 172, 240, 241, 254; successful vote-getter, 240, 241n; early political influences, 240, 244-45; background and education, 241-43; in political campaigns, 243-44, 246-47, 249-51; a raconteur, 245-46; appearance and personality, 247-48, 252; as